Nationalism and History Education

I0879775

History education, by nature, transmits an "official" version of national identity. National identity is not a fixed entity, and controversy over history teaching is an essential part of the process of redefining and regenerating the nation. France and the United States have in particular experienced demographic and cultural shifts since the 1960s that have resulted in intense debates over national identity. This volume examines how each country's national history is represented in primary schools' social studies textbooks and curricula and how they handle contemporary issues of ethnicity, diversity, gender, socioeconomic inequality, and patriotism. Analyzing each country separately and comparatively demonstrates how various groups (including academics, politicians, and citizen activists) have influenced education and how the process of writing and rewriting history perpetuates a nation.

Drawing on empirical studies of the United States and France, this volume provides insight into broader nationalist processes and instructive principles for similar countries in the modern world.

Rachel D. Hutchins is associate professor of American civilization at the University of Lorraine, France.

Routledge Research in International and Comparative Education

This is a series that offers a global platform to engage scholars in continuous academic debate on key challenges and the latest thinking on issues in the fast growing field of International and Comparative Education.

Books in the Series Include:

Transformative Learning through International Service-Learning
Towards an ethical ecology of education
Phillip Bamber

The Critical Global Educator
Global citizenship education as sustainable development
Maureen Ellis

Investigating Education in Germany
Historical studies from a British perspective
David Phillips

Knowledge Hierarchies in Transnational Education
Staging dissensus
Jing Qi

Global Identity in Multicultural and International Educational Contexts
Student identity formation in international schools
Nigel Bagnall

Teaching in Primary Schools in China and India
Contexts of learning
Nirmala Rao, Emma Pearson and Kai-ming Cheng with Margaret Taplin

A History of Higher Education Exchange
China and America
Teresa Brawner Bevis

National Identity and Educational Reform
Contested Classrooms
Elizabeth Anderson Worden

Citizenship Education around the World
Local Contexts and Global Possibilities
Edited by John E. Petrovic and Aaron M. Kuntz

Children's Voices
Studies of Interethnic Conflict and Violence in European Schools
Edited by Mateja Sedmak, Zorana Medarić and Sarah Walker

Culture, Transnational Education and Thinking
Case studies in global schooling
Niranjan Casinader

The Changing Landscape of International Schooling
Implications for theory and practice
Tristan Bunnell

Leading and Managing Indigenous Education in the Postcolonial World
Zane Ma Rhea

Multi-campus University Systems
Africa and the Kenyan Experience
Ishmael I. Munene

Education and the State
International perspectives on a changing relationship
Edited by Carla Aubry, Michael Geiss, Veronika Magyar-Haas and Jürgen Oelkers

Conflict, Reconciliation and Peace Education
Moving Burundi Toward a Sustainable Future
William M. Timpson, Elavie Ndura and Apollinaire Bangayimbaga

Citizenship Education and Migrant Youth in China
Pathways to the Urban Underclass
Miao Li

International Service Learning
Engaging Host Communities
Edited by Marianne A. Larsen

Educational Borrowing in China
Looking West or looking East?
Charlene Tan

Nationalism and History Education
Curricula and Textbooks in the United States and France
Rachel D. Hutchins

Nationalism and History Education

Curricula and Textbooks in the United States and France

Rachel D. Hutchins

Routledge
Taylor & Francis Group
LONDON AND NEW YORK

First published 2016 by Routledge

2 Park Square, Milton Park, Abingdon, Oxfordshire OX14 4RN
711 Third Avenue, New York, NY 10017

Routledge is an imprint of the Taylor & Francis Group, an informa business

First issued in paperback 2017

Library of Congress Cataloguing-in-Publication Data
Names: Hutchins, Rachel D., author.
Title: Nationalism and history education : curricula and textbooks in the United States and France / by Rachel D. Hutchins.
Description: New York : Routledge, [2016] | Series: Routledge research in international and comparative education ; 20
Identifiers: LCCN 2015041077 | ISBN 9781138801578 (hbk) | ISBN 9781315754857 (ebk)
Subjects: LCSH: United States—History—Study and teaching. | France—History—Study and teaching. | History—Study and teaching—United States. | History—Study and teaching—France. | Nationalism and education—United States. | Nationalism and education—France. | Education—Curricula—Political aspects—United States. | Education—Curricula—Political aspects—France. | Textbooks—Political aspects—United States. | Textbooks—Political aspects—France.
Classification: LCC E175.8 .H88 2016 | DDC 973.007—dc23
LC record available at http://lccn.loc.gov/2015041077

ISBN: 978-1-138-80157-8 (hbk)
ISBN: 978-0-8153-8192-1 (pbk)

Typeset in Sabon
by Apex CoVantage, LLC

For my parents

Contents

Tables and Figures

TABLES

FIGURES

Acknowledgments

I am very grateful to the many friends, colleagues, and family members whose feedback and support have been invaluable over the course of this project.

My thanks go to a large group of colleagues and friends at the *Université de Lorraine*: to the university for granting a research leave, which was instrumental in the progress of the manuscript; to the many colleagues of my research group, IDEA, who supported work on nationalism studies over the course of several years; in particular, to John Bak for guidance and support across the many stages of this project; to André Kaenel, who, as my PhD advisor, shaped my thinking as a young scholar and first guided me toward nationalism studies in my earliest work analyzing history education; to Dominique Hascoët for honing my translation skills; to Michael and Monica Latham and Anja and Matthew Smith for their encouragement and support over the years.

I would also like to thank friends and colleagues I know through the Association for the Study of Ethnicity and Nationalism at the London School of Economics who have improved this work through their thoughtful and thought-provoking questions and feedback (and—for those from the University of Edinburgh—who also gave me the opportunity to present work in progress as part of the Sociology Seminar Series). They are too numerous to name everyone individually; thank you in particular to Jonathan Hearn, John Hutchinson, James Kennedy, Liliana Riga, Michael Rosie, and Oliver Zimmer. In addition, several friends have read and offered much-appreciated suggestions on drafts of various chapters: Sarah Elzas, Jon Fox, Rouzbeh Parsi, and Kalil Smith-Nuevelle.

My thanks, also, to Tristan Lecoq of the *Inspection Générale de l'Education Nationale*, for inviting me to join and present my work in progress in the seminar series on history education at the *Sciences Po Centre d'histoire*. I have learned much from the whole group, and especially from Tristan Lecoq and his fellow *Inspecteur* Yves Poncelet, who have shared their feedback and expertise. Thanks also to Patricia Legris, for sharing her extensive knowledge of French curricula and offering me additional opportunities for feedback. I also appreciate James Loewen for taking time during a brief visit to New York City to meet with me and offer feedback.

I am very grateful to Jonathan Zimmerman of New York University, whose generosity with his time and ideas is truly exceptional. I thank him for his invaluable feedback on several chapters at various stages of the writing process, as well as for inviting me to join the historians of education writing group. Numerous people there offered enriching advice and criticism. Among them, I wish particularly to thank Zoë Burkholder and Natalia Mehlman Petrzela for their extended and thorough advice.

I cannot thank enough Daphne Halikiopoulou, who has encouraged me at every step of this project and whose advice and feedback have been as valuable as they have been generously given.

My parents, Jeff and Diane Hutchins, instilled in me a sense of inquisitiveness and raised me to question my own education, which is at the root of this book. I wish also to express my thanks to my sister, Nell, and brother-in-law, Daniel Shapiro, for their enthusiastic support and for sharing their inside knowledge of the American education system.

Finally, for his unwavering, extraordinary support and encouragement in innumerable ways throughout this project, thank you to Shafer Smith.

Introduction

Two weeks after the January 2015 terrorist attacks perpetuated in and near Paris by French citizens, the French government issued a directive calling for a large-scale "mobilization" of schools to promote secularism and the "values of the Republic." Faced with the criminal radicalization of a small subset of the country's marginalized Muslim minority, and amid reports of Muslim schoolchildren in socioeconomically disadvantaged areas refusing to honor the state-mandated minute of silence for the victims of the attacks, one of the most immediate policy responses thus came from the Ministry of Education, at the behest of the prime minister.

Though the measures advocated in this directive include expanding funding to assist disadvantaged children and increasing socioeconomic diversity in middle schools, the vast majority of these actions focus on renewed efforts to promote attachment to and understanding of national values and symbols. For instance, the document introduces a requirement that parents and children sign a "Secular Charter" with their schools, binding them to respect the "values of the Republic," under threat of (unspecified) punishment (République Française 2015).

The preamble to the summary of these measures on the government's homepage reveals in language at once ambiguous and explicit the belief in the schools' power to effect social change:

> Education reveals the tensions that traverse French society and the inequalities that mark it. Discriminations, the gap between professed values and experienced reality, and retreating into entrenched identities (*replis identitaires*) have undermined the goal of equality and fraternity borne by education. After the attacks that aimed at the heart of our values, the role of education is and will be reaffirmed in order to respond to the republican challenge to make secularism a reality.
>
> (République Française 2015)

Focusing on education in response to tragic, frightening events and social tensions is not limited to France. In the United States in June 2015, speaking the day after the racist terrorist attack in which a white man killed nine African American churchgoers in Charleston, South Carolina, the mayor of the city called for a national discussion on race and racism, adding: "We in America were not taught African-American history [. . .]. It was never in the history books, and we don't know the story" (Joseph Riley Jr., quoted in Stewart and Pérez-Peña 2015). Anger in the wake of the Charleston attack also focused on other representations of history, as calls increased to remove the Confederate flag that stood on the grounds of the South Carolina statehouse, and a nearby statue commemorating Confederate soldiers was spray-painted with the words "black lives matter." The protestors and the mayor's shared focus on representations of history highlights the widespread perception that history education and other forms of public history reflect society's vision of itself and the dominant power structure and can thus act as a vehicle for change.

Reactions to these events in France and the United States are representative of broader ongoing controversies. In both cases, ethnic minorities who face disproportionate socioeconomic disadvantage have fought against discrimination, in part by seeking greater visibility of their histories in school curricula and textbooks. Also in both cases, some members of the dominant ethnic majority perceive demographic, social, and epistemological changes as threats to national identity, unity, and security. These divisions have led to continuing conflicts over education and public history, particularly since the early 1980s. In the United States, these debates have commonly been known as the "culture wars" (Hunter 1991).[1]

To those in the middle of culture wars, their country seems irreconcilably divided. Yet controversy over national identity and history teaching is itself an essential part of the process of national regeneration. In arguing about who "we" are, citizens reaffirm belief in the nation and a sense of connection (Billig 1995: 95–96; Hutchinson 2005). The act of representing history and debating its meanings is a key component of this cycle. History education gives an official, or quasi-official, vision of national identity, showing who "we" think we are in the present, where we think we came from, and where we would like to go in the future (Smith 1999).

Despite the profound connections between nationalism and education, most research on teaching history and citizenship in the field of comparative and international education—particularly that which focuses on long-established Western nation-states—does not draw deeply on the nationalism literature.[2] This book aims to demonstrate how comparative studies of history and citizenship education can be made more meaningful through examination of the different conceptions of the nation that are at play and by studying how the nation-state and education sustain one another in practice. To this end, I propose a framework for conceptualizing the study of history education in a way that shows the connections between pedagogy, nationalism, and conceptions of national identity.

FRANCE AND THE UNITED STATES

The bonds between history education and national identity are elucidated by my comparative study of France and the United States. While there have always been significant differences between the two countries, they have enough in common to yield instructive comparison.[3] Both countries were founded on similar, though not identical, ideological underpinnings. Both modern nation-states began with revolutions based, at least partly, on Enlightenment philosophy, and both see themselves (and were traditionally seen in the literature) as examples of primarily civic nations, in which citizenship was based not on biological descent but on choice and adherence to the creed of the state. The countries share similar founding myths according to which they embody universal ideals. Both have histories of colonial expansionism that was justified in terms of spreading republicanism. They have long assigned similar roles to history and social studies education. Since the 1960s, France and the United States have faced parallel debates over national identity, immigration, exclusion, discrimination, historiography, and epistemology. During this time, both have also experienced a rise of the exclusionist right—the *Front National* in France and the New Right in the U.S.

I examine French and United States curricula and textbooks from the early 1980s to 2010. Specifically, I analyze 31 French textbooks, four French curricula, and 12 U.S. textbooks—all of which are used nationwide—as well as four U.S. curricula from Texas. I focus on Texas in particular because the state has exerted exceptional influence over the textbooks that are used across the country (as discussed further below). The evolution of history teaching in France and the U.S. in recent years reveals important similarities and significant differences, with implications for understanding the functioning of nationalism. In both countries, widespread popular concerns over national identity and unity have focused on education, leading to policies that reinforce the nationalistic aims of education, and especially history and social studies. This study focuses on curricula and textbooks because they embody official conceptions of national identity and determine, to a large extent, what is taught in classrooms.[4] As such, they are often the focus of efforts to influence education. As contentious as this process may be, since education cannot stop for ideological gridlock, curricula and textbooks necessarily reflect a working compromise. I begin with curricula and textbooks of the early 1980s because these were the first in both countries to follow the social, demographic, and epistemological debates and shifts of the 1960s and 1970s. I examine the evolution of national identity in the subsequent books and curricula through 2010, which were the most recently published in both countries when I began this study, because debates over education and national identity politics have remained prominent in both countries. The importance of these questions and the solutions that national communities find is reflected in the moments of trauma and tragedy that continue to highlight deep divisions within each country.

In studying textbooks, curricula, and the surrounding discourse and debate from 1980 to 2010, this book will demonstrate principal findings of two different but related types. First, it shows the continued salience of nationalism and its dominance in education, including widespread support for nationalism across the political and ideological spectrum. There have been many calls among cosmopolitan scholars to replace nation-centric history with world history (e.g., McDonough and Feinberg 2003; Nussbaum 1994; Schissler and Soysal 2005; VanSledright 2008: 135), but there is no evidence of significant political or public support for this shift in France or in the U.S. On the contrary, this book demonstrates that national history education has been reinforced and receives ideologically diverse support.

In addition to demonstrating the endurance of nationalism, this book also explores the specific evolution of national identity in curricula and textbooks as an outcome of various processes of official knowledge production in France and the United States. French identity as presented in curricula and textbooks is based on progressive yet assimilationist nationalism, whereas the vision of national identity presented in U.S. textbooks has become much more conservative yet pluralist. This book demonstrates that differences between French and U.S. history textbooks result partly from different means of producing knowledge. Similar historiographical and social science work has been done within the academy in both countries (and indeed, there has been ample cross-fertilization between them), yet there is a much more direct connection between the work of scholars and grade-school education in France than in the U.S. While this significant difference is largely attributable to institutional factors, these institutions themselves are grounded in different conceptions of democracy and the balance between popular power and the role of experts. I also demonstrate that, where they diverge, these different conceptions of national identity are tied to different pedagogical approaches, which are discussed below.

NATIONALISM, NATIONAL IDENTITY, AND EDUCATION

Before proceeding with discussion of the relationship between nationalism and education, it is necessary to clarify my usage of key concepts that are subject to multiple definitions. I adhere to the definition of nationalism as the belief that the state should represent a group of people who consider themselves as belonging to one nation and who share a territory. As such, nationalism is one of the dominant ideologies of the modern world, ascribing legitimacy to sovereign nation-states (Breuilly 1982/1993; Gellner 1997). The identity of the nation may be made up of a variety of factors, including but not limited to shared culture, religion, language, ethnicity, and/or political creed (Anderson 1983/2006; Billig 1995; Breuilly 1982/1993; Gellner 1983; Smith 1991, 1999). Early scholars of nationalism often adopted the dominant popular views of the U.S. and France as "civic" nations, where citizenship and national identity are based on voluntarist models of belonging, built around cores of universal, democratic values, which are traditionally seen as the opposite of "ethnic" nations (Kohn 1944). However, this dichotomy fails to account for the variety of ways in which people conceive of national membership and belonging.

Many recent scholars have commented on the inadequacy of the civic/ethnic model (see for instance: Kaufmann 2008; Kuzio 2002; Smith 1991; Thomas 2012; Zimmer 2003). In attempting to refine this model, nationalism scholars have introduced further distinctions within the category of civic nations, for instance, qualifying the U.S. as being based on a pluralist model, where citizens share political but not social culture (Smith 1999), whereas France embraces universalist assimilationism (Brubaker 1992, 2001; Jennings 2011; Thomas 2012). Yet, this book demonstrates that textbooks from both countries promote a form of nationalism that might better be described as "cultural" rather than purely civic (Calhoun 2007; Dieckhoff 2000; Thomas 2012).[5]

The contours of national identity within a cultural conception of national belonging are not only *open* to continual debate; such debate is arguably *required* in order to create a sense of national community. The process discussed above, in which each generation redefines who is a part of the nation and what values that nation represents, is perhaps especially important to cultural nationalism. Renegotiation of cultural national identity secures members' affective attachment to the nation and renews its legitimacy, thereby perpetuating the nation (Billig 1995: 95–96; Hutchinson 2005).

Nationalism is deeply connected to education. Modern education—and particularly history and social studies education—is inextricably linked to the development of nation-states in liberal democracies. In an industrialized, largely national economy and polity, the acquisition of a certain skill set and a sense of belonging to a community are seen as necessary and worthy goals to be administered by the state via mass public education (Gellner 1983). Thus, French unity and American identity have long been objects of concern by policymakers. From the early years of each modern state, and with renewed fervor in the late nineteenth and early twentieth centuries, leaders in each country saw education as one of the primary means of, respectively, turning "peasants into Frenchmen" (and avoiding repeated civil unrest in the wake of the Paris Commune) and immigrants into Americans (O'Leary 1999; Weber 1976).

In eras of conscious nation-building, French and U.S. leaders advocated teaching national history in order to shape citizens. The connection between history teaching and perpetuating the nation was enshrined in France by the Third Republic. Except for a brief interlude in the 1970s (discussed below), French history and geography have been continually taught with the explicit goal of promoting civic education and national identity (Bozec 2010; Citron 1987/2008; Durkheim 1922/1969; Mauss 1920/1969). Similarly, in the U.S., the connection between history, other social sciences, and civic nationalism has long been institutionalized via the subject of social studies, with its official place in curricula and professional organizations. Social studies was established as a discipline partly in response to mass immigration and was firmly anchored in the Progressive Education movement (Dewey 1916; Evans 2004; Marker and Mehlinger 1992). Social studies includes history, geography, and civic education, but historically, it has adopted different methods and objectives from the academic forms of the first and second of these disciplines.[6] In both countries, public schools were considered the primary site of nationalizing and unifying the population. Civic education has long been seen not only as supporting the nation-state but also as a source for positive social change.

In more recent times as well, when leaders and/or the public have perceived the nation to be facing a crisis—real or imagined, internal or external—renewed focus has often been directed toward education. This focus may be partly symbolic; in an increasingly globalized world, where important decisions are made on the supranational level, the power to educate citizens is one of the most visible domains of sovereignty remaining for the nation-state. It may also be a means of allowing politicians to act quickly by calling for change but with no immediately measurable impact and without disruption to the private sector. Nevertheless, the focus on education, whether symbolic or pragmatic, is widespread and appears genuine among many policy makers, commentators, and activists. It reflects a belief in the importance of socialization in early childhood and throughout the formative years. It also reflects the belief that change can be effected in the next generation through school, regardless of family and community influences. The focus on education perhaps above all reflects the enduring belief that the nation-state is the primary unit of social and political belonging and that affective attachment to it is necessary for social cohesion and functioning. Arguments advocating education reform are very often phrased not just in pragmatic terms but also in terms of national greatness and pride and often are framed in a context of international competition. The example of calls in the U.S. for improved education after the Soviet launch of Sputnik is particularly obvious, but the same principle applies to national attention to education in France and the U.S. in the 1980s.

In addition to the demographic and social changes that affected France and the U.S. in the 1960s and 1970s, other large-scale historical changes and events led to the growth of national soul-searching beginning in this period. These changes affected (and were affected by) academic research as well as politics in the broad sense. The academic study of history developed concurrently with nationalism. Historical work in Europe and the U.S., through most of the nineteenth century and into the twentieth, reflected periods of domestic nation-building and colonial and imperial expansion that were intricately tied to national self-conceptions and pride, including defining the nation in relation to its neighbors. Early national histories played a major role in defining national identity (e.g., Fichte 1808/2001;

Michelet 1847–1853/2007; see Kumar 2006b; Özkirimli 2010). However, nationalism itself gradually became an object of study. Renan's inquiry "What is a Nation?" was an early forerunner (1882/1994), and the subject attracted more attention after the First World War, and especially after the nationalistic catastrophes of the Second World War. Scholars began to question and examine the ideology that had contributed to such destruction—including genocide, territorial conquest, as well as the willingness to die for one's nation. In addition, memory of the use of nationalist propaganda during the war by the collaborationist Vichy government in France and by Nazi and fascist forces elsewhere made overt expressions of bellicose and exclusionist nationalism suspect in Western Europe in the years following the war.[7] The growth of nationalism studies was further fueled by decolonization (Özkirimli 2010). Thus, renewed scrutiny of nationalism coincided with newly visible and popular challenges to traditional conceptions of national identity in multiethnic societies and the growth of supranational power, which appeared to challenge the sovereignty of nation-states. That such a climate tends to heighten expressions and manifestations of nationalism is well established (Delannoi 1991: 14; Hobsbawm 1990/1992: 120–121, 170–171). National soul-searching by academics, politicians, and citizen groups of various ideological persuasions is thus all part of the same process.

CONTEMPORARY DEBATES

"Droit à la Différence" and Assimilationism in France

In France, during the 1970s, history was not taught as a separate subject in elementary schools but was included in a collective discipline called "activities of awakening" (*activités de l'éveil*). Following Piaget's theories on developmental psychology as well as the historiography of the *Annales* school, the *éveil* approach called for ceasing to teach history as a grand narrative and as a means of transmitting national memory. Instead, children were to "discover" the past of local as well as geographically distant civilizations through the study of primary source documents. Beginning in the final years of the 1970s and extending into the 1980s, a series of reports—some commissioned by the government, others under the impetus of academic researchers—questioned the efficacy of the *éveil* methods and the state of history education in France (with most notably the government-sponsored *Rapport Girault* of 1983). In a wide consensus, historians, politicians, primary and secondary school teachers, etc., charged that the schools were no longer teaching French history. They argued in these various reports and studies and in the press that history education must serve a civic agenda, in maintaining collective national memory (which was, they contended, in danger of being lost) and focusing on the nation's values through political and event-focused history (Garcia and Leduc 2003: 197, 205–206, 238; Legris 2014: 95–110).

These concerns over the schools' role in transmitting national identity paralleled broader fears among many French people of European origin that the growing Muslim population was "unassimilable" (de Laforcade 2006: 219, 226; Hargreaves 2007: 4–5). The major point of concern of European-French assimilationists is over the religion of newcomers and their descendants.[8] Without delving here into a long historical discussion (which could easily fill a book of its own), it is relevant to the study at hand to comment on recent developments. As the Muslim population in metropolitan France has grown, dominant (though not unchallenged) interpretations of *laïcité* (secularism) have emerged, which assert that the nation must be the primary locus of public identity, attachment, and loyalty for true citizenship and belonging (Scott 2007; Thomas 2012). In this view, religion must be relegated to the private sphere. This was, for example, the reasoning behind a 2004 law banning the wearing of "ostentatious" religious symbols in public schools (Scott 2007; Thomas 2012). If many people in French society so fear Islam, it is largely because they equate it with its fundamentalist fringe and believe that most Muslims will be loyal to Islam above France (Hargreaves 2007: 108–109).

These fears grew as the economy shrank, leaving many of these recent immigrants unemployed, as the deep recession that followed the three-decade post-war boom known as the *Trente glorieuses* raised alarm over national standing and identity. French self-conceptions were also shaken by the independence of France's colonies in the 1950s and 1960s. The rise in xenophobic sentiment contributed to a resurgence of assimilationism, which limited support for multiculturalism in France. In the 1970s, as the immigrant population from the Maghreb and sub-Saharan Africa grew and established more permanent roots in France, including having French-born children, a differentialist movement arose in opposition to traditional assimilationist policies and ideology. Proponents of *droit à la différence* (the right to be different) advocated preservation and promotion of traditional French regional cultures as well as those of recent immigrants (Bozec 2010: 305–306; Brubaker 2001: 536–537; Martigny 2012: 237–304). This movement had limited policy applications, but for a short time it gained support from both the right and the left, notably from President François Mitterrand and beyond national borders from the European Council (Bozec 2010: 306). As we will see, some prominent historians advocated for pluralism in the early 1980s, but the movement quickly lost momentum, and by the end of the decade, it had lost support. This shift is widely attributed to the rise in power of Jean-Marie Le Pen's *Front National*, which appropriated the discourse of differentialist cultural preservation from the movement (i.e., claiming that all cultures would be best protected by keeping them separate) in order to justify exclusionist policies. In response, more centrist parties and activists—including antiracist organizations, such as

SOS Racisme—aimed to undercut the far right by showing that they, too, wished to protect national identity and unity. Thus, what Rogers Brubaker has termed "neo-republican, neo-universalist, and at least hesitatingly neo-assimilationist discourse" came to dominate public discussions (Brubaker 2001: 537; see also for example: Bozec 2010; Hargreaves 2007; Legris 2014; Lewis 2011; Martigny 2012; Thomas 2012; Viguier 2011). This view is grounded in an essentialist conception of national identity that excludes the notion that identities change over time. It draws on a vision of an eternal France rooted in its history, territory, institutions, culture, and civic beliefs, whose continued existence requires the adherence of all residents.

While some pluralist voices remain (Noiriel 2007; Wieviorka 1996), they are a small minority. In addition, multiculturalism is often derided in France as being "un-French," a divisive force imported from Anglophone countries (Bozec 2010: 345; Scott 2007: 23). Thus, rejection of multiculturalism can also draw on a certain anti-Americanism and anti-British tradition (Meunier 2006). However, despite opposition to pluralism, French history education has become more inclusive of previously ignored ethnic groups (see Chapter One). This change is largely attributable to the activism of groups that have lobbied not for multiculturalism *per se* but rather for the inclusion of major historical events concerning minority groups that have been omitted from traditional narratives of French history (Legris 2014: 165–166). Such measures have received the support of government officials as well as the historians who write curricula and textbooks.

Multiculturalism and Conservatism in the United States

In the U.S., too, several concurrent changes led to ongoing debates over national identity and education. The Cold War, and particularly the space race, stirred fears of national decline and loss of the dominant status the U.S. had gained internationally (Hartman 2008). As a result, the federal government increasingly intervened in education, and this intervention often overlapped with other social concerns. The ensuing measures led to major changes as well as protest. Watershed moments include desegregation of public schools following the Supreme Court's 1954 decision, *Brown v. Board of Education*, the banning of school prayer by the court's 1962 decision, *Engel v. Vitale*, and later, the Bilingual Education Act of 1978 and President Jimmy Carter's creation of the Department of Education in 1979 (see Burkholder 2011; Hartman 2015; Zimmerman 2002). Following the desegregation of schools, calls for integrated textbooks increased, and an older tradition of African American curriculum and textbook activism merged with the Civil Rights Movement and subsequent minority rights and feminist movements and grew into what came to be known as multiculturalism (Zimmerman 2002).

The textbook publishing industry implemented some aspects of this early form of multiculturalism in the 1960s. Most publishers issued guidelines for their authors aimed at fighting stereotypes and incorporating more women and minorities (*Guidelines* 1975: x, 62–63; Moore 1977; Ravitch 2003: 40, 81, 85, 87; see also Zimmerman 2002).

At the same time, epistemological shifts led historians to challenge the traditional narratives and historiographical approaches, as part of the same intellectual movement as the *Annales* School and its poststructuralist offshoots in France (Cusset 2003; Hunt 1989). The resulting questions over the relationship between official knowledge and power fueled and were fueled by the ideological and political debates over discrimination, national identity, and unity.

I will present the different positions in these controversies in more detail than I did regarding the French case. In France, a wide consensus exists among educational actors around republican assimilationism, and there have been no significant challenges from pluralist activists. In the U.S., on the other hand, competing ideological groups affect the evolution of social studies education, so understanding their goals is an essential part of this study. In discussing these controversies, I will often refer to multiculturalist and conservative positions. However, these labels are not meant to imply that these are the only two options. Instead, I view these as two segments of a spectrum. When I refer to multiculturalism, I adopt the term as it is commonly used in practice by those who advocate it within U.S. education to describe progressive, antiracist pluralism, which grew out of the association of support for diversity, gender equality, and critical theory. I include within this definition those associated with what James Banks has called "transformative pedagogy" (Banks 1996). While some proponents of transformative pedagogy seem unconcerned with national identity, focusing more on social justice (e.g., Apple 2000), and some promote transnational framing of education in order to foster cosmopolitan solidarity (e.g., McDonough and Feinberg 2003; Nussbaum 1994; Soysal, Bertilotti, and Mannitz 2005), most seek to work within the dominant nationalist framework, as they often also argue that the United States has a national identity, which they accept and support. Many believe that national identity can and should be continually redefined in order to fully incorporate all members of the polity (e.g., Banks et al. 1981; Giroux 1981/1984).[9] They advocate including not just the faces but also the voices of minorities, women, and the underprivileged, teaching about history and society from multiple perspectives (see Nash, Crabtree, and Dunn 1997/2000). This approach is intended to promote social justice through critical examination of the relations between ethnicity, gender, and culture, on the one hand, and power, on the other. Variations on this progressive multiculturalism are fairly well represented within the academy and educational institutions (e.g., Banks et al. 1991; OAH 1991).

While progressive multiculturalism became dominant within the teaching profession and among historians and social scientists, conservative Christian educational activism also grew. Such activism, particularly in the South, has a long history (Zimmerman 2002), though the current wave has achieved exceptional levels of organization. This contemporary movement is commonly traced back to the early 1960s, when desegregation, the banning of prayer in schools, and (in the wake of concerns over lagging science education) the increased teaching of evolution led many white Southern conservative Christians to feel that the schools had become hostile to their conception of the common interest (Hartman 2015; Zimmerman 2002). Conservative evangelicals' educational activism grew through the 1980s and 1990s (Clark 1993; Delfattore 1992; Ravitch 2003).

To speak in generalizations, where progressive multiculturalists see national identity as subject to change, conservatives see it as fixed, its essence defined in the past. Progressives see identity as made up of multiple allegiances, where conservatives see it as unitary. This unchanging, unitary view of identity undergirds conservatives' strong desire to "protect" national identity. They adhere to a belief that theirs is the true vision of America, one they identify as the legacy of the Puritans' vision of a covenantal myth (see Smith 2008). That is, conservative Christians see themselves as Christian *Americans*—both aspects are central to their identity and are interwoven into what they see as a unified whole. This worldview represents a coherent form of religious nationalism (Brubaker 2012), which relates to almost all aspects of national identity studied in this book, as we will see. Overall, this view is incompatible with critical historiographical approaches to the past that reject teleology, as they challenge evangelicals' view that history reflects God's will (Hartman 2015: 213).

While multiculturalism was growing among educators, and conservative Christian groups were fighting to keep Judeo-Christian principles and traditional celebratory narratives of national history in the schools, a new wave of debate over educational reform began with the 1983 report, conducted by President Reagan's Secretary of Education, Terrel Bell, entitled *A Nation at Risk*, which raised alarm about the state of American students' knowledge, particularly concerning national history. This was the beginning of a series of efforts at reform, culminating in the widespread growth of standards on state and national levels. At times, these calls for reform brought together neoconservatives (who sought to increase the role of government in education in promoting a return to basics) and Christian conservatives. Though the positions of these different factions did not always align, the movement made education reform a prominent issue in electoral politics from local, to state, to national levels. The framing of education as being in crisis resonated widely, leading to multiple efforts to improve teaching in several subjects, including history. These efforts led to creation of new curricula in many states and especially the National History Standards (first proposed in 1994, then revised in 1996) that would spark serious controversy over multicultural education, all the while attracting more media attention to the aforementioned culture wars. These conflicts over national identity and history education continued through the 1990s, gaining new urgency again in the wake of September 11, 2001.

These clashes over education and national identity more broadly helped fuel the rise to power of the New Right. This has been the case on national, state, and local levels—as in Texas, where a long history of populist conservative evangelical Christian education activism fused with statewide and national politics (more on this below; see also Cunningham 2010; Farber 2010: 258).

Opposing factions in the "culture wars" all claim to speak for the nation, which is a powerful means of legitimizing claims to power (Breuilly 1982/1993). They also tend to frame these claims as part of a dichotomy. Yet, there are many more than two views of national identity and the public good. Framing the conversation as either/or, left versus right, not only oversimplifies debates but can be used as an effective strategy for discrediting one's opponents. This emphasis on polarization obscures divisions within each "side," but it also conceals important commonality. There are irreconcilable differences between critical, progressive multiculturalism and conservative views. Yet, if various participants in the "culture wars" disagree over which values should be taught or which events should be included in textbooks, they often fail to see the consensus that unites them: a fundamental focus on the nation as the primary social and political unit that is in need of protection.

The process of writing curricula and textbooks in the United States is a largely democratic one. As such, it must produce a functional compromise. The resulting compromise—this book will show—is inclusive and nationalistic and promotes a myth of unity. Though the French system defers much more to academic experts, its textbooks also demonstrate a reaffirmation of national identity and nationalism. Yet, these different education systems—which reflect different underlying ideologies—perpetuate distinctive visions of each nation's identity, which partly take dissimilar pedagogical forms.

PEDAGOGY AND NATIONALISM: THE HISTORY-MEMORY SPECTRUM

I propose conceptualizing pedagogical approaches to history as falling along a continuum: at one end is history as an academic discipline, and at the other is the past as a site of heritage or memory.[10] History as a discipline means that the past is not viewed as sacred. It is examined in an international context, rather than primarily in isolation, through a nationalist lens. This approach includes facts, of course, but also teaches how historians interpret the past, imparting something of the tools of the field and teaching about current historiographical debates in the process. Teaching academic-style history, combined with a critique of contemporary inequality from the other social studies, leads to a progressive, forward-looking study of society. In its purest form, this approach to teaching history is not nationalistic, as it does not instrumentalize the past in an effort to inculcate emotional attachment to the national community. At the other end of this spectrum is the past conceived of as a site of memory or heritage. Here, the past is idealized, viewed as the celebration of a series of events and people that have led to national greatness, the memory of which must be transmitted to each generation in order for them to share the national values and perpetuate that greatness. This approach presents the past as a story, made up of incontrovertible facts. It may also include a teleological vision, perhaps guided by divine intervention or design in a covenantal vision of a nation destined for glory and imbued with a providential mission. Pedagogically speaking, this approach takes an omniscient tone. It is the epitome of nationalism and is inherently conservative, wishing to preserve the essence of the nation, which it sees as fixed for eternity and firmly rooted in the past.

These are, of course, ideal types, but considering history education in these terms is instructive. France today is situated roughly in the middle of this continuum: it includes elements of memory in its history education, which is primarily national in its focus and which aims to impart a common culture, seen as essential for preserving national unity. However, French curricula and textbooks also aim to teach children to think like historians—to view representations of the past as at least partly contingent on point of view and to consider how the writing of history can change. That French curricula and textbooks have come to embrace this intermediary position on our spectrum is not surprising given the remarkable growth of memory as a subject for French historians, notably since Pierre Nora led many prominent historians to explore the sites of national memory (1984–1992). This scholarly interest in memory, identity, and historiography was, not coincidentally, concurrent with calls for school reform. Curricula and textbooks, like many historians, thus seem to seek balance between memory and history. For the most part, they do not idealize historical figures (though they do require students to be familiar with them). Regarding contemporary society, they take a critical approach, discussing economic difficulties in France and the importance of both the state and individuals helping the less fortunate. They teach adherence to the values of the French creed, *Liberté, égalité, fraternité*, in a way that celebrates national commitment to social justice, while simultaneously criticizing the status quo. This is nationalism of the left: French history education presents a vision of national identity grounded in pride in a culture of self-assessment that continually questions the past and the present. This is not to say that the curricula and textbooks are perfectly in tune with social justice or that this critical assessment is complete. Notably, they have moved away from discussing the inequalities recent immigrant groups face, consistent with their commitment to universalist assimilationism (see Chapters One, Three, and Four). Overall, however, this is a vision in which the nation's ideals include questioning the state and its leaders, past and present.

History education in the United States is much closer to the heritage and memory end of the spectrum. Despite attempts by progressive scholars to incorporate historians' methods and critical assessment of contemporary society into history teaching and social studies, evidence of this approach remains the exception, not the rule. U.S. textbooks emphasize continuity with the past. Despite some progressive changes (such as the inclusion of more African American and women's history), these textbooks primarily demonstrate commitment to a Crèvecoeurian image of the country, based on myths of equality of opportunity and of progress (Crèvecoeur 1782/1997). The books focus on celebrating "freedom," which they treat as an enduring ideal, rather than explaining its historical context, thereby ultimately turning it into a conservative national symbol. This is an approach to history grounded in idealization of the past and an identification with nation-builders, who are viewed as heroes—eidolons, rather than fallible people. In idealizing them, the historical specificity of their age melts away, helping to turn them into figures who transcend time and allowing them to be more connected to "us" in the present. This approach to history rests on something akin to filial piety, based on a sense of widespread gratitude to those who "gave us" the nation we know and love. In contrast, French history teaching might be said to draw more on filial rebelliousness (perhaps unsurprising for a country that beheaded its king, and then those who overthrew him, followed by nearly two centuries of changing regimes).

A memorial approach to teaching history, even if it is blended with teaching history as a discipline, promotes cultural nationalism and the belief that belonging to the nation requires knowledge of and attachment to a collective past. Thus, the different pedagogical approaches in France and the U.S. reflect and support different conceptions of the role of the state and the people's relationship to leaders, yet both are resolutely nationalist, asserting cultural and historical specificity.

CURRICULA AND TEXTBOOKS STUDIED[11]

My choice of which textbooks to study was dependent on the details of each country's primary education system. I focus on elementary education because these are the years of primary socialization. These first years in which the public schools introduce national history are also the years during which children develop the feeling of belonging to a nation and form their first ideas about the nature of that community. Even if secondary education (and extracurricular sources) can challenge and overcome certain overly simplistic impressions learned in primary school, these are the years in which children acquire the basis of national identity (Ichilov 1990; VanSledright 2008). In addition, primary education remains under-studied, as most studies of ideological themes in history curricula and textbooks concentrate on secondary education (e.g., FitzGerald 1979; Loewen 1995/2007; Moreau 2003; Zimmerman 2002. Keith Barton 2013 and Geraldine Bozec 2010 are notable exceptions).

French schools extend coverage of French history over three years in the primary grades. This study therefore includes books from the equivalent of Grades Three through Five (*Cours élementaire* 2, or CE2, *Cours moyen* 1 and 2, or CM1 and CM2). I examine all French history, geography, and civic education curricula for the primary schools adopted between the end of the *éveil* years and 2010. These curricula were implemented in 1985, 1995, 2002, and 2008. New textbooks were written for each curriculum. I have analyzed one history and geography textbook from each of the three publishing groups, corresponding to every curriculum published since 1985.[12]

Social studies in U.S. schools generally follow a progression of focus from local to global perspectives. The youngest children study the social units closest to home, and each year the focus moves to a larger group. Thus, studies of the school, neighborhood, town, etc. (in Grades K–3) give way to the study of the individual state in Grade Four, the United States in Grade Five, and the world in Grade Six. While elements of national culture are included in all of the earlier grades' curricula, my focus in this book is on the only year of the primary grades centered on U.S. history: Grade Five.

Though the U.S. system is decentralized, only a handful of publishers create textbooks for the primary schools. A small selection of books thus dominate markets nationwide. Nevertheless, as curricula are determined on a statewide basis, this book will focus on Texas as a sort of case study. Texas has long held extraordinary influence over the textbook industry due to its size, the centralization of its textbook selection system, and the power that the state gives to citizen groups and elected officials to influence the content of curricula and textbooks. While digital publishing and political changes discussed below may be on the cusp of diminishing Texas' influence, the state remained dominant throughout the period studied here. Also, as the number of textbook publishers for the elementary school market shrank since the 1970s, Texas' power to influence books grew (Finn and Ravitch 2004; Sewall and Cannon 1991). Thus, focusing on Texas is significant in itself, as the state is a microcosm of competing ideologies and interest groups, but also sheds light on debates and educational materials that affect much of the United States. Texas adopted new elementary social studies textbooks in 1982, 1988, 1997, and 2003. These textbooks were based on curriculum guidelines published in 1980, 1994, and 1998. In addition, Texas adopted new curriculum guidelines in 2010. Two new fifth-grade textbooks were approved for use starting in the fall of 2015, in line with these guidelines; however, for reasons explained below, the 2010 curriculum is included in the present study, but the new textbooks are not.

I have analyzed all of the textbooks approved for use in Texas in 1982, 1997, and 2003.[13] The U.S. books are social studies books. While there may be disagreement over which values to teach and how to teach them, there is broad agreement that social studies education should teach citizenship (Marker and Mehlinger 1992: 832; VanSledright 2008). This mission is made official and explicit in such documents as the Texas curriculum guidelines for elementary school social studies, which list requirements by topic, including "History," "Geography," and "Citizenship." The Texas Education Code defines these goals as a driving force of public education, stating: "A primary purpose of the public school curriculum is to prepare thoughtful, active citizens who understand the importance of patriotism and can function productively in a free enterprise society with appreciation for the basic democratic values of our state and national heritage" ("Texas Education Code" 1995). Statements stressing imparting patriotism as a goal of public education are common in other states as well (e.g., Michigan Department of Education 2007: 18; NYSED 1999: 29).

The organization of these subjects in textbooks is similar, but not identical, in France and the United States. In French books, while history, geography, and civic education are often included in the same textbook, they occupy separate sections; in the U.S., they are blended together. The U.S. books focus much more on history, generally devoting only a chapter to geography, and explicit citizenship lessons appear interspersed throughout the historical narrative. In the French books, history and geography generally receive equal and separate coverage (sometimes they are in entirely separate volumes), and it is more rare for books to include a civic education section. Since teachers often do not use a textbook for this subject, not as many publishers offer them. (Though this situation will most likely change following the release of the 2016 curriculum.)

This study, then, includes French history and geography textbooks (sometimes in the same volume, sometimes requiring two volumes) from three different publishers for each period studied here, for CM1 and CM2, as well as a selection of CE2 textbooks for the years in which the CE2 curriculum covered different historical periods than CM1. Some of these textbooks include civic education sections. In addition, two civic education textbooks from the late 1980s are included, as well as the only one published in accordance with the 2008 curriculum.

My analysis of these curricula and textbooks primarily employs a systematic qualitative comparison of French and U.S. educational materials, though for measuring the prevalence of different individuals as well as the visibility of women and various ethnic groups, the analysis draws on quantitative data. Generally speaking, textbooks in France and the U.S. have tended toward greater homogenization in recent years. Widely accepted explanations for this similarity include the declining number of competing publishers for the textbook market (Apple 1991; Ravitch 2003), as well as cooperation among publishers, and the tendency to adopt methods and narratives that have met with success (Colon 2015). Homogenization in the U.S. is also thought to reflect the growing politicization of the textbook production process and the financial risks of commercial failure (Apple 1991; Ravitch 2003). Thus, in this study, I analyze textbooks of each period in each country as a set (searching for consensus and for a big picture that emerges when considering textbooks published at the same time as a group) but also individually (seeking to discern outliers and opposing viewpoints, as well as changes in different editions of the same textbook). This individual consideration can reveal lack of consensus, which often marks a complex topic in history, but it can also highlight differing approaches, where one book favors heritage and others favor history. This approach can reveal likely influence of interest groups, particularly when the content changes significantly between two subsequent editions of the same book.

TEXTBOOK PRODUCTION PROCESSES AND SOURCES OF INFLUENCE

Curricula and textbooks are selected—and therefore written—in very different ways in each country. These differences, I argue, play a major role in determining the type of pedagogical approach and the related conceptions of national identity. In France and the U.S., textbooks are a commercial product in a lucrative market. In both cases, publishers follow curriculum guidelines but have freedom in how they present the material. However, many of the similarities end there.

Curricula and Textbooks in France

In France, historians are the primary actors in determining textbook content, though there has been recurring tension and conflict between historians and politicians since the end of the *éveil* years, as politicians have continually sought to influence history and civics education via increased control over curricula, and via a series of laws in the 1990s and early 2000s. The French system is highly centralized in some ways but freer in others. Curricula are commissioned and subject to approval by the national Education Ministry. Education ministers change more frequently than governments, following the political leanings of the prime minister. Because curricula are adopted for a minimum of five years, they do not change as often as education ministers but are certainly subject to government policies.

The French curricula of this study were written following different procedures. The 1985, 1995, and 2002 curricula were written by a group of historians appointed by the education minister and approved by the inspectors general, as well as the minister himself. In 1995 and 2002, the proposed curricula were submitted to various groups for their nonbinding input. These consultations included most teachers' unions, relevant interest groups, and parents' associations, as well as governmental expert panels (Legris 2014). The ministry has the final say and has made some changes, but it seems that from 1985 through 2002 the experts' role in the process was generally respected (Legris 2014).

There has been an increase in political intervention in curricula in recent years. Beginning in the mid-1990s, debate over memory of what came to be called "burning social questions" increased, particularly in the wake of President Jacques Chirac's public recognition in 1995 of France's role in deporting Jewish people during the Holocaust. Notably, people of Algerian origin came to demand similar recognition of atrocities committed by French soldiers in the Algerian War. These debates led to discord in classrooms and among teachers and historians (Legris 2014: 165). In the early 2000s, parliament stepped into what had been ministerial territory and passed a series laws (discussed in greater detail in Chapter One) requiring the inclusion of various previously excluded topics in history education. Historians protested vigorously what they called the "instrumentalization" of history. They have expressed their opposition to the Education Ministry, in the general press, and in various trade journals and associations (see e.g., Comité national de l'APHG 2005; de Cock and Picard 2009: 1; Garcia 2013: 11, 16).

The 2008 curriculum broke with the previous consultative approach, thus politicizing the process further. Written under the ministry of Xavier Darcos, this curriculum was created in great secrecy. Unlike his predecessors, the education minister did not convene a *Groupe d'Experts*, the *Conseil National des Programmes*, or the inspectors general. While previous curricula have identifiable authors, it is not known who wrote this one. Darcos' ministry did consult teachers' and parents' groups, but the curriculum and the process in which it was written met with widespread criticism from historians, teachers, and even former education ministers (Legris 2014: 175).

Though the process of curriculum creation is subject to political influence in France, textbooks are largely shielded from such direct intervention. While new textbooks do aim to conform to new curricula, they are under no legal obligation to do so. There is no ministerial control over textbooks, and neither does the ministry issue reviews or make recommendations. Publishers generally hire a small team of authors (usually approximately five) to write a series of books. For primary school texts, publishers select teacher training professors, historians and geographers, and usually one regional inspector (these inspectors start their careers as educators). In schools, textbooks are selected by individual teachers with no oversight by school authorities, parents, or communities.

Teachers' freedom, as well as that of the publishers, are guaranteed by French law, and are taken quite seriously in official texts (e.g., Borne 1997; Seré 2010). As such, publishers aim primarily to appeal to teachers. Publishers' concerns, then, seem to be predominantly pragmatic, making a tool that teachers will find easy to use in planning their lessons, which are centered on in-class activities. The cost of books is low, with an average retail price of about 12 euros for student editions. While developing new books, the publishers' association (Savoir Livre) organizes round table discussions for authors with teachers, so that they can better understand teachers' practical needs.

Publishers as well as individual authors might also agree to meet with representatives of various associations who try to convince authors to represent their point of view. Associations also seek audience with the historians and politicians involved in creating new curricula. These groups have little leverage, and their success seems to depend on whether they can genuinely convince those with the power to write curricula and textbooks of the validity of their viewpoints (Colon 2015; Legris 2014: 177). While several such groups promote the perspectives of various ethnic minorities or of feminists, the vast majority of the meetings between textbook authors and interested parties seem to involve more purely pedagogical questions: teachers' unions are most concerned with the pedagogical freedom of teachers to use the methods they prefer and to ensure that curricula create a realistic teaching load. Parents are more likely to complain about the physical weight of a textbook that children have to carry than to question its contents (Colon 2015; Seré 2010: 17–18).

Though there are different constituencies with different goals involved in the processes of creating curricula and textbooks, there are some key points of widespread consensus. Most historians, politicians, teachers, and parent groups involved in these processes want history to be taught following age-appropriate aspects of the academic discipline while imparting the foundations of national memory. If some groups wish to add events and people to the core vision of national identity, it is not fundamentally irreconcilable with the approach of the historians who are mainly responsible for writing curricula and textbooks. Above all, because teachers want to adhere to the curricula and want teaching tools that will help them do that, textbook publishers tend to follow the curriculum guidelines very closely. Even so, they have editorial freedom in their approach to most topics, as the curricula do not provide extensive explanations of the material to be covered.

Curricula and Textbooks in the United States[14]

In the U.S., curricula and textbook production is highly decentralized. Each state writes its own curricula (and this is still true as of 2015, as Common Core standards do not cover history) and has its own policies on textbooks. Most states do not exert statewide control over textbooks, leaving the choice up to districts, schools, or teachers themselves. However, a large minority of states—currently 19—establish a list of approved resources (Gewertz 2015). In some states compliance with this list is optional. In others, schools must choose most (but not all) of their textbooks from the state's list if they want the state to pay for them. Some states only provide funding for textbooks on the approved list. This was the case in Texas until a 2011 law, discussed below, changed the situation in that state. To be approved in Texas, technically, a textbook only needs to include half of the material in the state's curriculum guidelines and is free to include material that is not required (which makes it easier for textbooks to meet the guidelines for multiple states). However, the approval process—which Texas calls "adoption"—is long and complex.

The process of textbook selection is intricately connected to the production of the books and has become considerably more opaque over the years. It is helpful to bear in mind that U.S. textbooks are much longer and more costly than their French counterparts. Where the French textbooks generally devote about 100 pages to history and another 100 to geography, U.S. books published since the late 1990s are 600 to 800 pages long (those published in the early 1980s were approximately 400–500 pages long). Recent books retail for approximately $60 to $100 for a student book, though Texas negotiates a lower rate for the books on its list (typically, about $45 for the student edition). The excessive length of the U.S. books, which surpasses what a teacher can cover in a year, provides further evidence that they are not designed only as tools for teaching but also in order to meet political scrutiny, by including everything that various groups want to see.

In order to understand the textbook production process, it is essential to know that, in general, the U.S. textbooks from the major publishers (Houghton Mifflin Harcourt, McGraw-Hill, and Pearson Scott Foresman) are not written by the people whose names are listed as authors (Apple 1991; Loewen 1995: 283; Marshall 1991). These books list a great many authors and consultants (approximately 20–50)—and listed authors may be consulted by the publisher—but the real writers and managing editor are unknown.

In Texas, the process of selecting new textbooks begins with the creation of curriculum guidelines. These are drafted by the Texas Education Agency (TEA), but final approval rests with the elected State Board of Education (SBOE).[15] The curriculum guidelines serve as the basis for selecting new textbooks.

In order to be considered for adoption in Texas, publishers must submit their textbooks for review. All citizens of Texas are entitled to review the proposed books, submitting their comments to the State Board of Education. The board can then decide whether to demand editorial changes. Publishers must either comply with changes or withdraw their books from the adoption process.[16] Prior to 2014, publishers usually complied with Texas' requirements, since being selected by Texas not only meant access to that state's market of five million public school students but also improved sales in other states, as many prefer to rely on Texas' vetting process rather than investing their own resources in selecting textbooks. Publishers are further sensitive to the wishes of Texas citizen groups as these groups intervene in textbook selection after state-level adoption, ranking textbooks and mobilizing parents and teachers across the country to select the textbooks that they deem most appropriate.[17]

Politicization of this process is not new. Since the Cold War era, Texas' curriculum and textbook selection has been put under the authority of the elected State Board of Education.[18] Already by the 1980s, there was evidence that the TEA and SBOE removed material that was likely to cause protest (Marshall 1991). Public awareness about the politicization of Texas' curriculum and textbook adoption process has grown since the early 1980s, leading more individuals and groups with various agendas to intervene. Nearly all participants in the process seem to view it through the lens of the culture wars, so that any aspect of social studies education can be subject to ideologically charged debate. In recent years, more academic historians, for instance, have sought to influence the process through political channels (see Erekson 2012). However, the most prominent and influential groups have long been those of the Christian Right.

The current wave of conservative education activism is commonly traced back to Mel and Norma Gabler of Longview, Texas (1915–2004; 1923–2007). The Gablers, an oil-clerk who attended college briefly without graduating and a high-school-educated stay-at-home mother, began reviewing Texas textbooks in 1961, when they objected to material in their son's high-school government textbooks. They founded The Mel Gablers' Educational Research Analysts and became known for their meticulous reviews, systematically intervening in textbook adoption processes, and recruiting volunteers to expand their operations. The Gablers' organization (run today by Neal Frey) promotes a nationalistic conservative Christian worldview and opposes what they call "secular humanism," which they see as the dominant "religion" of the educational establishment (more on their views throughout this book).

As Christian Right opposition to education grew from the 1970s onward, in conjunction with the rise of the New Right more broadly, additional groups were formed. They, along with older organizations (such as Phyllis Schlafly's Eagle Forum), increasingly followed the Gablers' approach and joined them in petitioning the State Board and publishers in Texas and elsewhere. These groups now intervene in every stage of curricular development and textbook production and sales. In addition, in the early 1990s, conservative Christian organizations increasingly pursued a strategy of seeking election to state and local school boards. They were successful, partly due to the frequently low voter turnout for these elections.[19] Similarly, the Texas State Board of Education moved to the right, a process that continued into the 2000s.

Beginning in 1992, the Texas SBOE gave a more active role to conservative interest groups (Blakeslee 1999). For the 1996 social studies textbook adoption, the SBOE appointed members of Christian Right organizations to the State Textbook Committee, which was charged with the initial screening of proposed textbooks. Prior to 1996, the STC had been composed entirely of educators. There is also evidence that, as intervention from protest groups continued to rise into the 1990s (Clark 1993), textbook publishers began consulting increasingly with Christian Right groups early in the process of writing their books, to avoid costly rewrites later and to help ensure adoption and sales in Texas (Blakeslee 1999).[20]

Shortly thereafter, the state raised the stakes of its curriculum guidelines by establishing standardized testing in social studies for the elementary grades. In the process of drafting the 1998 standards (the Texas Essential

Knowledge and Skills), on which the tests would be based, the State Board of Education appointed a committee to review the proposed standards. This committee included at least three directors of conservative activist groups (Blakeslee 1999). The SBOE at that time included a majority of Republicans (nine out of the fifteen members), but in the 2000s the composition of the board shifted further rightward, as the Republican majority grew and more moderate Republicans were replaced by Christian conservatives (Erekson 2012).[21] When this board oversaw the revision of the 1998 TEKS in 2009–2010, they, too, appointed a committee to review the old document and rewrite it. This panel included two conservative pastors.[22] The resulting 2010 TEKS included striking instances of conservative influence, famously emphasizing Judeo-Christian influences on the writers of the U.S. Constitution and attempting to vindicate Joseph McCarthy—striking enough to invite ridicule by the national media (e.g., McKinley 2010; Texas Textbook Massacre 2010; see also Erekson 2012).

Perhaps partly spurred by this unflattering national attention, the state legislature passed a bill in 2011 with the power to reduce the SBOE's influence over what is taught in Texas classrooms, and by extension, the rest of the country. Up until 2011, Texas would only provide full funding for textbooks on the approved list. The new legislation made funding for textbooks much more flexible, providing funds for whatever teaching materials schools wish, as long as these adhere to the TEKS (Texas Legislature 2011: Section 31.004.). The selection of textbooks in 2014 thus seems considerably less significant than that of previous years. The SBOE only approved two publishers' submissions for fifth-grade social studies in 2014: Scott Foresman and Weekly Studies. Because for the first time in decades the majority of the major publishers for the primary grades (McGraw-Hill and Houghton Mifflin Harcourt) did not produce textbooks that met the SBOE's requirements, it seems likely (or at least possible) that they will instead produce textbooks freed from such overt political influence.

Media attention and pushback from the political center and left thus seem poised to curtail the extremes of Texan Christian conservative influence on the textbooks that are sold nationwide. The process of negotiating history and social studies education, though, will remain ongoing.

BOOK OUTLINE

This book is divided in two parts. Part One examines the ways in which ethnicity, gender, and class are represented as facets of national identity and the controversies that these representations entail in French and U.S. curricula and textbooks. Here the book demonstrates that the French and U.S. educational materials exhibit significant changes in their approaches to some previously ignored groups and topics. Chapter One focuses on ethnic diversity and the changing representations of various ethnic groups and their history. Chapter Two examines gender roles, focusing on the portrayal of women throughout national history. Chapter Three addresses issues of class and social justice, demonstrating that these issues constitute a key difference between French and U.S. textbooks and exploring the implications of these differences for nationalism and national identity.

Part Two examines more overt expressions of nationalism and demonstrates how these have become more prevalent in both countries' textbooks. This section focuses on the endurance of national myths and how these myths have evolved. Chapter Four explores textbook and curricula depictions of symbols of the nation, including objects that we typically picture when we think of symbols but also discourse about national greatness and values. Chapter Five focuses on the national hero as a key national symbol and the controversies implied in the representation of the heroes in France and the U.S. Chapter Six proceeds with an analysis of educational approaches to national territory in order to assess whether textbooks justify national boundaries in teleological terms. Finally the book concludes with a summary of the findings, contribution and policy implications, and avenues for future research.

This book demonstrates how depictions of national identity are shaped by a variety of factors reflecting broader tensions, debates, and power relations within societies. Through these changes, the founding nationalist myths and symbols have remained prevalent in French and U.S. educational materials. Social studies education remains committed to unifying these divided societies through traditional conceptions of the national essence.

NOTES

1. The expression "culture wars" was widely used in academic publications as well as those for the general public. Andrew Hartman has traced its first use in the contemporary U.S. to a piece by Todd Gitlin and Ruth Rosen in *The New York Times* in 1987 (Hartman 2015: 297). It was popularized in academic circles by James Hunter's 1991 book, among others.
2. Studies of history and citizenship education in Europe and North America that bring together comparative education and nationalism theories typically do so in a cursory manor, often simply acknowledging the historic relationship between education and nationalism (citing Anderson and Gellner, for instance) and perhaps examining conceptions of national identity within the context of Kohn's now-outdated ethnic-civic dichotomy. Notable exceptions to this treatment include Barton (2013) and Soysal et al. (2005). There are studies of history education within the field of comparative and international studies that do explore questions of national identity and nationalism, but based on a review of books and articles published in journals including *Comparative Education* and *Comparative Education Review* over the past 20 years, one finds that the vast majority of this work does not focus on Western democracies. As an indication of the state of the field, it is telling that in the annual bibliographical survey compiled by *Comparative Education Review*, "ethnicity, race, class" is listed as a category, but "nationalism" or "national identity"

is not. There is a need for more complex and systematized consideration of different conceptions of national identity that look beyond the dichotomies of civic versus ethnic, or national versus sub- or supra-national.

3. These differences between France and the U.S. notably include their views on the role of the state in redistribution of wealth. In addition, France is part of the European Union, and education is also situated within the European context. The U.S. is the current hegemonic power in the world, and that image informs its national identity and pride. By contrast, France's leading role on the world stage (which it shared with Great Britain [Kumar 2006a]) is behind it. It seems likely that the nationalism of a hegemon could differ from that of a state conscious of its diminished status. (Chapter Four explores this question, which reveals more nuanced answers than we might expect.) However, the similarities outweigh the differences and allow for meaningful comparison: France is also a leader in world affairs, is one of the world's major economies, and remains a notable cultural force. Despite their frequently ambiguous relationships with immigration, both countries take pride in their attraction for immigrants, in the present as well as through history. This status as "nations of immigrants" complements their status as exporters of culture: both conditions support a sense of cultural superiority and of a certain centrality, as a pole attracting people and diffusing cultural production. More significantly for the present study, though France faces greater external pressures on its sovereignty, the two countries' internal struggles are comparable, and these have dominated discussion over education in recent years.
4. Textbooks are used approximately 75 percent of the time in French primary school classrooms, and more frequently in history lessons (Borne 1997: 22). The majority of French teachers also rely on textbooks to prepare their classes (Séré 2010). Similarly, in the U.S., textbook use accounts for 80 to 90 percent of classroom time (Finn and Ravitch 2004), and this number rises for history education (Loewen 1995).
5. There are more typically ethnic views of national belonging that are based on a vision of the nation as a kinship community. However, this vision is now widely discredited and marginalized within Western democracies. There are also more purely civic conceptions, in which belief in the political values of the nation is the primary criterion for membership. This belief might be coupled with a sense of contract, in which membership requires contributing to the greater good, whether through social involvement, political responsibility, or economic means (i.e., productive work and paying taxes). However, these ethnic and civic categories leave out the idea of a cultural conception of national belonging, which goes beyond a "thin" political culture. Within cultural conceptions of national identity, different components may be more or less salient for different people, and the threshold at which one is considered to be a member of the community can vary widely. Thus, for example, for some, only a person born on the national soil to parents also born there can be truly part of the nation. To others, growing up in the country is sufficient, and for other cultural nationalists, even an adult immigrant might sufficiently adopt the dominant cultural practices to be seen as belonging. The same observer might hold different ethnic groups to different standards, as a result of what has been called "culturalist" or "differentialist" racism (Balibar and Wallerstein 1988/1991; Lentin 2000; Taguieff 1991). Major components of cultural nationalism can include language, religion, and perhaps even more elusively, affective attachment to the community, its values, and its history. I have adapted this description of typology from Elaine Thomas' recent work, in which she posited five membership categories: descent, culture, belief, contract, and monetized contract (Thomas 2012).

6. The term "social studies" was institutionalized by the National Education Association in 1916, with its founding of the Committee on the Social Studies. The NEA favored a focus on American culture over academic history as a means of assimilating immigrants (Marker and Mehlinger 1992: 833–834). Throughout the era of Progressive education, the gulf between history as an academic discipline and social studies grew, as educators saw history and geography as means of improving society, and did not see the value in teaching "history for history's sake" (Marker and Mehlinger 1992: 834).
7. The use of nationalist propaganda by the Vichy government was one of Suzanne Citron's major arguments against continuing to teach the "national myth" (see Bozec 2010: 120–123; Suzanne Citron, 1984, "Pour une mémoire plurielle," *Le Monde* 19 janvier 1984: 2; see also Citron 1987/2008).
8. Distrust of religion in France is not new. The Revolution was not only republican but also anticlerical, as the aristocracy and the church were united in their socioeconomic dominance during the *Ancien Régime*. The secular (*laïque*) republican left was thus long in conflict with the Catholic, more often royalist right, as shown by the frequent upheavals and reversals of regime of the nineteenth century. The push for universal public education during the Third Republic was partly intended to weaken the influence of the church, particularly in rural areas, liberating those in the provinces from superstition—turning not just "peasants into Frenchmen" (Weber 1976), but Catholics into nationalists. For many thinkers, the schools were the natural site for this secular conversion, as education could eradicate religion's "irrational" hold on citizens, which was seen as incompatible with the rationalist modern nation-state. (The parallels between the civic religion of nationalism and the methods of the Catholic Church do not need repeating here. See, for instance, Bell 2003; Bellah 1991; Zelinsky 1988.) Though the twentieth century finally witnessed the emergence of a republican consensus, thus easing much of the tension between religious and nonreligious factions (Amalvi 2011), the place of religion in French society is still controversial.
9. As Henry Giroux has written: "What educators need is a pedagogy that redefines national identity not through a primordial notion of ethnicity or a monolithic conception of culture, but as part of a postmodern politics of cultural difference in which identities are constantly being negotiated and reinvented within complex and contradictory notions of national belonging" (1981/1984: 55).
10. On the concepts of heritage or memory see Hartog (2003); Kammen (1989, 1991); Lowenthal (1998); Ricoeur (2000); VanSledright (2008).
11. For the complete list of the textbooks studied, see Chapter One.
12. This is another similarity between France and the U.S.: in each country the textbook market has been reduced to three major publishing groups. The three publishing conglomerates in France are Editis (which notably publishes Nathan, Bordas, and Retz, among others), Hachette Livre (which includes Hatier), and Albin Michel (which includes Sedrap and Magnard). The primary U.S. publishers for the public schools since the early 2000s are Houghton Mifflin Harcourt, McGraw-Hill, and Pearson Scott Foresman.
13. In addition to the three textbooks of 2003 studied here, there were two other works approved in Texas in 2003. These were not textbooks but multimedia systems that are interactive and much more expensive than traditional textbooks (priced at \$1275 for *History Alive!* and \$2000 for *Social Science 2000* per classroom). Their sales in Texas were far below those of traditional textbooks. (*Social Science 2000* did not sell any copies, and *History Alive!* sold only 322 copies by the 2008 school year. By contrast, by the same year, the three traditional textbooks had sold more than 131,000; 26,000; and 220,000 copies each [Harcourt, McGraw-Hill, and Scott Foresman, respectively; Texas Education Agency 2008].) I have read the textbook used with *History Alive!*

but have not consulted the full set of documents. I have not included this textbook in tallies of illustrations or in the analyses for two reasons. First, the format is too different from the traditional textbooks to allow for meaningful comparison. In addition to the fact that the textbook is only a part of the whole, *History Alive!* ends its detailed accounts of history with the Civil War, then skips ahead and summarizes the entire twentieth century in nine pages, whereas the other textbooks cover history to the present in detail. Second, and more importantly for the purposes of this study, the multimedia systems did not receive scrutiny from the citizen groups or from the State Board of Education. For instance, they were not reviewed by the Gablers' group, and there was almost no mention of them in the SBOE hearings. A board member asked a teacher testifying on behalf of *History Alive!* if there is anything offensive in it. The teacher affirmed that there was not, and her support of it seems to have been sufficient to secure its approval by the board (Texas Education Agency 2002). Thus, they are not products of the same process of knowledge production.

14. I described this process, as well as the history of the multiculturalist and conservative education activists, in greater detail in Hutchins 2005.
15. The TEA is staffed by political appointees at the top levels and education professionals below them. The TEA is also overseen by the SBOE. The SBOE consists of 15 members who are elected from districts of equal population across the state.
16. For more information on the current procedure, see: http://tea.texas.gov/interiorpage.aspx?id=2147485614 (accessed 17 March 2015). Previous procedures were detailed in "Overview of State Adoption/Distribution of Instructional Materials," Person Project, 13 Oct. 1999. Retrieved 24 June 2005 (http://www.youth.org/loco/PERSONProject/Handbook/States/texas2.1.html). See also: Marshall (1991); Wong (1991).
17. A great many studies and reports have documented various aspects of the influence exerted by the Texas State Board of Education and the state's citizen activists. See for example: Blakeslee (1999); Delfattore (1992); Keith (1991); Marshall (1991); Ravitch (2003).
18. Briefly in the 1980s, under Ross Perot's governorship, the elected board was replaced with an appointed board, in an attempt to depoliticize the process. However the elected board was reinstated in 1989, at the same time that conservative Christian groups were targeting such positions.
19. This was not a grassroots movement, as these candidates were often backed by large, national organizations. For instance, the Citizens for Excellence in Education, affiliated with the National Association of Christian Educators, boasted that they had obtained 12,000 seats on school boards across the country for their self-described fundamentalist Christian candidates between 1990 and 1994 (Kaplan 1994).
20. A listed textbook "author" of a 1997 textbook, who corresponded with me on condition of anonymity, confirmed this practice (personal e-mail to the author, 18 March 2005; 21 March 2005).
21. The 2010 board included ten Republicans, eight of whom were self-described "true Christian conservatives." Of the 15 board members in 2010, only one had extensive experience as a classroom teacher; the majority had worked in business (Erekson 2012).
22. One of these pastors was David Barton, who aside from being frequently featured in conservative media, was vice chairman of the Texas Republican Party from 1997 to 2006. In that capacity, Barton frequently worked with Texas billionaire James Leininger. Leininger has also financed the campaigns of all the conservative members of the SBOE, as well as having founded one of the citizen groups that has been active in reviewing textbooks since the 1990s (the Texas Public Policy Foundation) (Blakeslee 1999; King 2001; Miller et al. 2006; Stutz 2002).

REFERENCES

Curriculum Guidelines and Official Reports

Michigan Department of Education. 2007. Grades K-8 Social Studies Content Expectations. Retrieved 19 Jul. 2015 (https://www.michigan.gov/documents/mde/SSGLCE_218368_7.pdf).

NYSED (New York State Education Department). 1999. Social Studies Core Curriculum. Retrieved 19 Jul. 2015 (http://www.p12.nysed.gov/ciai/socst/ssrg.html).

République Française. 2015. Grande mobilisation de l'Ecole pour les valeurs de la République. Retrieved 26 Feb. 2015 (http://cache.media.education.gouv.fr/file/01-janvier/49/4/2015_DP_mobilisation_Ecole_complet_385494.pdf).

Texas Education Agency. 2002. Public Hearing on Textbooks Before the State Board of Education. 11 Sept. Retrieved 6 May 2005 (http://www.tea.state.tx.us/textbooks/proclamations/proc2000/sept11hearing.pdf).

Texas Education Agency. 2008. Interim Statement of Textbook Charges by MLC School Year: 2008. Retrieved 12 May 2009 (http://www.tea.state.tx.us/emat/sdinv_mlc.rtf).

"Texas Education Code §28.002 (h)." 1995. Retrieved 17 Sept. 2015 (http://www.statutes.legis.state.tx.us/Docs/ED/htm/ED.28.htm).

Texas Legislature. 2011. SB6, 82 (R). 82nd Texas Legislature. 14 Apr. Retrieved 19 Sept. 2015 (http://www.legis.state.tx.us/tlodocs/821/billtext/html/SB00006F.HTM).

Works of Reference

Amalvi, Christian. 2011. *Les héros des Français: Controverses autour de la mémoire nationale*. Paris: Larousse.

Anderson, Benedict. 1983/2006. *Imagined Communities: Reflections on the Origin and Spread of Nationalism*. Rev. ed. London; New York: Verso.

Apple, Michael W. 1991. "The Culture and Commerce of the Textbook." In M. Apple and L. Christian-Smith, eds., *The Politics of the Textbook*. New York; London: Routledge, pp. 22–40.

Apple, Michael W. 2000. *Official Knowledge: Democratic Education in a Conservative Age*. 2nd ed. New York; London: Routledge.

Apple, Michael W. and Linda K. Christian-Smith, eds. 1991. *The Politics of the Textbook*. New York; London: Routledge.

Balibar, Etienne and Immanuel Maurice Wallerstein. 1988/1991. *Race, Nation, Class: Ambiguous Identities*. Trans. Chris Turner. London; New York: Verso.

Banks, James A., ed. 1981. *Multiethnic Education: Theory and Practice*. Boston: Allyn and Bacon.

Banks, James A. 1996. *Multicultural Education, Transformative Knowledge, and Action: Historical and Contemporary Perspectives*. Multicultural Education Series. New York: Teachers College Press.

Banks, James A., et al. 1991. "Curriculum Guidelines for Multicultural Education." National Council for the Social Studies. Retrieved 30 Jan. 2002 (http://www.socialstudies.org/positions/multicultural/).

Barton, Keith C. 2013. "School History as a Resource for Constructing Identities: Implications of Research from the United States, Ireland, and New Zealand." In M. Carretero, M. Asensio, and M. Rodriguez-Moneo, eds., *History Education and the Construction of National Identities*. Charlotte, NC: Information Age Publishing, pp. 93–108.

Bell, David A. 2003. *The Cult of the Nation in France: Inventing Nationalism, 1680–1800*. Cambridge, MA: Harvard University Press.

Bellah, Robert N. 1991. *Beyond Belief: Essays on Religion in a Post-traditionalist World*. Berkeley: University of California Press.

Billig, Michael. 1995. *Banal Nationalism*. London: Sage.

Blakeslee, Nate. 1999. "McGraw-Hill Sees the Light." *The Texas Observer* 30 Apr. Retrieved 21 Mar. 2005 (http://www.texasobserver.org/showArticle.asp?ArticleID=1051).

Borne, Dominique, et al. 1997. *Le Manuel Scolaire*. Paris: Inspection Générale de l'Education Nationale.

Bozec, Géraldine. 2010. *Les héritiers de la République: Eduquer à la citoyenneté à l'école dans la France d'aujourd'hui*. Unpublished doctoral dissertation, Institut d'Etudes Politiques de Paris, Paris.

Breuilly, John. 1982/1993. *Nationalism and the State*. 2nd ed. Chicago: University of Chicago Press.

Brubaker, Rogers. 1992. *Citizenship and Nationhood in France and Germany*. Cambridge, MA: Harvard University Press.

Brubaker, Rogers. 2001. "The Return of Assimilation? Changing Perspectives on Immigration and Its Sequels in France, Germany, and the United States." *Ethnic and Racial Studies* 24.4: 531–548.

Brubaker, Rogers. 2012. "Religion and Nationalism: Four Approaches." *Nations and Nationalism* 18.1: 2–20.

Burkholder, Zoë. 2011. *Color in the Classroom: How American Schools Taught Race, 1900–1954*, Oxford; New York: Oxford University Press.

Calhoun, Craig. 2007. *Nations Matter: Culture, History, and the Cosmopolitan Dream*. New York; London: Routledge.

Clark, Charles S. 1993. "School Censorship." *The Congressional Quarterly Researcher* 19 Feb.: 145–168.

Colon, David. 2015. "La Fabrique du manuel d'histoire: enjeux et finalités d'un objet controversé." Paper presented at the Centre d'histoire de Sciences Po, 4 March, Paris, France.

Comité national de l'APHG. 2005. Il appartient aux historiens d'écrire l'histoire et aux enseignants de l'enseigner. Motion 22 May, Paris. Retrieved 17 Jul. 2015 (http://www.aphgaixmarseille.com/spip.php?article231).

Crèvecoeur, J. Hector St. John de. 1782/1997. *Letters from an American Farmer*. In Susan Manning, ed., Oxford; New York: Oxford University Press.

Cunningham, Sean P. 2010. *Cowboy Conservatism: Texas and the Rise of the Modern Right*. Lexington, KY: University Press of Kentucky.

Cusset, François. 2003. *French Theory: Foucault, Derrida, Deleuze & Cie et les mutations de la vie intellectuelle aux Etats-Unis*. Paris: La Découverte.

De Cock, Laurence and Emmanuelle Picard. 2009. *La Fabrique scolaire de l'histoire: Illusions et désillusions du roman national*. Marseille: Agone.

De Laforcade, Geoffrey. 2006. "'Foreigners,' Nationalism and the 'Colonial Fracture': Stigmatized Subjects of Historical Memory in France." *International Journal of Comparative Sociology* 47.3–4: 217–233.

Delannoi, Gil. 1991. "La Théorie de la nation et ses ambivalences." In G. Delannoi and P.-A. Taguieff, eds., *Théories du nationalisme*. Paris: Kimé, pp. 9–14

Delfattore, Joan. 1992. *What Johnny Shouldn't Read: Book Censorship in America*. New Haven: Yale University Press.

Dewey, John. 1916. *Democracy and Education*. New York: The Free Press.

Dieckhoff, Alain. 2000. *La nation dans tous ses Etats*. Paris: Champs/Flammarion, 2000.

Durkheim, Emile. 1922/1969. *Education et sociologie*. Paris: Presses Universitaires de France.

Erekson, Keith A. 2012. *Politics and the History Curriculum: The Struggle over Standards in Texas and the Nation*. New York: Palgrave Macmillan.

Evans, Ronald W. 2004. *The Social Studies Wars: What Should We Teach the Children?* New York: Teachers College Press.
Farber, David R. 2010. *The Rise and Fall of Modern American Conservatism: A Short History*. Princeton: Princeton University Press.
Fichte Johann Gottleib. 1808/2001. "Addresses to the German Nation." In V. Pecora, ed., *Nations and Identities: Classic Readings*. Oxford: Blackwell, pp. 114–127.
Finn, Chester and Diane Ravitch. 2004. *The Mad, Mad World of Textbook Adoption*. Washington, DC: Thomas B. Fordham Institute. 29 Sept. Retrieved 25 Feb. 2015 (http://edex.s3-us-west-2.amazonaws.com/publication/pdfs/Mad%20World_Test2_8.pdf).
FitzGerald, Frances. 1979. *America Revised: History Schoolbooks in the Twentieth Century*. New York: Vintage.
Frey, Neal. 2003a. [Director, Educational Research Analysts.] "Re: Fifth Grade Social Studies Textbooks." Personal email. 9 Apr.
Frey, Neal. 2003b. "Re: Fifth Grade Social Studies Textbooks." Personal email. 15 Apr.
Garcia, Patrick. 2013. "Les Péripéties de la discipline." *Le Débat* 175: 8–17.
Garcia, Patrick and Jean Leduc, 2003. *L'enseignement de l'histoire en France de l'Ancien Régime à nos jours*. Paris: Armand Colin.
Gellner, Ernest. 1983. *Nations and Nationalism*. Ithaca: Cornell University Press.
Gellner, Ernest. 1997. *Nationalism*. London: Weidenfeld & Nicholson.
Gewertz, Catherine. 2015. "States Ceding Power of Classroom Materials." *Education Week* 17 Feb. Retrieved 18 Sept. 2015 (http://www.edweek.org/ew/articles/2015/02/18/states-ceding-power-over-classroom-materials.html).
Giroux, Henry. 1981/1984. *Ideology, Culture, and the Process of Schooling*. Philadelphia: Temple University Press.
Guidelines for Creating Positive Sexual and Racial Images in Educational Materials. 1975. New York: Macmillan.
Hargreaves, Alec G. 2007. *Multi-ethnic France: Immigration, Politics, Culture, and Society*. 2nd ed. New York; London: Routledge.
Hartman, Andrew. 2008. *Education and the Cold War: The Battle for the American School*. New York: Palgrave Macmillan.
Hartman, Andrew. 2015. A *War for the Soul of America: A History of the Culture Wars*. Chicago: University of Chicago Press.
Hartog, François. 2003. *Régimes d'historicité: Présentisme et expériences du temps*. Paris: Seuil.
Hobsbawm, Eric J. 1990/1992. *Nations and Nationalism Since 1780: Programme, Myth, Reality*, Cambridge: Cambridge University Press.
Hunt, Lynn, ed. 1989. *The New Cultural History: Essays*. Studies on the History of Society and Culture. Berkeley: University of California Press.
Hunter, James. 1991. *Culture Wars: The Struggle to Define America*. New York: Basic Books.
Hutchins, Rachel. 2005. *Nationalisme et identité nationale dans les manuels d'histoire américaine de l'enseignement primaire (1982–1997)*. PhD dissertation, Université Nancy 2, Nancy, France.
Hutchinson, John. 2005. *Nations as Zones of Conflict*. London; Thousand Oaks; New Delhi: Sage Publications.
Ichilov, Orit, ed. 1990. *Political Socialization, Citizenship Education, and Democracy*. New York: Teachers College Press.
Jennings, Jeremy. 2011. "Universalism." In E. Berenson, V. Duclert, and C. Prochasson, eds., *The French Republic: History, Values, Debates*. Ithaca; London: Cornell University Press, pp. 145–153.
Kammen, Michael. 1989. "History Is Our Heritage: The Past in Contemporary American Culture." In P. Gagnon, ed., *Historical Literacy: The Case for History in American Education*. Boston: Houghton Mifflin, pp. 138–156.

Kammen, Michael. 1991. *Mystic Chords of Memory: The Transformation of Tradition in American Culture*. New York: Knopf.

Kaplan, George R. 1994. "Shotgun Wedding: Notes on Public Education's Encounter with the New Christian Right." *The Phi Delta Kappan* 75.9: K1–K12.

Kaufmann, Eric P. 2004. *The Rise and Fall of Anglo-America*. Cambridge, MA: Harvard University Press.

Kaufmann, Eric. 2008. "The Lenses of Nationhood: An Optical Model of Identity." *Nations and Nationalism* 14.3: 449–477.

Keith, Sherry. 1991. "The Determinants of Textbook Content." In P. Altbach, G. Kelly, H. Petrie and L. Weis, eds., *Textbooks in American Society: Politics, Policy, and Pedgagogy*. Albany: SUNY Press, pp. 43–59.

King, Michael. 2001. "Naked City: Not Quite by the Book." *Austin Chronicle* 30 Nov. Retrieved 27 Oct. 2002 (http://www. austinchronicle.com/issues/dispatch/2001-11-30/pols_naked4.html).

Kohn, Hans. 1944. *The Idea of Nationalism: A Study in Its Origins and Background*. New York: Macmillan.

Kumar, Krishan. 2006a. "English and French National Identity: Comparisons and Contrasts." *Nations and Nationalism* 12.3: 413–432.

Kumar, Krishan. 2006b. "Nationalism and the Historians." In G. Delanty and K. Kumar, eds., *The Sage Handbook of Nations and Nationalism*. London: Sage, pp. 7–20.

Kuzio, Taras. 2002. "The Myth of the Civic State: A Critical Survey of Hans Kohn's Framework for Understanding Nationalism." *Ethnic and Racial Studies* 251: 20–39.

Legris, Patricia. 2010. "Les Programmes d'histoire en France: la construction progressive d'une 'citoyenneté plurielle' (1980–2010)." *Histoire de l'éducation* 126: 121–154.

Legris, Patricia. 2014. *Qui écrit les programmes d'histoire?* Grenoble: Presses universitaires de Grenoble.

Lentin, Alana. 2000. "'Race,' Racism and Anti-racism: Challenging Contemporary Classifications." *Social Identities* 6.1: 91–106.

Loewen, James W. 1995/2007. *Lies My Teacher Told Me: Everything Your American History Textbook Got Wrong*. Revised Edition. New York: Touchstone.

Lowenthal, David. 1998. *The Heritage Crusade and the Spoils of History*. Cambridge, UK: Cambridge University Press.

Marker, Gerald and Howard Mehlinger. 1992. "Social Studies." In P. Jackson, ed., *Handbook of Research on Curriculum*. New York: Macmillan, pp. 830–851.

Marshall, J. Dan. 1991. "With a Little Help from Some Friends: Publishers, Protesters, and Texas Textbook Decisions." In M. Apple and L. Christian-Smith, eds., *The Politics of the Textbook*. New York; London: Routledge, pp. 56–77.

Martigny, Vincent. 2012. *Le Nationalisme culturel français: Récit national et usages politiques de la culture en France (1981–1995)*. PhD dissertation, Institut d'Etudes Politiques de Paris.

Mauss, Marcel. 1920/1969. "La Nation." *Oeuvres. 3, Cohésion sociale et divisions de la sociologie*. Paris: Editions de Minuit, 1969, pp. 573–625.

McDonough, Kevin and Walter Feinberg, eds. 2003. *Citizenship and Education in Liberal-Democratic Societies: Teaching for Cosmopolitan Values and Collective Identities*. Oxford; London: Oxford University Press.

McKinley, James C. 2010. "Texas Conservatives Win Curriculum Change." *The New York Times* 12 Mar. Retrieved 21 Sept. 2010 (http://www.nytimes.com/2010/03/13/education/13texas.html).

Meunier, Sophie. 2006. "The Distinctiveness of French Anti-Americanism." In P. Katzenstein and R. Keohane, eds., *Anti-Americanisms in World Politics*, Ithaca, NY: Cornell University Press, pp. 129–156.

Michelet, Jules. 1847–1853/2007. *Histoire de la Révolution Française.* 2 Vol. Paris: Folio Histoire.

Miller, Kathy, et al. 2006. "The Anatomy of Power: Texas and the Religious Right in 2006." *Texas Freedom Network.* Retrieved 12 Feb. 2015 (http://www.tfn.org/site/DocServer/SORR_06_ReportWEB.pdf?docID=222).

Moore, Robert. 1977. *Stereotypes, Distortions, and Omissions in U.S. History Textbooks.* New York: Council of Interracial Books for Children.

Moreau, Joseph. 2003/2004. *School Book Nation: Conflicts over American History Textbooks from the Civil War to the Present.* Ann Arbor, MI: University of Michigan Press.

Nash, Gary B., Charlotte Crabtree, and Ross E. Dunn. 1997/2000. *History on Trial: Culture Wars and the Teaching of the Past.* New York: Vintage Books.

Noiriel, Gérard. 2007. *A quoi sert « l'identité Nationale ».* Marseille: Agone.

Nora, Pierre. 1984–1992. *Les Lieux de mémoire.* 3 Vol. Paris: Gallimard.

Nora, Pierre. 2008. "Liberté pour l'histoire." *Le Monde* 10 Oct.

Nussbaum, Martha. 1994. "Patriotism and Cosmopolitanism." *Boston Review* Oct./Nov. Retrieved 1 Mar. 2015 (http://bostonreview.net/martha-nussbaum-patriotism-and-cosmopolitanism).

"OAH Statement on Multicultural History Education." 1991. Organization of American Historians, Spring. Retrieved 26 Jan. 2005 (http://www.oah.org/reports/mulitcultural.html).

O'Leary, Cecilia Elizabeth. 1999. *To Die For: The Paradox of American Patriotism.* Princeton, NJ: Princeton University Press.

Özkirimli, Umut. 2010. *Theories of Nationalism: A Critical Introduction.* 2nd ed. Basingstoke: Palgrave Macmillan.

Ravitch, Diane. 2003. *The Language Police: How Pressure Groups Restrict What Students Learn.* New York: Knopf.

Renan, Ernest. 1882/1994. "Qu'est-ce qu'une nation?" In J. Hutchinson and A. Smith, eds. Trans. Ida Mae Snyder. *Nationalism.* Oxford; New York: Oxford University Press, pp. 17–18.

Ricoeur, Paul. 2000. *La Mémoire, l'histoire, l'oubli.* Paris: Editions du Seuil.

Schissler, Hanna and Yasemin Nohuğlu Soysal, eds. 2005. *The Nation, Europe, and the World: Textbooks and Curricula in Transition.* New York; Oxford: Berghahn Books.

Schwartzmantel, J.J. 1987. "Class and Nation: Problems of Socialist Nationalism." *Political Studies* XXXV: 239–255.

Scott, Joan Wallach. 2007. *The Politics of the Veil.* Princeton, NJ: Princeton University Press.

Séré, Alain, et al. 2010. *Le manuel scolaire à l'heure du numérique: Une "nouvelle donne" de la politique de ressources pour l'enseignement.* Rapport à Monsieur le ministre de l'Education Nationale. Paris: Ministère de l'Education Nationale. Ministère de l'Enseignement Supérier de la Rercherche.

Sewall, Gilbert T. and Peter Cannon. 1991. "The New World of Textbooks: Industry Consolidation and Its Consequences." In P. Altbach, G. Kelly, H. Petrie, and L. Weis, eds., *Textbooks in American Society: Politics, Policy, and Pedgagogy.* Albany: SUNY Press, pp. 61–70.

Smith, Anthony D. 1991. *National Identity.* London; New York: Penguin.

Smith, Anthony D. 1999. *Myths and Memories of the Nation.* Oxford: Oxford University Press.

Smith, Anthony D. 2008. *The Cultural Foundations of Nations: Hierarchy, Covenant, and Republic.* Malden, MA: Blackwell.

Soysal, Yasemin Nohuğlu, Teresa Bertilotti, and Sabine Mannitz. 2005. "Projections of Identity in French and German History and Civics Textbooks." In H. Schissler and Y. Soysal, eds., *The Nation, Europe, and the World: Textbooks and Curricula in Transition.* New York; Oxford: Berghahn Books, pp. 13–34.

Stewart, Nikita and Richard Pérez-Peña. 2015. "In Charleston, Raw Emotion at Hearing for Suspect in Church Shooting." *The New York Times* 19 Jun. Retrieved 19 Jun. 2015 (http://www.nytimes.com/2015/06/20/us/charleston-shooting-dylann-storm-roof.html?smid=fb-nytimes&smtyp=cur&_r=0).
Stutz, Terrence. 2002. [Untitled.] *The Dallas Morning News* 10 Jul. Retrieved 13 Dec. 2004 (http://lists.wayne.edu/cgi-bin/wa?A2=ind0207&L=tamha&F=&S=&P=995).
Taguieff, Pierre-André. 1991. *Face au Racisme 1: Les moyens d'agir*. Paris: La Découverte.
Texas Freedom Network. 2004. "Profiles of the Religious Right." Retrieved 13 Dec. 2004 (http://www.tfn.org/religiousright.htm).
"Texas Textbook Massacre: 'Ultraconservatives' Approve Radical Changes to State Education Curriculum." 2010. *Huffington Post* 13 Mar. Retrieved 19 Sept. 2015 (http://www.huffingtonpost.com/2010/03/13/texas-textbook-massacre-u_n_498003.html).
Thomas, Elaine R. 2012. *Immigration, Islam, and the Politics of Belonging in France: A Comparative Framework*. Philadelphia: University of Pennsylvania Press.
VanSledright, Bruce. 2008. "Narratives of Nation-State, Historical Knowledge, and School History Education." *Review of Research in Education* 32.1: 109–146.
Weber, Max. 1905/1920/2001/2012. *The Protestant Ethic and the Spirit of Capitalism*. Trans. Stephen Kalberg. New York; London: Routledge.
Wieviorka, Michel. 1996 "Culture, société et démocratie." In M. Wieviorka, ed., *Une société fragmentée?: le muticulturalisme en débat*. Paris: La Découverte, pp. 11–60.
Wong, Sandra L. 1991. "Evaluating the Content of Textbooks: Public Interests and Professional Authority." *Sociology of Education* 64.1(Jan.): 11–18.
Zelinsky, Wilbur. 1988. *Nation into State: The Shifting Symbolic Foundations of American Nationalism*. Chapel Hill, NC; London: University of North Carolina Press.
Zimmer, Oliver. 2003. "Boundary Mechanisms and Symbolic Resources: Toward a Process-Oriented Approach to National Identity." *Nations and Nationalism* 9.1: 173–193.
Zimmerman, Jonathan. 2002. *Whose America? Culture Wars in the Public Schools*. Cambridge, MA; London: Harvard University Press.

Part One

Faces of the Nation

1 Ethnicity and the Nation

Increasing ethnic diversity and expansion of full citizenship rights to previously excluded ethnic groups has led, in many Western countries, to widespread reassessment of traditional conceptions of national belonging. Demographic and social changes beginning at roughly the same time in France and the United States have provoked similar questions over national identity, immigration policy, civil and civic rights, and education. This chapter demonstrates that, in French and U.S. curricula and textbooks, growing acceptance of ethnic diversity has contributed to reaffirmations of national sentiment and redefinitions of national identity. In both cases, explicit ethnic conceptions of national belonging have been marginalized while cultural nationalism has been strengthened.

In both countries, there are many who have seen demographic and social changes since the 1960s as threatening the established national way of life and who have considered certain ethnic minority populations to be unassimilable (de Laforcade 2006: 219, 226; Ngai 2004: 2, 267; Scott 2007: 60). Others have seen in these demographic changes more productive challenges to traditional visions of national identity. As the historic exclusion of minority groups came to be increasingly viewed by a majority as morally wrong (and legislated accordingly), it led many to question the accuracy of traditional conceptions of national identity and political and social belonging. These competing visions have been heavily publicized as part of the "culture wars" in the U.S. and in debates over national identity in France, which have been remarkably similar to one another in many respects. In both countries, these controversies have involved not just policy initiatives but have also led to changes in history and social studies teaching, because regardless of their position on these issues, participants in these debates agree that education is central to either perpetuating traditions or to changing the status quo in fighting exclusion.

Ultimately, though, our primary concern is the broader context beyond the "culture wars": these debates, however divisive, remain national. They highlight the salience of the nation as a primary locus of belonging for many people. They show how the nation is redefined—through conflict—in a process that renews attachment to the national polity.

There are a number of differences between the French and U.S. cases that we must bear in mind. Some of these differences are rooted in obvious contrasts between the two countries' histories. For instance, most disadvantaged minorities in France today are fairly recent immigrants, who came mainly from former French colonies in Africa and Asia, and their descendants. In the U.S., though recent immigration from Latin America and Asia has also contributed to debates over identity politics, these debates have much deeper roots in the history of African Americans' struggle for inclusion and equality. Conceptually, though scholars in France and the U.S. have influenced one another, historians, politicians, and pedagogues in France are much more likely to embrace colorblind republican assimilationism in response to socioeconomic inequality along ethnic lines, rather than pluralism. This view does not exclude a critical approach to national history. Since the 1990s, these decision-makers have increasingly seen the history of colonization, slavery, immigration, etc., as legitimate objects of study, partly thanks to the work of minority groups who have sought inclusion of their history in the national narrative. In the U.S., historians and educators tend to support varying forms of progressive multiculturalism. However, curricula and textbooks are subject to political approval from citizens and conservative elected bodies. As such, representations of past and present injustice regarding ethnic minorities constitute one of the main sources of conflict between competing education actors.

PRINCIPAL FINDINGS AND CHAPTER OUTLINE

Recent French and U.S. curricula and textbooks include more people of non-European origin in illustrations and narratives than did their predecessors, while promoting a narrative of progress and interethnic national unity.[1] The result is a sort of conservative, nationalist multiculturalism, which includes minorities and limited depictions of past discrimination, but only to the extent that these do not detract from a positive view of France and the United States today. The contemporary countries are shown as bastions of equality and unity.

French textbooks depict few people of color in national history and society, but more in recent textbooks than in the early 1980s. Since the 1990s, they have incorporated changes in academic historiography and public memory and now dedicate more attention and take a critical approach to injustice regarding non-European people in French history. However, they generally avoid discussing contemporary immigration and inequalities along ethnic lines. U.S. textbooks, on the other hand, render ethnic minorities much more visible in depictions of national history and contemporary society. While these books have absorbed certain, nonnegligible multiculturalist approaches, notably including more Native American and African American history, they exhibit a clear rightward shift between 1997 and

2003. They now relegate discussion of racist discrimination and inequality to the distant past and celebrate diversity and the contemporary status quo, thus avoiding addressing the depth and consequences of racism in American history and society.

Because this is the first chapter of analysis, it begins by providing some deeper background on the conflicts over identity in each country. It then examines changing conceptions of national identity as presented in curriculum guidelines. The bulk of the chapter is then dedicated to quantitative and qualitative comparative analysis of textbooks, showing first the ways in which they have incorporated more diversity and aspects of progressive multiculturalism, followed by a demonstration of the ways in which a more conservative nationalism shapes their presentations of the most controversial issues regarding ethno-racial equality.

DIFFERING CONCEPTIONS OF CULTURE AND IDENTITY

At the core of contemporary conflicts regarding national identity are different conceptions of the relations between different ethnic groups. Assimilationism, pluralism, different understandings of power, exclusion, and inclusion form the context of multiple political debates, including those over history and social studies education.

In France, most historians—including those writing curricula and textbooks—wish to transmit a sense of historians' methods to pupils. These methods are more conducive to learning a critical approach to history than were traditional narratives that celebrated the greatness of the nation-state, which were common in history education from the late nineteenth through mid-twentieth centuries (Citron 1987/2008). Despite this epistemological consensus, multiculturalism does not have the same standing among the French academy as it does in the U.S.

After briefly rising in popularity in the 1970s and early 1980s, cultural pluralism under the slogan *droit à la différence* (the right to be different) fell out of favor by the late 1980s (as discussed in the Introduction). Public discourse has been dominated since then by neo-assimilationist republicanism, as debates have continued to rage over the place of Maghrebi and sub-Saharan African immigrants and their descendants in French society. There is disagreement among different political factions over the best courses of action, but there is agreement that there is a rift in French society. The bulk of public discourse and debates take for granted that French residents and citizens of Maghrebi and sub-Saharan African origin are more likely to be unemployed, undereducated, and housed in the *cités*, the low-income housing generally on the outskirts of major cities (Viguier 2011). Beyond these facts, interpretations vary. However, what groups on the left, in the center, and on the right have in common is the framing of Islam as a problem and an obstacle to national cohesion (Scott 2007: 69–72; Viguier 2011:

262–267). In the most exclusionist view, these minority populations are too culturally different to assimilate, and the primary obstacle to their assimilation is Islam (de Laforcade 2006: 219, 226; Hargreaves 2007: 4–5). Far-right groups often depict these minorities as committed to fundamentalist Islam, which they show as a threat to French culture and security, seeing it as irreconcilable with republican values.

Most French historians and mainstream politicians adopt a more centrist assimilationist stance, which is officially colorblind, and in which they oppose exclusionary ethnic grounds for national membership. They may blame the far-right for discriminating against ethno-racial minorities and thereby exacerbating tensions. The corollary to this colorblind position is the broadly consensual notion that attachment to the nation should be the primary group allegiance, and the only one with which public education should concern itself (Bozec 2010; Garcia and Leduc 2003: 197, 205–206, 238, 251; Laborde 2001; Lebovics 2004; Legris 2014: 95–110; Martigny 2012: 376; Waldman 2009; for examples of this stance, see Schnapper 1991; Taguieff 1988). There has long been agreement among most historians, policy makers, and advocates on the left and the right in favor of assimilationism (Lewis 2011: 240–241; Thomas 2012: 136–150; Viguier 2011: 262–265).

In response to this consensus, there has recently been a split on the left, with some now advocating the official recognition of ethnic differences in order to face and thereby overcome discrimination. Despite colorblind rhetoric, there is much evidence of ethnic identification in France, as for example people of different national origins have come to unite under the terms *beur* or "black" (de Laforcade 2006: 226; Lewis 2011: 240). It thus seems likely that the widespread insistence on colorblindness can appear nonsensical or hypocritical to minority populations, and that it has added to their frustration, as they see discrimination against them as rampant and as a major obstacle to their integration (Hargreaves 2007: 10, 187; Lewis 2011: 240). Groups such as the *Indigènes de la République* have particularly given voice to this view that neo-colonialism and racism are the reasons for inequality, not minorities' culture or unwillingness to assimilate (Parti des Indigènes de la République 2005).

Such voices are still largely marginal (Amiraux and Simon 2006), though the tide may be turning. In the 1980s, the history of immigration, followed by that of colonization, began to gain legitimacy in French universities (Citron 1987/2008; Dosse 2007; Hargreaves 2007: 14; Lewis 2011: 238; Noiriel 1988). Shortly thereafter, some exceptions were made to the taboo on collecting data on ethnic groups, as some government-sponsored investigations and reports have examined socioeconomic inequalities and have found evidence of widespread discrimination in the labor market (Hargreaves 2007: 57–58; Tribalat 1995).

These broader debates inform the context of concerns over national identity. However, since the brief rise of pluralism in the early 1980s, education activists and policy makers have not issued calls for recognition of ethnic difference. They have, though, sought greater inclusion for colonial history and the history of slavery and greater visibility of the overseas French territories. These movements have been supported by memorial associations as well as by historians, as we will see in greater detail throughout this chapter.

In the U.S., respect for—and even celebration of—the ethnic diversity of the American people appears now to be a consensual value among all but the most extreme activists. However, in practice this principle means very different things, with very different implications for visions of national identity in educational materials.

For progressive multiculturalists, it is not enough to include multihued faces in textbooks; history teaching must incorporate a multiplicity of viewpoints—teaching that conflict, differing perspectives, and interpretations are inherent parts of the study of history. The more progressive forces among these activists want children to learn about injustice in the past as a means to understanding enduring inequality in the present. They do not want past injustices to be minimized or to be discussed only as part of a narrative of progress, as if discrimination, exploitation, and inequality were things of the past (Banks 1996; Nash 1997/2000). This is not to say that they oppose promoting unity: rather, they believe that unity can only be achieved through understanding, and thereby correcting, civic and socioeconomic divisions.[2] Progressive historians and pedagogues also generally believe in multiple identities—that is, that one can have a sense of national belonging that is not exclusive of other group allegiances and cultural practices.

Variations on this progressive multiculturalism are prominent among the academy and educational institutions. For instance, both the National Council for the Social Studies as well as the Organization of American Historians have issued statements that reflect this position. In 1991, as conflict surrounding multiculturalism was spreading through the media, the OAH made its position official through a statement published in its magazine and distributed to the press:

> The multiple objectives of history education can best be served by curricula that afford students the opportunity in the public schools to study both the history of the larger society and the history of minority groups and non-Western cultures. Whether the people of the United States regard themselves as one nation or many, or as some combination of both, most Americans will probably recognize that they share certain common traditions, values, and experiences arising out of their common humanity and their interactions with one another. These include our political and economic institutions, however imperfect, a mass culture that affects everyone, and a common entitlement to freedom, equality, and dignity. A successful history education should help students understand what binds Americans together while simultaneously promoting respect for America's pluralism and diversity. We hope it will

> contribute to realizing a common future of reconciliation and equality across the boundaries of race, ethnicity, gender, and class.
>
> (OAH 1991)

At the other end of the spectrum among prominent education activists, for assimilationists, the goal of history teaching is to instill national pride based on positive shared memory.[3] Celebrating America's identity as a "nation of immigrants" in which civil rights have continually been extended to greater segments of the population is in keeping with such a positive view. Indicating that divisions still exist in the U.S. and that these divisions might be the result of past discrimination and exploitation is not (e.g., Warren 1997). Assimilationism is prominent among conservative education activists, such as the Gablers' Educational Research Analysts, and reflects the view of many conservative Christians more generally.

Progressive multiculturalism and assimilationism, then, are fundamentally irreconcilable in some ways. Perhaps the deepest divide concerning visions of the nation in the U.S. is between progressives who (very broadly speaking) see national identity as continually changing and as a site for renegotiation of values and political membership, and conservatives who (as a generalization) see national identity as fixed in the past.

Nevertheless, though conservative Christians tend to depict national identity in essentialist terms, even their vision of it seems to have been somewhat reshaped by debates of the past thirty years. Most of the influential education activists of the Christian Right have now come to accept certain aspects of multiculturalism and adopt some elements of multiculturalist rhetoric. By the late 1990s, the Gablers and others had changed their approach to discussing diversity. Many conservative evangelicals now proclaim a commitment to multiculturalism, but they use this term quite differently than do progressives. Influential conservative Christian groups regularly declare their support for racial tolerance and for including previously excluded groups in curricula. This shift represents an important change from the days of overt racism. It also undergirds conservative claims to speak for a majority of Americans and to redefine national identity along ethnically inclusive but ideologically restrictive lines. By rejecting strict ethnic boundaries for national belonging, these groups may gain more widespread legitimacy in asserting their vision for the social and political culture of the nation. By asserting a belief in racial tolerance, and by equating this belief with true multiculturalism, they discursively discredit more progressive multiculturalism, condemning it as antipatriotic and divisive. In 2003, I asked executive director of the Gablers' Educational Research Analysts, Neal Frey, to explain the group's stance on multiculturalism. This was his response:

> Political correctness stereotypes whites as oppressors and people of color as victims, men as oppressors and women as victims, and/or Christians as oppressors and pagans as victims. We do not object to

> multiculturalism. We do oppose political correctness. Multiculturalism unites. Political correctness divides. Multiculturalism stresses consensus. Political correctness emphasizes conflict. Multiculturalism harmonizes groups. Political correctness alienates them. If the purpose of public education is to build democracy, it is most unprofessional to polarize multicultural populations. [. . .]
>
> (Frey 2003a)

In answer to a follow-up question, he added:

> Textbooks should speak of non-whites' brutalities to each other or to whites, as well as of whites' inhumanities to people of color.
>
> (Frey 2003b)

Conservative evangelical education activists, then, advocate a nationalist stance that brings together discourse of American exceptionalism, national pride and attachment, and racial tolerance. From this position, they challenge all the more strenuously what they deem the "excesses" of multiculturalism (framed as fractious threats that place group loyalty above national loyalty), as well as progressive ideologies, which they see as similarly dangerous and unpatriotic. Their discourse is thus one of cultural and ideological assimilationism, grounded in conservative nationalism.

While many conservatives today (unlike those of previous generations) generally reject a strict ethnic model of political membership and accept assimilation of certain previously excluded groups into the national polity, they accept this on their terms. Namely, Christian Right education activist groups define uncritical acceptance of the socioeconomic status quo and an embracing of conservative ideology centered around an unfettered market as the true "American way." As such, they see critical discourse that seeks to redress the effects of centuries of ethnic and gender discrimination as unpatriotic and inaccurate. For instance, in their review of Harcourt Brace's 1997 textbook, the Gablers' Educational Research Analysts demonstrate this equation of patriotism with traditional ("true"), triumphalist history education:

> A very "watered" down version of what is considered true American history. Over emphasis on multicultural to the point of ridiculous. Half of the pictures and content used to stress the point would have gotten the point across. Pictures of slavery and oppression number 25! Fifth graders are seeing a lot of degredation [sic] that is trying to diminish the patriotic aspect of studying our past. This text includes 72 pages of content where the cruelty to slaves and other minorities is heavily emphasized. It is basically "overkill". Fifth graders getting this presented to them would definitly [sic] not cherish "the Pledge of Allegiance" or singing the "Star Spangled Banner."
>
> (Jones 1997: 1)

Activists of the right, broadly speaking, eschew cultural pluralism when it seems to conflict with their view of national primacy and unity and their vision of history as sacred.

Changing conceptions of national identity and ethnic minorities' place in national history are reflected and made official in curriculum guidelines. Examining these documents offers an overview of dominant thinking and policy and constitutes a logical starting point for more in-depth analysis.

DIVERSITY IN CURRICULA

Curricula in France and Texas reflect broader evolutions in the consensus over the relationship between ethnic diversity and national identity in each country. Throughout the period studied here, both sets of curricula attribute great weight to the cultural component of national belonging and attachment. Both emphasize the transmission of national identity as an important goal of social studies education, in line with public and political discourse in each country. By framing this national identity in not just civic but also cultural terms at a time when minorities can no longer be ignored, the curricula must address the question of ethnic culture and belonging. The French official vision—while opposed to ethnic exclusion—is grounded in an assimilationist concept of the national culture and heritage. The emphasis on cultural and political assimilation through social studies education has grown throughout the period studied here, thus seemingly reflecting common public discourse depicting the culture of immigrants and their descendants (most notably, Muslims) as incompatible with traditional French society (Hargreaves 2007: 4–5). Texan curricula, on the other hand, adheres to a culturally inclusive vision in which U.S. culture is defined by its diverse members and influences, reflecting the widespread acceptance of a minimal or "thin" form of multiculturalism.[4]

As we have seen (in the Introduction), the demographic, social, and epistemological shifts and debates of the 1960s and 1970s contributed to multiple changes in conceptions of education. France and the U.S. experienced changes in dominant pedagogical styles during this period involving both form and content, followed by reactions against this new pedagogy. In both countries, these processes led to reflection over the nature and the goals of history teaching. This questioning intensified and expanded starting in the early 1980s. In both cases, questions over history teaching were often framed in terms of a "crisis" in education, involving national greatness, the financial and moral future of the country, as well as the definition of national identity.

In France, as the *éveil* experiment was winding down, the Cycle Moyen (CM, equivalent of fourth and fifth grades) history curriculum of 1980 was the first one written since 1945. The 1980 CM curriculum marked a return to renewed focus on events and chronology in history teaching associated explicitly with nationalist goals. The curriculum states that history and geography should help to foster a "feeling of belonging to the national collectivity" (44), and it explicitly tied learning national history to the education of future citizens. After laying out the pedagogical goals of the history program, the curriculum states:

> This set of goals thus contributes not only to the personal growth of the child, but also to developing his sense of belonging to a national collectivity. These goals are thus fundamental to the general objectives of moral and civic education.
>
> ("Horaires . . ." 1980: 44)

However, this point is not developed or emphasized nearly as much as it is in subsequent curricula, which also place more emphasis on various aspects of national culture. For instance, though the word *patrimoine* (loosely translated as "heritage") appears in the 1980 curriculum, it is not explicitly connected to national belonging or identity. Subsequent curricula refer frequently to *patrimoine* across all humanities subjects, repeatedly showing familiarity with it as an important part of national belonging.

The shift in the 1985 curriculum can be attributed to a variety of factors: ambient political and social concerns, the ongoing discussions among historians, educators, and politicians over the importance of transmitting national identity through history teaching, and the role of specific individuals. The 1985 curriculum marked the end of the *éveil* years and the implementation of an even more explicit conception of history teaching as a vehicle for the transmission of national memory. Jean-Pierre Chevènement—the French education minister who presided over the 1985 curriculum—opposed pluralism and advocated cultural assimilation to the dominant French culture (Legris 2010: 129–130). Mastery of French language and history are, in this view, keys to integration. His curriculum does, though, make several mentions of diversity (perhaps reflecting the pluralist strain advocated by such historians as Mona Ozouf, Jacques Le Goff, and Suzanne Citron [Bozec 2010: 118–123; Legris 2010: 129]). This curriculum emphasized the importance of knowing French culture to be a citizen and develop a "national consciousness":

> Knowledge of our historical heritage, assimilation of the political and cultural legacy (*patrimoine*) of France, and the discovery of the richness of our people and our country are indispensable to the shaping of the French citizen. History and geography contribute to the emergence of students' national consciousness; they can thus appreciate the contribution of other cultures, which they discover through studies, travel, or regular contact with immigrant communities.
>
> ("Horaires . . ." 1985: 17)

This passage attempts to show respect for foreign traditions. It is not, however, pluralist in its approach and is Franco-centric, regarding non-French cultures as "other," not as part of the national cultural repertoire (Géraldine Bozec has made a similar argument; 2010).

In later years, the focus turns further to integration and national unity. While memorial associations and immigrant groups demanded more recognition in the national memory and consciousness, the dominant political consensus on this issue continued to shift rightward (Bozec 2010; Martigny 2012; Thomas 2012). In the aftermath of the first *Affaire du foulard*,[5] a new policy for primary schools was proclaimed, which reaffirmed the emphasis on French language skills that appeared in the 1985 curriculum (language is discussed further in Chapter Four). This 1990 directive, drafted by Education Minister Lionel Jospin, heightens the emphasis on integration—along economic lines, but also along cultural lines:

> The [French] language is not only a key for scholastic success. It plays another role that, it seems to me, is essential for our schools to take on today. It is through language that children will become socially integrated. I am speaking of all the children who live on our land, all the children who will later participate in the economic, social, and cultural life of our country; that includes children of immigrants. Finally, mastering French is also a source of personal enrichment.
>
> (*Discours* . . . 1990: 607)

This assimilationist discourse dominates all the subsequent curricula. In particular, there is abundant, recurring emphasis on "common culture," which refers not just to political culture but to history. For instance, in the 2008 curriculum, following the list of topics that students are expected to know is this commentary: "These pillars of national history form the basis of a common culture. These references are to be joined with art history" ("Horaires . . ." 2008: 24). The definition of those cultural references becomes increasingly precise over time, as the subsequent curricula (up to and including 2002) become longer and more detailed.

Like the history curricula, the civic education curriculum writers since 1985 also emphasize cultural unity, centered around respect for French republican values, which are presented as universal. The only explicit reference to ethnic conflict and inequality in national history—past or present—that I have found in French primary school curricula since 1985 is in the 2008 civics curriculum:

> [The student] learns that, even if reality is never entirely in line with ideals, ideals should continue to be affirmed in order to guide behavior and structure action, starting from historic examples like slavery or the inequality between men and women.
>
> ("Horaires . . .": 71)

Among the values that civic education curricula emphasize is the "refusal of all types of discrimination." However, the curricula do not elaborate further on this precept and make no mention of ethnic categories. One might argue that this incitation is at least partly directed at establishing boundaries regarding Muslim culture, an interpretation that is subtly supported by this excerpt from the 2002 curriculum:

> Listening to others is the first form of respect and acceptance of difference. This respect for difference, to the extent that it does not infringe on the universal values of human rights, has multiple opportunities to be exercised: fighting against daily forms of rejection, welcoming a new, isolated student, integrating a disabled child. The different disciplinary fields reinforce this and show its value. Thus, experimental sciences allow better understanding of the differences between boys and girls, and history and geography or the arts do so for cultural differences.
> ("Horaires . . .": 71)

The implicit caveat that minority cultures can only be tolerated if they respect universal human rights seems to echo the common political discourse that unites the French left and right in opposing certain aspects of some immigrants' culture, framing them as sexist, which undergirds left-wing opposition to students' wearing headscarves (Scott 2007: 70–71; Thomas 2012).

The relationship between tolerance and religion is complex in contemporary France, as the events of early 2015 amply demonstrated, and as it has been since the founding of the First Republic. In 2002, the minister of education, Jack Lang, commissioned a report on teaching about religion, which concluded that secondary schools needed to teach about religions. The report cited a variety of reasons: a better understanding of history, but also to improve tolerance and freedom of thought, to fight against extremism, and to improve national cohesion. For instance, the report argues:

> If secularism is inseparable from a democratic goal of truth, then transcending prejudice, promoting values of discovery (India, Tibet, America), and loosening the vice-grip of identity in the heart of a society, which is more exposed than before to the partition of collective personalities, contributes to disarming various forms of fundamentalism [. . .].
> (Debray 2002: 21)

The report led to a legislative amendment in the 2005 law on education goals and curricula (Loi d'orientation . . . 2005). It is also connected to changes in the 2002 curriculum, which requires increased attention to historical events tied to religion (which remains in the 2008 curriculum).

This call to teach about the history of religion was intended to bridge cultural divides while reinforcing secularism. Teaching about religion in history had been advocated since 1993 by the Council of Europe as a means to fight extremism (Legris 2014: 176). The 2002 curriculum, as well as the 2005 law, established a connection between teaching *le fait religieux* and nationalist assimilation to republican values. For instance, the law states: "Beyond the transmission of knowledge, the Nation establishes as the primary mission of schools to make students share the values of the Republic" ("Loi d'orientation . . .": Article 2).

Laïcité as a French value is discussed further in Chapter Four. Because there is a religious dimension to current French identity politics, I will examine in this chapter textbooks' presentations of religion in national history. In adding *les faits religieux* to curricula, the Education Ministry required teaching more about medieval Christianity but also added references to the founding of Islam. These new guidelines present early interactions between Christians and Muslims as a source of both conflict and productive cultural exchange.

U.S. curricula, on the other hand, were quick to adopt certain multiculturalist approaches. The 1980 Texas curriculum guidelines featured a two-page section on Multicultural Education. Among 18 stated goals it lists: "examining cultural conflicts (past and present), how they arose, and what alternatives were found for resolving them" (*Framework* . . . 1980: 15). This reference to "cultural conflicts" may be a euphemism for racist discrimination—an approach that minimizes the possibilities for meaningful antiracist education. In addition, the focus then, as in more recent curricula, has consistently been much more on cultural diversity as a source of national pride than as a source of conflict. For instance, among the seven "Goals for Public School in Texas" (first adopted in 1970, reaffirmed in 1979) is: "Appreciation of Culture, Language, and Life Style Diversities and Their Corresponding Aesthetic Values" (*Framework* . . . 1980: 7). This emphasis on diversity and indirect approach to "conflict" is perhaps not surprising, given the well-established feel-good consensus of the time (cf. FitzGerald 1979; Loewen 1995; Zimmerman 2002). However, it would not have met with approval from progressive multiculturalists.

The 1980 Texas curriculum guidelines primarily emphasize the United States' past as being founded on the convergence of many cultures, which came together "to build a new and strong state and nation" (*Framework* . . . 1980: 5). They focus repeatedly on the "enrichment" of the national culture through the "contributions" and "achievements" of various ethnic groups (though they do not omit "problems"). This approach is largely typical of celebratory early multiculturalist efforts. This theme is repeated throughout the document, as in these passages:

> The confluence of many cultures has been characteristic of American life throughout our history. The great variety of cultures has been a powerful influence in structuring our social system, enriching our national heritage, and creating some of our most critical problems. The social studies curriculum should, wherever relevant, stress the contributions of individuals from many groups to our national development and the

> enrichment of our heritage by influences from all cultures represented in our population.
>
> (10)

Later curricula follow a different format and become increasingly positive in their presentations of diversity. Whereas in 1980, the curriculum guidelines consisted of explanations of goals and philosophies, by 1994, they do away with much of the explanation of their intentions and instead (like their French counterparts) list increasingly specific content to be covered. Like the guidelines of 1980, the later documents primarily emphasize the positive aspects of cultural diversity (e.g., listing it among the five "basic civic values of American society" [*Proclamation* . . . 1994: A-23]). In 1994 they continue to mention conflict, for example: "use major social issues, past and present, to analyze cooperation and conflict (e.g., voting rights, religious issues, slavery, status of women, displacement of American Indians)" (A-25). However "conflict" disappears as a general category from later curricula. Significantly, the 1998 and 2010 TEKS make no explicit, general negative statements about U.S. history or contemporary society. One meaningful addition to the 2010 TEKS does make room for potentially progressive study: in each grade level, K–5, they state: "Students identify and discuss how the actions of U.S. citizens and the local, state, and federal governments have either met or failed to meet the ideals espoused in the founding documents." Otherwise, they do not mention anything akin to conflict, inequality, discrimination, or exploitation. They do, though, require the teaching of specific events relating to conflict and oppression, as we will see below.

The general discourse regarding multiculturalism is one of celebration. For instance, the 1998 TEKS (on which the 2003 textbooks are based) require teaching the following:

> (23) Culture. The student understands the contributions of people of various racial, ethnic, and religious groups to the United States. The student is expected to:
>
> (A) identify the similarities and differences within and among selected racial, ethnic, and religious groups in the United States;
> (B) describe customs, celebrations, and traditions of selected racial, ethnic, and religious groups in the United States; and
> (C) summarize the contributions of people of selected racial, ethnic, and religious groups to our national identity.
>
> ("Chapter 113" 1998: §113.7.b)

We should note that in the 2010 curriculum guidelines, this language is changed, rendering it somewhat more in tune with the demands of multiculturalist advocate groups, who argue that talking about "contributions" and focusing on "customs" and "celebrations" limits minority groups to a status outside the mainstream of American culture. The 1998 passage just cited evolves in this way by 2010:

> Students describe the cultural impact of various racial, ethnic, and religious groups in the nation and identify the accomplishments of notable individuals in the fields of science and technology.
>
> ("Chapter 113" 2010: §113.16.a.1)

Textbooks in France and the U.S. adhere to curriculum guidelines. These guidelines, though, leave room for interpretation, leading to variations between competing textbooks. The following sections examine the broad, fairly consensual changes across time in each country as well as some striking differences between textbooks.

INCREASED DIVERSITY IN TEXTBOOKS

In many ways, French and U.S. textbooks demonstrate increased commitment to presenting a diverse picture of the nation. They do so literally through their illustrations.[6]

This analysis begins with an overview of the textbooks' illustrations, which occupy approximately half the page space in books for the primary schools and are an excellent indicator of editorial priorities. From a pedagogical standpoint, they reinforce key ideas and events (Amalvi 1984; Bliss 1990; Duchastel 1983). From a marketing standpoint, they make books more appealing and—touching on both marketing and politics—they provide a quick, efficient way for those reviewing textbooks to see whether the people and events that matter to them figure prominently in the books. In the U.S., in particular, the choice of illustrations is also ideologically charged, as textbook reviewers and critics will often flip through the books, looking primarily at illustrations in order to see what publishers have chosen to emphasize. In these books that, since the 1990s, surpass 600 pages, the so-called "flip test" can determine how these powerful critics react to a book (Farr and Tulley 1985: 470; Finn and Ravitch 2004; Marshall 1991: 127). Beyond pedagogical and ideological concerns, illustrations also contribute to making books more appealing to teachers or textbook selection committees—a nonnegligible concern in this competitive market.

Diversity in French Textbooks

Though numbers do not tell the whole story, they provide a clear starting point. Table 1.1 shows the percentages of illustrations depicting only people of European origin, and those that include at least one person of color for

Table 1.1 People of Color in Textbook Illustrations—France

	European origin only	Include people of color	Avg. per book total illustrations
1985 CM	93.6%	6.4%	115.5
1995 CM1	93.0%	7.0%	123
1995 CM2	88.1%	11.9%	150.7
2002 CM1	87.8%	12.2%	93
2002 CM2	78.2%	21.8%	117.7
2010 CM1	90.0%	10.0%	115
2010 CM2	80.2%	19.8%	138.3

all the French textbooks studied here published from 1985 to 2010 for CM1 and CM2 (equivalent of fourth and fifth grade).[7]

There is a great deal of change over time, but there is significant variation both among the competing textbooks published at the same time and between the history sections of the books and the geography and civics lessons. Most of the increased visibility of people of color in French textbooks comes from geography and civic education, particularly since the 2002 and 2008 curricula required teaching about the overseas territories and the Francophone world (*La Francophonie*), especially in CM2. The numbers and percentages of illustrations depicting people of color in these books vary widely, but some broad trends emerge. The majority of people of color in these books from 1985 through 2010 are in foreign countries and thus do not reflect on images of the French nation. Through the mid-2000s, the majority of books did not include any illustrations depicting people of color in the French overseas territories. Geography books examine many different aspects of life in France (social, industrial, economic, meteorological, topological, etc.), generally over the course of approximately 100 pages. Prior to 2008, when discussing these various themes, textbooks considered only continental European France. They generally attributed two separate pages (or perhaps four) to all of the overseas territories, usually toward the end of the book. These territories, which until the 2000s used the same curricula as mainland France, appear as an afterthought.[8] In these textbooks, the overseas territories appear truly peripheral to the French experience, rather than being represented as an integral part of the country.

All of the 2010 CM2 textbooks include illustrations depicting people in the overseas territories. The numbers vary greatly, indicating a remarkable lack of consensus on the place of the overseas territories within France, ranging from two such illustrations in Nathan's 2010 edition to 14 in Hatier's (Chevalier and Le Bourgeois 2010; Le Callennec 2011). Many of the newest books (and one early adopter—Hatier 2004 [Le Callennec]) have organized their geography sections to include the overseas territories more consistently, focusing on examples of industry, climate, regions, etc., not only from metropolitan France, but also from territories around the world. (We will return to this question in Chapter Six on territory.) Here, our primary concern is that this shows a rapid change toward greater sensitivity and inclusion of France's diversity.

The history sections of these books have also incorporated more people of color over time (following a dip in the 1990s), although this increase is slight, as shown in Table 1.2. This small change reflects the increased academic attention to the history of colonization and related changes in the curricula. Beginning in the 1990s and especially in the early 2000s, French textbooks incorporated a more critical approach to several aspects of national history that had previously often been ignored or presented in a way that reflected favorably upon the country. Notably, they increased their attention to questions of French imperialism, the French role in the slave trade, and in the Holocaust (see also Bonafoux, de Cock-Pierrepoint and Falaize 2007; Bozec 2010).

The most notable changes in French textbooks concern their presentation of colonization and decolonization. It was not until the 1990s that these topics came to be seen as legitimate for widespread university study and were integrated into the history curriculum at the university level (de Laforcade 2006: 227). This new perspective reached elementary school curricula in 2002 and has been more consistently represented in textbooks since then. The curricula prior to 2002 did not mention the French colonies at all. Since 2002, they include colonization, saying that Europeans, who were experiencing industrial and urban growth, sought new territories and markets (or perhaps this is better translated as "opportunities," as the text uses the polysemic noun *débouchés*), where they imposed their culture and diffused their values. This is the extent of the subject in the curricula, however, which do not indicate how colonization should be covered.

Though textbooks approach these subjects differently, they all now avoid the traditional approach that was still dominant (characterizing two of three books) in the 1980s, which consisted of showing French colonial conquests as a source of national pride and sign of strength. The older books exhibit a

Table 1.2 People of Color in Historical Illustrations—France

	European origin only	**Include People of Color**	**Avg. per book total illustrations**
1985 CM	93.6%	6.4%	197.7
1995 CM1	97.7%	2.3%	85.7
1995 CM2	94.0%	6.0%	121.3
2002 CM1	93.1%	6.9%	67.3
2002 CM2	91.5%	8.5%	90.7
2010 CM1	90.3%	9.7%	96.3
2010 CM2	90.8%	9.2%	108.3

clear identification with the French past, grounding the nation through time using deictic markers such as "our," which attach the present-day students to an older community. An excerpt from Nathan's 1985 edition illustrates this emotional attachment to the colonies and the colonialist thinking that justified imperialism, as well as the Eurocentrist view that led to discussing the colonies primarily in terms of European power struggles:

> Unfortunate wars brought about the loss of our colonies.
>
> The reign of Louis XV was interrupted by many wars. There was fighting in Europe with no results, but also on the seas and in the colonies. The English, thanks to their powerful navy, managed to take Canada. We had to cede it to them, as well as India in 1763 in the Treaty of Paris. All that we have left of our colonial empire is a few islands in the Antilles.
>
> (Vincent et al. 1985 CM1: 120)

This and other books of the mid-1980s make almost no mention of the people who were colonized. They do not show opposition to colonization, except as an isolated incident. Nathan includes Abd-el-Kader, the Algerian leader who resisted French colonization, as a sort of trouble-maker, who "harassed" French soldiers. The text indicates that following the defeat of Abd-el-Kader, French colonization was able to bring its civilizing benefits to Algerians: "Colonization could then start. [Governor-General] Bugeaud's former soldiers settled in the country, built farms, and established roads. Cities developed. Under the influence of France, Algeria was transformed" (Vincent et al. 1985 CM2: 34). Similarly, when discussing the imperialist wave of the late nineteenth century, this textbook entitles the chapter "The Triumph of the Republic" (72).

Despite such positive presentations of French colonialism, the 1985 books show the signs of breakdown of consensus. If Nathan's coverage (like that in Hachette) is Eurocentric and colonialist, Armand Colin's 1985 edition shows opposition to colonization, both from the people who were colonized and within France (Dorel-Ferré and Dhainaut: 135). It refers to colonization as "conquest" and "foreign domination" (135). In a seemingly well-meaning but paternalist approach, it indicates that colonization destroyed the pure, premodern civilizations it conquered, painting a utopic picture of Tahiti and India before Europeans arrived, where people's needs were all met. "These people are naturally gentle and kind; they are happy to live day-to-day, without the hassles of civilization" (105). Today, textbooks avoid this Rousseauan myth, while retaining the critical stance of this outlying textbook.

The 2010 textbooks demonstrate a certain consensus in their presentations of colonization. They explain the context of the time—that many Europeans believed in the superiority of their culture, which they saw as a justification for colonization. However, the textbooks present this view as being specific to its time and do not generally seem to adhere to this belief (though Nathan's coverage is somewhat ambiguous [Chevalier and Le Bourgeois 66–69]).

Overall, they give a negative presentation of colonization. Unlike most of the older textbooks, they clearly explain the profit motives, the competition among European countries for power and economic gain, the exploitation of local populations—including forced labor, which they compare to slavery—and the ways in which the system of colonization rendered occupied countries economically dependent on the metropolis, and impoverished the local populations while enriching the dominating power. Most cite anti-imperialist French voices of the time, which allows them to condemn colonization while showing that universalist values endured, and that France was not uniformly guilty (Boëche CM2: 27; Chevalier and Le Bourgeois 66).

Textbooks' handling of decolonization evolves similarly to that of colonization. In line with their traditional, positive presentation of colonization, two of the three books in 1985 present decolonization in a way that reflects positively on, or at least avoids criticizing, France.[9] For example, Nathan explained that, "France, which was proud of its colonial empire, hesitated to grant independence [to its colonies]," but that in Dien Bien Phu, Vietnam, in 1954, the French had to capitulate after two months of "heroic resistance" (Vincent et al. 1985 CM2: 102). Similarly, in the Algerian war (1954–1962), the French seem to have reacted to threats against them, seeking to "reestablish order" when "revolt broke out" rather than bearing major responsibility for the war (Nembrini et al. 144; Vincent et al. CM2: 104). The narrative thus echoes President Charles de Gaulle's interpretation, which Hachette reprints, basically justifying colonization, indicating that France had accomplished what it meant to, stating in overtly paternalist language that the children "are now grown up" (Nembrini et al. 144). All of the books of this period are sympathetic to the so-called *Pieds-Noirs* (i.e., the European French who had emigrated to Algeria), who appear as the primary victims of the conflict (Dorel-Ferré and Dhainaut 155; Nembrini et al. 144–145; Vincent et al. 104).

The more recent books, from 2002 onward, continue to vary in their presentations of the topic, though shifts in academic historiography and curricula have led to some clear changes. The textbooks move somewhat away from a purely Eurocentric approach, as they render more visible the role of people in the colonies in resisting and overthrowing French power, thus restoring their role as agents in their own history. For instance, both Nathan and Hatier emphasize indigenous movements for independence, citing Ho Chi Minh and Leopold Senghor on human rights and equality (Chevalier and Le Bourgeois 102–103; Le Callennec 2011: 90–91). Both textbooks show France opposing independence in the wars in Indochina and Algeria. Sedrap is an outlier and attributes very little space to the issue, adopting a more old-fashioned approach, in which Algeria is primarily presented as the "problem" that led to the Fifth Republic (Boëche CM2: 62–63). This difference shows how recent and unsettled these changes still are. Not surprisingly, the approaches to colonization and decolonization were extremely varied throughout the early-to-mid 2000s, even as the curricula were evolving.

The situation is similar regarding French textbooks' presentations of slavery. Textbooks now more clearly show France's role in the international slave trade and the presence of slaves in French overseas territories. Unlike U.S. textbooks (as we will see shortly), the French books of 1985 already explain and often illustrate the so-called Triangular Trade, through which Africans were captured and sold as slaves across the Atlantic, and these books show clearly how this practice enriched French merchants (Dorel-Ferré and Dhainaut 92–93; Nembrini et al. 79; Vincent et al. CM1: 123). Nevertheless, these older books minimize the extent of the role of slavery in French history and its presence on French territory. These older books sometimes emphasize the cruelty of Spanish treatment of Native Americans and slaves but not French mistreatment of them (Nembrini et al. 66–67). Still, they present slavery as a cruel system.

Textbooks' presentations shifted in later editions following changes in public perceptions. In the 1980s and 1990s, various advocacy groups organized campaigns demanding a reappraisal of national memory regarding slavery. This activism led 40,000 to 50,000 people to stage a march in Paris in 1998, protesting what they considered to be the French government's self-congratulatory commemorations of the 150th anniversary of the abolition of slavery. In response to this protest and continued resentment by people from the Caribbean, the French government passed a law in 2001 (the so-called *Loi Taubira*) declaring slavery to have been a "crime against humanity." This law directly involved education, by requiring that: "Textbooks and research programs in history and the humanities attribute to the longest and most massive deportation in the history of humanity the substantial attention that it deserves" (Loi n° 2001-434 . . . 2001).

In keeping with the 2001 law, more recent books differ from the older editions concerning their depictions of slavery in the French colonies, as they show its presence much more clearly. Though they still adopt different approaches with different levels of emphasis, all the recent books denounce slavery as a cruel system and discuss its existence in the French colonies, and they all state that slaves lived in terrible conditions.

The movements that led to legislation concerning representations of slavery and the changing historiography regarding colonization were preceded by a movement for recognition of France's role in the Holocaust, which began in the 1970s. Official acts of public recognition in the 1990s reflected changing norms. The Gayssot Law of 1990 criminalized Holocaust denial, and in a 1995 speech, President Chirac acknowledged French responsibility in enacting discriminatory legislation and deporting 76,000 Jews, nearly all of whom perished in Nazi camps.

The textbooks' presentation of the subject reflects these changes in public discourse and memory as well as changes in dominant historical scholarship. The textbooks of the early 1980s sometimes omitted the Holocaust or France's role in it. These older books also very much reflect what Henry Rousso has called the Gaullist "resistancialist" myth, that is, believing that most French people supported the Resistance against Nazi occupation and the Holocaust, and that the collaborators and government based in Vichy under the leadership of Marshall Pétain did not truly represent France.

Instead, collaboration is explained as the work of a minority who can alternatively be seen as cowardly and misguided (or misled) in their desire for peace, or—more rarely—as acting with racist intent (Rousso 1990/1994). One book (Hachette) does not, in fact, even mention the Holocaust. (It mentions "discrimination" against Jews in Nazi Germany and Vichy France, but this seems to have only concerned employment [Nembrini et al. 141].) The other two books clearly discuss deportation and "extermination camps" in Germany (Dorel-Ferré and Dhainaut 146–147; Vincent et al. CM2: 92–93), but all three attribute anti-Semitic actions on French soil to a misguided Pétain and his government. "France" is exonerated and equated with the Resistance. The books indicate that most French people were allied with the Resistance and minimize collaboration with the Nazis, indicating that the collaborators had disproportionate influence. For instance, Nathan states: "The 'collaborators' were few in number, but active" (Vincent et al. CM2: 92). Armand Colin shows French complicity in the Holocaust to have been entirely due to Nazi power (though the text uses harsh, straightforward language to describe killing): "To obey the Germans, the French arrested Jews and placed them in camps. They would be deported to Germany and exterminated" (Dorel-Ferré and Dhainaut 147).

Later textbooks change in some significant ways, discussing the Holocaust more clearly and in greater detail. They more directly show the responsibility of the Vichy government, instead of attributing its actions to Nazi pressure, stating that Pétain's government "actively participated" in discrimination and deportation of Jews (e.g., Chevalier and Le Bourgeois 2010: 90).

Recent textbooks also take their discussions of the Holocaust as an opportunity to explain and denounce racism as being based on an invalid concept. The books explain that the Holocaust was caused by racist thinking, and they define racism in terms like these:

> Racist: a person who thinks that humankind is divided into separate races and considers that certain races are superior to others. This conception is not scientific because there is only one race, the human race.
> (Chevalier and Le Bourgeois 2010: 81)

This explicit acknowledgment of the existence of racism is in keeping with the goals of tolerance that have recently been incorporated into curricula. It is interesting to note that textbooks do not condemn racism in moral terms but in scientific terms. This is consistent with their aims at disciplinary rigor and is in keeping with recommended practices of antiracist pedagogy (see Burkholder 2011).

The one civic education textbook published in conjunction with the 2008 curriculum dedicates two pages explicitly to fighting racism (Le Callennec 2008: 94–95), as well as six pages on tolerance and fighting discrimination in general (32–35, 96–97), including a moving, stark condemnation of racism toward immigrants in the lyrics of a song, "Lily," which it reprints (97).

The song is a poetic rendering of the disillusionment and suffering of an African immigrant, which clearly shows—and denounces—the existence of discrimination in France. At the end of a lengthy section on "The limits of tolerance" explaining that acts that impinge on people's dignity are not tolerable, the text states:

> For example, slavery and torture, racism and anti-Semitism are intolerable acts: they deny the humanity that is in every person.
>
> In every-day life, words or gestures that serve to reject someone because he is different from us due to his appearance, the color of his skin, his religion, his lifestyle, or his ideas are inacceptable.
>
> (35)

This antiracist discourse is grounded in the French law of 1972 (which the textbook also cites), forbidding incitation of racial hatred or violence.

This textbook is exceptional in its condemnation of racist discrimination in contemporary France, as we will see in greater detail below. However, all of the recent history textbooks address racism and do so in a way that is more sophisticated than older books. Until surprisingly recently, these books often taught about race as if it were a scientific fact. In its 1993 geography book, Armand Colin has a chapter entitled "Diversity of people—the Races" (*Diversité des peuples—les races*), which shows a map of the world color coded for "whites, yellows, blacks" (Figure 1.1 [Chagny and Forez 14]), and illustrates different countries with a photo of their "race"

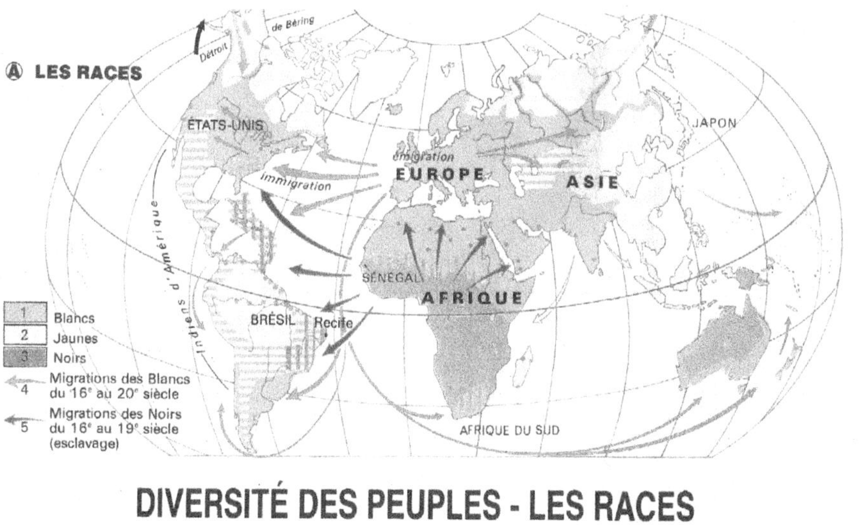

Figure 1.1 "Diversity of People—The Races."

Source: Chagny, Victor and Jean Forez. 1993. *Géographie. Cycle des approfondissements: CE2, CM1, CM2*. Paris: Armand Colin.

(including a very blond-looking family to represent the U.S.). Although it affirms that no race is superior to another, this presentation still perpetuates a biological definition of race long after it had been discredited. The textbooks have clearly evolved on this issue.

UNITED STATES TEXTBOOKS

U.S. textbooks have also added more ethnic minorities to their illustrations and have incorporated several aspects of progressive historiography into their narratives. As Tables 1.3 and 1.4 show, there is less fluctuation over time in the percentages of illustrations showing different ethnic groups in the U.S. books than in the French books. This holds true for historical illustrations as well as images of contemporary Americans.

By 1980, American textbook publishers had already adopted quotas and guidelines to ensure the representation of ethnic minorities (*Guidelines* 1975: 17, 63; Ravitch 2003: 35, 42, 47), so it is not surprising that the percentages remain approximately the same from the early 1980s to the 2000s. This aspect of multiculturalist reform was adopted early and seems to be well established. There is little variation among the competing textbooks, which further indicates consensus on this approach. There is, however, a noteworthy change, in that the total number of illustrations depicting people in U.S. textbooks is more than 2.5 times greater in 1997 than in 1982 (and rose further in 2003), leading to significant changes in the selection of people these books highlight. Less-expensive production methods and

Table 1.3 People of Color in Textbook Illustrations—United States

	European origin only	Include people of color	Avg. per book total illustrations
1982	58.3%	41.7%	153
1997	61.2%	38.8%	423.7
2003	59.5%	40.5%	472.9

Table 1.4 People of Color in Historical Illustrations—United States

	European origin only	Include people of color	Avg. per book total illustrations
1982	63.9%	36.1%	117.3
1997	65.7%	34.3%	372.3
2003	64.9%	35.1%	408.7

higher sales costs associated with a more polished-looking product are certainly factors contributing to the increased number of illustrations. There is also a well-known phenomenon of simply adding people to appeal to various activist groups (Tyson-Bernstein and Woodward 1991).

The percentage of illustrations depicting contemporary Americans that include people of color is much greater than in the illustrations of historic events, and it increases slightly, from 67.5 percent in 1982, to roughly 71 percent in 1997, to 75 percent in 2003. (The number of these illustrations increases roughly proportionately to the overall increase of illustrations in these books from 1982 to 2003.) With 35 percent of historical illustrations and three-quarters of contemporary illustrations including visible minorities, the most recent textbooks depict the United States as being more diverse than it actually is. These numbers indicate a clear commitment to projecting a multiethnic vision of the nation. The increased number of illustrations means that there are more pictures of every ethnic group. We need to look beyond these numbers to see the more meaningful changes in U.S. textbooks.

These books have shifted in several notable ways toward a more progressive stance. Since the 1990s, a new origins myth has come to replace the older focus on Columbus and his so-called discovery of the "new world" (e.g., Gross et al. 1980: 45–53; Helmus et al. 1982: 67–71; Klein et al. 1982: 55–63; discussed further in Chapter Six). Instead of the older triumphalist Eurocentric account of the navigator's daring, courage, and vision, the more recent textbooks present American colonial history as the meeting of three worlds (e.g., Banks et al. 2003: 92; Berson et al. 2003: 99; Boyd et al. 2003: 125). They show how contact between Europe and Asia as well as improved technology and science led to Columbus' voyage. The textbooks' emphasis has now shifted away from focusing on Columbus and instead concentrates on how European colonization in the Americas affected the indigenous populations as well as Africans, showing the link between colonization and the massive growth of the slave trade.

This approach includes much greater visibility for pre-Columbian Native American civilizations (as discussed further in Chapter Six). Where textbooks of the early 1980s dedicated on average 16 pages to this subject, the books of 1997 and 2003 accord it on average approximately 50 pages. This expanded coverage coincides with textbooks continuing to fight against stereotypes regarding Native Americans. For instance, in 1982 books, most pictures of Native Americans still showed bare-chested men; by 1997, fewer than 20 percent do, showing this as one style of dress among many others. Overall, the more recent books emphasize the variety of cultures among Native Americans, no longer giving a monolithic image of these groups. They highlight regional diversity and varied roles and actions of different individuals. Significantly, whereas 1982 textbooks mentioned only the Iroquois by name, by 1997, textbooks present many different tribes and nations and their cultures, referring to them individually, rather than lumped together under the generic name of "Indians."

In addition, the more recent books show more Native Americans throughout the historical narratives. The Native Americans and Pacific Islanders whom they have added include several individual people and groups whose history emphasizes agency and activism, in line with progressive multiculturalist wishes. Between 1982 and 2003 these books consistently added the following indigenous resisters of European colonialism: Queen Liliuokalani of Hawaii, Tecumseh, Tȟatȟáŋka Íyotȟake (a.k.a., Sitting Bull), Hinmatóowyalahtq'it (a.k.a., Chief Joseph), Metacomet (a.k.a., King Philip), and Pontiac (a.k.a., Obwandiyag). Textbooks show no historical illustrations depicting Native Americans after the land conflicts of the mid-nineteenth century. However, since 1997, they include more illustrations depicting contemporary Native Americans. Most of these photos show people practicing traditional aspects of their culture (e.g., creating art or performing dances and ceremonies in traditional dress [e.g., Banks et al. 59, 78–79, 94–95; Berson et al. 59, 65, 82; Boyd et al. 85, 91, 97]). Occasional photos show them integrated into urban environments, living in ways that are indistinguishable from other Americans (Boyd et al. 80–81).

In this same vein, focusing on the confluence of world civilizations leads to more inclusion of world history before the "three worlds" met, and allows for the addition of some Asian history (as textbooks now present illustrations of Kublai Khan and/or Zheng He [Banks et al. 2003: 94; Berson: 109; Boyd et al. 2003: 100, 105]). In their more ethnically inclusive approach to colonial history, textbooks now also allocate a great deal more space to discussing Spanish exploration and colonization in the Americas, instead of focusing almost exclusively on British colonization. The books of the early 1980s dedicated between five and 12 pages to Spanish exploration (after Columbus) and colonization, as compared to 30 to 35 pages on these topics in the 2003 textbooks. In addition, textbooks render Latinos somewhat more visible throughout U.S. history. For example, textbooks now all include photos of activists César Chávez and often Dolores Huerta and have increased their illustrations depicting anonymous Latinos in U.S. history (or territory before statehood) from just over three on average per book in 1982 to nine on average per book in 2003. (This change stems at least partly from Latino and multiculturalist activism in Texas, where Latinos make up approximately 38 percent of the population [Pew Research Center 2011]. Though such activists are far less numerous than those of the Christian Right, and did not began petitioning the board until the 2002 adoption cycle, the SBOE has been receptive to their concerns [May 2002; *Responses . . .* 1996].)

The biggest change overall in these books' presentations of ethnic minorities concerns African Americans, who are now shown in relation to nearly every major U.S. event and period. Older books tended to show African Americans only in relation to certain periods and topics, including slavery, Reconstruction, and the Civil Rights Movement of the 1950s and 1960s. More recent books have added certain topics relating to African American history, such as the Great Migration of the 1920s, and consistently show African Americans in a much broader array of roles and contexts, including as pioneers, cowboys, entrepreneurs, scientists and inventors, artists, social activists, and political leaders throughout American history.

Beyond simple inclusion of illustrations depicting minority groups, several individuals belonging to ethnic minorities are among the most frequently pictured people in the textbooks. (In decreasing order of frequency, Martin Luther King, Jr., Sacagawea, Frederick Douglass, and Harriet Tubman are all among the 28 people pictured on average more than twice per textbook in 2003).[10]

The presentation of several key historical topics regarding ethnic oppression or discrimination in U.S. history that are essential for understanding race relations today changed significantly from the early 1980s to 2003. Textbooks' depictions of slavery and Reconstruction, in particular, have incorporated aspects of academic historiography that are in line with progressive multiculturalism.

A significant aspect of this shift is quantitative: the books of 1997 and 2003 show slavery's role in American history in a greater number of contexts than did their predecessors. In 1982, slavery was generally only mentioned in the chapters on life in the British colonies, and then again regarding the Civil War. The textbooks of 1997 and 2003 show the effect of broader changes in American history on enslaved people and more consistently mention slavery at different points in the narrative. African American history is thus somewhat more integrated into American history as a whole.

Textbooks also changed their approach to the subject, so that they now more clearly show the extent of the slave trade and the cruelties of slavery, while moving away from the Eurocentrism of older textbooks and focusing more on the agency of Africans and African Americans. The textbooks of 1982 usually presented slavery from a white point of view, with only the rare book including source accounts from slaves' perspectives (Klein et al. is something of an exception, including a fictional letter, in which a former slave describes his past to his grandson [238]). Often, they only cite white people (both abolitionists and anti-abolitionists) on the issue. In one case, in an otherwise notably progressive textbook, the narrative includes a long fictional account of life on a plantation, where the fictional white planters' description of slavery is the only one students are given (Gross et al. 1980: 98–99). These books' pictorial representations of slavery are generally bland, showing work in cotton fields that does not appear difficult or forced. Many pictures show enslaved people smiling at their tasks, thus presenting a fairly benign picture of their day-to-day lives.

By 1997, several important changes occur. These books introduce multiple perspectives and make efforts to restore a voice to the slaves themselves, as all the books add primary source accounts from abolitionist former slaves. These books also demonstrate a major shift regarding the role of the North and merchants in the slave trade. In nearly all the books of

1982, slavery appeared only in conjunction with large Southern plantations. By 1997, textbooks clearly mention slave labor in the North, and more importantly, slavery is presented as a system that involved all of the British colonies, and then U.S. states, through triangular trade (e.g., Banks et al. 1997: 230–231; Boehm et al. 183–184). These books clearly show financial profit as the motivation that led Northern merchants to transport captured Africans in the horrible conditions of the Middle Passage. This change in presentation reflects a consensus: multiculturalists (who wish for the systemic extent of slavery to be exposed), as well as Southern conservatives (who wish to share "blame" across the Mason-Dixon line) advocate teaching about the North's role in slavery (e.g. Horne 1988: 41–59; Moore 1977: 19–22; *Responses* . . . 1996: 119, 163).

The 1997 and 2003 textbooks also more clearly show slaves' agency through varied acts of rebellion, from smaller daily tactics (slowing work, sabotaging equipment. . .), to violent insurrection, as well as their efforts to preserve cultural independence. In this vein, the 1997 and 2003 textbooks put greater emphasis on three resistance figures: Harriet Tubman, Sojourner Truth, and Frederick Douglass. Though these leaders were already present in the 1982 books, the later books are more likely to picture them and to quote them on the injustice of slavery, thereby giving them a greater voice. In the more recent textbooks, these people appear as heroes—Tubman in particular is shown as a model of courage and sacrifice.

Similarly, textbooks have moved away from the very uneven coverage of Reconstruction that characterized the early 1980s and now reliably present many key aspects of the history that were usually omitted. As Eric Foner has demonstrated, the historiography of Reconstruction has played a major role in race relations and policy in the U.S. After the collapse of Reconstruction, white people in the North and South reconciled around a myth that showed Reconstruction as a time of corrupt leadership in the war-ravaged South by a coalition of former slaves and greedy white profiteers. This vision of Reconstruction justified institutional racism for nearly a century (Foner 1988; see also Du Bois 1935).

Once again, the textbooks of the early 1980s took a fairly wide variety of approaches to the subject. Three books of the five analyzed here reflect the old white Southern view—presenting Republican governments in the South as made up of "scalawags, carpetbaggers, and blacks" who sought to become rich (King et al. 1981: 336; see also Helmus et al. 1982: 180; King et al. 1982: 119). Similarly, one of these books represents the conclusion (already rejected by mainstream historians) that Reconstruction ended because black people had attained freedom (King et al. 1982: 119), a view that dominated consensual narratives shared by Northern and Southern white people about Reconstruction from the end of the nineteenth century until the 1960s (Foner 1988). Two other textbooks, however, present narratives that reflect the influence of critical pedagogy and the consensus among historians (Gross et al. 1980: 275–276; and especially Helmus et al. 1982: 177–183). These accounts are similar to the more recent textbooks.

While there are differences in the details from book to book, the accounts in the 2003 editions are fairly similar to one another. Unlike the older books, all the recent textbooks show Reconstruction as a time when, after the injustices of the series of laws known as the Black Codes (which they describe as aiming to deprive black people of freedom in more stark terms than did many books of 1982), black people in the South briefly gained rights but were quickly again deprived of their rights by Southern white people through a combination of laws and intimidation, including violence. The textbooks show that resentment over black people attaining equal rights was a factor in this repression, rather than just ex-Confederates wanting representation in government (as older books implied, if they discussed the issue at all). The 2003 books all specifically mention the Ku Klux Klan. They show that segregation became the norm after Reconstruction, that black people were again deprived of the right to vote, and many became poor sharecroppers, since the government's failure to provide land or other means of earning a living limited their options.

Finally, changing topics somewhat, I wish to comment briefly on depictions of religion in these books. Though religion has not played the same role in current debates over national identity in the U.S. as it has in France, it is nonetheless relevant to the concerns of this chapter. Current debates over religion and education in the U.S. concern not so much the religion of ethnic minority groups as the religion of the waning, previously dominant group. For several decades, textbooks seemed to interpret the constitutional separation of church and state as meaning it was best to avoid discussing religion at all, except to emphasize freedom of religion as a founding American value (discussed further in Chapter Four). As we have seen, changing this situation has been one of the main goals of the Christian Right.

The approach of Christian Right activists is twofold. Partly, Christian groups have adopted multiculturalist logic to argue that if textbooks are going to discuss the cultures of various ethnic groups, they must also discuss the influence of Protestant Christian culture on American identity (Zimmerman 2002). In their arguments, they present themselves as the once-dominant group whose culture greatly shaped national identity, but who are now oppressed by hostile publishers who omit their history. While these groups may argue for equal time for their views in disciplines where science has marginalized them (as regarding evolution; see Introduction; Zimmerman 2002), in history, they argue that theirs is the true vision of America, because they equate the country with the heritage of the Puritans' covenantal mission. They lobby for textbooks to teach about the country's Christian heritage, and they want Christianity to be shown as the source of American ideals of freedom and tolerance. And yet, they are less protective of the Puritans themselves than of subsequent manifestations of Protestantism in American history. Notably, they want history textbooks to cover the

Great Awakening and show it as a major force in forging American identity leading to independence. They have also advocated an emphasis on the "Founding Fathers'" supposedly Christian goals.[11]

Their efforts appear to have met with some success regarding the Great Awakening, as textbooks generally did not cover these events in the early 1980s but do now discuss this major religious revival. One textbook particularly emphasizes the Great Awakening and credits it with being an early antecedent of national culture (as opposed to separate, regional cultures [Berson et al. 215–217]). Conservative Christian education activists have more recently achieved some of their deeper goals: the controversial 2010 Texas curriculum guidelines require that high school students learn about the biblical roots of American democracy including, as was widely reported in the media, listing Moses among those who influenced early American leaders (Chapter 113: §113.44.c.1.C). The changes in elementary social studies curriculum guidelines are more subtle—the most recent guidelines add Puritan leaders (William Bradford and John Wise) to the list of people with whom students should be familiar, thus putting the emphasis for this period not just on religious freedom but also on the religious roots of America (§5.b.1.B). These questions are discussed further in Chapter Four, on national values, and Chapter Six, on attachment to the national territory. For the moment, it is sufficient to note the appropriation by Christian Right groups of multiculturalist methods and the somewhat greater inclusion of religious history in recent textbooks, though it is far from an area of focus.

As these examples show, both French and U.S. textbooks have become increasingly diverse and have incorporated aspects of progressive historiography regarding historically excluded and oppressed groups. However, in many ways, these books remain Eurocentric, promoting what we might call nationalist multiculturalism, in which critical approaches to history stop short of questioning the unity and harmony of contemporary society.

NATIONALIST MULTICULTURALISM

French Textbooks

In the French history textbooks overall, ethnic minorities do not appear as an integral part of national history. The French overseas territories' history (and thus, much of the history of France's ethnic minorities) has become more visible in recent books. However, the overseas territories remain largely separated from the history of "France." Their history is discussed only in relation to colonization and the slave trade. Their role in other events or how those events affected them is omitted. In addition, most often, in the most recent books, "France" seems to refer only to the European continental territory, as the vast majority of maps depicting various aspects of the country's geography (climate, borders, topography, etc.) show only the mainland European territory (often omitting even Corsica). Though the overseas territories now receive more attention than they once did, most geography books discuss them in specially dedicated chapters, rather than including them as examples in other lessons (Hatier is a notable exception, as it uses multiple examples from the overseas territories mixed in with examples from metropolitan France). These regions are thus still separate and peripheral, their history mentioned only it relates to the history of continental France. They are thus not truly included in the national narrative or conception.

Showing further distinction between metropolitan France and the overseas territories, though the books of this study mostly adhere to the colorblind consensus when discussing metropolitan France, surprisingly, they do not apply it to the overseas territories. It is common throughout the period studied here—including in the most recent books—to inform students that the populations of various territories are "often black and *métissé*" (e.g. Le Callennec 2011: 158; Le Bourgeois 2010: 40). (Armand Colin's 1993 geography book referred to these populations using the retrograde, pejorative *mulâtres* ["mulatto"; 135].) The illustrations depicting people of color in the overseas territories also often emphasize their "otherness," whether through their exotic activities (which, for instance, often relate to growing bananas) or through their appearance. For instance, the only photo of people in the overseas territories in Nathan's 2010 CM2 edition shows male dancers in New Caledonia wearing dramatic-looking traditional costumes and makeup, dancing at the edge of the sea. The photo seems to have been taken with a filter that makes the water appear bluer and the people darker, thus further contributing to exoticizing them (Chevalier and Le Bourgeois: 150). Thus, while they have moved toward delegitimizing race as a scientific concept, the recent textbooks have not eradicated all traces of a racialized view of the world.

In presentations of contemporary metropolitan France, most textbooks show very few pictures representing ethnic diversity. The occasional photo (one on average per book) shows an interethnic group of children (usually in a school environment). Similarly, a handful of (mostly civic education) books show an image of a person of color or an interethnic group as part of a lesson against racism. For the most part, though, these books do not demonstrate an effort to present a multiethnic picture of France.

Even when these textbooks show faces of color in France, they never depict Muslims in any identifiable way (e.g., wearing traditional dress, in a mosque, or labeled as such). If French people in these books now have visibly diverse origins, their diversity is only mentioned as something that should be disregarded. Books written since 1985 do not promote cultural diversity. Most do not promote a multiethnic vision of metropolitan France, but those that do stress unity, not plurality. This is in keeping with dominant, official colorblind discourse and adheres to the curricula, which emphasize national unity and commonality above all.

This invisibility of Muslims and limited attention to showing ethnic minorities in metropolitan France is reinforced by the absence of recent immigration history in most books. While recent history textbooks briefly denounce the racism that led to the Holocaust, the majority of them do not discuss racism or discrimination in relation to immigration. Their presentation of this topic appears to be a reversal from earlier trends. The history and geography books of the 1980s discussed contemporary immigration, generally explaining the need for foreign labor in mostly unskilled jobs. While they often discussed the hardships immigrants faced, they did not discuss tensions or discrimination (e.g., Hinnewinkel, Sivirine, and Duchesne CM 1985: 122–123). In the intermediary years of this study, the occasional history and geography book discussed discrimination toward immigrants (e.g., Le Callennec 1998: 2004), but this was uncommon. The civic education books of the 1980s seemed to seek to combat discrimination but without directly acknowledging its existence in France. Thus, for example Bordas shows an antiracist demonstration in its chapter on immigrants but makes it sound like there was no racism to demonstrate against, focusing instead on the commitment of French people to diversity, saying that such demonstrations "express the attachment and respect of the population toward foreigners and immigrants" (Hanniet et al. 1987: 110).

The more recent books are less likely to discuss contemporary immigration at all, much less racial discrimination toward immigrants and their descendants. It appears that a consensus is lacking on this topic, as the most recent books take very different approaches. Among history and geography books, Nathan's 2010 edition makes no mention of immigration to France (Chevalier and Le Bourgeois). Hatier evokes it very briefly, stating that European, then African immigration contributed to the twentieth-century increase in the size of the French population (Le Callennec 2011: 98). Sedrap is a notable exception and is once again more progressive than its competitors. Not only does it state how and (briefly) why immigration was encouraged in the 1960s, it also mentions racist discrimination and the subsequent change in French immigration policy (Boëche 2011 CM2: 75). As mentioned above, the one recent civic education textbook (Le Callennec 2008) also deals directly with racialized discrimination in France, and civic education textbooks—whether from the late 1980s or produced recently—are also more likely than history and geography books to present a diverse picture of the country. Hatier's 2008 civic education textbook shows 28 illustrations of multiethnic groups in metropolitan France (i.e., approximately 20 percent of the total number of illustrations depicting people). The civic education curriculum, unlike history and geography curricula, requires teaching students to reject discrimination. This difference between the history/geography textbooks and the civic education textbook indicates the importance of the curriculum in effecting ideological change in France.

This Eurocentrism that characterizes most French textbooks' depictions of contemporary France also characterizes their historical narratives.

There are no individuals of minority origin who appear regularly in these textbooks. Appearing in at least two books of the same period indicates that a certain consensus exists concerning the importance of a given person. By this measurement, no minority figures seem to have entered the national history narrative.[12] The selection of featured people remains fairly consistent over time. These people are discussed in greater detail in Chapter Five. For the moment, we should note that most of them are men (41 of the 44), and most are known for actions in the political and/or military realms.

While most of these books do include specific individuals of color, there is not a consensual pantheon that appears in all or even most of the books of a given period. This absence reflects the curricula, which do not name any individuals of color. This situation is particularly surprising, given that five men of color are commemorated in the actual Pantheon in Paris. In 1949, Félix Eboué—the French-Guyanese-born colonial administrator who rallied African support for Charles de Gaulle and Free France during the Second World War—became the first person of color to be entombed in the Pantheon. Nearly fifty years went by before the next people of color were to be thus honored. These choices seem to reflect the "memorial turn" that was underway by the 1990s. In 1998, Toussaint Louverture and Louis Delgrès were commemorated with plaques in their names (as their remains were lost). These men are the only people honored in the Pantheon who opposed French metropolitan power, as both fought to abolish slavery and fought for the independence of Haiti and Guadeloupe, respectively. In 2002, the remains of author Alexandre Dumas, best known for *The Three Musketeers*, were transferred to the Pantheon. Dumas' father was the son of a French aristocratic military officer and an enslaved woman in Saint Domingue (though he was raised by his father in France and benefitted from his aristocratic status). In 2011, another plaque was added in the Pantheon, commemorating Aimé Césaire, the twentieth-century poet from Martinique known for helping to create the *negritude* movement. The fact that only one book of this study (Boëche 2011 CM2) mentions and pictures Toussaint Louverture and Louis Delgrès, and none mention Félix Eboué or other prominent black abolitionists such as Cyrille Bissette, indicates that French history textbooks do not necessarily overlap with official public memory, which seems more receptive to memorial movements.

Instead, the majority of recent books present the abolition of slavery in France and its territories from a Eurocentric perspective and as a triumph of the Republic. They emphasize the role of abolitionist journalist-turned-politician Victor Schoelcher and often, a second (European) voice, such as Victor Hugo or Tocqueville, as well as the state, omitting the major role played by enslaved people themselves. This narrative of progress is in line with the official version of the 1998 sesquicentennial commemoration of abolition and is consistent with recent curricula, which name Schoelcher but no abolitionists of color.

Thus, while French textbooks take a critical approach to discussing the horrors of slavery and showing its existence in the national history, their perspective remains largely Eurocentric and to a degree, paternalist. The majority of these books show slaves as victims while depicting white French men as eventual liberators. This Eurocentrism is epitomized by the illustration that most books (including all three of the most recent editions) include depicting a white political leader in Guadeloupe declaring the abolition of slavery, in which the newly emancipated people thank him and other white people in subservient positions, including on their knees (Figure 1.2 [e.g., Boëche 2011 CM2: 25; Chevalier and Le Bourgeois 2010: 55; Le Callennec 2011: 47]). In this way, the textbooks reconcile the 2001 Taubira law, requiring them to show the importance of slavery, with the myth of progress and residual belief in the *mission civilisatrice* that underscored opposition to such "memorial laws."

Following the passage of these laws, a right-wing backlash occurred, notably in the form of the 2005 Mékachera law. The fourth article of this law required that: "Curricula recognize in particular the positive role of the French presence overseas, notably in North Africa, and attribute to the history and sacrifices of the soldiers of the French Army from these territories the eminent consideration which they deserve" (Loi n° 2005–158 . . . 2005). This provision was advocated by conservatives who saw the 2001 law on

Figure 1.2 François Biard, *L'abolition de l'esclavage (27 avril 1848)*, 1849.
Source: Wiki Commons. Retrieved 29 Sept. 2015 (https://commons.wikimedia.org/wiki/File:Biard_Abolition_de_l%27esclavage_1849.jpg).

slavery as reflecting and promoting "anti-French" sentiment or "anti-white racism" and excessive self-criticism (de Laforcade 2006: 228). This article was repealed following public outcry, including protest from dozens of prominent historians (Azéma et al. 2005).

Though the relevant provision of the Mékachera law did not stand, these books still often show decolonization as a sign of French progress. They now mention the role of certain leaders of independence movements such as Ho Chi Minh and Leopold Senghor. However, they ultimately claim moral victory for France, rather than military defeat. For instance, the main heading in Hatier's chapter on decolonization states, "One of the major accomplishments of the Fifth Republic was decolonization: the French colonies became independent states" (Le Callennec 2011: 90). This impression of French benevolence is reinforced by the emphasis on *la Francophonie* and the good relations between France and its former French-speaking colonies (which is discussed further in Chapter Four).

Most French textbooks also protect the image of the nation in their presentations of the Holocaust. While they discuss the subject and recognize the French government's role more than older editions did, most of the recent books still adhere to aspects of the "resistancialist" myth. Blame is attributed entirely to the government, while the population is associated with the Resistance. Vichy is always shown as an aberration, while the true France is with the Allies (e.g., Boëche 2011 CM2: 58–61). This approach matches the official line as set by the curriculum of 2002: "In France, the 'collaboration' of the Vichy government greatly facilitated deportations to the death camps, while civil and military resistance allowed many Jews to be saved" (Ministère . . . 17). Among the most recent textbooks, however, there is one major exception. Hatier clearly shows that the Resistance, while meaningful, only included about 1 percent of the French population—the same number, they state, as of active Nazi collaborators (Le Callennec 2011: 41). The textbooks overall take an antiracist approach to the topic, but still struggle with assessing the responsibility of the French. While these books denounce racism in their lessons on the Holocaust, they attribute racism only to the Axis Powers, and do not explicitly associate it with France (Boëche CM2: 57; Chevalier and Le Bourgeois 90, 93; Le Callennec 2011: 75).

Finally, Eurocentrism pervades the presentation of topics relating to more distant history, notably the Crusades and the "discovery," as most French textbooks still call it, of America and Africa (Boëche CM1: 43; Le Bourgois 65). This last point needs no further clarification, but the presentation of the Crusades and Muslim culture is worth attention. Textbooks of the 1980s present Islam and its early expansion as a threat to European societies. All these books show Muslim territorial expansion in the seventh and eighth centuries and state that Muslim "invaders" "threatened" France (Dorel-Ferré and Dhainaut 39; Nembrini et al. 35; Vincent et al. CM1: 35). If they do not praise Charles Martel (the eighth-century Frankish military leader and statesman known for stopping an Arab invasion at Poitiers) at length in the way that pre-1980s books did (see Citron 1987/2008), some books of the 1980s still depict him as a hero for stopping the advance of Islam into "France" (Vincent et al. 1985 CM1: 35). The more recent books mention Martel only briefly, if at all. They still describe the "Arab invasions" but use more neutral language, referring to "conquest" rather than "threats" (Boëche CM1: 25; Le Bourgeois 16; Le Callennec 2010: 43).

Given the emphasis on secularism in contemporary France, one might expect that the Crusades would be presented according to historiographical norms, omitting modern judgment as well as avoiding legitimizing a Eurocentrist view. However, most books retain a European perspective, indicating that the Christian Crusaders were reacting to "Arab expansion" and were merely trying to reclaim their holy city of Jerusalem from the Muslim conquerors. All of the most recent books use the term "retake" or "recapture" (*reprendre*), thus implying a certain legitimacy in the Christian action (Boëche 2011 CM1: 26; Chevalier and Le Bourgeois 2010: 16; Le Callennec 2010: 46). Otherwise, though, the textbooks take rather different approaches, thus indicating a lack of consensus over how to handle this sensitive subject. Sedrap presents events in a way that is sympathetic to the Christian point of view and relates "the crusade of the poor," who seem touching, pathetic, and devout (Boëche CM1: 26–27). Nathan, on the other hand, is unique in giving, in addition to a Christian perspective, a Muslim point of view, which shows the Christian crusaders as cruel and violent (Chevalier and Le Bourgeois 47).

Nevertheless, regarding Louis IX's role in the Crusades, even Nathan says that the French king went to fight Muslims to recapture (again, *reprendre*) Jerusalem (Le Bourgeois 2010: 27). Hatier goes arguably further in its positive representation of Louis's role in the Crusades, stating "Profoundly Christian, Louis IX did not hesitate to make war in order to convert people to Christianity" (Le Callennec 2010: 16). His involvement in the Crusades thus appears to be the natural result of his religious devotion, which the book praises (more on Louis IX in Chapter Five).

Curricula show the importance of Christianity in providing a "first form of religious, cultural, and artistic unity" for Europe (Horaires . . . 2002: 79). Recent textbooks all include chapters on the role of the Church in medieval life. However, if this more chronologically distant history contains some favorable references to the role of religion in French society, the closer the narrative gets to modern times, the more critical textbooks become. Though there are variations from one book to another (see, for instance, discussions of Joan of Arc and Louis IX in Chapter Five), most focus increasingly on the violence that has resulted from religious intolerance (notably regarding the wars of religion between Catholics and Protestants in the sixteenth century) and on the material advantages enjoyed by the Catholic Church prior to the Revolution. These narratives reflect a secularist interpretation that has long undergirded French republican visions of the pre-Revolutionary past. Though textbooks consistently show religion to have been the cause of conflict, intolerance, and racism, they also show it as inspiration for great Christian art, and they are even more expansive regarding the beauty of Islamic art.

Most older books and all of the most recent ones make additional positive references to Islam by citing its cultural and scientific advances, and stating that the Crusades brought western Europeans into contact with these achievements. The sections on religious art permit textbook editors to satisfy curriculum requirements regarding the *fait religieux* and art history simultaneously, so it is hardly surprising that they have become common features. Given the Europhilic tendencies regarding the motives behind the Crusades, these complimentary mentions of Islamic civilization seem to be a rather minimal effort at a conciliatory approach that cedes no moral ground, while presenting Islam somewhat favorably, yet maintaining its foreignness.

Aside from its very early role in extending the borders of the Frankish kingdom (more on this in Chapter Six), some medieval social progress (led mainly by monks and nuns who took vows of charity and service), and the contributions in the name of faith to art and architecture, religion appears primarily in these books as opposed to republican principles. In keeping with the curricula, textbooks emphasize that the universal public education that was established under the Third Republic was free and secular, and they stress the importance of the 1905 law separating church and state. The textbooks seem to have struck something of a balance, in which Christianity is included among the older roots of national identity but is relegated, along with religion in general, to the premodern, nonrepublican past, thus contributing to reaffirming secularism.

These textbooks reflect official commitments not only to colorblindness but also to "religion-blindness." They show that religion was an important historical force in the distant past, but that its only place now is in the private sphere, for the greater good. Combined with the decreased attention to recent immigration in the most recent textbooks, almost all of these books render Muslim immigrants and their descendants invisible. This invisibility is justified in assimilationist thought.

Overall, the recent French textbooks dedicate more space to national and global history of French ethnic minorities than their predecessors did, but in most books, these groups remain confined to the margins, and events are generally related from the point of view of French people of European descent. In addition, while these textbooks seem to aim at fighting racism and denouncing injustice, they tend to portray people of color almost exclusively as victims, both in French history and worldwide, frequently discussing global poverty and child labor (more on this in Chapter Three). They very rarely depict the agency of people of color in historical or contemporary events, thus exhibiting remnants of paternalist Eurocentrism.

United States Textbooks

French textbooks have become increasingly critical of injustice committed by the ethnic majority against minorities in the past, though they take a variety of approaches regarding contemporary diversity and discrimination. American textbooks' trajectory has been more uniform, but less linear. From

1982 to 1997, U.S. textbooks more systematically incorporated aspects of progressive multiculturalist historiography. After 1997, however, the books show the effects of a conservative reaction against the more critical pedagogy. This rightward shift is evident in the books' selection of people to feature in illustrations, as well as in their presentations of slavery, Reconstruction, discrimination during the years often called the "nadir" of race relations (1877–1950s), and the Civil Rights Movement of the 1950s and 1960s.

U.S. textbooks present a multiethnic vision of the country, rendering minorities visible throughout the historical narrative and especially in illustrations depicting contemporary Americans. Nevertheless, their selection of people and events to emphasize promotes a narrative of progress, minimizing the perception of conflict and disparities. This positive emphasis is perhaps not surprising, given the context of textbook production. While progressive scholars and educators advocate more critical pedagogy, there is also some overlap between the wishes of conservative and minority activist groups, in that many minority advocates do not wish to be shown only as victims, but want to teach children pride in their heritage (see also Zimmerman 2002; e.g., Horne 1988; Moore 1977). This approach can take the more conservative form of emphasizing unity and showing minority figures as patriots and nation-builders.

In their historical as well as contemporary illustrations, these textbooks promote an image of interethnic harmony and national unity. In some ways, this approach is consensual and would appeal to many progressive multiculturalists as well as conservatives. For instance, the books show multiethnic professional groups. Sometimes the focus of these images is the historical breaking of color barriers. Sometimes questions of ethnicity are tangential to the illustrations. However, in some cases, these textbooks feature individuals who have traditionally been part of European-American folklore but are rejected by progressive multiculturalists and minority activists as atypical representatives of intergroup relations. For instance, in 1981, the Council on Interracial Books for Children (CIBC) advocated this guideline: "If Native American heroes are described, are those who were hostile to whites also included? Or are the heroes selected only those known to have been friendly and helpful to whites (e.g., Pocahontas, Sascatchewea [aka Sacajawea], Squanto)?" (58). Elsewhere, they elaborated:

> Pocahontas and Sacajawea were not typical of Native American women.
>
> If texts make any mention of individual Native American women, it is inevitably of Pocahontas, Sacajawea, Nancy Ward or Mary Brant [. . .] women who, in some way, aided Europeans.
>
> The vast majority of Native women—who learned that their own interests were opposed to European interests and who suffered greatly, along with their people, when they fought to defend their homelands—are not discussed in textbooks.
>
> (Moore: 106)

Pocahontas and especially Sacagawea continue to hold prominent places in these textbooks. Sacagawea is among the 15 most frequently pictured people in the recent editions and is the only Native American among the top 28 featured people (see endnote 10). The image of these women continues to be used in a way that implicitly justifies European colonization, promoting a vision of more harmonious relations. In illustrations depicting Native Americans' relations with European-Americans, more recent textbooks include more pictures showing interethnic meetings, most of which are peaceful and demonstrate cooperation. For example, almost all the textbooks feature the scene of William Penn and the Lenape signing a treaty of friendship (Figure 1.3 [Banks et al. 2003: 179; Berson et al. 2003: 214]). There is little evolution over time in these books' illustrations regarding the presentation of harm inflicted on Native Americans by European-Americans. For instance, nearly all books from 1982 to 2003 show illustrations of the Trail of Tears, but it is the only example of forced displacement to be pictured. Similarly, while textbooks sometimes show illustrations of battles between Spanish conquistadors and native populations, these tend to be highly stylized, and more significantly, there are almost no illustrations showing battles between Anglo-Americans and Native Americans. As a result, these books' illustrations do not emphasize victimization or conflict. This largely attenuated

Figure 1.3 Benjamin West, *William Penn's Treaty with the Indians when he founded the Province of Pennsylvania in North America*, 1771.

Source: Wiki Commons. Retrieved 29 Sept. 2015 (https://commons.wikimedia.org/wiki/File:Treaty_of_Penn_with_Indians_by_Benjamin_West.jpg).

image of relations between Native Americans and European colonizers contrasts, however, with most of the books' text, as discussed in Chapter Six. We can only guess at the reasons for this discrepancy. Perhaps publishers hope that images will influence textbook critics and adoption committees more than the text. Perhaps they seek to avoid showing children images that may be upsetting or violent.

Beyond Pocahontas and Sacagawea, despite the addition of more minority figures in these books' illustrations, the images in recent textbooks reflect the dominance of conservatism and demonstrate a rightward shift between 1997 and 2003. Because the percentages of different ethnic groups depicted remain the same while the numbers increase, most of the people added from 1982 to 2003 are men of European origin. These men, as well as the women (discussed in the next chapter) and the minority figures (especially African Americans) who have been added tend to be nation-builders. They consist mostly of explorers, pioneers, and soldiers of various wars, but the largest group by far are leaders of the founding generation, those who led the Revolution, wrote the Constitution, and ran the government in the early years of the United States.

In an ostensibly multiculturalist approach, these books have added more illustrations of enslaved people. However, it is noteworthy that these figures—Harriet Tubman, Frederick Douglass, Sojourner Truth, Olaudah Equiano, Phillis Wheatley, Crispus Attucks, and James Armistead—were all freed during their lifetimes. By showing only people who escaped slavery apparently through a combination of intelligence, will, and hard work—plus the occasional consenting master—these textbooks mask or minimize to a certain degree the unbreakable hold slavery held over the vast majority of its victims. This process could attenuate the view of slavery as an institution.

Similarly, though 1997 and 2003 textbooks more consistently incorporate the subject of slavery into their narratives, slavery is not shown where it would tarnish certain myths, notably in connection with the founders, as we will see in Chapter Five on heroes. In this way, where the multiculturalist approach was irreconcilable with a conservative position, the conservative position often triumphed.

This observation notably holds true regarding the most controversial aspects of slavery, as well as all the ensuing civil rights struggles, which are those that have the most powerful ramifications today. Namely, textbooks do not address the role and development of racism as a justification for slavery, thereby rejecting antiracist pedagogy. That is, they do not present racial discrimination as a cause or justification for slavery or regarding systematic efforts to deprive African Americans of their rights after Reconstruction. They also do not discuss the continued effects of slavery—its legacy of racism and persistent socioeconomic inequality. (We will examine this question in more detail in Chapter Three, on social class.)

Although the textbooks of 1997 and 2003 present Reconstruction more clearly than the older books did, it seems that the progressivism of the narrative in many books has been tempered by compromise with conservative groups. Harcourt's editions from 1997 and 2003 offer the most striking evidence of this shift regarding Reconstruction, as for many other topics discussed throughout the present study. Harcourt Brace's 1997 edition dedicates the most content among books of that year to Reconstruction. The narrative emphasizes the emotional reactions of the recently freed slaves to their freedom and highlights the hardships that they faced, including primary source documents and other narrative accounts on how former slaves sought their family members who had been taken from them, which make this idea more concrete and emotionally moving. This textbook shows (as does McGraw-Hill) that despite promises to the contrary, the government did not give most black people land, because white people wanted it. Harcourt Brace also contains the most stark and dramatized depiction of the KKK's action among the books of 1997, explaining that Klansmen broke into black people's homes, where they attacked and killed them:

> [. . .] some white Southerners formed secret groups to keep Africans from having their rights as free persons. [. . .] One such group was the Ku Klux Klan, or the KKK. Dressed in white robes and hoods, its members delivered nighttime message of hate. Klan members broke into homes and attacked and killed Africans. They burned schools and churches. They hurt anyone who helped former slaves. It was a time of terror for many people.
>
> (Boehm et al. 437)

This textbook concludes its chapter on Reconstruction by explicitly connecting the retraction of African Americans' rights after 1877 to the need for the Civil Rights Movement of the twentieth century in a section entitled "Making Social Studies Relevant: The Fight for Freedom goes on" (442–443).

This textbook's historiographically grounded approach was met by virulent opposition from the powerful Gabler's Educational Research Analysts after the book was approved for use in Texas. The Gablers' group distributed a review of this textbook designed to help volunteers persuade schools not to use the book, in which they argued:

> Half-truths, selective disinformation, and false editorial stereotypes flaw *America's Story's* discussion of Reconstruction. Here its whites-as-oppressors, blacks-as-victims editorial agenda results in politically-correct tunnel vision. On Reconstruction *America's Story* consistently violates Texas Administrative Code section 67.7 (a)(4), which provides that "instructional materials shall treat divergent groups fairly without stereotyping." Yet the following passages stress white disfranchisement of blacks but never mention Radicals' disfranchisement of ex-Confederates between 1867 and 1872 [. . .].
>
> (Gabler et al. 1997: 22)

They thus advocate a Confederate viewpoint, in which white Southerners are to be seen as victims of aggression (presumably from white and black Republicans). It is noteworthy that the reviewers do not focus on removing depictions of injustice suffered by black people, but instead seek to show that the injustice inflicted on white Southerners was equivalent, thereby minimizing centuries of racist oppression. As we have seen, though, they generally advocated limiting discussions of discrimination in the country's past, in the belief that a more harmonious vision would promote unity and patriotism (e.g., Jones 1997; Warren 1997).

The hypothesis of direct conservative influence on this textbook is supported by the fact that while the 1997 edition was the lowest rated by the Gablers' group, the 2003 edition received their highest endorsement (Educational Research Analysts 2003a). The passage cited above, in which Harcourt's 1997 edition describes the KKK's use of violence, disappears from the 2003 edition, which retains only a brief section mentioning the KKK using unspecified violence to prevent black people from voting (Berson et al. 438–439). Without the earlier explanation of what that violence entailed, this passage becomes much less vivid and clear. The more recent Harcourt edition also reverses its earlier emphasis on the injustice of the sharecropping system, so that, instead of offering the clearest accounts of sharecropping and the KKK's use of violence, this textbook discusses these topics the least among the 2003 textbooks.

Overall, textbooks could all still go much further toward incorporating the view of the current historiographical consensus (as epitomized by Eric Foner's work). For instance, the books say little about the progressive aims and achievements of the radical Reconstruction governments. This has the effect of bolstering the case for white Southern opposition to these governments, as it makes it more difficult to understand why they raised taxes so sharply. In addition, this omission means books do not show how deeply progressive these governments were and how much all poor Americans lost with the collapse of Reconstruction. Perhaps most importantly, the textbooks do not show that widespread racism was a major factor in the failure of Reconstruction to establish enduring civic equality. Most books simply state that the Northern troops withdrew, either without citing reasons or saying it was because the South had met the required conditions. For instance, McGraw-Hill provides a rather confusing account of how Reconstruction ended: the text cites a Northerner saying they had tried Reconstruction long enough, which may imply different causes, but is far from explicit (Banks et al. 498). None of these books mention white people's widespread lack of concern with the wellbeing of former slaves. Without discussing the role of racism in the end of Reconstruction, it is—as McGraw-Hill's confusing account demonstrates—difficult to provide a coherent narrative, as it is difficult to explain the many decades of racial inequality that were to follow in both the South and the North.

After the 1980s, in keeping with multiculturalist scholarship, most textbooks made more of an effort to include African American voices, and they more consistently render visible black people's fight against discrimination. Notably, Booker T. Washington and W.E.B. Du Bois, who appeared only sporadically in the 1982 textbooks, were added to curricula and have become standard figures in these books (in the text, if not always in illustrations). Textbooks do not, however, transmit their critical ideas, rendering them more moderate than they were. Most books indicate that Washington advocated education and self-improvement, and they credit Du Bois with helping to found the NAACP, but of his ideas, they only state that he wanted to end discriminatory state laws immediately. Only one book indicates that Du Bois' preoccupations went beyond the institutional realm, hinting at the persistence and more pernicious effects of racism:

> W.E.B. Du Bois was proud of being black. "Beauty is black," he said. He wanted all African Americans to be proud of their African heritage. [. . .] As a teacher and a writer, he devoted his career to improving life for African Americans. In his later years, Du Bois believed that prejudice in the United States would never be broken down. He left the United States in 1961 and spent the rest of his life in the African country of Ghana.
>
> (Boehm et al. 1997: 526)

Textbooks similarly neutralize many other figures' radicalism. This is true of Rosa Parks, whose refusal to give up her bus seat appears not as a deliberate, focused act of civil disobedience undertaken by a long-time activist in a powerful social movement but almost as unwitting—a tired woman did not want to give up her seat and took a spontaneous stand against racism (Banks et al. 579; Berson et al. 586; Boyd et al. 644). Rosa Parks' courage, agency, and intelligence are minimized by this account. As we see in more detail in Chapter Three, the same is true of Martin Luther King, Jr. and of the Civil Rights Movement in general.

Consistent with the importance they accord to Parks and the bus boycott, recent textbooks focus only on the legal measures achieved by the Civil Rights Movement. This emphasis limits the scope of activists' ideas and gives the impression that by eradicating legal segregation in public facilities and obstacles to voting, equality has been achieved. Again, as we will see in more depth in Chapter Three, some books do mention economic inequality, but overwhelmingly the focus is on segregation and, to a lesser extent, voting rights. They thus depict the movement as mostly unified and moderate in its aims. The most recent books do, however, allude to departure from this consensus, as they mention Malcolm X (though only one book from 1997 pictures him [Boehm et al. 590], and none from 2003 do). They indicate that he was dissatisfied with the pace of change, but do not generally relate his ideas sufficiently to be coherent. The most cogent presentation is in Scott Foresman, which says that Malcolm X felt that white people would never cease to feel prejudice toward black people, so he advised self-reliance (Boyd et al. 646). But all the books either present his ideas more benignly from the beginning (Banks et al. 585) or indicate that he adopted a more moderate view and embraced unity before his death (Berson et al. 588; Boyd et al. 646). They do not discuss other figures of black radicalism, nor do they mention other divisions within the movement. Thus, radicalism is reduced to one man's youthful pessimism, which maturity corrected.

Perhaps more strikingly, textbooks also bowdlerize the Civil Rights Movement by largely omitting the role of violence. As with most other topics covered in this chapter, this one was handled in a variety of ways by the books of 1982. The textbooks of 1997 then more consistently adhered to historians' views, giving a clearer presentation of the extent of racism in American history, while the 2003 books make a decisive shift away from progressive historiography.

The textbooks of 1997 all show to varying degrees the role of violent opposition to the Civil Rights Movement as a catalyst that helped galvanize support for change. For instance, McGraw-Hill discusses the murder of Medgar Evers and the beatings and arrest of Freedom Summer workers in Mississippi: "At the same time the response to the struggle grew more violent. [. . .] Much of this violence was broadcast on television sets across the United States. Millions of Americans were shocked by what they saw" (Banks et al. 620). Houghton Mifflin emphasizes this violence by including a photo of white police officers attacking a black man with what the text describes as "snarling dogs" (Bednarz et al. 566).

The recent books demonstrate a clear shift away from what appeared in the 1990s textbooks to be a growing emphasis on the role of violence in the history of the Civil Rights Movement. The recent books omit almost completely the violence and opposition that Civil Rights activists faced.[13] They focus instead on peaceful protest, the support of Presidents Kennedy and Johnson, and the successful changes achieved. For instance, the only mention in any of these books of resistance to school desegregation is in Harcourt, which simply states that many states were "slow to obey that order," so many schools remained segregated (Berson et al. 586). By contrast, half of the books of 1997 showed photos of the National Guard, visibly armed as they escorted black children and college students to their recently desegregated schools (Banks et al. 623; Garcia et al. 499). In 2003 books, the only reference to opposition of any kind to the movement in general is in McGraw-Hill, which states that the march from Selma was forced back by law enforcement, and that many people were "hurt." The text says that many people were shocked by the violence of the protest, but this ambiguous statement and lack of details make it very unclear who was committing violence, for what reasons, and how widespread and systemic it was (Banks et al. 2003: 581).

Looking beyond individual topics to consider the textbooks in their entirety, it bears repeating that, generally speaking, these books mitigate the ongoing, pervasive role played by racial discrimination in U.S. history. As a counterexample, one textbook of 1997 commented on the ubiquity of discrimination in the U.S., but this book did not sell well in Texas, and its more critical approach to social justice is not echoed in any recent textbooks. This book set the stage for the Civil Rights Movement in this way:

> Discrimination was certainly not new to African Americans. All their lives, they had dealt with discrimination—even hatred—shown by some white Americans. At the start of World War II, for example, black workers were kept out of many jobs. They did not have equal access to housing or medical care. Still, discrimination became especially clear during the war. Black Americans were ready to die in the service of their country, yet their country was treating them poorly.
>
> (Garcia et al. 1997: 474)

Similarly, a telling change occurs between the 1997 and 2003 editions of McGraw-Hill's textbook. In the introductory section of the older book, after celebrating the diversity of the American people, the text explains:

> However, the acceptance of differences has not always come easily. Many ethnic groups have faced prejudice because their backgrounds, skin color, or beliefs were different from those of other groups. Prejudice is a negative opinion formed without proof.
>
> (Banks et al. 1997: 11)

This statement vanishes from the later edition. By commenting immediately on historical prejudice, this textbook set the stage for an antiracist approach to U.S. social studies. In removing this paragraph, the textbook instead focuses on a rosier view of diversity (as we will see in more detail in Chapter Four). Still, this textbook is the only one in 2003 to give any explicit indication that discrimination still exists in the U.S. The book ends its chapter on the Civil Rights Movement with this statement: "Discrimination still exists, but our country has come closer to the ideal of 'liberty and justice for all.' Leaders such as Jesse Jackson and Coretta Scott King, Martin Luther King's widow, have carried the legacy of the movement into the new millennium" (Banks et al. 583).

The other recent books avoid commenting on discrimination in contemporary U.S. society and end their chapters on the Civil Rights Movement rather vaguely. Both the Scott Foresman and Harcourt texts conclude their discussion of the Civil Rights Movement with the assassinations of Malcolm X and Martin Luther King, Jr., saying that they did not live to see all the progress of the movement (Berson et al. 588; Boyd et al. 646), and Harcourt adds that African Americans kept working for justice after the death of these leaders (Berson et al. 588).

We should also note that textbooks' focus on these few figures takes attention away from the broader movement, thereby limiting the view of how widespread anger was, and also delegitimizing protest as a force for social change. This narrative continues the "great people" approach to history, which is ultimately conservative, as it limits the perceived impact of "ordinary" people, constructing eidolons instead of teaching history (as we will see in greater detail in Chapter Five).

Between 1982 and 2003, U.S. textbooks took some important steps to showing the role of discrimination in some key historical developments, but the scope is still limited, and the variation from one book to another shows that official curriculum guidelines and public opinion are still leaving publishers free to skirt around this driving force of American history. Teaching about the pervasiveness and extensive repercussions of institutional racism in the United States represents a commercial risk. Defenders of the status quo might argue that this topic is too disturbing for children, but that certainly has not held back French publishers (at least regarding discrimination in the past). Clearly, U.S. publishers find it easier to talk about segregation—a problem that has, at least officially, been resolved—than about the deep roots and repercussions of racism and racist violence across U.S. history (see also Loewen 1995; Zimmerman 2002).

Before concluding the discussion of how American textbooks handle racial diversity, we should note that, following the example of the U.S. Census, these textbooks continue to promulgate the concept of race as if it were uncontested fact. They often reprint Census Bureau figures on "ethnicity," thus promoting the narrow ethnic categories used by the Census, and missing the opportunity to challenge this construction and show the simplifications and amalgamations it promotes (e.g., Banks et al. 2003: 20; Berson et al. 2003: 622). Teaching an anthropological definition of culture as a fluid process, rather than a static mainstream against which minority cultures are compared, can challenge essentialized notions of both national culture and minority identity (see Burkholder 2011 on antiracist pedagogy). But current textbooks do neither of these. U.S. textbooks reify racialized categories, failing to show how these have been historically created. In so doing, they group minorities into monolithic blocks, obscuring the internal diversity and the complexity of these categories, thus creating a clear demarcation between a majority defined as white and others defined as ethnic minorities.

CONCLUSION

From the mid-1980s to 2010, French textbooks came to show slightly greater diversity of phenotypes in national history, as U.S. textbooks have done (to a higher degree) since the 1960s. In both countries, this visual diversity aims to reinforce national unity: by including the images of previously excluded groups in official depictions of the nation and its history, these textbooks aim to emphasize the nation's egalitarian, open, and voluntaristic nature. In so doing, they reinforce the nation's primacy, promoting assimilation to dominant beliefs, including a myth of progress and equality in both countries, and in France, the elevation of secularism to the status of core value.

French textbooks have come to adopt a more critical assessment of injustice in the country's past, but this does not generally lead to questioning inequality today. French textbooks and curricula reveal mixed results regarding the place of previously excluded ethnic minorities in the nation. Overall, they give a slightly more diverse picture of the nation today than they did in the 1980s. They all demonstrate greater inclusion of France's overseas lands (departments and territories in the Caribbean and Indian Ocean), though in most textbooks these are still not fully incorporated into their vision of "France" and remain somewhat "other." Few people of minority origin are shown in pictures of metropolitan France (though the few existing civic education textbooks, from the 1980s as from the 2000s, are more inclusive). No contemporary, identifiable Muslims, Christians, or Jews are pictured in any book; these books reflect the official interpretation of secularism in curricula and public discourse, in which religious affiliation is relegated to the private sphere. The books are assimilationist, as they do not show other cultures in contemporary metropolitan France. Similarly, most of the recent textbooks omit discussion of contemporary immigration to France. If they do discuss it, they do so on their own initiative, as the curricula are silent on this issue. Recent textbooks do, though, make an effort to combat exclusionist ethnic conceptions of national belonging. These efforts follow traditional French discursive commitments to a colorblind polity, which places national unity above all other affiliations.

On some topics, French textbooks are Eurocentric, promoting a traditional interpretation of events that ignores perspectives of other ethnic or national groups. This is the case regarding the Crusades and European exploration of the Americas and Africa. Similarly, in their acknowledgement of past injustices, French textbooks adhere to a narrative of progress, which consistently features metropolitan (white) French liberators and protectors of oppressed minorities.

However, recent trends in public memory and related changes in academic historiography are reflected in some changes to textbooks published since the mid-1990s and especially since 2002. The books are more critical of the French government's role regarding colonization, the wars of decolonization, and the Holocaust. Most, though, attribute negative actions only to the government and do not identify the French people as a whole with discriminatory or exploitative practices.

In the U.S. textbooks studied here, an apparent shift between the 1980s and the 1990s toward a more widespread academic, critical approach to ethnic injustice in national history was reversed in many ways in the early 2000s. There have been some real changes toward greater inclusion that endured into the 2000s: the new origin myth in these books of America as the meeting of three worlds, more consistent inclusion of Native Americans' history, and discussing African Americans throughout U.S. history (including more "negative" aspects of the national past). However, the most recent books also reject antiracist pedagogy in avoiding frank discussions of the historical role of racism and its enduring legacy, and they retreat from emphasizing perspectives of those who endured racist oppression and from presenting radical figures.

Looking at U.S. textbooks in a longer perspective, going back to the mid-twentieth century, we see that the increased inclusion of diversity dating from the 1970s seems to have become sufficiently consensual to remain an enduring feature. However, there is less change over time regarding the most profound aspects of critical historiography, which only seems to have influenced these books sporadically and briefly, before being reversed by a reactionary backlash. The state of recent U.S. textbooks confirms many of Frances FitzGerald's findings in her 1979 study, as well as those of Jonathan Zimmerman in 2002: previously excluded groups have typically wanted "a place at the table" (Zimmerman 2002: 7) (i.e., to be included in the patriotic national story), not to overturn the triumphalist narrative. This continuity shows the resilience and conservative power of U.S. nationalism. It also points to the strength of the Christian Right in the U.S. and their power in defining national identity as taught in schools. More broadly, the lack of critical discourse in social studies textbooks for elementary schools shows the disconnect between academic history and primary education.

The contrast is particularly striking in comparison to the French textbooks. While French academic historians have been slower to legitimize the study of France's colonial history, dominant academic views do influence French curricula and textbooks more reliably than in the U.S. (albeit with a lag of several years). This difference can largely be attributed to structural and institutional factors, as discussed in the Introduction, as the U.S. system allows for more involvement of the lay public, treating history education more as a public good than as the province of experts.

Nevertheless, despite these differences, similar processes are at work in both countries. Social studies education in France and the United States reflects officially antiracist viewpoints. Curricula and textbooks of the past thirty years aim to eradicate residual ethnic conceptions of national belonging. However, in so doing, they reinforce nationalism. While greater awareness of diversity has changed the picture of who constitutes the nation, history education has only heightened its efforts to connect the contemporary community to a shared national past. Nationalistic historiography requires that the modern "we" see the past "them" as "us." Curricula and textbooks have changed who is part of the in-group, "we," but as we will see in subsequent chapters, this greater inclusion has not fundamentally changed underlying myths and narratives about what "we" believe in, the fairness of "our" society, and social cohesion. It is perhaps not surprising that by debating who comprises the nation in ethnic or ethno-cultural terms at a time when majorities already oppose racism, the result should be an officially colorblind celebration of progress, which reaffirms national unity but could well stall efforts to promote greater social justice. This colorblind approach prevents textbooks from addressing discrimination and the resulting inequality in contemporary society. Omitting lucid discussion of the historical role of racism provides a means of uniting liberal-to-moderate and conservative white people, at the price of continuing to exclude many minorities. Though the symbols have certainly changed to become more inclusive, the absence of racist pedagogy is not the same thing as antiracist pedagogy.

NOTES

1. This result shows similar trends as the findings of Frances FitzGerald (1979), James Loewen (1995), and Jonathan Zimmerman (2002), when analyzing textbooks written primarily in the 1960s and 1970s.
2. While there are advocates of more extreme versions of a "politics of recognition" (Taylor 1994), who reject the notion of an overarching national culture (e.g., Asante 1988), their voices are not generally heard in national debates regarding the teaching of national history in the primary schools. Afrocentrism is perhaps the primary example of this type of thinking, and it has influenced curricula in several cities, mainly in the Northeast and industrial northern Midwest. In addition, proponents of ethnic pride, inspired by Afrocentrism, have participated in debates over curricula and textbooks, and this type of thinking has certainly influenced more mainstream multiculturalist thought (see, e.g., Gitlin 1995; Glazer 1991; Ravitch 2003). However, Afrocentrism *per se* is beyond the scope of this book, as it has not been a recognizable force in determining social studies textbook content from the early 1980s to the present. Afrocentric challenges to education have been more localized, seeking to serve a specific community, rather than seeking to rewrite the curriculum for the nation (see Binder 2002). (For a concise overview of the varieties of multiculturalism, see Petrzela 2013; for an external perspective, see Lacorne 1997.)
3. For more on the concept of memory (as opposed to history) see the Introduction in this book as well as Hartog (2003); Kammen (1989, 1991); Lowenthal (1998); Ricoeur (2000); VanSledright (2008).
4. I apply the concept of "thinness" here to refer to a conception of multiculturalism that sets aside more transformative social justice goals, focusing instead on limited cultural pluralism, where national unity remains predominant.
5. There have been several *affaires du foulard*. The first was in 1989, when three female students were suspended from a middle school in Creil for refusing to remove their hijabs in class. The resulting controversy led to a decision by the Council of State, essentially allowing school authorities to decide on a case-by-case basis whether to allow students to wear hijabs. However, generally, this decision established narrow grounds for prohibiting the hijab, so that allowing it was the default (Thomas 2012: 189–190). This decision led to many local conflicts and efforts by school principals to obtain stricter, less ambiguous legislation. This controversy eventually led to the passage in 2004 of the law banning wearing of "ostentatious" religious symbols in schools.
6. On the subject of antiracist pedagogy, this would be a good point at which to address one of the ethical dilemmas posed by this chapter. In the course of this chapter, I will examine curricula and textbooks' representations of subjects

involving racist discrimination and inequality. I will also examine the visual representations of the population in France and the U.S. Examining depictions of diversity without reifying "racial" categories raises serious theoretical and methodological questions. I have decided that the most productive way to address depictions of diversity in textbooks is to apply, in adapted form, the same logic used by the publishers. In this decision, I adhere to the reasoning of such scholars as Richard Alba, who argues that ethno-racial categories are still useful in measuring inequalities in order to redress them (Alba 2015).

Examining textbooks in terms of ethno-racial categories reflects the reality of the publishing industry. From the quotas in use since the 1960s and 1970s by textbook publishers to regulate the inclusion of ethno-racial minorities in illustrations, to the categories used by the companies that sell art to the publishers (see for example the catalogs of services such as Photo Edit, available at: Photoeditinc.com [accessed 12 June 2015]), to ethno-racial descriptions in textbooks, this industry has institutionalized these categories.

Nevertheless, there is no perfect way of quantifying ethnic groups in illustrations. Generally, regarding historical illustrations, I have been able to rely on the text itself to indicate the ethnic identity of pictured individuals. The context generally shows how a person was categorized during his or her lifetime. Beyond such historically relevant categories, U.S. textbooks often explicitly label featured people (e.g., "African American inventor" or "Native American artist"). For illustrations depicting contemporary people, I have often had to rely on phenotype. This regrettable approach is, I believe, justified by the fact that textbooks very deliberately include people of different phenotypes as part of their efforts to combat discrimination. For the history sections of the textbooks, my analysis thus often employs the same categories as the U.S. Census and the stock photo companies: African American (or black), Asian, Hispanic (or Latino), Native American (or Indian), and white. The use of all of these categories erases internal differences and reinforces arbitrary boundaries. The inclusion of "Hispanic" as a category raises additional difficulties (and highlights the absurdity of using fixed ethno-racial categories to describe fluid conceptions of identity). To some extent, I evaluate the integration of these various groups' history into the general narrative. However, regarding contemporary Americans, I have chosen to limit my analysis to "white" and "people of color" in an effort to measure diversity and understand textbooks' policies. While this approach still reifies a dichotomous racialized view, it is my hope that it helps elucidate the ways in which depictions of the nation are changing.

7. Please note: I have chosen to count Nathan's CM1 and CM2 books as one volume, in order to be comparable to the other books of the period, which both cover CM1 and CM2 in a single volume. The 1985 textbooks include the history books published in 1985 and three geography books published between 1985 and 1993. The 2010 CM1 books include two integrated history and geography textbooks (Hatier and Sedrap) and Nathan's volumes, which separate history and geography (for the per-book average number of total illustrations, I have counted the Nathan volumes as one). Otherwise, each set of books refers to three textbooks that combine history, geography, and sometimes civic education. I have chosen not to include here the two civic education books published in 1987 and the one published in 2008, as the lack of civic education textbooks in the samples from other years would make this a flawed comparison.
8. In a departure from traditional centralized practice, the overseas territories were permitted to create their own curricula in 2004.
9. Armand Colin is once again something of an outlier and is ahead of its time. This 1985 textbook indicates that France bears responsibility for losing its colonies and for engaging in war in Indochina and Algeria, as it failed to

grant equal rights to colonized people, despite their support in the World Wars (Dorel-Ferré and Dhainaut 155).

10. In declining order by the number of illustrations in the most recent books, the top 28 most frequently pictured people in U.S. textbooks—who appear on average at least twice per book in the recent books—are: George Washington, Benjamin Franklin, Thomas Jefferson, Abraham Lincoln, Theodore Roosevelt, Christopher Columbus, Martin Luther King Jr., Robert E. Lee, Ulysses S. Grant, James Madison, John Adams, Alexander Hamilton, Meriwether Lewis and William Clark, Sacagawea, William Penn, Marco Polo, George W. Bush, Franklin Roosevelt, Hernando Cortés, Frederick Douglass, Andrew Jackson, Stephen Austin, Dwight D. Eisenhower, John F. Kennedy, James Oglethorpe, Abigail Adams, and Ronald Reagan. (Please note: Harriet Tubman appears 1.7 times on average per book in 2003, but she was the tenth most visible person in the books of 1997, appearing 2.8 times on average in those editions.)
11. This religious vision of U.S. identity appears only sporadically in public testimony and efforts but infuses documents that the Gablers' group circulates internally. In public efforts, for instance, the Gablers' Educational Research Analysts publish checklists to advise people who wish to review educational materials. These checklists include making sure that textbooks show that "colonial religion fostered independence," through relating how "church polity encouraged self-rule," "Calvinist covenant theology nurtured constitutionalism," and "The Great Awakening promoted self-determination" (Educational Research Analysts 2003b). In the newsletter that they send to their mailing list, they advise like-minded activists to employ new strategies in order to get textbooks of various subjects to reflect their Christian beliefs. The banner on the newsletter cover sets the tone, with a slogan proclaiming, "Besting foes on their own ground." The newsletter then explains the content that activists must make sure U.S. history textbooks cover, which provides coded "evidence of supernatural inspiration" in national history and in economic and government structure. That these strategies are meant to be covertly applied to public school education is made clear in several different ways. For instance, the newsletter includes a poster on how to teach "American Exceptionalism" (which was required in the 2010 TEKS for high-school U.S. history courses). A note on the poster informs the reader that the chart shows how U.S. history fits with "Biblical principles" but that if they would like to use the poster for public schools, Educational Research Analysts can provide a different version of it, which keeps the same list of facts, but removes the blurbs around the margins, explaining the connections between theology and the content to be advocated for classroom teaching. This "secular version" also removes the group's byline. In addition, another chart sent out with the newsletter explains how Christian teachers in the public schools can subtly teach religious content: "Christian teachers who communicate implied, unstated Biblical principles in public school classes are functionally Christocentric. [. . .] Teachers forced to 'align' classes with scripted humanistic lesson plans can antidote them with quick handouts incorporating this enrichment" (Educational Research Analysts 2013: n.p.).
12. The people who appear in at least two of three books of any of the four periods studied are: Léon Blum, Charlemagne, Charles le Téméraire, Charles VII, Jacques Chirac, Christopher Columbus, Georges Clémenceau, Clovis, Jean-Baptiste Colbert, Copernicus, Marie Curie, Georges Danton, Charles de Gaulle, Denis Diderot, Jules Ferry, François I, Galileo, Valéry Giscard d'Estaing, Henri IV, Adolf Hitler, Victor Hugo, Hugues Capet, Jean Jaurès, Joan of Arc, Helmut Kohl, Louis IX, Louis XI, Louis XIII, Louis XIV, Louis XVI, Louise Michel, François Mitterrand, Jean Moulin, Napoléon I, Napoléon III, Louis Pasteur,

Philippe Pétain, Georges Pompidou, Cardinal Richelieu, Maximilien Robespierre, Jean-Jacques Rousseau, Nicolas Sarkozy, Joseph Stalin, and Voltaire.

13. This omission of violence in U.S. history also applies to lynching, which the recent textbooks do not mention. Among older textbooks, Gross et al. is exceptional in mentioning Ida B. Wells-Barnett, to whom the textbook dedicates a half-page biography that focuses on lynching (1980: 251). While it omits gory details, it is much clearer than almost all the textbooks studied here—from 1982 to 2003—on this point. In addition to stating that lynching declined in frequency—partly thanks to Wells-Barnett's work—but continued into the 1960s, the book relates that she moved north to escape opposition to her activism, including the burning of her office by "a mob." In 2003 textbooks, only McGraw-Hill alludes to violence in the early twentieth century, as it mentions Ida B. Wells-Barnett's articles against violence—though without any details about who committed that violence, their reasons, and what it consisted of (Banks et al. 544–545 [483 in the 1997 edition]).

REFERENCES

French Textbooks

Baillat, Gilles, et al. 1996. *Histoire, géographie, éducation civique: Cycle 3, niveau 3*. Collection Gulliver. Paris: Nathan.

Bendjebbar, André, et al. 2003. *Multi-livre CM1: Histoire, géographie, sciences*. Paris: Istra.

Bendjebbar, André, et al. 2004. *Multi-livre CM2: Histoire, géographie, sciences*. Paris: Istra.

Beyria, Patrick, et al. 1998. *A Nous le monde! Cycle 3, 2e année, CM1: Histoire, géographie, sciences, éducation civique*. Paris: Sedrap.

Beyria, Patrick, et al. 2003. *A Nous le monde! Cycle 3, 2e année, CM1: Histoire, géographie, sciences, éducation civique*. Paris: Sedrap.

Beyria, Patrick, et al. 2003. *A Nous le monde! Cycle 3, 3e année, CM2: Histoire, géographie, sciences, éducation civique*. Paris: Sedrap.

Billard, Jacques, et al. 1986. *Education civique CM: "Vivre ensemble."* Paris: Nathan.

Boëche, Sandra, ed. 2011. *CE2: Les Reporteurs histoire, géographie, histoire des arts, développement durable*. Toulouse: Sedrap.

Boëche, Sandra, ed. 2011. *CM1: Les Reporteurs histoire, géographie, histoire des arts, développement durable*. Toulouse: Sedrap.

Boëche, Sandra, ed. 2011. *CM2: Les Reporteurs histoire, géographie, histoire des arts, développement durable*. Toulouse: Sedrap.

Chagny, Victor and Jean Forez. 1993. *Géographie. Cycle des approfondissements: CE2, CM1, CM2*. Paris: Armand Colin.

Chapier-Legal, Geneviève. 2010. *Histoire, géographie, histoire des arts, CE2*. Paris: Belin.

Chevalier, Jean-Pierre and Martine Picrel. 2010. *Géographie: CM1*. Paris: Nathan.

Chevalier, Jean-Pierre and Roselyne Le Bourgeois, eds. 2010. *Histoire, histoire des arts, instruction civique, CM2*. Paris: Nathan.

Dorel-Ferré, Gracia and M. Dhainaut. 1985. *Cours moyen: Histoire*. Paris: Armand Colin.

Dorel-Ferré, Gracia, et al. 1998. *Histoire, géographie, CM2 Cycle 3: Une Terre, des hommes*. Paris: Magnard écoles.

Hanniet, J.-P., et al. 1987. *Education civique, CM1, CM2*. Paris: Bordas.

Hinnewinkel, Jean-Claude, Jean-Michel Sivirine, and Anne Duchesne. 1985. *CE Histoire, Géographie*. Paris: Nathan.
Hinnewinkel, Jean-Claude, Jean-Michel Sivirine, and Anne Duchesne. 1985. *CM Géographie*. Paris: Nathan.
Le Bourgeois, Roselyne, ed. 2010. *Histoire, histoire des arts, CM1*. Paris: Nathan.
Le Callennec, Sophie, ed. 1997. *Histoire-géographie, Cycle 3, niveau 2, CM1*. Paris: Hatier.
Le Callennec, Sophie, ed. 1998. *Histoire-géographie, Cycle 3, niveau 3, CM2*. Paris: Hatier.
Le Callennec, Sophie, ed. 2004. *Histoire, géographie, CM2, Cycle 3*. Collection Magellan. Paris: Hatier.
Le Callennec, Sophie, ed. 2008. *Education à la citoyenneté, Cycle 3*. Collection Magellan. Paris: Hatier.
Le Callennec, Sophie, ed. 2010. *Histoire, géographie, CM1*. Collection Magellan. Paris: Hatier.
Le Callennec, Sophie, ed. 2011. *Histoire, géographie, CM2*. Collection Magellan. Paris: Hatier.
Lécharny, Hugues, et al. 2007. *Histoire géographie CM1 Cycle 3*. Collection Vers le monde. Paris: Nathan.
Nembrini, Jean-Louis, Pierre Polivka, and Jean Bordes. 1985. *Histoire CM*. Pour connaître la France. Paris: Hachette écoles.
Nembrini, Jean-Louis, Pierre Polivka, and Jean Bordes. 1985/1991. *Géographie CM*. Collection Pour connaître la France. Paris: Hachette écoles.
Vincent, Marc, et al. 1985. *CM1: Histoire: La France au fil du temps, de la Préhistoire à 1789*. Collection Télémaque. Paris: Nathan.
Vincent, Marc, et al. 1985. *CM2: Histoire: La France au fil du temps, de 1789 à nos jours*. Collection Télémaque. Paris: Nathan.

United States Textbooks

Banks, James. A., et al. 1997. *United States: Adventures in Time and Place*. New York: Macmillan McGraw-Hill.
Banks, James. A., et al. 2003. *Our Nation*. New York: Macmillan McGraw-Hill.
Bednarz, Sarah, et al. 1997. *Build Our Nation. We the People*. Boston: Houghton Mifflin.
Berson, Michael, et al. 2003. *Harcourt Horizons: United States History*. Orlando, FL: Harcourt.
Boehm, Richard G., et al. 1997. *America's Story: Stories in Time*. New York: Harcourt-Brace.
Boyd, Candy Dawson, et al. 2003. *The United States, Social Studies*. Glenview, IL: Scott Foresman.
Garcia, Juan R., et al. 1997. *Our United States: Social Studies*. Parsippany, NJ: Silver Burdett Ginn.
Gross, Herbert, et al. 1980. *Exploring Our World: Americas*. 2nd ed. Chicago: Follett.
Helmus, Timothy M., et al. 1982. *The United States and Its Neighbors*. Morristown, NJ: Silver Burdett.
King, Allen Y., et al. 1982. *The United States and the Other Americas*. New York: Macmillan.
King, Frederick M., et al. 1981. *Understanding Our Country*. River Forest, IL: Laidlaw.
Klein, Stanley, et al. 1982. *Our Country's History: Level E*. New York: Scholastic.

Curriculum Guidelines, Official Reports, and Legislation

"Chapter 113: Texas Essential Knowledge and Skills for Social Studies." 1998. *Texas Essential Knowledge and Skills*. Texas Education Agency. Retrieved 20 Dec. 2000 (http://www.tea.state.tx.us/rules/tac/ch113.html#s1137).

"Chapter 113: Texas Essential Knowledge and Skills for Social Studies." 2010. *Texas Essential Knowledge and Skills*. Texas Education Agency. Retrieved 5 Nov. 2013 (http://ritter.tea.state.tx.us/rules/tac/chapter113/index.html).

Discours du Ministre d'Etat, Ministre de l'Education Nationale, de la Jeunesse et des Sports [Jospin, Lionel]. 1990. "Une nouvelle politique pour l'école primaire." *Bulletin officiel de l'Education nationale* 9 (1 Mar.): 601–608.

Framework for the Social Studies. 1980. Austin: Texas Education Agency.

"Horaires et programmes d'enseignement de l'école primaire." 2002. *Bulletin officiel de l'Education nationale*. Special issue 1 (14 Feb.).

"Horaires et programmes d'enseignement de l'école primaire." 2008. *Bulletin officiel de l'Education nationale*. Special issue 3 (19 Jun.).

"Horaires, programmes et instructions pour l'école élémentaire, 1985." 1986. *Bulletin officiel de l'Education nationale*. Special issue 1 (16 Jan.).

"Horaires, objectifs et programmes. Cycle Moyen." 1980. *R.L.R. 514–3*.

"Loi d'orientation et de programme pour l'avenir de l'école." 2005. *Bulletin official* 18 (5 May). Retrieved 20 Aug. 2015 (http://www.education.gouv.fr/bo/2005/18/MENX0400282L.htm#loi).

Loi n° 2001-434 du 21 mai 2001 tendant à la reconnaissance de la traite et de l'esclavage en tant que crime contre l'humanité. 2001. République Française. Retrieved 20 Aug. 2015 (http://www.legifrance.gouv.fr/affichTexte.do?cidTexte=JORFTEXT000000405369&categorieLien=id).

Loi n° 2005–158 du 23 février 2005 portant reconnaissance de la Nation et contribution nationale en faveur des Français rapatriés. 2005. République Française. Retrieved 20 Aug. 2015 (http://legifrance.gouv.fr/affichTexte.do?cidTexte=JORFTEXT000000444898).

Ministère de la Jeunesse, de l'Éducation nationale et de la Recherche: Direction de l'enseignement scolaire. 2002. "Histoire et géographie cycle des approfondissements (cycle 3)." Collection Ecole: Documents d'application des programmes. Paris: Centre national de documentation pédagogique.

Proclamation 1994 of the State Board of Education Advertising for Bids on Instructional Materials. 1994. Austin: Texas Education Agency.

"Programmes de l'école primaire." 1995. *Bulletin officiel de l'Education nationale* 48 (28 Dec.).

Works of Reference

Alba, Richard. 2015. "The Myth of a White Minority." *The New York Times* 11 Jun. Retrieved 12 Jun. 2015 (http://www.nytimes.com/2015/06/11/opinion/the-myth-of-a-white-minority.html?_r=0).

Amalvi, Christian. 1981. "L'Iconographie des manuels d'histoire et la mémoire collective: de la mémoire scolaire à la mémoire buissonière. 1871–1950." In H. Moniot, ed., *Manuels d'histoire et mémoire collective*. Paris: Université Paris, p. 7.

Amiraux, Valérie and Patrick Simon. 2006. "There Are No Minorities Here: Cultures of Scholarship and Public Debate on Immigrants and Integration in France." *International Journal of Comparative Sociology* 47.3–4: 191–215.

Apple, Michael W. 2000. *Official Knowledge: Democratic Education in a Conservative Age*. 2nd ed. New York: Routledge.

Appleby, Joyce. 1995. "Controversy Over the National History Standards." *OAH Magazine of History* 9.3: 4. Retrieved 27 Jan. 2005 (http://www.oah.org/pubs/magazine/standards/appleby.html).

Asante, Molefi Kete. 1988. *Afrocentricity*. Trenton, NJ: Africa World Press.

Azéma et al. 2005. "La Liberté pour l'Histoire." Petition. Retrieved 11 Feb. 2014 (http://www.lph-asso.fr/index.php?option=com_content&view=article&id=2&Itemid=13&lang=fr).

Balibar, Etienne and Immanuel Wallerstein. 1988/1991. *Race, Nation, Class: Ambiguous Identities*. London: Verso.

Banks, James A. 1996. *Multicultural Education, Transformative Knowledge, and Action: Historical and Contemporary Perspectives*. Multicultural Education Series. New York: Teachers College Press.

Binder, Amy J. 2002. *Contentious Curricula: Afrocentrism and Creationism in American Public Schools*. Princeton, NJ: Princeton University Press.

Blanchard, Pascal, Nicolas Bancel and Sandrine Lemaire, eds. 2005. *La Fracture Coloniale: La société française au prisme de l'héritage colonial*. Paris: La Découverte.

Bliss, Traci. 1990. "Visuals in Perspective: An Analysis of U.S. History Textbooks." *The Social Studies* 81.1(Jan./Feb.): 10–14.

Bonafoux, Corinne, Laurence de Cock-Pierrepont, and Benoît Falaize. 2007. *Mémoires et histoire à l'Ecole de la République: quels enjeux?* Paris: Armand Colin.

Bozec, Géraldine. 2010. *Les héritiers de la République: Eduquer à la citoyenneté à l'école dans la France d'aujourd'hui*. Unpublished doctoral dissertation, Institut d'Etudes Politiques de Paris, Paris.

Burkholder, Zoë. 2011. *Color in the Classroom: How American Schools Taught Race, 1900–1954*, Oxford: Oxford University Press.

Camus, Jean-Yves. 2006. "The Commemoration of Slavery in France and the Emergence of a Black Political Consciousness." *The European Legacy: Toward New Paradigms* 11.6: 647–655.

CIBC (Council on Interracial Books for Children). 1981. *Guidelines for Selecting Bias-Free Textbooks and Storybooks*. New York: Council on Interracial Books for Children.

Citron, Suzanne. 1987/2008. *Le Mythe national: L'histoire de France revisitée*. Rev. ed. Paris: Les éditions de l'Atelier.

Debray, Régis. 2002. *L'enseignement du fait religieux dans l'Ecole laïque, Rapport au Ministre de l'Education Nationale*.

De Laforcade, Geoffrey. 2006. "'Foreigners,' Nationalism and the 'Colonial Fracture': Stigmatized Subjects of Historical Memory in France." *International Journal of Comparative Sociology* 47.3–4: 217–233.

Deltombe, Thomas and Mathieu Rigouste. 2005. "L'ennemi intérieur: la construction médiatique de la figure de l' « Arabe »." In P. Bancel, N. Blanchard, and S. Lemaire, eds., *La Fracture Coloniale*. Paris: La Découverte, pp. 191–198.

Dosse, François. 2007. "Les remises en cause du roman national." In C. Delacroix, F. Dosse, and P. Garcia, eds., *Les courants historiques en France XIXe-XXe siècles*. 2nd ed. Paris: Gallimard, pp. 472–483.

Du Bois, W.E.B. 1935/1995. *Black Reconstruction in America*. New York: Simon & Schuster.

Duchastel, Philippe C. 1983. "Text Illustrations." *Performance & Instruction Journal* 22.4(May): 3–5.

Educational Research Analysts. 1982a. *1982 Textbook Ratings*. Longview, TX: Educational Research Analysts.

Educational Research Analysts. 1982b. *Comparison of Social Studies Series, Grades 4–6*. Longview, TX: Educational Research Analysts.

Educational Research Analysts. 1997a. *1997 Elementary Social Studies Information*. Longview, TX: Educational Research Analysts.

Educational Research Analysts. 1997b. *Strengths of United States (Macmillan, 1997) 5th Grade Social Studies Textbook Approved for 1997 Texas Local Adoption (Compiled from Reviews by Carol Warren, Pam Morse, and Jeanie Jones)*. Longview, TX: Educational Research Analysts.

Educational Research Analysts. 2003a. *2003 5th Grade Social Studies Textbook Rating*. Longview, TX: Educational Research Analysts.

Educational Research Analysts. 2003b. *U.S. History Textbook Standard Review Criteria*. Longview, TX: Educational Research Analysts.

Educational Research Analysts. 2013. *Newsletter* Oct. Longview, TX: Educational Research Analysts.

Farr, Roger and Michael A. Tulley. 1985. "Do Adoption Committees Perpetuate Mediocre Textbooks?" *Phi Delta Kappan* 66.7(Mar.): 467–471.

Finn, Chester and Diane Ravitch. *The Mad, Mad World of Textbook Adoption*. Washington, DC: Thomas B. Fordham Institute. 29 Sept. 2004. Retrieved 25 Feb. 2015 (http://edex.s3-us-west-2.amazonaws.com/publication/pdfs/Mad%20World_Test2_8.pdf).

FitzGerald, Frances. 1979/1980. *America Revised*. New York: Vintage.

Foner, Eric. 1988. *Reconstruction: America's Unfinished Revolution, 1863–1877*. New York: Harper & Row.

Frey, Neal. 2003a. [Director, Educational Research Analysts.] "Re: Fifth Grade Social Studies Textbooks." Personal email. 9 Apr.

Frey, Neal. 2003b. "Re: Fifth Grade Social Studies Textbooks." Personal email. 15 Apr.

Gabler, Mel, Norma Gabler, and Neal Frey. 1997. Review of Harcourt Brace and Company, *America's Story*. Longview, TX: Educational Research Analysts.

Garcia, Patrick and Jean Leduc. 2003. *L'enseignement de l'histoire en France de l'Ancien Régime à nos jours*. Paris: Armand Colin.

Giroux, Henry. 1981/1984. *Ideology, Culture, and the Process of Schooling*. Philadelphia: Temple University Press.

Gitlin, Todd. 1995. *The Twilight of Common Dreams*. New York: Metropolitan Books.

Glazer, Nathan. 1991. "In Defense of Multiculturalism." *New Republic* 205.1(Sept.): 18–22.

Guidelines for Creating Positive Sexual and Racial Images in Educational Materials. 1975. New York: Macmillan.

Hargreaves, Alec G. 2007. *Multi-ethnic France: Immigration, Politics, Culture, and Society*. 2nd ed. New York: Routledge.

Hartog, François. 2003. *Régimes d'historicité: Présentisme et expériences du temps*. Paris: Seuil.

Horne, Gerald, ed. 1988. *Thinking and Rethinking U.S. History*. New York: Council on Interracial Books for Children.

Hunter, James. 1991. *Culture Wars: The Struggle to Define America*. New York: Basic Books.

Jones, Arnita A. 1995. "Our Stake in the History Standards." *OAH Magazine of History* 9.3: 5–6. Retrieved 27 Jan. 2005 (http://www.oah.org/pubs/magazine/standards/jones.html#Anchor-Ou-23757).

Jones, Jeanie. 1997. "Reviews of 5th Grade U.S. History Texts." *1997 Elementary Social Studies Information*. Longview, TX: Educational Research Analysts.

Kammen, Michael. 1989. "History Is Our Heritage: The Past in Contemporary American Culture." In P. Gagnon, ed., *Historical Literacy: The Case for History in American Education*. Boston: Houghton Mifflin, pp. 138–156.

Kammen, Michael. 1991. *Mystic Chords of Memory: The Transformation of Tradition in American Culture*. New York: Knopf.

Kumar, Krishan. 2006. "English and French National Identity: Comparisons and Contrasts." *Nations and Nationalism* 12.3: 413–432.

Laborde, Cécile. 2001. "The Cultures of the Republic: Nationalism and Multiculturalism in French Republican Thought." *Political Theory* 29.5: 716–735.

Lacorne, Denis. 1997. *La Crise de l'identité américaine: Du Melting-pot au multiculturalisme.* Paris: Fayard.

Lebovics, Herman. 2004. *Bringing the Empire Back Home: France in the Golden Age.* Durham, NC: Duke University Press.

Le Débat. 2013. "Définir les programmes: Entretien avec Laurent Wirth." *Le Débat* 175: 23–34.

Legris, Patricia. 2010. "Les Programmes d'histoire en France: la construction progressive d'une 'citoyenneté plurielle' (1980–2010)." *Histoire de l'éducation*, 126: 121–154.

Legris, Patricia. 2014 *Qui écrit les programmes d'histoire ?* Grenoble: Presses universitaires de Grenoble.

Lepore, Jill. 2010. *The Whites of Their Eyes: The Tea Party's Revolution and the Battle over American History.* Princeton, NJ: Princeton University Press.

Lewis, Mary Dewhurst. 2011. "Immigration." In E. Berenson, V. Duclert, and C. Prochasson, eds., *The French Republic: History, Values, Debates.* Ithaca, NY: Cornell University Press, pp. 232–241.

Loewen, James W. 1995/2007. *Lies My Teacher Told Me: Everything Your American History Textbook Got Wrong.* Revised Edition. New York: Touchstone.

Lowenthal, David. 1998. *The Heritage Crusade and the Spoils of History.* Cambridge, UK: Cambridge University Press.

Marshall, J. Dan. 1991. "State-Level Textbook Selection Reform: Toward the Recognition of Fundamental Control." In P. Altbach, et al., eds., *Textbooks in American Society: Politics, Policy, and Pedagogy.* Albany, NY: SUNY, pp. 117–144.

Martigny, Vincent. 2012. *Le Nationalisme culturel français: Récit national et usages politiques de la culture en France (1981–1995).* Unpublished doctoral dissertation, Institut d'Etudes Politiques de Paris.

May, Michael. 2002. "War by the (Text)book." *The Austin Chronicle* 26 Jul. Retrieved 31 Jan. 2003 (http://www.austinchronicle.com/issues/dispatch/2002–07–26/pols_feature5.html).

Moore, Robert. 1977. *Stereotypes, Distortions, and Omissions in U.S. History Textbooks.* New York: Council of Interracial Books for Children.

Nash, Gary B. 1999. "The Lawrence F. Brewster Lecture in History: The History Wars of the 1990s." East Carolina University, 9 Feb. Retrieved 20 May 2001 (http:// www.ecu.edu/history/ Brewster/bl96.htm).

Nash, Gary B., Charlotte Crabtree, and Ross E. 1997/2000. *History on Trial: Culture Wars and the Teaching of the Past.* New York: Vintage Books.

Ngai, Mae M. 2004. *Impossible Subjects: Illegal Aliens and the Making of Modern America.* Princeton, NJ: Princeton University Press.

Noiriel, Gérard. 1988. *Le Creuset français: Histoire de l'immigration, XIXe-XXe siècles.* Paris: Seuil.

Noiriel, Gérard. 2007. *A quoi sert "l'identité nationale"?* Marseille: Agone.

Nora, Pierre. 2008. "Liberté pour l'histoire." *Le Monde*, 10 Oct. Retrieved 23 Nov. 2015 (http://www.lemonde.fr/idees/article/2008/10/10/liberte-pour-l-histoire-par-pierre-nora_1105435_3232.html).

"OAH Statement on Multicultural History Education." 1991. Organization of American Historians, Spring. Retrieved 26 Jan. 2005 (http://www.oah.org/reports/mulitcultural.html).

Parti des Indigènes de la République. 2005. "Nous sommes les indigènes de la République!" Retrieved 22 Aug. 2015 (http://indigenes-republique.fr/le-p-i-r/appel-des-indigenes-de-la-republique/).

Petrzela, Natalia Mehlman. 2013. "Multiculturalism." In I. Ness, ed., *The Encyclopedia of Global Human Migration*. Hoboken, NJ: Wiley-Blackwell.

Pew Research Center. 2011. Demographic Profile of Hispanics in Texas, 2011. Retrieved 14 Aug. 2015 (http://www.pewhispanic.org/states/state/tx/).

Ravitch, Diane. 2003. *The Language Police: How Pressure Groups Restrict What Students Learn*. New York: Knopf.

Responses to Written Comments and Oral Testimony Regarding Instructional Materials Reviewed by the State Textbook English Social Studies Committee 1996 Adoption. 1996. Austin: Texas Education Agency.

Ricoeur, Paul. 2000. *La Mémoire, l'histoire, l'oubli*. Paris: Editions du Seuil.

Rousso, Henry. 1990/1994. *The Vichy Syndrome: History and Memory in France since 1944*. Trans. Arthur Goldhammer. Cambridge, MA: Harvard University Press.

Schnapper, Dominique. 1991. *La France de l'intégration: Sociologie de la nation en 1990*. Paris: Gallimard.

Scott, Joan Wallach. 2007. *The Politics of the Veil*. Princeton, NJ: Princeton University Press.

Sleeter, Christine E. and Peter L. McLaren, eds. 1995. *Multicultural Education, Critical Pedagogy, and the Politics of Difference*. SUNY Series, Social Context of Education. Albany, NY: SUNY Press.

Taguieff, Pierre-André. 1988. *La Force du préjugé. Essai sur le racisme et ses doubles*. Paris: La Découverte.

Taylor, Charles, ed. 1994. *Multiculturalism: Examining the Politics of Recognition*. Princeton, NJ: Princeton University Press.

Thomas, Elaine R. 2012. *Immigration, Islam, and the Politics of Belonging in France: A Comparative Framework*. Philadelphia: University of Pennsylvania Press.

Tison, Hubert. 2013. "La Bataille de l'enseignement: L'histoire sous la Ve République." *Le Débat* 175: 18–22.

Tribalat, Michelè. 1995. *Faire France: une enquête sur les immigrés et leurs enfants*. Paris: La Découverte.

Tyson-Bernstein, Harriet and Arthur Woodward. 1991. "Nineteenth Century Policies for Twenty-first Century Practice." In P. Altbach, et al., eds., *Textbooks in American Society: Politics, Policy, and Pedgagogy*. Albany: SUNY, pp. 91–104.

VanSledright, Bruce. 2008. "Narratives of Nation-State, Historical Knowledge, and School History Education." *Review of Research in Education* 32.1: 109–146.

Viguier, Frédéric. 2011. "The Suburbs." In E. Berenson, V. Duclert, and C. Prochasson, eds., *The French Republic: History, Values, Debates*. Ithaca, NY: Cornell University Press, pp. 262–271.

Waldman, Abby. 2009. "The Politics of History Teaching in England and France During the 1980s." *History Workshop Journal* 68: 199–221.

Warren, Carol. 1997. "Reviews of 5th Grade U.S. Social Studies Texts." *1997 Elementary Social Studies Information*. Longview, TX: Educational Research Analysts.

Zimmerman, Jonathan. 2002. *Whose America? Culture Wars in the Public Schools*. Cambridge, MA: Harvard University Press.

2 Gender and the Nation

Gender differences and inequalities are central to modern nationalism as it has been practiced in most Western countries. The very centrality and rootedness of gendered divisions in the functioning of modern nations and the constructions of national identities continue to obscure the relations between the two in much public opinion. The limitation of women's power (social, economic, and political) is intricately tied to modern nationalism. In defining the national citizenry during the revolutionary era, ruling elites in both France and the United States deliberately excluded women from many political and economic rights. In so doing, they created starkly different roles for men and women in the modern nation-state (Accampo 2004; Hunt 1992; Scott 1996). While, of course, these roles drew on existing gender norms, tying them to nationalism legitimized and reinforced them over time, imbuing them with patriotic associations, in which fulfilling traditional gender roles is seen to promote the good of the nation (Mosse 1996; Nash 2005; Yuval-Davis 1997).

Feminism, then, presents something of an inherent challenge to nationalism as it has traditionally manifested itself in the West. Feminism not only challenges the confinement of women to a supposedly apolitical domestic sphere or to a limited range of related nurturing occupations (as biological and cultural reproducers of the nation), as opposed to men's roles as actors in a variety of capacities in the public sphere. Feminism also demands an examination of how nationalism has limited women's and men's roles, and therefore how it can limit individual freedom. Thus, feminism (like other critical theory) shows the gap between nationalist myths of equality and the reality of exclusion that underlay those myths. It shows how male dominance required female sacrifice and how prizing "masculine" attributes as patriotic and therefore noble contributed to devaluing women and "feminine" attributes.

Yet, feminism is not inherently opposed to nationalism. Indeed, feminism, like multiculturalism, arguably was and is most successful when it has been allied with nationalism, rather than opposed to it. This chapter demonstrates that, in response to feminist movements, French and U.S. social studies curricula and textbooks have incorporated more women but have not fundamentally altered their narratives. In both countries, conceptions of nationalism and national identity constrain and shape presentations of women's history. These educational materials only legitimize the strains of multiculturalism and feminism that have adopted nationalist discourse, thus delegitimizing more radical strains and rendering them invisible in their historical narratives, which remain focused on the history of the nation-state. By omitting ideological challenges to the nation-state's hegemony, curricula and textbooks reify the nation, showing it as natural, the only possible primary community of belonging and political organization.

Whereas positions regarding multiculturalism vary between France and the U.S. (see Chapter One), the aims of feminists are more similar in both countries, as they advocate not just adding women to the curriculum and textbooks but also teaching about the construction of gender differences and inequality in history and systematically questioning women's exclusion from historical narratives (e.g., Cott and Faust 2005; Dermenjian et al. 2010).

Similarly, in both countries, opposition to feminism and women's history takes the form of essentialism tied to nationalism. In this view, traditional gender roles are a part of the national heritage. Family structure and nationalism are connected in several ways. The nuclear family is seen by many as the basic unit of modern society, and family is often used as a metaphor for the nation. Some forms of feminism and related questioning of gender norms can be seen as challenging this family structure, which many see as eternal and natural. Thus, feminism is seen by its opponents as a threat to basic social order and the nation in practical as well as symbolic terms. In France, much of the population embraces—in explicitly nationalist terms—different gender roles, which, in effect, contribute to inequalities. This opposition to the specter of the erasing of gender differences is frequently framed as defending French society and identity against the threat of American-style feminism (Ezekiel 2002; Fassin 1999). Indeed, the image of France as characterized by harmonious relations between "feminine" women and "masculine" men is a recurring antifeminist myth. Regarding education in particular, while there is occasional antifeminist protest from the far right, it is generally directed at broader educational policies, rather than at history teaching (as, for instance, was the case with the "ABCs of equality" program [*ABCD de l'égalité*] in 2014, which aimed to challenge gender inequality beginning with preschoolers [Battaglia 2014]). In the U.S., feminism has been one of the major targets of conservative Christian politics more broadly as well as education activists in particular. They promote traditional gender roles in a variety of school subjects, from sex education (Petrzela 2015) to social studies, and they oppose teaching critical women's history (e.g., Gabler et al. 1982: 8–10; Jones 1997: 3, 5).

PRINCIPAL FINDINGS AND CHAPTER OUTLINE

French curricula and textbooks have undergone a major recent shift, which reflects broader changes in political and academic trends. Though they still show few women in French history, they have begun to include slightly more. More significantly, they have also begun to adopt a critical approach to women's absence from traditional historical narratives and toward enduring sexism.

Where French curricula and textbooks have moved toward a more critical approach to sexism in history and contemporary society, U.S. textbooks have moved in the opposite direction. This rejection of feminist aims demonstrates once again the success of the Christian Right in promoting its vision of U.S. national identity. As this chapter will show, women have been added throughout national U.S. history, yet the narrative of progress dominates coverage of women's history, obscuring the inequality that remains and optimistically showing only how far the nation has come toward gender equality.

This chapter begins by examining how curricula reflect changing historiographical trends and other ideological influences in their presentations of women's history and contemporary gender inequality. It then analyzes images of women in the different countries' textbooks, looking both at the changing percentages of women in relation to men in these books' illustrations and at the types of roles in which women are depicted. The final section looks beyond the images of women, at how textbooks discuss women's exclusion from civic rights, continuing inequalities today, and whether they address the longstanding invisibility of women from historical narratives.

WOMEN'S HISTORY AND GENDER EQUALITY IN CURRICULA

Changes in most French textbooks regarding gender begin with changes in the 2002 curriculum. Whereas women's history and its aims were largely absent from older curricula, those of 2002 adopt a much more critical stance. However, while the recent curricula encourage students to learn about and criticize women's absence from history, they do not for the most part add many individual women.

Curricula mandated these changes beginning with the 2002 guidelines created under the supervision of historian Philippe Joutard, who (as we saw in the Introduction) actively incorporated current historiographical trends to the curricula. These changes echo shifts in political policy as well as academic scholarship. French feminism scholar Christine Bard sees 1995 as a critical turning point in feminism studies in France and in the reception of feminism in society more generally. Though feminism studies have existed since the 1970s in France, the field struggled to gain institutional recognition. The political and academic climate changed notably after the United Nations' 1995 World Conference on Women in Beijing as well as protests held in France that same year. Notably, the law on parity in electoral lists (2000) as well as other policies to reduce inequality date from that period (Bard 2003: 24). In the realm of education, in 2001 the wing of the Education Ministry in charge of higher education commissioned a report on the state of gender studies in France (Andriocci et al. 2003), and in 2003 the Economic and Social Council commissioned another report on the place of women in history teaching (Wieviorka 2004). The Wieviorka report has been credited by textbook authors with increasing their sensitivity to including more women's history, as have the actions of various feminist associations, most notably Mnémosyne, which seeks audience with writers of curricula and textbooks and has recently published its own high school history textbook (Colon 2015; Dermenjian et al. 2010).

Where the 1985 curriculum did not list specific names of people to be covered, the 1995 curriculum introduced a small list of 20 names, including two women: Joan of Arc and Marie Curie. The *Documents d'accompagnement*, which list the specific content to be covered for the 2002 curriculum, build on the 1995 list, naming 14 individuals as part of the required curriculum, plus an additional 21 optional figures. Of these 35 people, seven are women (to Joan of Arc and Marie Curie are added: George Sand, Queen Victoria, Louise Michel, Hélène Boucher, Anne Frank, plus a suggested additional activity mentions Camille Claudel). In addition, the 2002 *Documents* list twelve groups of people under either required or suggested content, and these include two groups that are explicitly women only (women of the Revolution; women at work), and one that is explicitly men and women (*résistantes et résistants* (Ministère . . . 2002: 11–17); which could, one might wonder, imply that curriculum writers were not too concerned about including women with all social categories, such as peasants or craftspeople, as they only give the masculine form of these words.

Beyond the few names listed, this shift toward including more women in 2002 is more marked in the presentation and choice of topics to be covered. The French curricula tend to pay more attention to social history in general than do their U.S. counterparts. These descriptions of social history, while not explicitly including women, allow for their inclusion. Women do not explicitly appear in either the 1985 or 1995 history curricula, though there is a brief mention of "racial and sexual equality" among the basic rules for life in society, as taught in civic education for the *classes préparatoires* (i.e., ages 6–7). The 2002 curriculum adds one specific event pertaining to women's history, by including the "right to vote for women" in 1944 on the twentieth-century timeline (Ministère . . . 2002: 16). More importantly, however, the 2002 curriculum (both in the *Programmes* and in the accompanying documents) makes several critical statements that require using a historiographical approach to teaching history, explicitly studying women's absence from traditional historical narratives ("Horaires . . ." 2002: 78; Ministère . . . 2002: 9). In addition, the curriculum clearly points out the exclusion of women from voting rights and their relegation to inferior status in France and throughout Europe in the early republic ("Horaires . . ." 2002: 79). It highlights this issue, stating for instance:

> Inequality between men and women: exclusion from voting and legal inferiority. The progress of democracy highlights the persistence of women's unequal situation, which, at times, was made worse on the

> legal level. While some of them held significant roles in artistic or scientific realms, and in increasing number obtained access to education and paid work, they were most often legally considered as minors and did not have the right to vote.
>
> (Ministère . . . 2002: 16)

The mysteriously written, highly criticized 2008 curriculum, however, marks a reversal from its more feminist predecessor. In negating the *Documents d'accompagnement*, it eliminates the emphasis on feminist discourse and critical approach to history. It also greatly reduces the number of women mentioned. The 2008 curriculum for *troisième cycle* (Grades Three through Five) reduces the 35 people named in the 2002 curriculum to 25, reverting to the same two women named in the 1995 curriculum, Joan of Arc and Marie Curie. However, as we will see, these changes appear to have had little effect on textbooks, which generally continue to adhere to the spirit of the 2002 documents. This lack of change seems to indicate historians' dominance in writing the textbooks and their independence from certain political whims.

As for the U.S., the optional National History Standards, written in 1996 (after an initial attempt in 1994; see Nash, Crabtree, and Dunn 1997/2000) by a team of historians and educators, largely reflect the state of the academic field. Because they propose studying national history in a way that incorporates many of the objectives and approaches of women's history, it is instructive to consider their suggestions. The NHS seek to teach students—even from Grade Five—to look critically and directly at women's deprivation of rights throughout U.S. history. For instance, in the section on 1800–1861, the standards state: "students will see that the evolution of political democracy was not a smooth, one-way street as free African Americans were disenfranchised in much of the North and woman's suffrage was blocked even while white male suffrage spread throughout the states and into the newly developed territories" ("United States History Standards . . ." 1996). Though the NHS still primarily focus on political and military history, they regularly incorporate aspects of social history, which would allow for the inclusion of women's perspectives. The standards at least mention women in conjunction with each era of American history, addressing, for instance, how the significant events of the time impacted them specifically and their role in those events. While women's history may not have revolutionized the standards (i.e., it does not act as a filter through which all of American history is viewed), it has nevertheless influenced them.

Among conservative Christian education activists, on the other hand, critical approaches of women's history meet with sharp opposition. As Rogers Brubaker, building on work by Roger Friedland, has argued, norms regarding gender roles are an integral part of a religious form of nationalism:

> Religious nationalism joins state, territory and culture primarily by focusing on family, gender and sexuality: by defending the traditional

> family, as the key generative site of social reproduction and moral socialisation, against economic and cultural forces that weaken its authority or socialising power; by upholding traditional gendered divisions of labour within and outside the family; and by promoting a restrictive regulation of sexuality, seeking to contain sexuality within the family.
>
> (Brubaker 2012: 13)

Indeed, antifeminism and gender politics have played a major role in mobilizing evangelical activists (Hartman 2015: 134–170), and traditional views of family structure and gender roles are intricately bound to their conceptions of national identity and the good of the nation.

State curriculum standards are often more compatible with this traditionalist vision than with critical women's history. I cite the NHS approach to these issues not because it seems to have had a strong influence on state standards but mainly to show the gap between academic efforts and primary history education.

Turning now to the Texas curricula, the amount of attention given to women has increased slightly since 1980. The 1980 curriculum guidelines contained little detail and do not list specific people to be included in the curriculum. Instead, they laid out broad goals in general terms. While they repeatedly emphasize the importance of ethnic and cultural diversity, they make no mention at all of gender diversity or of women's history. The 1994 standards are somewhat more detailed. They retain the earlier document's focus on ethnic and cultural diversity and add only one mention (for all the K-6 curricula) of women: in the very last point of grade five content, they require that students: "use major social issues, past and present, to analyze cooperation and conflict (e.g., voting rights, religious issues, slavery, status of women, displacement of American Indians)" (*Proclamation* . . . 1994: A-25). This statement is too vague for clear interpretation, but it is certainly not normative in its implications. Furthermore, these standards include very few women. When specific figures are mentioned, they are almost all men (a list of 13 names in Grade Four on Texas history are all men; the lone woman mentioned in these standards is Texas politician Barbara Jordan in the Grade Two content requirements) (*Proclamation* . . . 1994: A-13). In Grade Five, the 1994 curriculum mentions no specific figures but does require teaching about "significant Americans of various racial, ethnic, and cultural groups who contributed to change in the United States, e.g., explorers, statesmen, reformers, inventors, military leaders, entertainers, sports figures, literary figures" (*Proclamation* . . . 1994: A-24)—a list that would include few women. Gender considerations do not, therefore, have the same consensual status and attention as does ethno-cultural diversity.

With the more detailed TEKS of 1998, some changes occur. From mentioning only 16 individuals in 1994, the TEKS include 73 names in 1998 and 139 in 2010. Of these, in 1998, 14 are women (about 19 percent of the total) and in 2010, 29 are women (including one group, rather than an individual, for about 21 percent of the total). There is some evolution between 1998 and 2010 in the types of women included and the reasons given for their inclusion. The women listed in 1998 are: Jane Addams, Clara Barton, Carrie Chapman Catt, Amelia Earhart, Miriam Ferguson, Anne Hutchinson, Barbara Jordan, Helen Keller, Henrietta King (a Texas rancher and philanthropist who also opposed the Union during the Civil War), Florence Nightingale, Rosa Parks, Eleanor Roosevelt, Sojourner Truth, and Harriet Tubman. Half of these women are included as models of "good citizenship," under the instructions: "identify characteristics of good citizenship such as a belief in justice, truth, equality, and responsibility for the common good," which these women are said to exemplify (i.e., Addams, Barton, Keller, Nightingale, Roosevelt, Truth, and Tubman; "Chapter 113" 1998). In a related category, the TEKS list Barbara Jordan, who is included for having "modeled active participation in the democratic process." The other six women are singled out for their accomplishments. These include Chapman Catt and Rosa Parks who are mentioned in conjunction with: "accomplishments of notable individuals . . . who have made contributions to society in the areas of civil rights, women's rights, military actions, and politics" ("Chapter 113" 1998 §113.7.b.5.b). The percentage of women who are included for good citizenship is much higher than is the case for men. Arguably, these traits—belief in basic civic values and responsibility for the common good—are more traditionally associated with the feminine sphere than is action. Men are, overwhelmingly, noted for their "accomplishments" or "actions." Indeed, only two men in the 1998 TEKS are noted as examples of "good citizenship," and even one of these two changes categories in 2010 (Nathan Hale is now noted as a "Founding Father and Patriot hero"; "Chapter 113" 2010 §113.16.b.2.b).

In the 2010 TEKS, though most of those listed for "good citizenship" are still women, the majority of women listed are now credited with other achievements. Nine of the 29 are listed for good citizenship (to which we might add two more for "active participation in the democratic process"). Three women are listed under "accomplishments of individuals and groups [. . .] who have made contributions to society in the areas of civil rights, women's rights, military actions, and politics" (Jane Addams, Susan B. Anthony [who apparently replaces Carrie Chapman Catt], and Rosa Parks, as before). These standards demonstrate an effort to increase representation of women in nontraditional roles, as they include two astronauts, three pilots (in addition to the already present Amelia Earhart, they add Bessie Coleman and the "World War II Women Airforce Service Pilots"—who are included under "good citizenship"), two writers, one artist, two cattle ranchers, and several Texas politicians. (We might also note that in all of these categories, the women cited are of varied ethnicities.) Despite this apparent effort to expand the roles in which women are depicted, their proportion remains ostensibly the same (19.2 percent in 1998, 20.8 percent in 2010).

Beyond the inclusion of more specific women in the curricula, the TEKS do not incorporate many of the aims or approaches of women's history. The

TEKS of both 1998 and 2010 mention women's rights only once, and this concerns only suffrage movements of the nineteenth and early twentieth centuries. In addition, though these documents frequently refer to "equality," the term is never used in conjunction with women; it is, instead, undefined and vague (as we will discuss in Chapter Four). None of the Texas curriculum guidelines explicitly mention discrimination toward women or question or explain their relative absence in history, or gender inequality. They do not, as such, advocate a critical approach to U.S. history and social studies in line with women's history or feminism.

Both French and U.S. curricula are vague to varying degrees and affect more or less directly the classroom materials in each country. In particular, it is difficult to measure their emphasis on social history. Where French textbooks seem to reflect the same approach as curricula until the two part ways in 2008, U.S. textbooks' approach to gender issues was independent of curricula in the early 1980s, but in more recent years, it seems to follow similar trends as the curriculum guidelines.

REPRESENTATIONS OF WOMEN IN TEXTBOOK ILLUSTRATIONS

In many ways, the French and U.S. textbooks follow very different trajectories from 1980 to 2010. The French textbooks have become more attentive to women in French history, though they have not fully integrated women's history into the national narrative, nor do they systematically adopt the critical approach required by the 2002 curriculum. The U.S. books, on the other hand, were considerably more attuned to women's history and to issues of gender equality in the early 1980s than in later years.

Tallying textbooks' illustrations makes for dry reading but shows which historical and public figures publishers choose to emphasize and provides a clear overview of the books' content. Tables 2.1 and 2.2 show the

Table 2.1 Women and Men in Textbook Illustrations—France

	Percentage of illustrations including women	Percentage of illustrations including men	Avg. per book total illustrations
1985 CM	33%	95%	115.5
1995 CM1	34%	95%	123
1995 CM2	42%	93%	150.7
2002 CM1	37%	93%	93
2002 CM2	48%	87%	117.7
2010 CM1	36%	95%	115
2010 CM2	43%	89%	138.3

Table 2.2 Women and Men in Textbook Illustrations—United States

	Percentage of illustrations including women	Percentage of illustrations including men	Avg. per book total illustrations
1982	42%	85%	153
1997	36%	83%	423.7
2003	35%	87%	472.9

percentages of illustrations that include women and men in the French and U.S. books, respectively, in their entirety (i.e., history and contemporary sections).

While the percentage of illustrations including women grows in the French books after 1985, it does not follow a linear progression, nor did this increase follow directly from the curricular changes of 2002, as the percentage of women in illustrations had already risen in the 1990s (in CM2 books—the equivalent of U.S. Grade Five). While the number of illustrations including women rose, men's visibility did not diminish in proportion, as textbooks have added more illustrations of mixed groups, rather than adding many images of only women. In the U.S. books, on the other hand, the evolution has been quite a bit clearer: the percentage of illustrations including women decreased after the early 1980s while the percentage of illustrations depicting men has remained about the same. Because the number of illustrations in U.S. textbooks has risen greatly since the 1980s, the decline in the percentage of illustrations showing women does not reflect a drop in the number of such images, but rather the addition of illustrations showing men. This shift largely reflects changes in the approach to history.

If we look separately at only the historical images in the textbooks (Tables 2.3 and 2.4), not surprisingly, when contemporary illustrations are subtracted from the totals, the disparity between the sexes is greater in France as well as the U.S.

Though the numbers indicate that women are more visible in the recent French books than in their American counterparts, this impression is somewhat misleading. In reality, the majority of images depicting only women (and many that show men and women together) include not real women, but allegories or works of art, such as the allegory of the French Republic, Marianne, Delacroix's *Liberty Leading the People* (Figure 2.1 [e.g., Boëche 2011 CM2: 24; Chevalier and Le Bourgeois 53; Le Callennec 2011: 10–11]), or the *Mona Lisa*. In addition, when they are depicted with men, women are sometimes passive or background figures, rather than essential to the scene. Thus, if we include only images where real or realistic women are not purely background figures, then instead of 31 percent and 38 percent of historical illustrations

Table 2.3 Women and Men in Historical Illustrations—France

	Percentage of historical illustrations including women	Percentage of historical illustrations including men	Avg. per book total illustrations
1985 CM	29%	96%	197.7
1995 CM1	25%	96%	85.7
1995 CM2	39%	93%	121.3
2002 CM1	30%	93%	67.3
2002 CM2	41%	87%	90.7
2010 CM1	31%	96%	96.3
2010 CM2	38%	90%	108.3

Table 2.4 Women and Men in Historical Illustrations—United States

	Percentage of historical illustrations including women	Percentage of historical illustrations including men	Avg. per book total illustrations
1982	39%	86%	128
1997	30%	84%	372.3
2003	30%	90%	408.7

Figure 2.1 Eugène Delacroix, *Le 28 Juillet. La Liberté guidant le people*, 1830.

Source: Wiki Commons. Retrieved 29 Sept. 2015 (https://commons.wikimedia.org/wiki/File:Eug%C3%A8ne_Delacroix_-_Le_28_Juillet._La_Libert%C3%A9_guidant_le_peuple.jpg).

including women in the most recent CM1 and CM2 books respectively, the percentages drop to fewer than 20 percent (and this number drops further to 15 percent if we remove images of Joan of Arc) and 26 percent. The American books also include illustrations where women are incidental: if we remove historical illustrations where women are passive background figures, the percentages for 2003, for instance, drop to 27 percent of historical illustrations featuring women. If we also remove from this tally the illustrations where the people are incidental (such as street scenes where the focus is on the scenery), the percentage of women drops below 26 percent. These adjustments, then, put the French CM2 textbooks on similar footing with the most recent American books.

In both France and the United States, textbooks have increasingly included women in contemporary illustrations (Tables 2.5 and 2.6). Though the French books have added more illustrations including women in the geography and civic education sections, this change has not entailed a significant decrease in the number of men, as these illustrations are largely

Table 2.5 Women and Men in Contemporary Illustrations—France

	Percentage of contemporary illustrations including women	Percentage of contemporary illustrations including men	Avg. per book total illustrations
1985 CM Geo.	61%	87%	33
1985 CM Civ. ed. (2 books)	50%	90%	136.5
1995 CM1 Geo. & civ. ed.	56%	92%	37
1995 CM2 Geo. & civ. ed.	52%	92%	29.3
2002 CM1 Geo. & civ. ed.	53%	92%	25.7
2002 CM2 Geo. & civ. ed.	69%	89%	27
2008 CM1 Geo. & civ. ed.	61%	88%	19
2008 CM2 Geo.	58%	87%	33.3
2008 CM Civ. ed. (1 book)	69%	81%	129

Table 2.6 Women and Men in Contemporary Illustrations—United States

	Percentage of historical illustrations including women	Percentage of historical illustrations including men	Avg. per book total illustrations
1982	55%	79%	24.6
1997	73%	66%	51.5
2003	71%	73%	64.3

made up of group scenes, including many street scenes where the people are incidental. The U.S. books have shown a more consistent concerted effort to include women via contemporary images since the 1990s, as they are included in more than half of such illustrations (roughly the same amount as men).

Looking beyond the numbers, though the French books have added more illustrations showing women, they are not systematically attentive to the ways in which they depict women. Notably, the vast majority of professional situations feature only men. When the books do show women working, it is usually as teachers or doing unskilled labor. For instance, though Nathan's most recent CM2 edition does show a woman working on a computer to illustrate meteorological science, all but three of its 18 professional illustrations depict only men. This textbook promotes gender stereotypes by showing men in the more prestigious professions ("a surgeon" is shown and mentioned in the masculine, *un chirurgien*) and women in unskilled labor (a cashier is illustrated and labeled in the feminine, *une hôtesse*) (Chevalier and Le Bourgeois 2010: 126–127).

In addition to the images in French textbooks depicting women as allegories or in works of art, they are also shown in (often very stylized, sexualized) advertisements for various household products (Figure 2.2 [e.g., Le Callennec 2004: 18]). The percentage of such images has declined but still remains high. In Nembrini et al.'s 1985 edition, 100 percent of the illustrations depicting only women were of allegories, art, or advertisements, as are 64 percent in Armand Colin's 1985 edition. In the most recent books, this number has declined, and now between one-third and one-half of images depicting only women show these types of figures. In nearly all cases, these images are presented without questioning or commenting on the ways in which women are represented. Among the books in this study, none look critically at allegories or artistic renderings of women, and only one (Hatier's most recent CM2 edition) takes a critical approach to an advertisement, specifically regarding the evolution of marital relations. The advertisement in question dates from 1961 and is not the most sexualized, but it shows a man offering his grateful wife a gift of a food processor. The textbook points out that the document shows older relationships within families: that wives were at their husbands' disposal to take care of them, adding that today such an advertisement would be considered shocking, and it asks students to explain why (Le Callennec 2011: 100). This exercise, which combines social history with social commentary, is extremely rare and highlights other textbooks' indifference to such issues.

Aside from these types of images, those where women are onlookers, and the street scenes, in which all of the people are incidental, women appear primarily in illustrations relating to social history. They are depicted in the textbooks in families, illustrating cultural changes or the lifestyle of their time. They are also shown illustrating labor, particularly in factories during the Second

Figure 2.2 Jean de Paleologue, "Rayon d'or, dernier mot de l'éclairage," Paris: Paul Dupont, 1895.

Source: Library of Congress, Prints and Photographs Online Catalog, Retrieved 2 April 2015 (http://www.loc.gov/pictures/item/2004675013/).

World War, or sometimes in various stereotypically female professions, such as clerical work or in textile plants. As we will discuss below, some textbooks show the movement for women's suffrage, and most now illustrate the first elections in which women could cast ballots. Women also often appear in situations in which they are victims, such as Jewish people in the Holocaust, the French exodus during the Second World War, or the Saint Bathélemy massacre (Figure 2.3 [e.g., Boëche CM1: 58; Le Callennec 2010: 81]).

French textbooks regularly present social history, showing how people lived in various time periods and how major events and transitions affected them. Nevertheless, they remain largely focused on military and especially political history, which largely accounts for the greater prevalence of men in their illustrations. For instance, in the most recent CM1 and CM2 textbooks, 23 percent and 26 percent (respectively) of historical illustrations focus on political figures. They include a smaller percentage of military figures (not quite 10 percent in the CM1 books, and 18 percent in CM2). While this leaves more than half of the French books available for social history, in the case of the CM1 books, this does not necessarily mean a greater focus on women. These books often illustrate premodern historical periods using only images of men, for instance, as clergy, farmers, and knights.

In addition, a very limited number of individual historical women appear in all or most French textbooks. For the most part, only the women who are required by the curricula are regularly pictured (i.e., in at least two books of the same period): Joan of Arc and Marie Curie, plus Joséphine de Beauharnais, who appears in two books of most periods, but usually

Figure 2.3 François Dubois, *Le Massacre de la Saint Barthélemy*, c. 1572–84.
Source: Wiki Commons. Retrieved 29 Sept. 2015 (https://commons.wikimedia.org/wiki/File:Francois_Dubois_001.jpg).

this is because she is pictured with Napoleon I at his coronation ceremony (as depicted by the painter Jacques-Louis David). However, Simone Veil appears in two of the most recent CM2 books. This is a significant addition, as Veil is not mentioned in the curriculum. In one of these books she is shown—with no explanation—with Jacques Chirac, looking at the names engraved on the Holocaust memorial, and no further mention of her is made (Le Callennec 2011: 77). However, Sedrap features her in a brief half-page biography that includes her deportation from Nice, survival of Auschwitz, political career in France and in the European Union, specifically crediting her with legalizing abortion, and her current activities as a Holocaust survivor (Boëche 2011 CM2: 65). Considering how briefly this textbook covers the Fifth Republic (just four pages), attributing half a page to Veil is significant. Though Sedrap offers no explicit commentary on women's rights via Veil, the focus on her and the inclusion of abortion rights (in a textbook for ten-year-olds) demonstrates Sedrap's commitment to a more progressive women's history. As for the most prominent women in these books, Marie Curie is a fairly recent addition to textbooks, following her inclusion in the 1995 curriculum. A 1985 textbook (Nathan) illustrates the shift in her status: in this edition, Curie is pictured with her husband Pierre, and the emphasis is on him. In addition to a photo showing both of them in their lab, the textbook includes a portrait of him alone, with a caption saying he pursued his research "with his wife Marie" (Vincent et al. 54). In later books, Marie Curie is always featured in a portrait on her own and discussed in greater detail in the text. Most of these books emphasize Curie's importance in breaking down gender barriers (Chevalier and Le Bourgeois 2010: 63; Le Callennec 2011: 37). Joan of Arc (who is discussed in more detail in Chapter Five) already figured prominently in the books of 1985. She is the second most frequently pictured person in the French textbooks (after Charles de Gaulle). Other women whom feminist scholars would like to see featured appear only sporadically. For example, Olympe de Gouges appears only in two books of this study (Bendjebbar et al. 2004; Boëche 2011 CM2). Louise Michel's visibility declines (from two out of three books in 1985 and 1995, to one [Bendjebbar] in 2004, and now she no longer appears at all). Even such major cultural figures as Diane de Poitiers and Catherine de' Medici appear only in Dorel-Ferré and Dhainaut's 1985 edition (79, 85) plus Hatier's most recent edition, where a statue of Diana, goddess of the hunt, displays the former's likeness (Le Callennec 2010: 68). The remaining women who appear in any French textbooks (usually in just one or two volumes across the four periods of publication studied here) are mostly included as wives of leaders. Indeed, some are listed simply as "and his wife" (e.g., Dorel-Ferré and Dhainaut 69, 73). Thus, the books do not generally go beyond the curricula to feature additional women.

This overview of illustrations has shown that, even when women are included, they are most often shown in traditional roles, as weak, or as victimized. Consistent with curricula, though, textbooks now show women in the Revolution and Marie Curie, all of whom serve (often explicitly) to counter sexism. Such figures are, however, very few in number.

Regarding the U.S. books, the decline in women's visibility partly reflects a decline in social history in favor of military and political history. The shifting focus of these books also affects the ways in which men are represented. Where images of anonymous people (including soldiers) made up 59 percent of historical illustrations in 1980, they were only 51 percent of such images in 1997, and 32 percent in 2003. Even illustrations depicting anonymous people reflect the renewed emphasis on traditional political and military history, as more of these now show battles. If we count only illustrations that truly focus on social history, by removing from this tally the images of military scenes or of official political bodies, the number declines sharply, so that these images constitute only 19 percent of the total historical illustrations in the most recent textbooks. Anonymous women (whether alone or with men) mainly appear in illustrations depicting social history (87 percent and 85 percent, respectively). As in the French books, groups of anonymous women tend to adhere to traditional roles, and these images change little over the period studied here. Though the percentage of such illustrations drops from 1982 to 1997 and 2003, the number is higher, as the more recent books include many more total illustrations. Women of all ethnic groups are shown with their families, especially in colonial times, as immigrants and pioneers. There is slightly more emphasis on women's work in 1997 and 2003 than in 1982. They are shown (alone or with men) working at tasks typically done by women in colonial and pre-Columbian periods. Women of European origin are shown working in factories during the Second World War. They are shown without men working as nurses, in textile plants of the nineteenth century, and demonstrating for their civil rights, whether in the nineteenth century, the 1920s, or the 1970s (more on this below). Although the number of women shown lags far behind that of men, the books seem to make a consistent effort to show women in varied roles.

The emphasis on military and political history not only contributes to marginalizing women, but it also limits men's roles. The majority of images of anonymous men depict soldiers or more rarely, politicians—on average, there are 51 images of anonymous soldiers per textbook in 2003. When added to the named figures, men associated with the military make up a plurality of images in these textbooks. In the 2003 textbooks, military images of men make up 27 percent of historical illustrations and 23 percent of all illustrations.[1] By contrast, in the books of 1982, just under 20 percent of historical illustrations depict military figures. Considering that the more recent textbooks include on average 3.5 times more historical illustrations than the older editions (409 versus 117), this represents not only a shift in focus in relative terms but also a noteworthy numerical increase. The more recent books also include more political history. In the books of the early 1980s, just below 15 percent of historical illustrations show political figures. The percentage rises by 10 points in 2003 (to 25 percent), but again, this increase reflects a significant numerical increase. Where textbooks in 1982 included on average 23 illustrations depicting military figures (the plurality, if not the majority, of which relate to the Revolutionary War) and 17 illustrations depicting political figures, in 2003, an average of 110 illustrations per book depict people in military scenes, and another 109 show politicians.

Individual men are also shown primarily in military and political roles, and this is particularly true of men of European origin. Among the two largest ethnic groups shown in these books, white men are by far more often shown in military and political roles than are African American men. For example, among named figures, about 70 percent of named men of European origin in 1982 are shown in military and/or political roles. This figure rises slightly to about 75 percent in 1997 and 72 percent in 2003. By contrast, about 28 percent of named men of African origin in the most recent books are politicians or military personnel. Partly, of course, this reflects a history of racist exclusion and discrimination. Thus white men continue to be shown predominantly in roles typically associated with traditional nationalism, where "masculinity" is tied to military and political leadership. Yet African American men are also shown in prestigious roles—authors, inventors, scientists, and in archetypically American roles such as cowboys and pioneers (which are also more traditionally "masculine"), as well as soldiers. White men are, of course, also shown in these roles. Thus national history continues to be dominated by white men and traditional images of masculinity. Yet, by increasing the inclusion of African American men, in particular, textbooks offer some alternative visions of how men can build the nation.

U.S. textbooks differ more notably from the French books concerning individual women: the U.S. books include considerably more named women than do their French counterparts, both in number and in proportion. Between 20 and 25 percent of illustrations showing named individuals feature women in U.S. textbooks from 1982 to 2003. In French textbooks, women account for only 11 to 13 percent of such figures. However, unlike France, where Joan of Arc is the second most frequently pictured person, the most frequently pictured individuals in U.S. textbooks are all men. The most visible woman is Sacagawea, in fifteenth place. (She was the Native American who led Lewis and Clark across the continent and is usually pictured with the two men, with her baby on her back.) Of the 28 individuals who are emphasized in the textbooks (i.e., shown on average twice per book in a given period), only three are women—in addition to Sacagawea, we find Abigail Adams and Harriet Tubman (for the complete list, see Chapter One, note 10).

The basically steady percentage of women among named figures over the period studied mainly reflects the addition of new figures (as well as repeated images of some already present in 1982). Between 1982 and 1997, twelve new women were added in at least two books: Abigail Adams, Queen Elizabeth I, Mary Ludwig Hays (a.k.a., Molly Pitcher), Mary Harris "Mother"

Jones, Malintzin (the Aztec translator who assisted Cortés), Queen Liliuokalani, Dolley Madison, Sandra Day O'Connor, Sacagawea, Harriet Beecher Stowe, Mercy Otis Warren, Martha Washington, and Phillis Wheatley. The books of 2003 further added: Linda Brown, Carrie Chapman Catt, Miriam Amanda Ferguson, Dolores Huerta, Pocahontas, and the semifictional Rosie the Riveter. In addition to these new figures, the visibility of Jane Addams, Clara Barton, Anne Hutchinson, Rosa Parks, and Harriet Tubman increased over this time. These women are the most frequently pictured in the most recent textbooks, appearing in at least two of the three books, as do Eleanor Roosevelt and Sojourner Truth. The visibility of Roosevelt and Truth, however, declined from 1997 to 2003. All of these choices call for further scrutiny.

The three Native American women who have recently been added to U.S. textbooks (Malintzin, Sacagawea, and Pocahontas) are legendary figures, all of whom promote an image of harmony between European settlers and indigenous people. In U.S. history in particular, Pocahontas and Sacagawea evoke an idyllic and romanticized vision of these relations, and thereby legitimate European colonization and U.S. territorial expansion. These women can be viewed as symbols of the territory welcoming and merging with the future United States. Their images have been appropriated by white America, particularly as multiculturalist groups have specifically advocated against allowing them to stand as representatives of European-indigenous relations (Moore 1977: 106; see also Chapter One). Beyond the ethno-cultural issues their inclusion raises, this choice also has significant implications for the depiction of women in general and Native American women in particular. These women's gender is an integral part of their place in U.S. history, and their representations support traditional gender roles. The Pocahontas myth (though it is presented as a possible fabrication by John Smith in the recent books that still include it [Berson et al. 162; Boyd et al. 160]) relies on and perpetuates the representation of indigenous women as a sexual, exotic "other." Both Pocahontas and Sacagawea are shown as nurturing and wise in their acceptance of and assistance to English and American settlers, respectively.

Similarly, Phillis Wheatley, who despite being enslaved for much of her life, became a published patriotic poet best known for her ode to George Washington. While a remarkable figure, Wheatley is hardly representative of the conditions endured by most female slaves of her time. She has become a prominent figure in recent books, which accentuate different aspects of her life. McGraw-Hill emphasizes her abolitionist poetry (Banks et al. 1997: 291; Banks et al. 2003: 229), which Scott Foresman also cites (Boyd et al. 2003: 309). However, Harcourt and Scott Foresman largely focus on Wheatley's patriotism. Harcourt features biographies of 22 people and labels each one with a "character trait" (more on this in Chapter Five). It dedicates one such biography to Wheatley, highlighting "patriotism" as her defining trait and focusing on her reverence for Washington (Berson et al. 2003: 296).

This presentation of Wheatley provides another example of conservative nationalist multiculturalism that ultimately promotes a myth of ethnic unity at the moment of the nation's founding. Her peaceful passion for the United States and amicable relations with the Wheatley family are another example of gentle, patriotic womanhood, such that she, too, becomes a nationalist symbol.

The same could be said of Mercy Otis Warren, Martha Washington, and Dolley Madison (the first lady best known for saving such national treasures as the Gilbert Stuart portrait of George Washington, when the British burned down the White House during the War of 1812). Those three women acted in support of the new country, but beyond showing their portraits, textbooks pay little attention to them. Mary Ludwig Hays, whom the textbooks identify as "Molly Pitcher," is presented as having accompanied her husband into battle during the Revolutionary War, brought water to soldiers on the battlefield, and according to some books, replaced her husband at the cannon when he fell. This icon of female dedication—to her husband, his brothers in arms, and the nation—is another powerful symbol. Unfortunately, she is also a historically inaccurate one; Molly Pitcher is, most likely, a legend, an amalgamation of several real camp wives, who were not so heroically regarded during their lifetimes, but who were transformed into national symbols by later generations (Raphael 2004: 27–44). The variations in the story between the different textbooks seem to indicate their lack of certainty regarding the story of Molly Pitcher. It appears, then, that they choose to include this tale for nationalist, rather than historical, reasons (for example, McGraw-Hill's 2003 edition is more accurate than those of Harcourt or Scott Foresman [Banks et al. 291; Berson et al. 319; Boyd et al. 307, respectively]).

Abigail Adams is the lone representative of more progressive thinking regarding women's rights, as most textbooks include her for having implored her husband to "remember the ladies" as he helped write the Articles of Confederation. However, due to changes in the way textbooks present her, she is discussed further in the next section.

Some of these featured women are depicted in more progressive roles: as civic reformers, whether opposing slavery (Harriet Beecher Stowe, Sojourner Truth, and Harriet Tubman) or advocating civil rights for African Americans (Linda Brown, Rosa Parks) or for laborers and those struggling during times of economic hardship (Dolores Huerta, Mary Harris "Mother" Jones, Eleanor Roosevelt). Some are shown as political leaders and groundbreakers for women in leadership roles (Queen Elizabeth I, Sandra Day O'Connor, and Miriam Ferguson). Some are shown in traditional, specifically nurturing roles (Clara Barton and Jane Addams; I list Addams here because the books do not mention her more radical ideas).

Queen Liliuokalani of Hawaii, however, breaks with norms regarding gender as well as ethnic minority representation, as she opposed the U.S. takeover (see also Chapter Six). Anne Hutchison is also a somewhat more controversial figure; as a woman who opposed Puritan rule and founded a new settlement, she was not only an iconoclast of her time but is also a reviled figure by conservative Christian education activist groups today. However, it seems that as long as the texts give a globally positive presentation of the Puritans, conservative evangelical groups accept the inclusion of Hutchinson.[2]

As important as it is to analyze the meanings attributed to the women who are included in these books, the choices to omit certain women are at least as revealing. Several of these will be discussed below, in relation to the presentations of the topics with which they are associated: namely, the three key periods of women's rights movements. For the moment, I wish to note the disappearance after 1982 of Frances Perkins (labor secretary under Franklin Roosevelt and first woman appointed to the cabinet) and the anthropologist Margaret Mead. The Gablers' group specifically opposed both of these figures' inclusion in textbooks of the 1980s (Educational Research Analysts 1982). Their subsequent removal, therefore, may have been politically motivated.

Overall, then, the women highlighted in illustrations in U.S. textbooks—whether anonymous or individually known—adhere to a vision of women's roles that would be acceptable to most conservative Christians, even if some of these figures had rather radical ideas for their time (such as support for women's suffrage). Like the men mentioned in Chapter One, these women illustrate above all dedication to the nation-state.

NARRATIVES AND WOMEN'S HISTORY

French Textbooks

If the U.S. textbooks make more of an effort than their French counterparts to depict women in a variety of roles, the French books have recently begun showing greater commitment to the more critical goals of feminism through their presentation of certain aspects of women's history. Since 2002 French textbooks have made significant changes in the ways in which they present women's history.[3] Perhaps because these changes are so recent, the results are not yet as homogenous across books as is their presentation of more established subjects. When a topic or issue is clearly and explicitly explained in the curricula, it appears in all the textbooks. Nevertheless, the curricula are vague enough to leave specific interpretation up to textbook authors. Thus, there are major differences in tone and approach between the different books, and it is worth looking at them in some detail.

Overall, all of the recent French textbooks in this study take a critical stance regarding women's exclusion from certain civil rights. In some cases, the critical comments and questions appear only in the coverage of a few specific topics in history. For instance, all three recent books both point out that women were excluded from the rights granted by the Revolutionary government in the 1790s (Boëche CM2: 14; Chevalier and Le Bourgeois 37; Le Callennec 2011: 18). Some books also note the inequalities inherent in Napoleon's civil code (which defined wives as legally beholden to their husbands) or the exclusion of women when men were granted universal suffrage in 1848 (Boëche CM2: 25; Chevalier and Le Bourgeois 37, 54; Le Callennec 2011: 46). Some textbooks include a separate section (the standard two-page format used for most topics) on women's rights in general, as in Hatier, which explains how women's options were limited throughout history and in different socioeconomic classes (Le Callennec 2011: 82–83). The textbook clearly refers to the situation of unequal rights as "unfair," cites Victor Hugo's powerful denunciation of sexism, and includes the following statement denouncing the irony of France's poor record on women's suffrage: "France, '*patrie des droits de l'homme*' ("home of human rights"), was one of the last countries in Europe to recognize women's right to vote: they voted for the first time in 1945. That is when suffrage became universal" (83). This book also denounces current inequalities under the heading "The persistence of inequalities," stating: "Inequalities persist. Few women are elected mayor or appointed as ministers. And many, in their personal lives, are still subject to men's authority" (83). This statement is accompanied by a photo of brochures against forced marriage, sexual aggression, and conjugal violence. (In its civic education textbook, Hatier also addresses pay inequalities, but not in the history-geography textbook [Le Callennec 2008: 92–93].) Similarly, Sedrap clearly denounces inequality and women's exclusion from civil rights. It questions women's absence from history narratives, notably featuring the revolutionary and proto-feminist Olympe de Gouges, including the question, "Why doesn't Olympe de Gouges have a bigger place in our history?" (Boëche CM2: 14). Sedrap also includes a short section on "Women in French Society," discussing recent laws (including on contraception, abortion, and parity on electoral lists), and states that inequality persists, as women often earn less than men for the same work and are underrepresented in politics (Boëche CM2: 77). Though Nathan's textbook does mention women's exclusion from voting rights, it does not engage in the same critical approach to the contemporary situation as do its competitors. Hatier and Sedrap's clear critiques of gender inequalities are certainly a strong step toward integrating the feminist objectives recently added to curricula. However, this approach has the disadvantage of segregating women's history from the rest, as it is discussed in separate, limited sections.

The focus in all books remains mainly on political and military events and on men. On occasion, textbooks present aspects of social history drawing on female examples. For instance, some books show women or girls working in textile plants (Chevalier and Le Bourgeois 38) or mines (Boëche CM2: 33) to illustrate the industrial revolution (though most focus on men). We should note, however, that feminist scholars often object to showing women only in textile plants, as this gives a falsely limited view of their work and their abilities and supports the stereotype of women as physically weak, best suited to delicate work (Berton-Schmitt 2015). Overall, textbooks often focus on men's actions where they could just as easily show women. For instance, women as well as men were involved in the Resistance during the Second World War, and two women whose work in the Resistance is well known, Germaine Tillion and Geneviève de Gaulle-Anthonioz, were added to the Pantheon in 2015. Yet, no textbooks picture women in their presentations of the Resistance movement. Instead, they show Charles de Gaulle (see Chapter Five), Jean Moulin, anonymous men sabotaging rails, men facing Axis firing squads, and men on various military and paramilitary expeditions.

Textbooks miss many such opportunities to include women and to follow the 2002 curriculum's instructions to take a critical approach to women's absence in history. For instance, the CM1 books dedicate a great deal of space to monarchs and religious leaders in the Middle Ages and *Ancien Régime*. Yet, they never explain or explore women's exclusion from power within the monarchy or the church. Similarly, when presenting premodern society, the textbooks generally only show women as peasants, along with their families, and as nuns tending the ill. The books do not discuss the restrictions that limited many women to these roles, nor do they show the women who worked in other capacities or held political power. Men, on the other hand, are shown in multiple active roles in all sectors of society (clergy, aristocrats, feudal lords, etc.). There are two small exceptions in the most recent books that are more in line with the curriculum and that may therefore point to the future direction of these publications. In its presentation of pre-Revolutionary society, Nathan presents different social groups via women (i.e., a poor woman with several children and a caption that explains the high child mortality rates of the time, and a low-skilled and low-status profession (*petit métier*) illustrated by a clothing saleswoman [Le Bourgeois 2010: 86–87]). In this way, women are integrated into the main narrative. Hatier takes a more critical approach, showing the famous Enlightenment salon of Marie-Thérèse Geoffrin. Unlike other works, which may include this illustration seemingly as a form of tokenism, Hatier specifically asks: "How many women are there in this salon? In your opinion, why are there so few of them?" (Le Callennec 2010: 97).

It is generally more difficult and controversial to critically approach questions of justice and inequality regarding more recent history. Not surprisingly, then, the results here vary across different textbooks. While the recent books (unlike most of the older books) at least mention that French women obtained suffrage in 1944, not all show the efforts of activists to obtain this right. For instance, in its most recent edition, Nathan simply states that women did not have the vote before, and then it was given to them (Chevalier and Le Bourgeois 95). There is no mention of movements or struggles, nor any comments on inequality in general. In this way, women's agency and historical roles are rendered invisible. By contrast, Hatier (Le Callennec 2011: 82–83) and Sedrap (Boëche CM2: 15, 25, 77) both emphasize the struggle to obtain women's suffrage, consistently with their emphasis on injustice in the past and the persistence of inequalities today. However, even then, focusing on suffrage is a moderate approach to feminism, as suffragists are aligned with modern views, and their struggle was a successful one.

Curricula and textbooks do not discuss the more radical feminism that engendered suffrage movements. Perhaps this omission results from habit or a sense that this history is outside the narrative arc. Perhaps this history is not in the textbooks because it has been delegitimized for so long, and this delegitimization is partly rooted in nationalism. Feminism grew as an international movement in the mid-to-late nineteenth century (see Offen 2000). That Louise Michel is both one of the major figures of the Commune and a radical feminist is not surprising. Michel and many of her feminist cohort were universalists, who advocated either international socialism or anarchy. The Third Republic reasserted nationalism as a reaction against the devastating loss in the Franco-Prussian War, also to prevent the resurgence of another revolt like the Commune. In reasserting nationalism, the Third Republic sought to crush internationalism as well as feminism.

Textbooks today largely continue to uphold this tradition, focusing on the nation-state and the narrative of progress. Thus, regarding more contemporary history, Sedrap presents Simone Veil and her work in legalizing abortion (Boëche CM2: 65) as well as a 1997 law regarding parity on electoral lists (77), and Hatier shows pamphlets opposing violence toward women (Le Callennec 2011: 83), but none of the French textbooks discuss contemporary feminist movements.

United States Textbooks

As the French textbooks have taken some steps toward a more critical vision of women's place in national history and society, U.S. books have demonstrated a stark decline in progressivism regarding women's history and contemporary situation. This shift appears clearly when comparing the books of the early 1980s to later publications, and in some cases, the continued decline in teaching about women's exclusion appears with remarkable clarity as more progressive passages disappear between 1997 and 2003 editions of the same book. Approaches to women's history vary so considerably among the most recent books that it is worthwhile to examine them individually. The remainder of this analysis will compare the most recent books' presentations of key topics in women's history with those of the older editions.

Overall, McGraw-Hill and Scott Foresman attribute considerably more importance than does Harcourt to struggles for women's rights throughout U.S. history. Nevertheless, none of these books adopt a strong critical approach of the issue and of the current state of gender equality. None of these books comment on women's minority status in leadership roles, either in the past or in the present, or on women's historical deprivation of citizenship rights. As such, women's legally and politically subordinate status can seem natural and normal.

Beginning with the Revolutionary era, though textbooks picture Mercy Otis Warren and Abigail Adams, their inclusion in the textbooks paradoxically highlights a significant—and more widespread—shift away from critical feminism in the most recent books. The textbooks only mention Warren for her role in leading boycotts against the British in the years before the war, and occasionally they mention that she was a historian. They omit completely that she was an early advocate for women's civic rights. Similarly, regarding Adams, McGraw-Hill (Banks et al. 2003: 312) and Scott Foresman (Boyd et al. 2003: 307) both mention Adams' letter to her husband asking him to "remember the ladies," but they do so without explaining the context in which Adams wrote the letter or offering any commentary regarding women's rights. These books each include a large portrait of her and quote her in bold print, but without any follow-up; there is no further mention of Adams or of women's rights in general regarding either the Articles of Confederation or the Constitution. It is not simply that these publishers have perhaps not thought to engage in a more critical presentation of this topic: both McGraw-Hill and Harcourt have removed more progressive material that appeared in their 1997 editions. In its older edition, McGraw-Hill included a clear statement on women's lack of rights in the colonies and their agency in improving their lives:

> Although the work of colonial women helped to keep farms and businesses running, they had few rights except for those allowed by their husbands. To improve their lives, some women began to start their own shops and businesses. A number of colonial women became highly successful.
>
> (Banks et al. 247)

There is nothing similar in the 2003 edition. Harcourt's 2003 edition contains no mention of Abigail Adams' letter at all. In fact, there is no mention of her in the text, though the editors display her portrait along with three others to illustrate the subchapter entitled "Women and the War," which primarily relates women's roles in nurturing and assisting soldiers (Berson et al. 311). In stark contrast, the older edition contains a longer version of the section "Women and the War" that explicitly mentions Adams' egalitarian concerns and quotes her at some length regarding the importance of giving women a voice in the new government (Boehm et al. 1997: 242).

Similar changes occur regarding social history and social justice in descriptions of the Constitutional Convention. Harcourt's 1997 edition dedicates a paragraph to the "ordinary" people who were excluded from participating in the Convention that drafted the new Constitution: frontier farmers, women, Native Americans, and Africans—enslaved and free (Boehm et al. 1997: 274). This paragraph and any similar observations disappear from the 2003 edition. The other 2003 textbooks likewise do not discuss women's exclusion from the Constitutional Convention or lack of voting rights.

Moving chronologically ahead to the mid-nineteenth century movement for women's rights and the women's suffrage movement, among the books of 2003, McGraw-Hill and Scott Foresman place considerably more emphasis on the topic than does Harcourt. The first two books dedicate approximately three and four times as much content as Harcourt to these topics. In their discussions of the Seneca Falls Convention of 1848, both McGraw-Hill and Scott Foresman cite the Declaration of Rights and Sentiments, picture the early leaders of the movement, and quote them, thus giving them a voice and emphasizing their own words. These books also discuss issues of equality beyond voting (e.g., property rights and equal social, civil, and economic rights with men), and indicate in some ways the intensity of debates. McGraw-Hill cites one of the Declaration's more explicitly critical passages: "The history of mankind is a history of repeated injuries . . . on the part of man toward women" (Banks et al. 420). Scott Foresman shows the harsh opposition to the movement, citing a newspaper report of the event that declared, "A woman is a nobody" (Boyd et al. 419). These textbooks emphasize the movement itself—its size and the scope of its efforts. For instance, McGraw-Hill mentions a "suffrage army" of one million volunteers and shows a photo of an anonymous group of women suffragists to illustrate the movement (Banks et al. 549). Both Scott Foresman and McGraw-Hill accentuate the notion of "struggle." For example, McGraw-Hill explains, "After more than 50 years of struggle and hard work, women finally won the right to vote in national elections in 1920" (Banks et al. 549). These books relate that women were arrested for voting, and that it took many attempts to get the amendment passed. They both discuss Susan B. Anthony and show goals of the movement beyond voting, presenting suffrage as the starting point of movement, not its final aim. This approach is reasonably well in line with what many feminist historians advocate, as well as the guidelines of the NHS.

Harcourt, on the other hand, mentions only Elizabeth Cady Stanton in its presentation of the Seneca Falls convention. This textbook includes no pictures of the other leaders of that time, and even omits mentioning Sojourner Truth and Frederick Douglass's involvement, which the other books highlight, and which shows the movement's widespread support and connections to other key human rights issues of the time. Harcourt ignores other aspects of the fight for gender equality, mentioning only civic rights (voting, holding office, and jury duty). Similarly, regarding later suffragist leaders, Harcourt does not even mention Susan B. Anthony. It focuses instead on Carrie Chapman Catt, referring to the rest of the movement in only a few lines. Harcourt thereby downplays the size, scope, and importance of women's rights movements. By mentioning only one person in relation to each period and limiting the discussion to political rights, this textbook takes a state-centered approach to this topic and avoids social history, focusing instead on structures, institutions, laws, and individual action, rather than collective action.

McGraw-Hill and Scott Foresman's 2003 editions are similar to those of 1997 and 1982 in how they present these topics. Only Harcourt demonstrates this abrupt rightward shift, which is apparent not only in comparing the textbook to its contemporaries but also to its previous edition, whose presentation of these subjects was similar to those in other textbooks (Boehm et al. 371–372).

Related to our earlier discussion of illustrations, we should note here that Susan B. Anthony and Elizabeth Cady Stanton were more prevalent in the 1997 textbooks, and their disappearance from most of the 2003 books seems particularly surprising. Though we can only guess at explanations, the fact alone is noteworthy. It seems significant that Carrie Chapman Catt—who effectively stands in for the whole women's suffrage movement of the late nineteenth and early twentieth centuries in Harcourt and is its only face in two books—was less radical than Anthony and Stanton. Voting rights were Catt's primary goal (though she focused on other issues after the passage of the Nineteenth Amendment), unlike Stanton and Anthony, who also fought for property rights for married women, more lenient divorce laws, etc. Perhaps Catt is also featured because she lived to see the passage of the Nineteenth Amendment—a success story, rather than a more complex narrative of a struggle that involved several generations.

Feminist movements of the 1960s and 1970s represent even more fraught terrain for textbook publishers, as more contemporary issues of social justice generally do. It is thus not surprising that there is no consensus among the 2003 textbooks, and their presentation of the topic varies greatly. Again, Harcourt dedicates only about one-third of a page to the subject, mentioning only that certain jobs were previously closed to women and that there had been a pay gap, excluding all other issues. Though Harcourt mentions that women "organized" for change, no groups are shown, nor are any individuals mentioned or pictured (unlike for all other civil rights movements covered in the section). The text states: "By the 1970s new laws had been passed saying that employers must treat men and women equally" (Berson et al. 589). The unexplained passage of these laws in the 1970s seems to have resolved any inequality, as women then "began careers in jobs that were once held only by men" (589). The text makes no mention of the ERA or other controversy. The only data given simply shows the increased number of women in the workforce from 1950 to 2000 (in a chart that accounts for half of the total page space given to the issue).

McGraw-Hill seems to have a confused approach to the subject, to which the publishers dedicate one and a half pages. This book shows several leaders of the movement (including Shirley Chisholm, Bella Abzug, Gloria Steinem, and Betty Friedan). The text mentions controversy over the ERA but not what its proponents were really aiming to do. The publishers paraphrase Phyllis Schlafly's arguments against the ERA, mentioning twice that "many women disagreed with NOW" in advocating the ERA. However, they cite no arguments in favor of the ERA. By focusing only the trajectory of the ERA, McGraw-Hill leaves out more substantive coverage of the movement. Like Harcourt, McGraw-Hill ends the section with a focus on women's new roles in public life, notably emphasizing Shirley Chisholm and Sandra Day O'Connor (Banks et al. 592, 593). Harcourt chooses O'Connor and Geraldine Ferraro (Berson et al. 589).

Finally, Scott Foresman dedicates one page to women's rights. While this book also focuses on jobs and Justice O'Connor, the publishers take a different approach than their competitors, as they emphasize the discrimination that existed against women in many professions by citing O'Connor's comments on the issue. Scott Foresman thus gives gender inequality more weight and a voice (Boyd et al. 647). Though they also mention Schlafly, she seems to speak only for herself, not to represent "many women" as she does in McGraw-Hill (Banks et al. 632). Thus, in many ways, Scott Foresman presents the most coherent view of the issue and the one that most clearly evokes the difficulties women faced. However, all of these recent textbooks end in an upbeat manner, and all avoid more troubling questions of persistent gender inequality.

These presentations of feminism since the 1960s represent one of the clearest shifts toward conservative nationalism in these textbooks. The books of the early 1980s show overwhelming support for the ERA and the contemporary feminist movement. They present women's rights as a continuous and ongoing struggle. When these books were published, the ERA was still pending, and their presentations of it, as well as women's rights movements more generally, were normative. This stance ranged from simply demonstrating enthusiasm for the movements' progress (as Silver Burdett did when discussing the difficulties faced in ratifying the Nineteenth Amendment: "Finally in 1919—success!" [Helmus et al. 1982: 249]) to presenting the ERA as a necessary antidote to prejudice and discrimination against women. Macmillan for instance, states:

> The struggle for equal rights for women continues. Many women and men in the 1970s and 1980s worked to ratify a new amendment to the Constitution. This amendment, called the Equal Rights Amendment, or ERA for short, states that equality shall not be denied on account of sex. When three-fourths of the states ratify it, the ERA will become law.
>
> (King et al. 1982: 144)

These books' overall presentations of the 1960s and 1970s movement are similarly positive. For example:

> The movement for full equality was reborn in the 1960's. In 1963, Betty Friedan's book, *The Feminine Mystique*, was published. It raised again the basic issue of equality. Friedan urged women to express themselves outside the home as well as in it. In 1966 she helped start the National

> Organization of Women (NOW). The group aimed to "take action to bring women into full participation in the mainstream of America *now*."
>
> Stanton, Bethune, and Friedan. These are just three of the many Americans—both women and men—who have worked for full equality. The courage and drive of these people have been gifts to us all.
>
> (Gross et al. 1980: 83)

It goes nearly without saying at this point that there are no equivalent statements in the U.S. textbooks of the 1990s or 2000s. Similarly, each of the books of the early 1980s ends the section on the contemporary movement with a statement along the lines of this one: "There is still a way to go in the struggle for equal rights for women" (Helmus et al. 1982: 249). This assessment is in direct opposition to more recent books' indications that equality has been achieved through their assertions that women are now able to do the same jobs as men, as evidenced by Sandra Day O'Connor or Geraldine Ferraro.

Though the narrative in textbooks had already changed by the late 1990s, the six years between the publications of the most recent editions brought further retreat from feminist approaches. Once again, comparing the 1997 and 2003 editions of Harcourt and McGraw-Hill's textbooks demonstrates that, as was the case regarding presentations of Abigail Adams and women's rights in the early republic, these publishers scale back their coverage of feminism since the 1960s. Harcourt's 1997 and 2003 editions include very similar prose on the topic—much of the text is identical, except for approximately one third of the earlier text that vanishes from the more recent edition (Berson et al. 2003: 589; Boehm et al. 1997: 592). The deleted text discusses Betty Friedan, NOW, and the organization's work in getting women elected. In the more recent edition, women just "won elections" without the work of the movement; again, in this way, progress seems more natural, and the textbook hides conflict and the efforts of much of society. The older text also lists some of the new professional fields into which women entered, thus emphasizing the scope of change. Likewise, McGraw-Hill makes changes from 1997 to 2003 that reduce the visibility of the movement and the breadth of its aims. Though the 1997 version also indicated that Schlafly's point of view was representative of "many" women who opposed NOW's aims, the textbook's presentation was clearer and more indicative of a pro-feminist stance. It cited Friedan and NOW's aims (rather than talking only vaguely about the ERA), for instance, stating that *The Feminine Mystique*, "raised questions about women's traditional roles. 'Who knows what women's intelligence will contribute when it can be nourished?' Friedan asked" (Banks et al. 1997: 632). Another significant change concerns the removal of a chart from the earlier edition that shows women's earnings as a percentage of men's, including contemporary data (1997: 632). The older edition shows its support for gender equality when it states that women's newfound representation in electoral politics was not the only domain in which they made "gains" (631).

Thus, already by the 1990s, textbooks reached a mostly positive conclusion regarding women's rights, emphasizing the progress achieved and making no explicit mention of remaining inequalities. (Even McGraw-Hill, despite its chart, does not draw attention to this aspect, leaving it up to teachers' discretion, apparently.) The books of the 1980s show greater commitment to social justice; they teach not just history but progressive social studies.

CONCLUSION

In France and the U.S., the history of the nation is still primarily a history of men. In French curricula and textbooks, however, there is a recent and growing awareness of this disparity and a resulting effort to approach it critically and in so doing, attempt to combat gender inequality. French left-leaning nationalism is more compatible with feminism and its challenges to traditional national narratives. French textbooks and curricula once again demonstrate a tendency to view the national past critically, constructing national identity above all as a forward-looking quest for greater equality and social justice.

Arguably, French textbooks are more committed to gender equality than to ethnic equality. Where the books generally avoid discussing discrimination along ethnic lines in contemporary France, they face sexism more directly. A particularity of dominant French thought may partly explain this difference. As Joan Wallach Scott has written, in a culture that widely embraces universalist republican rhetoric, which does not allow for official recognition of demographic differences, gender is a major exception. By viewing gender in essentializing terms, it can be seen as a "real" difference, one that can legitimately be addressed without fear of reifying a social construct. Thus, gender inequalities can be recognized and combated through government intervention (e.g., the parity law) and through education. Antisexist education is thereby on much stronger footing than is antiracist education in France. Still, these reforms are very recent and could go much further to be truly integrated into the textbooks, in order for women to have a larger place in historical narratives and in visions of national identity.

In the U.S., once again, nationalism and a conservative vision of national identity are stronger than progressive forces. Much like multiculturalism, feminism has led to some changes in textbooks, but the progressive core of the movement has been weakened. Though multiculturalism has certainly been adapted to a more conservative ideology in many ways, it has still made significant strides, including in challenging stereotypes, in marginalizing racism, and in creating an ethnically (if not ideologically) diverse portrait of America. Arguably, feminism has had less enduring impact. Even more than regarding multiculturalism, the stronger feminist stance of many books of 1980 has disappeared, leaving only a narrative of progress in its wake. The most recent books take a tokenist approach to women's history, supporting women's most long-standing, consensual rights—namely, suffrage and working in a variety of professions—without taking a critical stance toward the status quo or advocating greater equality. Not only do these books not challenge positive images and myths of the nation through critical feminism, but they primarily ground patriotism, the nation, and its history in men's actions and masculinity. Perhaps feminism challenges traditional, conservative nationalism in the U.S. more directly than does multiculturalism. Most proponents of progressive multiculturalism advocate a shared national identity built around core civic beliefs, and they therefore have some grounds for compromise with conservatism. Feminism, by contrast, inherently challenges the core beliefs of religious conservative nationalists. Christian conservative groups in Texas, then, have achieved many of their aims regarding representations of gender roles in recent years, as textbooks now include a superficial version of feminism akin to their substitution of diversity for progressive multiculturalism. In addition, the continued emphasis on politics and wars—with women's limited visibility in both—continues not only to relegate women to a lesser role in national history but also to maintain the distinction between social history and military-political history, and thus the private and public spheres, which depoliticizes everyday life and the government's involvement therein.

Despite these differences, the curricula and textbooks of both countries remain focused on the history of the nation-state. Feminism constitutes a challenge to traditional nationalism, built as it is on gender disparities. In addition, feminism has often been allied with ideologies that lead to challenging not only the gender norms of modern nation-states, but challenge the very legitimacy of a world order composed of democratic, capitalistic nation-states. Feminists have embraced universalism, internationalism, pacifism, and socialism. Curricula and textbooks, to the extent that they show feminism at all, only do so when it coincides with the story of the nation-state and furthers the narrative of national progress.

NOTES

1. A note on methodology: I have counted here only illustrations where the military aspect is the primary focus of the illustration. In other words, an illustration showing George Washington in battle counts as a military image, but one showing him as president does not.
2. The Gablers wrote, for instance, in their 1982 textbook evaluations: "The text continues to withhold important information from the students. Students need to have an understanding of the hard work, faith, courage, and perseverance of the people who settled this country. They did not just come over and set up colonies—they endured great hardships and formed the very foundations our country is

based on. Also, why does the text choose to elevate the deviants to positions of honor? Students have no understanding of why this colony was governed as it was. [. . .] The text is determined to portray the Puritans as tyrants when in fact they were hardworking people trying to make their government work. Students do not understand the situation or why the Puritans believed as they did. For some reason, the text only portrays them negatively when they were actually very inspirational people" (Educational Research Analysts 1982: 7). However, they no longer criticize inclusion of Hutchinson and Williams in later books (at least, not in the reviews that they distribute), focusing instead on ensuring that the textbooks present the Puritans' religion and government favorably.

3. Some earlier textbooks (notably Le Callennec 1997) also included critical perspectives on women's history, even before the curricular reforms of 2002, but these were outliers.

REFERENCES

For the complete list of textbooks analyzed, see Chapter One.

French Textbooks Cited

Bendjebbar, André, et al. 2004. *Multi-livre CM2: Histoire, géographie, sciences.* Paris: Istra.

Boëche, Sandra, ed. 2011. *CM1: Les Reporteurs histoire, géographie, histoire des arts, développement durable.* Paris: Sedrap.

Boëche, Sandra, ed. 2011. *CM2: Les Reporteurs histoire, géographie, histoire des arts, développement durable.* Paris: Sedrap.

Chevalier, Jean-Pierre and Roselyn Le Bourgeois, eds. 2010. *Histoire, histoire des arts, instruction civique, CM2.* Paris: Nathan.

Dorel-Ferré, Gracia and M. Dhainaut. 1985. *Cours moyen: Histoire.* Paris: Armand Colin.

Le Bourgeois, Roselyne. 2010. *Histoire, histoire des arts, CM1.* Paris: Nathan.

Le Callennec, Sophie, ed. 1997. *Histoire-géographie, Cycle 3, niveau 2, CM1.* Paris: Hatier.

Le Callennec, Sophie, ed. 2004. *Histoire, géographie, CM2, Cycle 3.* Collection Magellan. Paris: Hatier.

Le Callennec, Sophie, ed. 2008. *Education à la citoyenneté, Cycle 3.* Collection Magellan. Paris: Hatier.

Le Callennec, Sophie, ed. 2010. *Histoire, géographie, CM1.* Collection Magellan. Paris: Hatier.

Le Callennec, Sophie, ed. 2011. *Histoire, géographie, CM2.* Collection Magellan. Paris: Hatier.

Nembrini, Jean-Louis, Pierre Polivka, and Jean Bordes. 1985. *Histoire CM.* Pour connaître la France. Paris: Hachette écoles.

Vincent, Marc, et al. 1985. *CM2: Histoire: La France au fil du temps, de 1789 à nos jours.* Collection Télémaque. Paris: Nathan.

United States Textbooks

Banks, James. A., et al. 1997. *United States: Adventures in Time and Place.* New York: Macmillan McGraw-Hill.

Banks, James. A., et al. 2003. *Our Nation*. New York: Macmillan McGraw-Hill.
Bednarz, Sarah, et al. 1997. *Build Our Nation. We the People*. Boston: Houghton Mifflin
Berson, Michael, et al. 2003. *Harcourt Horizons: United States History*. Orlando, FL: Harcourt.
Boehm, Richard G., et al. 1997. *America's Story: Stories in Time*. New York: Harcourt-Brace.
Boyd, Candy Dawson, et al. 2003. *The United States, Social Studies*. Glenview, IL: Scott Foresman.
Gross, Herbert, et al. 1980. *Exploring Our World: Americas*. 2nd ed. Chicago, IL: Follett.
Helmus, Timothy M., et al. 1982. *The United States and Its Neighbors*. Morristown, NJ: Silver Burdett.
King, Allen Y., et al. 1982. *The United States and the Other Americas*. New York: Macmillan.

Curriculum Guidelines and Official Reports

"Chapter 113: Texas Essential Knowledge and Skills for Social Studies." 1998. *Texas Essential Knowledge and Skills*. Texas Education Agency. Retrieved 20 Dec. 2000 (http://www.tea.state.tx.us/rules/tac/ch113.html#s1137).
"Chapter 113: Texas Essential Knowledge and Skills for Social Studies." 2010. *Texas Essential Knowledge and Skills*. Texas Education Agency. Retrieved 5 Nov. 2013 (http://ritter.tea.state.tx.us/rules/tac/chapter113/index.html).
Discours du Ministre d'Etat, Ministre de l'Education Nationale, de la Jeunesse et des Sports [Jospin, Lionel]. 1990. "Une nouvelle politique pour l'école primaire." *Bulletin officiel de l'Education nationale* 9 (1 Mar.): 601–608.
Framework for the Social Studies. 1980. Austin: Texas Education Agency.
"Horaires et programmes d'enseignement de l'école primaire." 2002. *Bulletin officiel de l'Education nationale*. Special issue 1 (14 Feb.).
"Horaires et programmes d'enseignement de l'école primaire." 2008. *Bulletin officiel de l'Education nationale*. Special issue 3 (19 Jun.).
"Horaires, programmes et instructions pour l'école élémentaire, 1985." 1986. *Bulletin officiel de l'Education nationale*. Special issue 1 (16 Jan.).
"Horaires, objectifs et programmes. Cycle Moyen." 1980. *R.L.R. 514–3*.
Loi d'orientation et de programme pour l'avenir de l'école. 2005. *Bulletin official* 18 (5 May). Retrieved 20 Aug. 2015 (http://www.education.gouv.fr/bo/2005/18/MENX0400282L.htm#loi).
Ministère de la Jeunesse, de l'Éducation nationale et de la Recherche: Direction de l'enseignement scolaire. 2002. "Histoire et géographie cycle des approfondissements (cycle 3)." Collection Ecole: Documents d'application des programmes. Paris: Centre national de documentation pédagogique.
Proclamation 1994 of the State Board of Education Advertising for Bids on Instructional Materials. 1994. Austin: Texas Education Agency.
"Programmes de l'école primaire." 1995. *Bulletin officiel de l'Education nationale* 48 (28 Dec.).

Works of Reference

Accampo, Elinor. 2004. "Integrating Women and Gender into the Teaching of French History, 1789 to the Present." *French Historical Studies* 27.2: 267–292.
Andriocci, Muriel, et al. 2003. *Premier recensement national des enseignements et des recherches sur le genre en France. Rapport final aux Ministère des affaires*

sociales, du travail et de la solidarité, et al. Association Nationale des Etudes Féministes.

Association Nationale des Etudes Féministes. 2014. *Le genre dans l'enseignement supérieur et la recherche.* Paris: La Dispute.

Bard, Christine. 2003. "Jalons pour une histoire des études féministes en France (1970–2002)." *Nouvelles Questions Féministes* 22.1: 14–30.

Battaglia, Mattea. 2014. "L'appel au boycott qui alarme l'école." *Le Monde* 30 Jan.: 6.

Berton-Schmitt, Amandine, ed. 2015. *Les Femmes dans les manuels scolaires.* Proceedings of the conference *Les Femmes dans les manuels scolaires*, 2 Jul. 2014, French Senate. Paris: Centre Hubertine Auclert.

Brubaker, Rogers. 2012. "Religion and Nationalism: Four Approaches." *Nations and Nationalism* 18.1: 2–20.

Colon, David. 2015. "La Fabrique du manuel d'histoire: enjeux et finalités d'un objet controversé." Paper presented at the Centre d'histoire de Sciences Po, 4 March, Paris, France.

Cott, Nancy F. and Drew Gilpin Faust. 2005. "Recent Directions in Gender and Women's History." *OAH Magazine of History* 19.2: 4–5.

Dermenjian, Geneviève, et al., eds. 2010. *La Place des femmes dans l'histoire: une histoire mixte.* Paris: Belin.

Educational Research Analysts. 1982. *1982 Textbook Ratings.* Longview, TX: Educational Research Analysts.

Ezekiel, Judith. 2002. "Le *Women's Lib*: Made in France." *European Journal of Women's Studies* 9.3: 345–361.

Fassin, Eric. 1999. "The Purloined Gender: American Feminism in a French Mirror." *French Historical Studies* 22.1: 113–138.

Gabler, Mel and Norma, W. Kelley Haralson, and Jackie Cobb. 1982. Review of Macmillan Publishing, *The Mel Gablers Educational Research Analysts 1982 Textbook Ratings.* Longview, TX: Educational Research Analysts.

Gambaudo, Sylvie. 2007. "French Feminism vs Anglo-American Feminism: A Reconstruction." *European Journal of Women's Studies* 14.2: 93–108.

Hartman, Andrew. 2015. *A War for the Soul of America: A History of the Culture Wars.* Chicago: University of Chicago Press.

Hunt, Lynn. 1992. *The Family Romance of the French Revolution.* Berkeley: University of California Press.

Jones, Jeanie. 1997. "Reviews of 5th Grade U.S. History Texts." *1997 Elementary Social Studies Information.* Longview, TX: Educational Research Analysts.

Legris, Patricia. 2014. *Qui écrit les programmes d'histoire?* Grenoble: Presses universitaires de Grenoble.

Moore, Robert. 1977. *Stereotypes, Distortions, and Omissions in U.S. History Textbooks.* New York: Council of Interracial Books for Children.

Moses, Claire Goldberg. 1998. "Made in America: "French Feminism" in Academia." *Feminist Studies* 24.2: 241–274.

Mosse, George. 1996. *The Image of Man: The Creation of Modern Masculinity.* Studies in the History of Sexuality. Oxford: Oxford University Press.

Nash, Gary B., Chartlotte Crabtree, and Ross E. 1997/2000. *History on Trial: Culture Wars and the Teaching of the Past.* New York: Vintage Books.

Nash, Margaret A. 2005. *Women's Education in the United States, 1780–1840.* New York: Palgrave Macmillan.

Offen, Karen. 2000. *European Feminisms, 1700–1950: A Political History.* Stanford: Stanford University Press.

Petrzela, Natalia Mehlman. 2015. *Classroom Wars: Language, Sex, and the Making of Modern Political Culture.* Oxford: Oxford University Press.

Raphael, Ray. 2004. *Founding Myths: Stories that Hide our Patriotic Past.* New York: New Press.

Scott, Joan Wallach. 1996. *Only Paradoxes to Offer: French Feminists and the Rights of Man.* Cambridge, MA: Harvard University Press.
Scott, Joan Wallach. 2009. *The Politics of the Veil.* Princeton, NJ: Princeton University Press.
"United States History Standards for Grades 5–12: Era 4: Expansion and Reform (1801–1861)." 1996. National History Standards. Retrieved 21 Aug. 2015 (http://www.nchs.ucla.edu/history-standards/us-history-content-standards/united-states-era-4).
Wieviorka, Annette. 2004. *Quelle place pour les femmes dans l'histoire enseignée?* République française, Avis et rapports du Conseil économique et social.
Yuval-Davis, Nira. 1997. *Gender & Nation.* London: Sage.

3 Class and the Nation

Conceptions of solidarity are intricately connected to nationalism and national identity. Myths of economic equality and of national unity that transcends entrenched socioeconomic divisions are powerful means by which nationalism can be antithetical to social justice. Inversely, this relationship can be a progressive force, in which nationalism allied with awareness of inequality can foster a sense of solidarity and social justice. This chapter demonstrates how diverging founding myths regarding equality and solidarity remain salient in France and the U.S.

Approaches to socioeconomic inequality have come to constitute one of the most significant differences between French and American textbooks. This issue represents a key point of divergence between the two countries' self-conceptions as presented in these books, with French books showing commitment to social justice (within the limits of colorblindness), while U.S. curricula and textbooks have moved steadily away from criticism of the status quo and historical events that have led to it. Yet, despite these different conceptions of national identity and belonging, both countries' curricula and textbooks reveal heightened expressions of nationalism and reaffirmation of national unity through their presentations of socioeconomic aspects of history and contemporary society.

Equality is a founding ideal in both France and the United States yet, historically, they have defined it differently. The French Revolution was a social revolution (Skocpol 1979), in which class-based revolt overturned the existing social order, doing away with feudal privilege, and laying the groundwork for a sense of national identity and pride that is allied with commitment to a certain equality of opportunity as well as a degree of equality of outcome (Schwarzmantel 1987). The U.S. Revolutionary War, on the other hand, was not a social revolution (as Skocpol defines it) but a colonial revolution that also sought freedom in pursuit of Enlightenment ideals, which did not overturn the existing social order when it overthrew the political order. The U.S., then, does not have the same historical, founding commitment as does France to socioeconomic equality.

Accordingly, whether or not to teach about socioeconomic inequality does not seem to be much of a question in France. There is apparent consensus among the educational community that society is unequal and that government has a responsibility to redistribute some wealth to assure minimal wellbeing, as this chapter will show.

In the U.S., on the other hand, a myth of equality of opportunity—that with sufficiently hard work, anyone can overcome hardship and attain material success—has deep roots and remains prevalent. Attitudes may be shifting, particularly among younger age cohorts in the wake of the recent recession. However, in the early 2000s when the most recent books of this study were published, a majority of Americans continued to profess belief in this axiom (Scott and Leonhardt 2005). Americans' loyalty and attachment to their state has deep roots in economic factors. From colonial times, America offered inhabitants of European descent greater access to land and possibilities of owning property than they had had in Europe. This situation contributed to a sense of better individual financial prospects, and from the United States' beginning, many Americans conflated a lack of formal, hierarchical class structure with the belief that socioeconomic classes did not exist in the new country (Marienstras 1976: 295). Americans' sense of economic superiority and optimism regarding their personal fortunes have long formed the basis for an attachment to the nation-state as the source of this wellbeing (Curti 1946/1968: 102, 119). To challenge the belief in a level playing field and the myth of opportunity is, for many Americans, to challenge the nation's greatness.

The French welfare state improves quality of life for low-income residents more so than in the U.S. (Viguier 2011: 266; Wacquant 2008). Yet, in both countries, socioeconomic status is largely hereditary, indicating entrenched inequality (Hargreaves 2007: 56; Mangum, Mangum, and Sum 2003). Also in both countries, certain ethnic minorities are disproportionately represented among the disadvantaged. This inequality along ethnic lines is the result of a complex legacy of historic deprivation of rights, which limited accumulation of economic as well as cultural capital over generations, in addition to ongoing discriminatory labor, housing, and education practices (Bonilla-Silva 2014: 56–62; Hargreaves 2007: 54–58). It is thus impossible to talk about class without also discussing socioeconomic inequality along ethnic lines.

In France and the United States, the existence of persistent socioeconomic inequality challenges the traditional view of the country as a bastion of equality. Such inequalities are antithetical to national unity. If the nation is conceived of as a metaphorical kinship community, it is understood that a certain sense of solidarity unites its members. The fact that ethnic minorities are disproportionately disadvantaged renders discussion of socioeconomic inequality more controversial. Socioeconomic inequality along ethnic lines can undermine national unity and solidarity for all groups. Those in dominant groups might believe that more marginalized groups are economically disadvantaged because they choose not to work (first in school, then in a profession), and thus that they reject national values. This view reflects a belief among the more privileged that national belonging is asserted through contribution to the national economy, and that such contribution is possible for all citizens, thanks to systemic equality (see Thomas [2012] on "monetized contract" models of national belonging). In this way, some members of dominant groups justify their rejection of more radical redistribution by depicting the marginalized as outsiders to the national community. In turn, marginalized groups may perceive racist exclusion as the cause of inequality. This controversy makes the topic of socioeconomic inequality one of the most ideologically charged for history and social studies education.

PRINCIPAL FINDINGS AND CHAPTER OUTLINE

Nationalism and class interact in sharply opposed ways in recent French and United States textbooks. The presentations of this topic were more similar to one another in the early 1980s and have diverged since then. This divergence may not seem surprising to many readers, given the different scope in each country of the welfare state. Yet, the differences between French and American textbooks are so striking—and have become so much more pronounced over the past three decades—that they point not just to an ideological difference between the countries but to a profound rightward shift in educational materials in the United States.

French textbooks show wealth disparities throughout national history and strive to impart a sense of social justice and the conviction that economic redistribution and helping the less fortunate are key national values, which have helped to improve the quality of life in France, and which students must continue to pursue in the face of inequalities driven by globalization. Most of these books, though, do not connect questions of socioeconomic inequality to more controversial questions of contemporary ethno-racial discrimination or disparities. U.S. textbooks of 2003 take a very different approach from French textbooks, but also from U.S. books of 1982, as they show poverty and socioeconomic inequality as a thing of the (increasingly distant) past and adopt a celebratory tone regarding the state of contemporary American society and the global economy.

This chapter begins with an overview of the different debates that could influence how this topic is taught in each country, along with an analysis of official approaches as represented in curricula. It then examines textbooks, looking first at their presentations of class awareness and class divisions in history. This section focuses on the chapters in textbooks where issues of class, inequality, social justice, and the role of the state are most likely to be salient. These include the books' general introductions or summaries of national identity, the French textbooks' presentations of the medieval period and the monarchy prior to the establishment of the republic, presentations of each country's founding revolution, industrialization and urbanization, and the Great Depression in the U.S. The next section examines presentations of contemporary poverty and inequality, focusing on the boom of the post-war years and the contemporary period since the 1960s (including, in France, the economic decline that followed the *Trente glorieuses* years of post-war prosperity and in the U.S., the Civil Rights Movement and War on Poverty, the growing wealth gap since the 1980s, and the curtailing of the welfare state).

SOCIAL JUSTICE AND EQUALITY IN CURRICULA AND SURROUNDING DEBATES

Before delving into our analysis, it is helpful to frame it within the context of debate in each country. While a certain commitment to redistribution of wealth is widely consensual in France, discussions of socioeconomic inequality are subject to controversy regarding the situation of French citizens and residents of non-European origin. Data measuring inequality along ethnic lines is limited, due to France's official ban on ethnic statistics. However, public discourse reflects general awareness that Maghrebi and sub-Saharan African immigrants and their descendants are more likely to be socioeconomically disadvantaged than is the population of European descent (Viguier 2011: 269–270). Indeed, discussion about "immigration" (often a euphemism for residents and citizens of Maghrebi and sub-Saharan African origin, which frequently includes the French-born children of immigrants) or social tensions tends to frame this community as a problem precisely because they exhibit higher levels of unemployment, lower levels of education, and greater geographical segregation within low-income housing projects (Scott 2007: 69–72; Viguier 2011: 262–267). While majorities on both the left and the right continue to adhere to the universalist norm that prohibits measuring equality along ethnic lines, a split is occurring on the left. Many on the left continue to advocate colorblind policies and increasing commitment to traditional left-wing approaches to promoting equality, such as economic redistribution and improving education for all. An increasing number of more radical voices, however, argue that traditional colorblind approaches are ineffective and, contrary to their stated intentions, promote a myth of national unity and equality and heighten divisions, as the marginalized members of society see these policies as hypocritical (Amiraux and Simon 2006; Lorcerie 1994; Viguier 2011: 264–265).

This dissenting view, however, has not entered education debates. So far, the efforts of groups such as *SOS Racisme* to influence curriculum and textbook authors have focused mainly on inclusion of the history of colonization and slavery.[1] In many ways, this approach appears similar to the early efforts of multiculturalist reformers in the U.S. Perhaps in time, these groups will also seek support for their concerns with socioeconomic inequality. For the moment, though, most reform efforts have focused on inclusion and denouncing racism in more general terms (see Chapter One). Thus, there has not yet been a significant challenge to left-leaning but colorblind consensus regarding social justice in France.

French curricula demonstrate a commitment to education for creating a just society. They express goals of providing equal opportunity through the schools and their power to provide needed skills, sociocultural integration, and to level the playing field. They also reflect dedication to a self-consciously left-leaning nationalism, which takes pride in a shared commitment to social justice within the country and worldwide. Critiques of globalization in more recent curricula also reveal an inherent defining of French identity in opposition to American-style capitalism, thus perhaps strengthening the symbolic power of progressive nationalism. Expressions of these goals become increasingly explicit in subsequent curricula through 2002, retracting somewhat in 2008.

The brief French primary school curriculum of 1985 does not contain anything explicit about socioeconomic inequality but does include a couple of points that imply a left-leaning consensus. In a list of fundamental freedoms, which includes freedom of assembly and expression, this curriculum includes the right to strike and various forms of what it terms "social progress" since the establishment of that right ("Horaires . . ." 1985: 21). The other indication of a commitment to social justice is in the section on civic education, where the instructions require teachers to "engage students in cooperative life, lead students to practice equal rights and to participate in humanitarian organizations' national and international campaigns" (20).

France's 1995 curriculum focuses much more on social equality, discussing the issue in its mission statements, emphasizing the social role of teachers and the school, especially in the *zones défavorisées* (underprivileged areas; "Programmes . . .": 6). This curriculum charges schools with helping disadvantaged students to overcome obstacles to social and professional success. For instance, in the mission statement regarding early childhood education (*école maternelle*, approximately ages three through five), the curriculum states:

> The *école maternelle* is the primary site where children build the foundations of their future learning. The variety and richness of their experiences allow them to construct their knowledge and to prepare themselves, through structured learning, for the more systematic learning of elementary school. Language is learned in the same way: it is through the richness of their experiences that children learn to better understand the language that is addressed to them and to speak better. This is why the role of the *école maternelle* is capital, especially in underprivileged neighborhoods.
>
> ("Programmes . . .": 6)

(The emphasis on language in curricula is discussed further in the next chapter.) In addition to advocating education as a means of integration, this curriculum also lays out content guidelines aiming to instill a sense of social justice in all students. For example, the geography section of the curriculum makes several references to socioeconomic inequality, requiring that students learn about "rich and poor countries," that they be taught a "sense of personal and collective responsibility regarding problems linked to [. . .] individual, collective, and social resources and their limited nature," and be taught about "social protection and solidarity" as a defining feature of "civic life in society" ("Programmes . . .": 45).

These themes are even more thoroughly developed in the 2002 curriculum and accompanying documents. The opening line of the preamble to the curriculum states: "At the beginning of the twenty-first century, the primary schools must remain true to the inspired idea of republican education: offer to all children equal chances and successful integration into French society" ("Horaires . . .": 13). The curriculum guidelines also focus on socioeconomic inequality in their approach to history. They discuss the issue regarding several periods in the past, emphasizing its ubiquity under the feudal system, its role in leading to the Revolution, and the harsh labor conditions of the nineteenth century, which the curriculum credits organized labor, strikes, and socialism, in general, with having improved. The curriculum's presentation of France since the mid-twentieth century clearly states that, though many people enjoyed newfound prosperity, the benefits were unequal throughout society, and that today, "Despite legislation for social protection, this rapid progress has not prevented unemployment, exclusion, and great poverty" ("Horaires . . .": 17). The 2002 curriculum guidelines on history and geography also repeatedly discuss the inequalities created on an international scale by globalization. For example, the geography instructions include this explanation:

> France in the age of globalization
>
> The exchange of capital, the circulation of people, of industrial products, of services and information, pushed by several major urban centers, take on international and global dimensions that surpass the authority of states at the same time that disparities and inequalities are being accentuated, both between developed countries and poor countries, as well as within national spaces. Parallel to this, current events highlight the resistances, oppositions, and the fragility of globalization. Does France have a specific place in this process?
>
> ("Horaires . . .": 29)

The more concise 2008 curriculum removes these explanations as well as the focus on socioeconomic factors in French history. Nevertheless, the 2008 curriculum still includes solidarity and economic redistribution among the fundamental national values students must study. For instance, in its civic education requirements, the document stresses the importance of "the stakes of national solidarity (social protection, responsibility between generations)" ("Horaires . . .": 27).

The subject is much more contentious in education debates in the United States where demographically detailed statistics make clear the hereditary nature of socioeconomic status and the disproportionate representation of certain ethnic minorities among the disadvantaged. Progressive multiculturalists in the U.S. advocate facing these inequalities head-on: understanding the depth and breadth of inequality, the causes, and the historical roots. They believe that the only way to level the playing field is to begin by acknowledging that it is not level. They also believe that teaching how discriminatory policies have contributed to the current state of socioeconomic inequality is essential for combating racist and sexist stereotypes (see for example Banks 1996; Giroux 1992). The approach to the topic is contentious even on the left, though, as some multiculturalists (particularly in the earlier manifestations of the movement) have opposed depicting ethnic groups as impoverished, as they felt it conveyed a negative stereotype (CIBC 1981: 53).

Lack of consensus around the state's redistributive role in the U.S. reflects many Americans' faith in the fairness of capitalism and the levelness of the playing field. Such a vision is central to the positive image of the United States that Christian Right educational activists advocate. A Protestant capitalist ethos (Weber 1905/1920/2012) is at the heart of their conception of the nation. They thus believe that teaching about inequality in the American past—and even more so in the present—is "antipatriotic" and undermines the image of the nation. For instance, in 1985, the Mel Gablers' Educational Research Analysts published the following critique of a high-school history textbook:

> This book is not a comprehensive and balanced study of history. It is subtle anti-American propaganda. Social problems get top billing while U.S. accomplishments and advantages go virtually unnoticed.
>
> In numerous history texts poverty, protests, and crime are covered far out of proportion to the positive happenings and advances in America. Problems are stressed while solutions achieved through the American system are largely censored. Society and capitalism are blamed for practically everything negative.
>
> Ponder this quote:
>
>> But a major reason [for poverty] lies with our society's tragic legacy of prejudice, ignorance, and exploitation, which has left the great majority of adults on welfare poorly equipped for employment by training, education, and even general health.
>
> This, when free enterprise and open opportunity have rendered the lower classes and minorities more upwardly mobile in America than anywhere else on earth.
>
> (Gabler and Hefley 1985: 55–56)

Because theirs is a religious nationalism, they see criticism of the country's economic system not only as misguided but as heretical. In their textbook activism, these groups consistently support pure capitalism: they oppose government redistribution (and hence, positive presentations of the New Deal or Great Society), and they believe that the higher wages negotiated by unions undermine the economy and consumers' purchasing power. They believe that poverty is an individual rather than a structural phenomenon and see it as a reflection of personal moral qualities. For instance, the Gablers criticize redistributive programs in the following terms: "The Great Society no longer distinguished between the 'deserving' and the 'undeserving' poor. Instead it blamed 'the system' for poverty and granted welfare as a 'right,' debunking the work ethic" (Educational Research Analysts 2003b: 9).

Turning now to an opposing viewpoint, it is useful once again to begin with a look at the National History Standards of 1996, as they offer an overview of many historians' suggestions. The NHS incorporate several aspects of labor history, which can offer a window into questions of socioeconomic equality and can render visible nonelite sections of society. The NHS advocate, for example, teaching about labor conflict, and the different working conditions in different industries for different workers (by "gender, race, ethnicity, and skill" [Standard 3]). However, the NHS grade-level recommendations indicate that they advise teaching about inequality only in high school, rather than to younger students. For instance, when discussing the U.S. economy since 1945, the standards recommend that students in grades nine through twelve be able to "Analyze the continued gap between poverty and the rising affluence of the middle class" (NHS 1996). For the same historical era, the guideline that includes fifth graders focuses much more on positive aspects of the period: "Explain the reasons for the sustained growth of the postwar consumer economy" (NHS 1996).

Given the lack of focus on questions of socioeconomic equality in NHS recommendations for the primary schools, it is not, perhaps, surprising that state-level curricula for elementary school are not particularly progressive.[2] This observation holds true both for history curriculum guidelines as well as other aspects of social studies education. As Texas curricula became more detailed from 1980 to 2010, they increasingly emphasized capitalism as a key source of national identity and pride. The conservative tenor of these documents is heightened by their lack of attention to labor history and socioeconomic issues in history and contemporary society.

The Texas curriculum guidelines, while similar to those of many other states in many regards, have a particularity in this domain. In each of its curricula since 1980, Texas emphasizes teaching about the "benefits" of the "free enterprise system." For example, the 1980 curriculum guidelines state: "The social studies program shall help students to develop and examine their own values and attitudes and those of others, including: [. . .] appreciation for the nature of and demonstration of positive support for the American economic system" (*Framework* . . . 1980: 8). This curriculum repeats the injunction to teach students: "the essentials and benefits of the free enterprise system" (*Framework* . . . 1980: 11, 16). Subsequent curricula are even more insistent on this point. For example, at least once per grade level, the 1995 curriculum guidelines reiterate the requirement of "emphasizing the free enterprise system and its benefits." In a similar shift, the 1980 curriculum, overall, does not adopt a celebratory tone in its descriptions of the U.S. economy, but it says nothing on inequality or disadvantages, either. The 1995 curriculum becomes more expansive and explicitly includes the economy as a guiding force in defining national identity: "Analyze the development of the basic cultural institutions (e.g., family, religion, education, government, economy) that have shaped our national identity" (*Proclamation* 1994: A-24). All the curricula of this study (1980–2010) also focus on teaching students a work ethic, stressing the value of work and positive attitudes, and the sense of satisfaction that a job well done imparts.

With the advent of the conservative-board-approved, lengthier TEKS in 1998 (and in 2010), the curricula repeatedly and consistently emphasize the transmission of memory grounded in positive interpretations of U.S. culture and history. In keeping with this focus on progress in U.S. history and celebration of the current quality of life in the U.S., these curricula place loyalty to the country's economic system at the center of national identity, wellbeing, and pride. For example, the fifth-grade content requires that students learn to: "explain the impact of American ideas about progress and equality of opportunity on the economic development and growth of the United States" ("Chapter 113": §113.7.b.14.f). While this emphasis on celebrating capitalism is new, the invisibility of socioeconomic concerns is not. As in the older curricula, the 1998 and 2010 TEKS omit mentioning the existence of classes or anything reminiscent of class conflict (even regarding eras of industrialization). The TEKS do not mention the New Deal or the Great Society, nor socioeconomic inequality in any capacity. There are vague mentions of "equality" as a national value, but the concept is undefined, and presumably refers to political equality (discussed further in Chapter Four).

SOCIOECONOMIC INEQUALITY IN TEXTBOOKS

Class Awareness and Class Divisions

Generally speaking, class awareness pervades the French textbooks, whether published in the 1980s or in the 2010s. It is a recurring theme that the books emphasize explicitly, regularly presenting the differences in lifestyle between rich and poor at different periods in history, as well as in contemporary society, and showing socioeconomic inequality to be a driving force for social change over time. This topic dominates coverage of the Middle Ages, the Enlightenment and the French Revolution, the Industrial Revolution, and contemporary society. For instance, when discussing the Middle Ages and the *Ancien Régime*, the textbooks all explain in detail that the vast majority of the population (90 percent) were beholden to the landowning lords and had to work for them. The books also explain that many of the peasants were very poor and often struggled to meet their basic needs, especially in the years of famine preceding the Revolution. Some textbooks (such as Hatier [Le Callennec 2010: 18–19] and Sedrap [Boëche 2011 CM1: 12–14]) explicitly and repeatedly emphasize that medieval society was inegalitarian, and all the books emphasize the inequalities that led up to the Revolution. For instance, Sedrap, after a long description of the many demands placed on peasants by the lords, adds: "Sometimes peasants, crushed by debt, barely able to feed their families, revolted against their lord. These revolts often ended with the massacre of the peasants." This text is followed by an illustration showing one of these massacres (Boëche 2011 CM1: 14). Whether or not the textbooks use the term "exploitation," they give the unmistakable impression of an unjust society. The textbooks also all show that class inequalities persisted after the Revolution, notably with the bourgeoisie being the primary economic beneficiaries of the new order.

Similarly, while the books of both countries (with a notable exception among U.S. books, as we will see below) show workers' struggle to obtain better conditions during the Industrial Revolution, French textbooks are more likely to frame the topic in terms of growing disparities between socioeconomic classes. The books emphasize harsh treatment of workers, especially children. For instance, Nathan cites an eleven-year-old girl's description of her 12-hour days in the mine where she had worked since she was eight. The girl explains in detail how much she has to carry up a steep slope, concluding: "I have to do 20 trips to fill the five wagons. When I cannot do it, I get a beating. I am happy when the work is done because it exhausts me" (Chevalier and Le Bourgeois 2010: 44). The books all show in one way or another that the bourgeoisie distanced itself from the working class (Le Callennec 2011: 43), becoming richer as opposed to the laborers, whose lives were difficult (Chevalier and Le Bourgeois 2010: 45). Sedrap shows most explicitly that the capitalist class deliberately decreased workers' pay while increasing their hours and emphasizes more than its competitors the obstacles against organizing labor unions. It states:

> Industrialists organized work to produce:
>
> - the maximum amount at maximum speed (mechanization, increased speed of work and length of the work-day, especially with the use of lighting)
> - as cheaply as possible (very low salaries . . .). [. . .]
>
> In the factories and in the mines, the labor conditions were often inhuman. Laborers worked 12 to 15 hours a day, without days off or holidays.
>
> Badly paid, often mistreated, victims of numerous work accidents, workers could be fired overnight.

> In France, strikes were prohibited until 1864, and those who dared to rebel were arrested and imprisoned. [. . .]
>
> Little by little and following many revolts in the factories, workers organized to defend their rights. [. . .]
>
> (Boëche 2011 CM2: 32–33)

This book also attributes improvements in workers' conditions to the Socialist Party (which it does not differentiate from the contemporary party), thus reinforcing the impression that an alliance of solidarity and national progress lies with the left. In this manner, to varying degrees, the French books impart a sense of historic class divisions and opposing interests, which the U.S. books generally do not do.

Overall, U.S. books mention poverty and wealth inequality, but this is not a recurring theme, and it is not accorded the same importance as a historical force for change as in French books. U.S. textbooks reflect traditional views characterizing America as a classless society, in which socioeconomic differences do not constitute an aspect of individual or national identity. Some of these textbooks mention socioeconomic differences in early American society, but they do not show these as having enduring political significance. For instance, if the books mention the poverty of the farmers who rebelled against the new state in the 1780s, as in the uprising known as Shays's Rebellion, this conflict does not seem to reflect on the current U.S. state, as this period predated—and led to—the creation of the Constitution. All of the U.S. textbooks in the present study cover poverty in the Gilded Age, notably among immigrants and factory workers during the Second Industrial Revolution. Almost all of these books dedicate at least two or three pages to the poverty endured by laborers and tend to emphasize child labor. However, there is one remarkable exception: the coverage in Harcourt's 2003 edition of the living conditions of laborers during the Gilded Age is qualitatively very different from that of its competitors. Harcourt offers an overwhelmingly positive account of immigration and life during the Second Industrial Revolution. It does mention the hardship endured by workers, but only very briefly, with no detail, no first-person accounts, and much less emphasis than French books of either period studied, older U.S. books, as well as its contemporary competitors. Perhaps even more significantly, once Harcourt has mentioned this poverty, it immediately puts a very positive (and patriotic) spin on it. After explaining that most of the new immigrants were poor and were seeking a better life in the U.S., Harcourt dedicates only 60 words to describing the immigrants' lives in the U.S., stating that many of them lived in crowded apartments, and children often had to work, as adults' wages were too low to support a family. The text then comments:

> In spite of the difficult conditions, many new immigrants succeeded. One of these people was Irving Berlin. [. . .] During his life, Berlin wrote

> more than 800 songs, including "God Bless America," perhaps his most famous song.
>
> (Berson et al. 2003: 503)

In most U.S. textbooks, presentations of the inequalities of the Gilded Age lead to discussions of the rise of labor unions and reform. The books of the U.S., like those of France, present labor unions as a positive force for change. Some U.S. books show opposition between labor and management, stating that business owners were reluctant to improve workers' conditions and pay, and that conflict sometimes turned violent (Banks et al. 2003: 508). However, in the U.S. books, unions are only mentioned before 1945, whereas in France, they are presented as still standing up for workers' rights in contemporary society. Harcourt (Berson et al. 2003) is again a significant exception, as it does not mention labor unions at all. As such, it appears that laws protecting workers' rights were passed on the sole initiative of governments (533). This is not only a stunning concession to conservative pressure but is also a powerful rejection of a social history approach to historiography, in favor of a more traditional political (i.e., top-down) approach.

The differences between Harcourt's 2003 edition and all the other U.S. textbooks are particularly striking because the 1997 edition of this same book contained a detailed chapter emphasizing management's responsibility for workers' harsh conditions during the Gilded Age. This chapter includes a three-and-a-half-page subchapter entitled "Owners against Workers," which relates the use of military force against strikers, and the section concludes by showing the support among many in government for unregulated business (Boehm: 461–464). Like other progressively inclined sections of this textbook that disappeared between 1997 and 2003 (as seen in the previous chapters), this section garnered staunch criticism from the Gablers' group:

> On the subject of labor relations from 1865 to 1914 *America's Story* stresses defects but not benefits of industrial capitalism and benefits but not defects of unions. Workers' purchasing power rose in this era. Millions of immigrants saw in urban factory jobs at market wages a golden opportunity. *America's Story* speaks as if industrial capitalism invented child labor. In fact it had existed for millennia, and only mature industrial capitalism made possible its abolition. It is a serious error in a history textbook to compare developing industrial capitalism to an ideal rather than to its context in economic historical reality. Nor does *America's Story* link improved wages, hours, and working conditions to increased productivity from reinvested profits not distributed as above-market union wages. The following passages nowhere explain that higher prices of unionmade [sic] goods cut sales and purchasing power, or how above-market union wages reduce the number of available unionized jobs.
>
> (Gabler, Gabler and Frey 1997: 31)

The removal of this entire chapter detailing the hardships workers faced and depicting class conflict (combined with the removal of many other passages featuring a critical approach) seems to reflect the influence of conservative activist groups, as Harcourt's 1997 edition was the lowest-ranked textbook by the Gablers' group and its 2003 edition received the Gablers' highest ranking (Educational Research Analysts 1997; 2003a). These changes (along with the Gablers' endorsement) may have contributed to greater financial success, as the 2003 edition accounted for approximately 35 percent of statewide sales of fifth grade social studies textbooks in Texas, up from approximately 24 percent for the 1997 edition (TEA 2001; TEA 2008). Though Harcourt's 2003 edition is not representative of all of the U.S. textbooks, neither is it marginal, as it accounts for over a third of textbook sales in its category.

In addition, while this textbook is extreme in omitting all references to labor unions and in removing any discussions of harsh labor conditions of the industrial age, it resembles its competitors, in that they relegate discussion of unions to the past. Textbooks of 1982 and 1997 were more likely to show unions as still active in contemporary society. For instance, after crediting labor unions with improving harsh, dangerous working conditions, several older books mention that the AFL-CIO is still active today (e.g., Bednarz et al. 1997: 515; Helmus et al. 1982: 211). The older books are also more likely to state that unions are still relevant in safeguarding workers' quality of life today (e.g., Banks et al. 1997: 545), and all the 1997 books (and many from 1982) list the National Farm Workers Association founded in the 1970s under "labor unions" in the index, showing the continued relevance of and need for labor organizing. McGraw-Hill's 2003 edition does not change as significantly in relation to its 1997 edition as does Harcourt's, but it does remove contemporary references to labor unions. For instance, the 1997 edition concluded the chapter on "The Labor Movement" of the late nineteenth and early twentieth centuries under the heading "Why it Matters," explaining the importance of these issues today: "Industry has also changed in response to the struggles of the labor unions. Workers in most industries today work eight hours a day, five days a week. Many also receive paid vacations and other benefits" (545). There is no equivalent passage in the 2003 edition. In a subtle, yet similar, change, the 2003 edition no longer refers to La Causa (or the National Farm Workers Association) under "labor unions" in the index, thus reducing the visibility of the concept in contemporary times.

Furthermore, among U.S. books, those published in 1982 and 1997 were much more likely than the more recent editions to show opposition between labor and management. The older books generally state that business owners were reluctant to improve workers' conditions and pay, and show the intensity of that conflict. For instance, Houghton Mifflin describes the Great Uprising of 1877 and explains: "In some cities, the state militia and federal troops battled angry mobs" (Bednarz et al. 1997: 514). The text goes on to state that the use of strikes increased thereafter and that: "Strikes often led to violence and bloodshed." It also uses the word "battle" again to refer to the Carnegie Steel strike in Homestead, Pennsylvania of 1892 (514). Among the most recent books, only Scott Foresman still mentions the Homestead Steel Works violence. This textbook says that "at times" conflict led to violence but offers no other examples (Boyd et al. 2003: 573). In addition, it avoids showing complete opposition between classes, as it also explains that "some business owners, religious organizations, and political leaders" worked with labor unions to improve workers' conditions (574). McGraw-Hill again removes details from its 1997 edition that emphasized conflict and reflected badly on the capitalist class. The older edition explains that, in response to strikes, "owners often hired men called strikebreakers to beat up strikers. Owners also hired nonunion workers to replace those on strike" (Banks et al. 1997: 544). In the 2003 edition, strikebreakers are no longer defined, and the text is sufficiently ambiguous that the term might be taken to be synonymous with the nonunion replacement workers: "When unions organized a strike, owners hired strikebreakers, or nonunion workers who replaced the striking workers" (Banks et al. 2003: 508). Overall, then, representations of labor unions have subtly reduced the sense of their relevance today, thus reducing impressions of the importance of collective action, and have reduced the emphasis on class conflict, thus showing a more unified society.

Thus, French textbooks attribute much more historical importance to class divisions. However, even in the French books, this opposition has increasingly come to appear as being mostly confined to the past.

CONTEMPORARY POVERTY AND INEQUALITY

The books of both France and the U.S. show poverty in the more distant past. However, they differ even more in their presentations of contemporary poverty and inequality.

Though they do not emphasize class divisions or antagonism, all French books clearly, explicitly emphasize wealth inequalities in contemporary society. The books focus on broad causes of poverty and inequality in the contemporary era, rather than presenting the situation as the result of deliberate, selfish aims of a capitalist class (as they do for example, regarding the age of industrialization or the *Ancien Régime*). The most recent books discuss contemporary wealth inequalities, but they show these as a shared concern among the national community, not as a source of antagonism or divisiveness. For instance, Sedrap's 2010 edition, like its competitors, focuses its coverage of post-1945 France on the post-war economic boom, followed by recession, and how these situations have affected the population. This publication's summary of key points includes the following statement:

> Starting in 1974, there have been a series of economic crises in France and in the whole world. Many people lost their jobs and unemployment continues to rise.

> As in many other countries, suffering (*la misère*) continues to grow in France despite new social laws and the work of many associations to help the least fortunate.
>
> (Boëche 2011 CM2: 79)

This clear statement of the widespread, systemic nature of poverty and the suffering it causes, both in France and worldwide, is typical of the French books. They offer explicit criticism of globalization as being responsible for France's economic decline, and they imply that it perpetuates inequalities worldwide, or at least allows them to persist. For instance, one book dedicates four pages to showing contrasts between rich and poor countries, including two pages featuring photographs illustrating these vast disparities. These images include water use (American sprinklers abundantly watering lush lawns and the adjacent street, versus women carrying jugs of water from a well across desolate, barren land in Mali), schools (children in a dilapidated building, sitting on the floor, looking at a decrepit blackboard in Somalia, versus Swedish children—one of whom is of African origin—in a classroom, each using their own laptop computer on individual desks), and agriculture (mechanized harvest of plentiful wheat in France, versus people bending down to harvest sparse rice crops by hand in Bali) (Boëche 2011 CM2: 138–141). This critique of globalization and graphic depiction of worldwide inequalities seems to constitute a criticism primarily of other countries, notably the U.S., and it perhaps allows France to appear as morally superior to some other Western countries thanks to its commitment to equality. (Anti-Americanism and French claims to moral superiority are discussed in greater detail in Chapter Four.) However, textbooks are careful to point out that there are wealth inequalities and poor people within rich countries including France, as well (e.g., Boëche 2011 CM2: 178–179; Le Callennec 2011: 170–171). In another recent French textbook's critical approach to contemporary global inequality, the authors include a caricature, which emphasizes not only disparity, but also implies that the wealthy countries are benefiting at the poor countries' expense: the cartoon depicts a globe, the top half of which is occupied by two white men in suits, seated at a dinner table where they are clearly finishing a copious meal. They are drunk, waving around glasses of wine, and generally making merry. The bottom half of the globe contains a man of color, inadequately clothed, in an empty room, banging a broom handle on the ceiling (in the hope that his noisy, inconsiderate upstairs neighbors will be more respectful) (Le Callennec 2011: 170). These books thus condemn "consumer society" (*la société de consommation*) for accentuating differences between rich and poor worldwide, and they associate consumer society with the growing wealth gap in France.

Beyond history and geography textbooks, the themes of social justice are also heavily emphasized in French civic education books and lessons and are presented in very similar manners whether in the books of 1980 or the most recent editions. As we will see in more detail in Chapter Four, these books present solidarity as a founding national value and source of pride. The development of the welfare state is presented as a sign of national progress, built on a shared commitment to solidarity and the collective responsibility of the polity (Boëche 2011 CM2: 33; Chevalier and Le Bourgeois 2010: 95; Le Callennec 2008: 98–99; Le Callennec 2011: 45). Social justice is thus presented as a source of national pride and means of truly belonging to the nation. Civic education and geography textbooks or sections of books impart a sense of national community, but are careful to state that this bond should not exclude others, as they also teach students that they are part of the worldwide community. These books highlight the work of governments and NGOs in France and worldwide, encouraging children to participate with regard to many different types of problems (poverty, but also human rights abuses, disability, natural disasters, etc. [Boëche 2011 CM2: 142–143; Chevalier 111; Le Callennec 2008: 39).

These books, therefore, are not radically leftist, as they do not argue that the rich exploit the poor. They do, though, represent a more moderate left-wing position: there is continued wealth inequality, and it is government's, society's, and individuals' responsibility to bridge the gap (both within France and worldwide). They thus emphasize solidarity, rather than antipathy.

However, as we saw in Chapter One, most of the recent books do not discuss recent immigration or socioeconomic inequalities between recent immigrants or their descendants and the rest of French society, in keeping with the colorblind consensus. Only Hatier's 2008 civic education textbook mentions, in a lesson on fighting racism, that racist discrimination can make it difficult for some people to find jobs (Le Callennec 2008: 94–95). They do not, though, discuss inequality as such or the broader effects of such discrimination. Thus, systemic reasons for poverty are discussed, but discrimination and related effects are not, thereby avoiding the (arguably) most controversial aspect of socioeconomic inequality in France today.

In U.S. books, by contrast, more recent poverty has become increasingly invisible over time. In recent editions, problems of poverty and inequality seem to have been resolved and do not appear to be a feature of contemporary society. In the U.S. books of the early 1980s, President Lyndon Johnson's so-called "War on Poverty" of the 1960s figured in all but one (King et al. 1982) of the books. However, the 1982 books take some very different approaches to discussing the persistence of poverty in the U.S. after Johnson's (seemingly successful) campaign. Most mention it in passing (Klein et al. 389) or show it as a marginal problem, affecting only small, specific segments of the population (recent immigrants, for example, or rural areas, such as Appalachia [Helmus et al. 342; King et al. 1982: 130; King et al. 1981: 430]). As we will see, by 2003, however, not only is contemporary poverty not discussed by any of the U.S. books, but only one of the three even mentions the 1960s War on Poverty (Banks et al. 2003: 585).

The salient difference between presentations of poverty in French and U.S. textbooks is not just whether or not it is mentioned but whether it is shown as a structural and societal problem, or simply as an individual phenomenon. In American books, poverty is generally minimalized and marginalized. No explanations are given, and to the extent that it appears at all, it seems to be an individual issue. For instance, the shift of population away from urban centers to suburbs in the mid-twentieth century is a key part of social history and is essential to understanding contemporary demography and socioeconomic inequalities. Yet, most textbooks either do not mention this topic at all or do not present the socioeconomic implications of this shift. This situation, like most of the other examples discussed in this chapter, has moved further away from social justice considerations in more recent textbooks. While most textbooks of all three periods studied here show a general increase in individual wealth as characteristic of the 1950s, it is mostly the older books that associate this change with the move to the suburbs. Yet, even then, the textbooks are often not very sensitive to socioeconomic inequalities. Most textbooks mention the growth of suburbs (Gross et al. 165; Helmus et al. 395, 429; King et al. 1982: 130; Klein et al. 383 from 1981–1982, Banks et al. 611; Bednarz et al. 562; Garcia et al. 501 from 1997, but only Banks et al. from 2003: 569). However, most do not explain or elaborate on this change; they simply present it as desirable, indicating that suburbs offer the best quality of life (as they are quiet and clean, with space for children to play). These books seem to assume that their readership will be middle-class students for whom the suburbs represent a positive, familiar environment. Money does not appear to be a factor in the decision to move to suburbs except in one book of 1980s (King et al. 1982: 130). This is also the only book of any period studied here to discuss the effect of this population shift on cities, and is worth citing as a counterexample:

> Many businesses and services of the cities followed people to the suburbs. As people and businesses began to move away from the large cities, life in the cities changed too. Some city businesses lost their customers. Factories moved away from cities to suburban areas with lower rents. In many neighborhoods unskilled workers were left without jobs. Buildings were left in need of repair. Yet many people could not afford to live anywhere else. Because they became costly to repair, many buildings were left vacant. Entire neighborhoods became run-down.
>
> (King et al. 1982: 130)

However, the book then concludes on an upbeat note, stating: "Many people are again finding it preferable to live in the cities," citing the high cost of fuel and proximity to culture as reasons. This book, like most others, presents contemporary society largely through the lens of leisure time and activities, without commenting on those who cannot afford such luxuries.

The more recent textbooks are not only more likely than older editions to present only positive aspects of suburban development. More significantly, they also demonstrate a clear shift away from discussing contemporary poverty and from associating socioeconomic inequality with the legacy of racism. Textbooks of the early 1980s often present poverty as a consequence of racial discrimination (Gross et al.; Helmus et al.; Klein et al.). For instance, Gross et al. shows a photo of a man in silhouette in a rundown urban environment, who appears to be African American, accompanied by this caption: "If one lacks education and skills and is sometimes discriminated against, finding a job can be a difficult and discouraging task" (351). This textbook also contains a lengthy explanation of how newcomers to cities often have to take low-paying jobs and live in tenements and that many groups of newcomers have been subject to rejection and fear:

> Sometimes groups of people have found that they are not welcome in the city [. . .]. When large numbers of Irish people first came to America from Europe, many people in America were fearful that the newcomers would take their jobs or spoil their neighborhood. Many people did not want to have anything to do with them. Blacks, Jews, Orientals, and others also had to work hard to overcome fear and distrust.
>
> (166–167)

By 1997, only two of the four textbooks studied here mention poverty after the Great Depression, and one of these (Banks et al.) implies that it was eradicated (or in the process of being eradicated) by Lyndon Johnson's War on Poverty. This book does, though, explain poverty in the past in relation to discrimination. In its discussion of life for African Americans after the passage of civil rights legislation, it states: "Many African Americans still suffered from discrimination and poverty. In 1965 almost 5 out of every 10 nonwhite Americans were officially considered poor by the government. About 2 out of every 10 white Americans were this poor" (Banks et al. 1997: 626). This is the only textbook of 1997 to associate poverty and racism and the only one to discuss poverty regarding the Civil Rights Movement: "Poverty and discrimination in the cities drew the attention of many leaders, including Martin Luther King, Jr. King began a new program, which he called 'The Poor People's Campaign.' Its goal was to end poverty for both blacks and whites" (627). The textbook does not, however, show poverty or racism as institutionalized, only as the acts of individuals. This type of explanation is acceptable to conservative groups.

Indeed, most U.S. textbooks do not look at poverty in a systemic way. The older books are slightly more likely to do so, with, for instance, Laidlaw and Gross et al. showing, at least implicitly, the cycle of poverty as linked to subpar education. In discussing the 1950s and 1960s, Laidlaw states:

> Even though large numbers of people moved to the suburbs, other people moved to cities. Most of these people were looking for jobs. Many

> of these people were Puerto Ricans, Mexican Americans, and southern blacks. These people often came from poor, rural areas. [. . .] The poor people in American cities could afford to live only in run-down neighborhoods. They had trouble finding jobs and often received poor health care. Their children had to attend run-down and highly crowded schools.
>
> (King et al. 1981: 430)

Gross et al. emphasizes even more the injustice of wealth inequality:

> While America has a high standard of living, it also has many people who live in poverty. They live in city slums and country shacks. They have little education, little food or clothing, and little hope. There are many who have to live on money from the government. Some are members of minority groups, but most are whites. We need to work on our system to make sure that everyone has a fair chance.
>
> (1980: 351)

By 1997, only one textbook discusses wealth inequality in the contemporary U.S. (This outlier—Silver Burdett Ginn—had by far the lowest sales in Texas [Garcia et al.].) Because this book's approach to this issue is so different from any other, it is worth examining in some detail. The text begins by explaining that "Reaganomics worked in some ways and for some people," leading many to become millionaires (Garcia et al. 541). However, it states, "For many others the 1980s was a time of failure. The gap between the rich and the poor grew larger" (541). The text continues, asserting, "To make things worse, many more people lost jobs during the 1980s," and it attributes much of this job loss to mergers, which increased corporate profits but laid off newly redundant workers. The text also cites the shift from a manufacturing to a service economy, as well as the displacement of jobs overseas (541–542). The book covers this topic further in another section:

> **The Nation Gets Richer.** Like the 1920s, the 1980s was a good time to make money. Business executives earned huge salaries. People enjoyed spending money on luxuries. This spending helped fuel the economy. In the 1980s some Americans saw being rich and having power as important goals. Even those who weren't rich and powerful spent time finding out about those who were. Popular TV shows featured wealthy, glamorous people. Best-selling books promised to help people become successful quickly. [. . .]
>
> There was another side to the story. Not all Americans did well during the 1980s. Twenty percent of American families earned less money at the end of the 1980s than at the beginning. The number of people living in poverty rose from 26 million to 32 million.
>
> **The Nation Gets Poorer.** Joblessness and homelessness became major problems. This was especially true in cities. Many workers lost their

> jobs as industries had work done in other countries with less expensive labor costs. Wages for other jobs remained low, which meant that people had to struggle to pay their bills. Costs of renting or buying a place to live went up everywhere. As a result, more people ended up living on the streets than at any time since the Great Depression. By 1985, hundreds of thousands of Americans were homeless.
>
> (551)

Though it does not go so far as to criticize capitalism itself, this textbook is the only one of 1997 to indicate explicitly that the economic system contributes to inequality and poverty. On the contrary, other textbooks present lifestyles and culture of the 1950s and 1960s favorably, while Silver Burdett Ginn questions materialism and television culture, as—to a lesser degree—do two books of 1980, which warn against watching too much television (Klein et al. 389; Helmus et al. 461). The positive presentation of popular culture in most U.S. books represents another stark contrast with French textbooks, which more often criticize consumer society.

In the U.S. textbooks of 2003, issues of socioeconomic justice disappear even further. The text cited above in McGraw-Hill's 1997 edition is altered in the 2003 edition, where the statement about discrimination contributing to poverty of African Americans is removed (though the textbook still mentions poverty rates for people of color and white Americans [Banks et al.: 585]). The older edition also included a chart showing the persistence of unequal salaries between African Americans and white Americans; this chart has been removed from the 2003 edition. The recent edition does add an activity in the chapter-end questions that encourages a sense of social justice: "Write a paragraph in which you propose a program like the 'Great Society' or 'War on Poverty' to Congress. Explain the need for the program and how it will help" (587). However, this lone indication of a possible need for government intervention is separate from the narrative and hardly accentuates the issue. Overall, the 2003 edition no longer emphasizes the link between discrimination and poverty, thus moving further away from progressive multiculturalism than its predecessor.

The other textbooks of 2003 avoid completely the issue of poverty and socioeconomic inequality. They do not mention Johnson's antipoverty programs or the place of these questions in the Civil Rights Movement. They only mention La Causa and action led by César Chávez and Dolores Huerta to help migrant farm workers. They do refer to discrimination against Mexican migrants in the mid-twentieth century (Berson et al. 588–589; Boyd et al. 648–649), which represents a small victory for multiculturalists. However, this approach limits discussion of discrimination to only one group, and the text indicates that the problem has been resolved.

In further contrast to French books' commitment to economic solidarity, discussion of redistribution is now limited in most U.S. books to the New Deal era, where the expansion of the welfare state is now usually presented along with accounts of skepticism. Notably, when discussing Franklin Roosevelt's New Deal, the textbooks state that unemployment still remained high by the early 1940s (Banks et al. 556–557; Berson et al. 548–549; Boyd et al. 622). Most books add that many people today doubt whether these programs helped to end or mitigate the Great Depression, and that many people believe that government should have a smaller role in the economy (Banks et al. 556–557; Boyd et al. 622). It seems probable that these statements are the direct result of conservative activists' intervention in the textbook production process. Thus, French books largely take for granted that the government runs programs to help those in difficulty, and often state that this redistribution does not go far enough. U.S. textbooks on the other hand mention welfare programs of the New Deal and some protections of Progressive era, but generally indicate that that was sufficient to have solved the problem (and may have made government too big).

In a final noteworthy difference between the two countries' books, U.S. textbooks give positive presentations of globalization, indicating that it is mutually beneficial for the different countries involved, and that it leads to progress for all. Harcourt, for instance, gives a resoundingly positive account of the effects of NAFTA (the North American Free Trade Agreement) for all three partners, the U.S., Mexico, and Canada, stating it has given them all "a chance to compete better," leading to an increased "number of goods and services available to people in all three nations." The text goes on to discuss the global economy, asserting that, "International trade adds much to the economy of the United States" (Berson et al. 2003: 636).

Thus, United States textbooks have come to present the economy as a benevolent force for opportunity worldwide as they have rendered socioeconomic inequality within the country's borders invisible. (Dedication to capitalism is discussed further in the next chapter.)

CONCLUSION

French textbooks of the whole period studied here stress commitment to social justice and show this commitment as a source of pride. These books reserve their final lessons to emphasizing children's responsibility to work toward greater socioeconomic equality, both in France and worldwide. They direct blame for inequality at global (especially American) markets, obscuring the legacy of French imperialism. Thus, a certain anti-Americanism or opposition to global capitalism is combined with official colorblind policies so that most textbooks avoid the most controversial questions of contemporary inequalities and exclusion. Still, curricula and textbooks do strive to transmit a sense of justice that incorporates humanity as a whole. Progressive nationalism dominates French textbooks and seeks to bind the nation together in the quest for a more equal future. This progressive nationalism embraces national self-criticism (again, within the limits of colorblindness) in the service of national self-improvement, and French identity is clearly grounded in a shared commitment to solidarity.

U.S. books, by contrast, have moved further away from aiming to impart a sense of social justice. Once again, this chapter demonstrates that these textbooks have embraced a conservative approach that favors celebration of the status quo over a commitment to a more just collective future. Conservative cultural nationalism—which has come to dominate American textbooks—eschews social criticism as unpatriotic and thus perpetuates inequality in the name of national pride and unity. There may be additional reasons, beyond the political and commercial pressure exerted by Christian Right activists, for the retreat from progressive nationalism. While the textbooks of the early 1980s were critical of the country's shortcomings, they were also fundamentally optimistic that, with effort, the situation could continue to improve. This optimism was, in many ways, misplaced, as the wealth gap continued to grow throughout the 1980s, and racism and sexism have not been eradicated. It seems, then, the more recent textbooks' conservative emphasis does not in fact stem from the optimism that these books project, but rather from a deeper underlying pessimism, from which they shield children.

Part One of this book has shown that French primary school textbooks incorporate many of the methods of teaching history as a discipline. This approach lends itself to promoting progressive nationalism. U.S. textbooks, by contrast, treat history as a shrine, thus promoting conservative nationalism. Yet, in both cases, curricula and textbooks since the early 1980s have sought to reinforce a sense of national unity. They have partly done so via including citizens regardless of their origin, while avoiding discussions of socioeconomic divisions in contemporary society and subtly excluding those deemed "other" along ideological lines, as the next chapter will continue to demonstrate.

NOTES

1. On activism regarding the history of colonization, see Bozec 2010: 169. Studies such as those by Bozec (2010) and Legris (2014) mention efforts by these groups only regarding specific historical topics, not regarding socioeconomic inequalities.
2. Though I am focusing on Texas curriculum guidelines for the reasons explained in the Introduction, I would like to note that the curricula of other states differ slightly on this point, though none that I have found treat issues of socioeconomic equality as a central concern. For instance, the curriculum standards of California (2005; to be replaced in 2015) and Michigan (2007; to be replaced in 2015) barely allude to the existence of socioeconomic differences in their primary school content requirements. In general guidelines for K–12 history and social sciences, the California curriculum framework states that "students need opportunities to examine some of the local, national, and global problems of the nation's mixed economy, including [. . .] the persistence of poverty in a generally

productive economy" (18). The curriculum does not, however, develop this point any further. The New York State curriculum (1999, still in effect as of 2015) is an exception. This document draws on the National History Standards and advocates teaching children a historiographical approach, mentioning several times the importance of comparing different perspectives on events. The Social Studies Overview thus explains: "In examining different perspectives about events and issues and how ethnic, racial, gender, religious, and socioeconomic background can influence opinion, students should understand that all members of a given group will not necessarily share the same view" (1999: 6). Nevertheless, the document gives no further detail or specific examples in the content guidelines for U.S. history in the elementary school years (NYSED 1999).

REFERENCES

For the complete list of textbooks analyzed, see Chapter One.

French Textbooks Cited

Boëche, Sandra, ed. 2011. *CM1: Les Reporteurs histoire, géographie, histoire des arts, développement durable.* Paris: Sedrap.

Boëche, Sandra, ed. 2011. *CM2: Les Reporteurs histoire, géographie, histoire des arts, développement durable.* Paris: Sedrap.

Chevalier, Jean-Pierre and Roselyne Le Bourgeois, eds. 2010. *Histoire, histoire des arts, instruction civique, CM2.* Paris: Nathan.

Le Callennec, Sophie, ed. 2008. *Education à la citoyenneté, Cycle 3.* Collection Magellan. Paris: Hatier.

Le Callennec, Sophie, ed. 2010. *Histoire, géographie, CM1.* Collection Magellan. Paris: Hatier.

Le Callennec, Sophie, ed. 2011. *Histoire, géographie, CM2.* Collection Magellan. Paris: Hatier.

United States Textbooks Cited

Banks, James A., et al. 1997. *United States: Adventures in Time and Place.* New York: Macmillan McGraw-Hill.

Banks, James A., et al. 2003. *Our Nation.* New York: Macmillan McGraw-Hill.

Bednarz, Sarah, et al. 1997. *Build Our Nation. We the People.* Boston: Houghton Mifflin

Berson, Michael, et al. 2003. *Harcourt Horizons: United States History.* Orlando, FL: Harcourt.

Boehm, Richard G., et al. 1997. *America's Story: Stories in Time.* New York: Harcourt-Brace.

Boyd, Candy Dawson, et al. 2003. *The United States, Social Studies.* Glenview, IL: Scott Foresman.

Garcia, Juan R., et al. 1997. *Our United States: Social Studies.* Parsippany, NJ: Silver Burdett Ginn.

Gross, Herbert, et al. 1980. *Exploring Our World: Americas.* 2nd ed. Chicago: Follett.

Helmus, Timothy M., et al. 1982. *The United States and Its Neighbors.* Morristown, NJ: Silver Burdett.

King, Allen Y., et al. 1982. *The United States and the Other Americas.* New York: Macmillan.

King, Frederick M., et al. 1981. *Understanding Our Country*. River Forest, IL: Laidlaw.
Klein, Stanley, et al. 1982. *Our Country's History: Level E*. New York: Scholastic.

Curriculum Guidelines and Official Reports

California Department of Education. 2000/2005. History-Social Science Framework for California Public Schools. Retrieved 19 Jul. 2015 (http://www.cde.ca.gov/ci/cr/cf/documents/histsocsciframe.pdf).

"Chapter 113: Texas Essential Knowledge and Skills for Social Studies." 1998. *Texas Essential Knowledge and Skills*. Texas Education Agency. Retrieved 20 Dec. 2000 (http://www.tea.state.tx.us/rules/tac/ch113.html#s1137).

"Chapter 113: Texas Essential Knowledge and Skills for Social Studies." 2010. *Texas Essential Knowledge and Skills*. Texas Education Agency. Retrieved 5 Nov. 2013 (http://ritter.tea.state.tx.us/rules/tac/chapter113/index.html).

Discours du Ministre d'Etat, Ministre de l'Education Nationale, de la Jeunesse et des Sports [Jospin, Lionel]. 1990. "Une nouvelle politique pour l'école primaire." *Bulletin officiel de l'Education nationale* 9 (1 Mar.): 601–608.

Framework for the Social Studies. 1980. Austin: Texas Education Agency.

"Horaires et programmes d'enseignement de l'école primaire." 2002. *Bulletin officiel de l'Education nationale*. Special issue 1 (14 Feb.).

"Horaires et programmes d'enseignement de l'école primaire." 2008. *Bulletin officiel de l'Education nationale*. Special issue 3 (19 Jun.).

"Horaires, programmes et instructions pour l'école élémentaire, 1985." 1986. *Bulletin officiel de l'Education nationale*. Special issue 1 (16 Jan.).

"Horaires, objectifs et programmes. Cycle Moyen." 1980. *R.L.R. 514–3*.

"Loi d'orientation et de programme pour l'avenir de l'école." 2005. *Bulletin official* 18 (5 May). Retrieved 20 Aug. 2015 (http://www.education.gouv.fr/bo/2005/18/MENX0400282L.htm#loi).

Michigan Department of Education. 2007. Grades K-8 Social Studies Content Expectations. Retrieved 19 Jul. 2015 (https://www.michigan.gov/documents/mde/SSGLCE_218368_7.pdf).

Ministère de la Jeunesse, de l'Éducation nationale et de la Recherche: Direction de l'enseignement scolaire. 2002. "Histoire et géographie cycle des approfondissements (cycle 3)." Collection Ecole: Documents d'application des programmes. Paris: Centre national de documentation pédagogique.

NYSED (New York State Education Department). 1999. Social Studies Core Curriculum. Retrieved 19 Jul. 2015 (http://www.p12.nysed.gov/ciai/socst/ssrg.html).

Proclamation 1994 of the State Board of Education Advertising for Bids on Instructional Materials. 1994. Austin: Texas Education Agency.

"Programmes de l'école primaire." 1995. *Bulletin officiel de l'Education nationale* 48 (28 Dec.).

TEA. 2001. "Interim Statement of Textbook Charges by MLC School Year: 2001." Texas Education Agency. 6 Jun. 2001. Retrieved 29 Apr. 2001 (http://www.tea.state. tx.us/emat/sdinv_mlc.htm).

TEA. 2008. "Interim Statement of Textbook Charges by MLC School Year: 2008." Texas Education Agency. 6 Jun. 2001. Retrieved 7 May 2008 (http://www.tea.state. tx.us/emat/sdinv_mlc.htm).

Works of Reference

Banks, James A. 1996. *Multicultural Education, Transformative Knowledge, and Action: Historical and Contemporary Perspectives*. Multicultural Education Series. New York: Teachers College Press.

Bonilla-Silva, Eduardo. 2014. *Racism without Racists: Color-Blind Racism and the Persistence of Racial Inequality in America*. 4th ed. Lanham, MD: Rowman & Littlefield.

Bozec, Géraldine. 2010. *Les héritiers de la République : Eduquer à la citoyenneté à l'école dans la France d'aujourd'hui*. Ph.D. dissertation, Institut d'Etudes Politiques de Paris, Paris.

CIBC (Council on Interracial Books for Children). 1981. *Guidelines for Selecting Bias-Free Textbooks and Storybooks*. New York: Council on Interracial Books for Children.

Curti, Merle. 1946/1968. *The Roots of American Loyalty*. New York: Atheneum.

Educational Research Analysts. 1997. *1997 Elementary Social Studies Information*. Longview, TX: Educational Research Analysts.

Educational Research Analysts. 2003a. *2003 5th Grade Social Studies Textbook Ranking*. Longview, TX: Educational Research Analysts.

Educational Research Analysts. 2003b. *U.S. History Textbook Standard Review Criteria*. Longview, TX: Educational Research Analysts.

Gabler, Mel, Norma Gabler, and James C. Hefley. 1985. *What Are They Teaching Our Children?* Wheaton, IL: Victor Books.

Gabler, Mel, Norma Gabler, and Neal Frey. 1997. Review of Harcourt Brace and Company, *America's Story*. Longview, TX: Educational Research Analysts.

Giroux, Henry A. 1992. Curriculum, Multiculturalism, and the Politics of Identity. *NASSP Bulletin* 76.1: 1–11.

Hargreaves, Alec G. 2007. *Multi-ethnic France: Immigration, Politics, Culture, and Society*. 2nd ed. New York: Routledge.

Legris, Patricia. 2014. *Qui écrit les programmes d'histoire?* Grenoble: Presses universitaires de Grenoble.

Lorcerie, Françoise. 1994. "Les sciences sociales au service de 1'identité nationale: Le débat sur l'intégration en France au début des années 1990." In Denis-Constant Martin, ed. *Cartes d'identité: Comment dit-on "nous" en politique?* Paris: Les Presses de Sciences Po, pp. 245–281.

Maberry, Barbara. 1997. "Review of 1st and 2nd Grade Social Studies Texts." *1997 Elementary Social Studies Information*. Longview, TX: Educational Research Analysts [n.p].

Mangum, Garth L., Stephen L. Mangum, and Andrew M. Sum. 2003. *The Persistence of Poverty in the United States*. Baltimore: Johns Hopkins University Press.

Marienstras, Elise. 1976. *Les Mythes fondateurs de la nation américaine*. Paris: François Maspero.

NHS. 1996. "United States History Standards for Grades 5–12: Era 9: Postwar United States (1945 to early 1970s)." National History Standards. Retrieved 20 Aug. 2015 (http://nchs.ucla.edu/standards/era9–5–12.html).

Scott, Janny and David Leonhardt. 2005. "Shadowy Lines That Still Divide." [Dossier special] *The New York Times* 15 May. Retrieved 20 Aug. 2015 (http://www.nytimes.com/2005/05/15/us/class/shadowy-lines-that-still-divide.html?_r=0).

Scott, Joan Wallach. 2007. *The Politics of the Veil*. Princeton, NJ: Princeton University Press.

Skocpol, Theda. 1979. *States and Social Revolutions: A Comparative Analysis of France, Russia, and China*. Cambridge, UK: Cambridge University Press.

Schwarzmantel, J.J. 1987. "Class and Nation: Problems of Socialist Nationalism." *Political Studies* 35.2: 239–255.

Viguier, Frédéric. 2011. "The Suburbs." In E. Berenson, V. Duclert, and C. Prochasson, eds., *The French Republic: History, Values, Debates*. Ithaca, NY: Cornell University Press, pp. 262–271.

Wacquant, Loïc J.D. 2008. *Urban Outcasts: A Comparative Sociology of Advanced Marginality*. Cambridge: Polity.

Weber, Max. 1905/1920/2001/2012. *The Protestant Ethic and the Spirit of Capitalism*. Trans. Stephen Kalberg. New York; London: Routledge.

Part Two

Symbols of the Nation

4 National Symbols and Values

National symbols and discourse play a key role in promoting the affective attachment and sense of belonging necessary to perpetuating the nation. This chapter demonstrates that nationalist symbols and discourse have become more prominent in French and U.S. textbooks following decades of public debate over diversity and its implications for national identity. The national values that textbooks thus promote reflect a resurgence of cultural assimilationism in France and conservatism in the U.S.

In France as well as the United States, mass public education was originally established for nationalistic purposes: to legitimize and strengthen the state via the forging of a national identity and consciousness through greater cultural and ideological unity while training future citizens for productive work in a modern economy. Education retains this nationalizing purpose today. Schools are charged with shaping citizens capable of participating in the polity and with perpetuating the national community via affective attachment to national culture and a sense of belonging.

Symbols and myths act as useful shorthand, providing a focal point for who "we" are, what we believe in, and how we came to be the way we are. They act as signifiers of unity, they denote boundaries (literally and figuratively), and they help members envision the nation-state. Symbols can be in the background, quietly, continually reasserting the nation-state's omnipresence (Billig 1995). They can also be more actively used, in ceremonies both large (such as national days) and small (like pledging to the flag). In both ways, symbols provide a shared, physical point of focus, often becoming objects of affection in their own right, as they infuse our lives with a sense of collective belonging. Their meanings—like those of national identity, itself—are open to interpretation, and this malleability allows for their widespread use (Breuilly 1982/1993: 64–68; Elgenius 2011; Eriksen 2007; Smith 1999). National symbols represent the nation-state and unity but can represent different values and different versions of national identity to different people. They can effectively be appropriated by various groups in various contexts to confer patriotic associations upon a variety of objects, people, and ideas. Contesting the meanings of myths and symbols is ultimately a proxy for (and part of the process of) contesting the definition of the nation. Values, as this chapter will show, can also be enshrined, and can fulfill the same functions as myths and symbols.

In many ways, the multiplicity of meanings that can be attributed to symbols as well as the labels used as shorthand for values mean that there is little to no controversy surrounding their inclusion in textbooks in France or the U.S. The nationalizing role of schools is so deeply entrenched in both countries that they have long familiarized students with national symbols, and civic education has continually focused on the political values associated with the founding of the modern state. In the politicized debates over national identity in both countries, there have been renewed calls to reinforce emphasis on these symbols and values, which have not met with opposition.

PRINCIPAL FINDINGS AND OUTLINE

While the books of each country emphasize similar founding Enlightenment values, they define these concepts differently. French textbooks emphasize solidarity as a necessary condition for achieving equality and liberty, thus continuing to promote social justice as a national trait and source of pride. Textbooks published throughout the period studied here (1985–2010) emphasize these values. However, the most recent directives and the lone civic education textbook published since the implementation of the 2008 curriculum demonstrate a significant addition to this collection of national values, as they now also emphasize secularism,[1] or *laïcité*, as a central belief. This change appears to indicate a connection between increased emphasis on "republican values" and concerns over the assimilability of Muslim immigrants and their children, as this chapter will show. Presentations of national symbols and values in United States textbooks reveal similar trends to those discussed in Part One of this book, as textbooks have rejected the emphasis on social justice that dominated the books of the 1980s. They move instead toward conservative conceptions of national identity, notably highlighting capitalism as a fundamental freedom. These textbooks make an ostentatious shift toward visibly displaying patriotism, further indicating the growth of a pedagogy of memory over historical or critical pedagogy. This chapter begins by examining curricula and textbooks' presentations of national symbols, followed by an analysis of the depictions of national values in educational materials.

NATIONAL SYMBOLS IN CURRICULA AND TEXTBOOKS

Both French and U.S. curricula require familiarizing students with certain symbols. The French curricula have undergone a significant change in recent years. Whereas curricula since 1985 have required that students be acquainted with national symbols ("Horaires . . ." 1985: 21), the 2008 curriculum states: "They learn to recognize and to respect the emblems and symbols of the Republic (the 'Marseillaise,' the tricolor flag, the bust of Marianne, the motto 'Liberty, Equality, Fraternity')" ("Horaires . . ." 2008: 19). In light of the emphasis on national identity in Nicolas Sarkozy's successful 2007 presidential campaign, this shift in language might well reflect a reaction against the booing of the "Marseillaise,"[2] in addition to broader trends (Noiriel 2007). (Indeed, Sarkozy's close friend and minister of immigration and national identity, Brice Hortefeux, proposed in 2008 that immigrants be required to learn and understand the anthem, and earlier that year, Sarkozy himself had said that soccer games at which the anthem was booed should be cancelled. Previously, in 2005, members of the French parliament had voted to require schools to teach the song, thus emphasizing the politicized nature of the subject.)

The Texas curricula have increasingly emphasized patriotism and patriotic symbols over the years. The 1980 curriculum guidelines mention patriotism only once, and they do not refer to patriotic symbols at all. On the contrary, their emphasis is on civic competence and participation, and their only reference to patriotism as such is that civic values might be put into "practical application" through "participating in meaningful patriotic activities" (*Framework* . . .: 13). This statement challenges the validity of blind displays of flag waving. The 1994 curriculum guidelines introduce patriotic symbols, but only for first-grade (six-year-old) pupils. They require that first-grade students learn to:

> Identify anthems, patriotic customs, symbols and mottoes of Texas and the United States through songs, visuals, and stories [and] explain the importance of patriotic customs, celebrations, and traditions of the community, Texas, and the United States.
>
> (*Proclamation* . . .: A-11)

Still, the curriculum guidelines emphasize civic values much more than patriotic symbols (as we will see in the next section), and they ground patriotism in practice more than in symbols. The General Requirements for Grades One and Two state that these children should "begin to acquire a personal sense of patriotism through the study of the heritage and traditions of Texas and the United States" (*Proclamation* . . .: A-9).

A significant shift occurs in the four years between this curriculum and the next. The 1998 Texas Essential Knowledge and Skills standards emphasize patriotic symbols as a key component of citizenship education. In every elementary grade level (except, for some reason, third grade), these standards list under "Citizenship" the following requirements: "The student understands important customs, symbols, and celebrations that represent American beliefs and principles and contribute to our national identity." In fifth grade, for instance,

The student is expected to:

(A) explain selected patriotic symbols and landmarks such as the Statue of Liberty and the White House and political symbols such as the donkey and elephant;
(B) sing or recite The Star-Spangled Banner and explain its history;
(C) recite and explain the meaning of the Pledge of Allegiance; and
(D) describe the origins and significance of national celebrations such as Memorial Day, Labor Day, and Columbus Day.

("Chapter 113": §113.7.b.18)

This trend remains mainly the same in the 2010 TEKS, with a few small changes. Notably, the instructions added "landmarks" ("including the White House, Statue of Liberty, and Mount Rushmore") to "customs, symbols, and celebrations," thus expanding the patriotic repertoire. Similarly, they also lengthen the list of national celebrations ("Chapter 113": §113.16.b.17). The 2010 TEKS also add Constitution Day and Celebrate Freedom Week (discussed further in the next section) among required patriotic symbols and events.

Reflecting these changes in curricula, French and U.S. social studies textbooks include increased numbers of national symbols over the past thirty years. In French textbooks (considering in the aggregate history, geography, and civic education books) the number of illustrations in which flags are a focal point or figure prominently increases approximately threefold from 1985 to 2010 (from approximately three per book on average to ten). The books also show increased numbers of images depicting the allegory of the Republic, Marianne, a 1792 illustrated printing of the "Marseillaise" sheet music, a painting showing its composer Leconte de Lisle singing it in an exalted state (Figure 4.1 [e.g., Le Callennec 2011: 21]), the Arc de Triomphe (particularly in association with the liberation of Paris in 1944), and the Bastille fortress along with an explanation of its symbolic importance. From 1985 to 2010, French textbooks have shown an approximately consistent number of illustrations showing David's painting of the *Serment du Jeu de Paume* and Delacroix's *Liberty Leading the People* (see Figure 2.1), both of which appear at least once in nearly all the books of all periods studied here.

Depictions of the French flag have evolved over this time. In the books of the 1980s, most images containing the flag were photographs primarily depicting state buildings, aiming to familiarize students with the institutions of government. These were often flags of the "unwaved" variety (Billig 1995), included either incidentally or to show an institution's national affiliation. In the more recent books, the flag is associated with a broader array of meanings and takes on a more active, present role. The flag is a particularly malleable symbol, as it represents the state and/or the republic but is devoid of specific content as to the nature of the state and interpretation

Figure 4.1 Isidore Pils, *Rouget de Lisle chantant la Marseillaise*, 1849.
Source: Wiki Commons. Retrieved 29 Sept. 2015 (https://commons.wikimedia.org/wiki/File:Pils_-_Rouget_de_Lisle_chantant_la_Marseillaise.jpg).

of its values (Elgenius 2011: 15; Eriksen 2007: 3–5). The French flag now appears often in relation to Charles de Gaulle and the Resistance and in the liberation of France in 1944. For example, it is pictured emblazoned on de Gaulle's 1940 call to resist Nazi occupation or surrounding the Arc de Triomphe during the parade celebrating the liberation of Paris in 1944. It also appears in the illustrations used to accompany discussions on the abolition of slavery in France and its territories in 1848 (see Figure 1.2) as well as the creation that same year of universal manhood suffrage. In this way, the flag, along with these other icons, is a powerful symbol of the state and is associated with key national events. These events are thus highlighted as sources of national pride and identity. This increased emphasis on these symbols seems to reflect the renewed commitment to transmitting "national culture." Yet, there is some distance from these icons in French textbooks, as they now often teach the history of certain symbols in a way that shows the historic importance of their status as symbols. For instance, French books now often emphasize that storming the Bastille was important for symbolic rather than pragmatic reasons in galvanizing support for the French Revolution (e.g., Le Callennec CM2 2011: 14–15). Certain art history lessons analyze the structure of Delacroix's famous painting, thus underscoring that it is a Romantic, not realistic depiction of the events of the 1830 revolution (Chevalier and Le Bourgeois 2010: 53; Le Callennec 2011: 30).

The meaning of the Arc de Triomphe is not as clear as it is for other symbols. The Arc may represent the city of Paris, rather than the nation as a whole. It may be associated with military might, as Napoleon intended. In the photos of the liberation of Paris, it may represent all of these aspects at once. Whatever its meanings, the Arc seems to have its place in this list of national symbols. The Arc overshadows the Eiffel Tower in recent textbooks, in which the Tower appears generally in illustrations of Paris, of the 1889 World's Fair, or in Jean Effel's famous cartoon in which an anthropomorphized Tower wearing Marianne's Phrygian cap stretches out her arms to welcome de Gaulle as the liberator of Paris (Figure 4.2 [e.g., Dorel-Ferré and Dhainaut 1985: 149]).

Figure 4.2 Jean Effel, 25 August 1944 *"Mon Grand!"*

While the number of images of national symbols increases over time in French textbooks, this increase is dwarfed by that in United States textbooks. The number of flags in U.S. textbooks has been multiplied by ten, with an average of 2.5 featured flags per book in the early 1980s, 11 each in 1997, and 25 per book in 2003. Similarly, the Statue of Liberty, which appeared in only two of the five books of 1982, is now featured at least once in large photos in each book. The U.S. books also introduce several new patriotic symbols, including the Liberty Bell (which rang when the Declaration of Independence was first read), Independence Hall (where the Declaration and the Constitution were written), the chair upon which George Washington sat during the Constitutional Convention (which features half of a sun, reportedly prompting Benjamin Franklin to state—as the books all now relate—"I have often looked at that behind the president without being able to tell whether it was rising or setting. But now I [. . .] know that it is a rising [. . .] sun"). The books also feature the Capitol as a symbol of the nation-state and its democratic institutions in Washington, D.C., as well as early patriotic symbols that the first U.S. citizens collected, thus creating a link between contemporary patriots and their forebears. These symbols of the state particularly enshrine the country's founding.

As in French textbooks, the meanings associated with the U.S. flag change over time. For many Americans, then flag has sacred status as evidenced, for example, by existing laws regulating its use and treatment as well as by repeated attempts between 1989 and 2005 to pass a constitutional amendment prohibiting desecration of the flag (see also Billig 1995; Zelinsky 1988: 243). Its increased visibility in textbooks and the meanings attributed to it are thus significant in assessing nationalism and visions of the nation in these textbooks. Certain uses of the flag have remained essentially constant over time, though their frequency has increased in more recent books. For instance, the flag is often shown alone, to acquaint students with the symbol and to signify patriotism in the abstract. It is also associated with other events, objects, or people, thus conferring on them a nationalist significance. In this way, the flag illustrates important moments in the United States' history, such as the American Revolution, advances in civil rights and liberties, and the expansion of national borders and growing power abroad, including the space race. All these events are marked in this manner as examples of progress in the United States, whether politically, militarily, or toward civic ideals. One particular association of the flag stands out for being much more prominent in the books of 1997 than in earlier editions. In these books, the flag is shown in conjunction with various ethnic groups, thus indicating that diversity is a characteristic trait of American culture and constitutes a source of national pride. These books, which included 11 illustrations on average featuring the U.S. flag, contain at least three images per book in which the flag helps celebrate diversity. While this type of image persists in the textbooks of 2003, it constitutes a much smaller percentage of illustrations showing the flag—the books now only contain one such illustration each, out of 25 total illustrations showing the flag. In the 2003 books, the flag is still associated with defining moments in American history, including the advancement of ethnic equality, but many more images are military in nature. These military illustrations also include diverse ethnic groups (as discussed in Chapter One), which is typical of the conservative nationalist multiculturalism discussed in the first part of this book, as well as by other scholars (see Jonathan Zimmerman on minorities' desire to be shown as patriotic members of the national community; 2002).

Overall, then, symbols in both countries' textbooks since the 1980s show a renewed commitment to nationalism and emphasize the omnipresence of the nation-state as the primary framework for current society and past events, particularly those meant to invoke shared pride. Like symbols, the meanings and use of values change over time and shed further light on the interpretations of these symbols.

NATIONAL VALUES IN CURRICULA

French Curricula and Official Documents

Consistent with the historically established role of history and social studies education in forming citizens, curricula in France and the United States include statements on civic national identity. French curricula contain lengthy mission statements that expound upon these themes. Since 1985, with the return to more clearly defined subject areas after the *éveil* years, these curricula have become increasingly explicit, emphasizing the importance of a shared culture for turning the country's diverse inhabitants into unified citizens. As we have seen, this largely consensual, renewed emphasis on shared national identity coincided with growing concerns over and politicization of questions regarding the assimilability of recent immigrants and their children (see Chapter One; Hargreaves 2007; Scott 2007; Viguier 2011). The renewed focus on the stakes of history teaching brought about reflection on the nature of citizenship. The national culture that the resulting curricula advocate is twofold: a civic dimension emphasizes republican values while a cultural dimension stresses French language, arts, and history. For instance, the 2002 curriculum explicitly associates goals of integration with republican values and advocates not a purely civic nationalism but a culturally assimilationist national community. Through these techniques, education is charged with shaping citizens and promoting equality. In the preface to the 2002 curriculum, Education Minister Jack Lang wrote:

> At the beginning of the twenty-first century, the primary schools must remain true to the inspired idea of republican education: to offer all children equal chances and successful integration into French society. [. . .] Two major axes structure primary education: the mastery of the

> French language and civic education. Transmitting the national language is the fundamental goal. Feeling at home in the French language is indispensable in order to access all knowledge.
>
> ("Horaires . . ." 2002: 13)

Similarly, in the preface to the 2008 curriculum, Education Minister Xavier Darcos writes:

> Education is a common good. I have, in the name of the State, the responsibility to define the national curriculum to ensure for all students the equality of access to instruction in order to permit each child to become a free and enlightened citizen.
>
> ("Horaires . . ." 2008: 4)

Jack Lang made explicit the vision that came to dominate curricula from the end of the *éveil* years. The 1985 curriculum, in its renewed focus on transmitting national identity, highlighted civic values as well as language and culture. For instance, its statements on the goals of civic education emphasize belonging to the national community:

> Civic education teaches the child that he does not live alone, that he comes from a history, that he has rights that are recognized, but also duties. Eminently moral, civic education develops honesty, courage, the refusal of racism, and love of the Republic.
>
> ("Horaires . . ." 1985: 20)

The objective here, as in more recent curricula cited above, is not framed in purely civic terms but in terms of emotional attachment and moral obligations, and the republic is not merely a source of rights and responsibilities but an object of love.

Likewise, curricula have placed renewed emphasis on the language since 1985, showing it to be at the heart of national culture. Curricula also state that mastery of the language is the key to rational thought, which they depict as a core value of the French Republic. In addition, the curricula embrace French not only as an instrument of education and the key to accessing national literature and culture but also as aesthetically worthy in itself. The following passage from the 1985 curriculum shows the combination of practical goals—including the integration of immigrants—and aesthetic appreciation for the language itself, and through it, the culture:

> Mastery of the French language is the key to success in primary school. It is, on the one hand, the prerequisite for all learning; on the other hand, it shapes clear thinking, which is organized and self-assured. Finally, it fosters success in social and professional life. That is why it is the first instrument of liberty.

> [. . .] For children for whom French is not the native language, school offers a means of integration into the French community, as well as a culture that is always open to diversity.
>
> For all children, whatever their origin, the French language in its richness and rigor is learned at school. [. . .] This study leads to the discovery of usage, rules, and functional principles: it is the initial access to scientific knowledge. The regulated practice of the language, which allows the necessary space for playfulness, engenders an aesthetic pleasure that is indispensable for initial learning.
>
> Everything should be done to develop students' taste for reading as well as the set of skills that this requires; under this condition, the teaching of the French language allows them to dispose of a rich and diverse language of communication, but also to appropriate the living culture of humanity.
>
> ("Horaires . . ." 1985: 5)

It is noteworthy that this text includes value judgments about the language itself, referring to its "richness and rigor," perhaps as if these were special traits of French, conflating the language as medium with traditional views of French identity as grounded in exceptional rational, universal thought. More recent curricula emphasize this national culture throughout, including in their mission statements regarding art history and literature. (Though they also refer to other works of the Western cannon, the focus is on immersion in French national culture.) Since 1995, curricula have added the requirement to teach about *Francophonie*, the French-speaking world. The 1995 curriculum includes this requirement under the heading "France in the World," thus indicating the persistence of a colonialist mind-set, equating French language with "France" and its international power and presence. Subsequent curricula revise this organization.

A strong case can be made that this emphasis on republican values and national culture is a reaction to the growth of France's Muslim population (see also Chapter One; Brubaker 2001; Lewis 2011; Scott 2007; Thomas 2012). In particular, public discourse and education policy in recent years have increasingly focused on secularism as a core founding value that is explicitly opposed to *communautarisme* (the pejorative term used to describe allegiance to a community, usually ethnic and/or religious, above the nation). Collective memory about the place of secularism in French society has played a key role in defining parameters of public life in recent years. Discourse regarding *laïcité* and the assimilability of religious Muslim immigrants and their descendants has underscored multiple discussions, from controversy surrounding citizenship laws to varied interpretations of and reactions to the *Front National*'s success, to the widely discussed 2004 law banning ostentatious religious signs in schools (Baubérot 2011; Scott 2007; Thomas 2012).

In less mediatized, more consensual ways, secularism has also spurred recent changes in education policy. Contemporary reformers have chosen innovative ways of addressing religion in the history, geography, and civic education curricula, and in education policy more broadly. Amid tensions over national identity and the perceived compatibility of Islam with the values of the republic, education policy-makers have drawn on historical conceptions of education as the antidote to supposed antirepublican religious ignorance. Their rhetoric is at times subtle, referring less frequently to *laïcité* and more often to the increasing diversity of French schools.

However, the relationship between *laïcité*, religion, and education has been more explicitly focused upon over time, and it was defined more overtly beginning with the Debray report of 2002. As discussed in Chapter One, in 2002, then Minister of Education Jack Lang commissioned a report regarding teaching about religion. This report concluded that secondary schools needed to teach about religions to promote a better understanding of history, to improve tolerance and freedom of thought, and to fight against extremism (Debray 2002). The report was careful to state—as was the resulting legislative amendment in the 2005 law on goals and curricula of schools (*Loi d'orientation et de programme pour l'avenir de l'école*)—that teaching about religion required an even firmer commitment than before to freedom of thought and *laïcité* (Debray 2002: 19). This report and this law resulted from decades of debate over the place of religion in French society, but also from the events of September 11, 2001, as Debray stated (Debray 2002: 6).

This report highlights the complexities and ambivalence of dominant attitudes toward religion, tolerance, and national identity. The report aims above all to foster tolerance. However, in so doing, it reasserts the framing of Islam as a problem. The report posits intolerance as intolerable, which is philosophically sound in itself. However, it equates tolerance with *laïcité* and equates *laïcité* with "us," understood as the national community, thus positioning those whose practices clash with the dominant norms as being outside the national community. The text states:

> Secularism is not one spiritual option among others, it is what makes their coexistence possible, because rights that are shared by all men should take precedence over what separates them in fact. The ability to have access to the entirety of human experience, which is inherent to all individuals endowed with reason, implies in so doing that we fight against religious illiteracy through the study of systems of existing beliefs. Thus we cannot separate the principle of secularism and the teaching of religious history [. . .]. Even better: it is important to *begin* with a first lesson on the foundations and duties of a principle that is after all not so banal, that we would be mistaken to believe has become normal practice, and of which the surrounding furies continue to increase the relevance. [. . .] To bring to fruition the projects outlined here demands that public schools be not a little less but be even more secular, grounding themselves from the beginning in a set of values for which they clearly take responsibility, which are no less demanding than

> those of religious believers and which can counter them if necessary. (To each his own credo. We respect yours. Respect ours . . .).
>
> (Debray 2002: 19)

This final phrase, whose direct, simple style differs so sharply from the long, complex phrases that characterize the rest of the report, gives one of several indications of the "us/them" mentality behind this report. This impression is strengthened by Debray's explicit reference to Islam. He attempts to frame the meeting of Islam and France as providing the opportunity to develop a more sophisticated understanding of secularism to replace the clashes between republicanism and Catholicism of centuries past. He thus states, "*laïcité* is an opportunity (*une chance*) for Islam in France, and Islam in France is an opportunity for *laïcité*" (21). Finally, Debray reflects the framing of minority religions as problematic in his suggestion that the government support school principals who are:

> confronted daily with these current issues (refusal to take biology or civic education courses, wearing headscarves, coeducation), for it is they who are primarily led to communicate (*discuter*) with minority groups who invoke presumed religious knowledge to obtain modifications of internal rules.
>
> (33–34)

The connection between *laïcité* and schools as a major locus of integration was the justification for the 2004 law banning ostentatious religious symbols in schools. It was also the impetus for the 2009 and 2010 reports (under the Sarkozy presidency) on, respectively, the knowledge and transmission of republican values and the related report entitled *Les défis de l'intégration à l'école et Recommandations du Haut Conseil à l'intégration au Premier ministre relatives à l'expression religieuse dans les espaces publics de la République* (Challenges of Integration in Schools and Recommendations of the High Council on Integration to the Prime Minister regarding Religious Expression in Public Spaces of the Republic), which advised "a pedagogy of *laïcité*" in order to help "immigrants and the descendants of recent immigrants" (not very subtle euphemisms for Muslims) to integrate and understand that they must not "impose" their religious convictions in public spaces. These issues were again emphasized by the 2015 directive, discussed in the introduction to this book (République Française 2015: 2, 4).

Unlike these official government reports, curricula do not explicitly discuss *laïcité* in their general goals or in the civic education guidelines, focusing instead on civic education more broadly and acculturation. *Laïcité* is only mentioned briefly in the history curricula, beginning in 1985. The 1985 curriculum mentions the *lois laïques* (secular laws) of the Third Republic. In subsequent curricula, this becomes *l'école laïque, gratuite et obligatoire* (secular, free, obligatory education) of the Third Republic, and the 2008 curriculum adds the 1905 law separating church and state. Despite the more subtle discourse regarding secularism, curricula beginning in 2002 seem to adhere to the ideas and suggestions of Debray's report, as the primary school curriculum that was published in the same year, under the instructions of the same education minister, also gave increased attention to historical events tied to religion (which remains in the 2008 curriculum).

Viewing the emphasis on freedom of thought, citizenship, integration, and national culture in the context of the increased emphasis on teaching religious history, including the history of secularism, demonstrates the link between reaffirmed assimilationist nationalism and recent immigration. The increasingly explicit references to Muslims in official documents seems to indicate a shift away from a more robust belief in the power of assimilation (and the attendant commitment to colorblind discourse) in the early 1980s.

U.S. Curricula and Surrounding Influences

Curricula in the United States, by contrast, are generally less detailed and do not include the long mission statements that are common in their French counterparts. Still, a sampling of several states' curricula confirms that they all include statements about the importance of educating future citizens.[3] The Texas curricula are within the norm when they define the aims of social studies in these terms:

> Throughout social studies in Kindergarten-Grade 12, students build a foundation in history; geography; economics; government; citizenship; culture; science, technology, and society; and social studies skills. The content, as appropriate for the grade level or course, enables students to understand the importance of patriotism, function in a free enterprise society, and appreciate the basic values of our state and nation as referenced in the Texas Education Code, §28.002(h).
>
> ("Chapter 113" 1998: §113.2.a.4)

In addition to such overt statements, the social studies curricula also often include connections to citizenship education. For instance, the 1998 TEKS state:

> Students identify the roots of representative government in this nation as well as the important ideas in the Declaration of Independence and the U.S. Constitution. Students recite and explain the meaning of the Pledge of Allegiance. Students examine the importance of effective leadership in a democratic society and identify important leaders in the national government. Students examine fundamental rights guaranteed in the Bill of Rights.
>
> ("Chapter 113" 1998: §113.7.a.1)

This statement remains the same in the 2010 TEKS except that they replace "democratic society" with "constitutional republic." This change adheres to the wishes of conservative activist groups, who reject the use of the term "democratic," preferring "republican" (e.g., see comments by Texas Public Policy Foundation activists in Texas Education Agency 2002).

These curricula also include lists of knowledge, values, and skills under the heading "Citizenship" for each grade level. In addition to the patriotic symbols previously mentioned, the 1998 fifth-grade curriculum focuses primarily on electoral politics, requiring that students understand: "the importance of individual participation in the democratic process [. . .]; the importance of effective leadership in a democratic society; [. . . and] the fundamental rights of American citizens guaranteed in the Bill of Rights and other amendments to the U.S. Constitution" (§113.7.b.19, 20, 21). Each of these instructions is developed in several more specific points (e.g., "the student is expected to explain how to contact elected and appointed leaders in the national governments" [19.d]).

While the headings and most of the supporting points remain the same between the 1998 and 2010 versions of the TEKS, there are a few noteworthy changes. Most remarkably, the more recent document adds that students must "explain the contributions of the Founding Fathers to the development of the national government" (19.a). It also adds "the right to keep and bear arms" to the list of rights with which students must be familiar (20.a). In addition, the 1998 TEKS contained only one instruction that does not relate directly to electoral procedures or to the Constitution: "the student is expected to identify significant individuals such as César Chávez and Benjamin Franklin who modeled active participation in the democratic process" (19.c). This example is removed from the 2010 TEKS, which no longer mention Chávez, thus removing any (even implicit) reference to collective action, protest, and labor unionization as legitimate forms of civic participation. Citizenship skills and values are thus defined in fairly narrow political terms, focusing on electoral politics and a few basic freedoms and protections (discussed further below). The 2010 TEKS also demonstrate incorporation of conservatives' wishes, with their renewed emphasis on the "founding fathers" and the Second Amendment.

The 1998 and 2010 TEKS represent a conservative shift from the older curricula, which emphasized broader goals of self-improvement and development. For instance, the 1980 curriculum guidelines state:

> Although all of public education prepares students for citizenship, the social studies program has the major role and responsibility for citizenship education (iii). [. . .]
>
> The primary purpose of the social studies program is to provide learning experiences for all students that will lead to the acquisition and development of the knowledge, attitudes, processes, and competencies essential for self-development, positive human relationships, and participation in a democratic society.
>
> (1)

The 1994 curriculum was similar, and was also more international in its scope. For instance, it states:

> The goal of social studies education is to develop thoughtful citizens who have the capacities for living effective personal and public lives in the 21st century. Therefore, the social studies program in Grades 1–6 should provide for all students active learning experiences that lead to the acquisition and development of knowledge, attitudes, and skills essential for responsible behavior, positive self-concept, effective interpersonal relations, and active civic participation in a society that is both democratic and international.
>
> (*Proclamation* . . . A-8)

Thus, once again, the 1998 TEKS mark a departure from more progressive (though still nationalist) education, as they present a much more narrowly defined vision of citizenship than their predecessors.

Both French and U.S. curricula frame the goals of education in nationalist terms, emphasizing the education of future citizens and affective attachment to the national community. The French curricula emphasize more than their recent U.S. counterparts liberty, equality, and the quest for knowledge (for the common good and for individual enlightenment, we might infer). This conception of liberty seems to rest on Enlightenment ideals of individual autonomy, for which rational thought and therefore education are essential preconditions. The American texts, one might argue, emphasize a less reflexive vision of nationalism. This impression, as we will now see, is confirmed by an analysis of symbols and values in each country's textbooks.

NATIONAL VALUES IN TEXTBOOKS

Between French and U.S. textbooks, there is some overlap in values, but there are also significant differences in these values and how their depiction has evolved in the past thirty years. In France as well as the United States, founding values are defined in the country's official documents, and these definitions are reflected in textbooks. For their definitions of national values, French textbooks draw in particular on the Declaration of the Rights of Man of 1789 and the Constitution of the Fifth Republic of 1958. American textbooks refer to the Declaration of Independence, the original articles of the Constitution, and especially the Bill of Rights. The French documents (and textbooks' summaries of them) define "Liberty, Equality, Fraternity" as the national credo and refer to specific liberties, such as freedom of speech and assembly. The Declaration of 1789 also defines liberty expansively as the freedom to do anything that does not harm others. The Constitution of the Fifth Republic proclaims France to be "an indivisible, secular, democratic, social Republic." While the American documents (as well as curricula and textbooks) name specific liberties, such as freedom of speech, religion, and the press, they do not offer a broader, more philosophically grounded definition of liberty, as the French legal documents do. This difference has important repercussions for textbooks.

The more recent textbooks of both countries pay increased attention to the founding documents themselves. Where these documents are rarely pictured in the books of the 1980s, they appear in all recent books and constitute national symbols in their own right. Both countries' textbooks thus glorify their official national values. However, how they define these values differs, with significant implications for conceptions of national identity. Similarly, each country's textbooks also present different values and features as sources of national pride.

French textbooks express pride over three types of traits and accomplishments: France's development of and influence over Enlightenment ideas and ideals; the French language; and France's power, influence, and independence on the world stage. We will now examine each of these in turn.

Enlightenment Ideals in French Textbooks

French textbooks throughout the period studied here make sweeping statements celebrating the accomplishments of the French Revolution and establish continuity between the ideals and legal precedents of the time and France today. For instance, in its most recent edition, Nathan cites the French Romantic author Lamartine on how to interpret the Revolution and its legacy:

> "[. . .] Certainly, a nation must mourn for its dead and should not console itself over a single unjustifiably guillotined head; but she must not regret it when this allowed eternal truths. The history of the Revolution is glorious and sad, as is the day after a victory and as is the night before another battle."
>
> (Quoted in Chevalier and Le Bourgeois 2010: 36)

In its summary of the Revolution and Napoleon's reign, this same edition states:

> Between 1789 and 1815, certain decisions transformed France; they show the continuity of the ideas of the eighteenth century. These social, economic, and political changes influenced the following centuries and still mark France today. Some of these reforms are still in practice. These founding ideas constitute our heritage.
>
> (34)

This Romantic nationalist grounding of French civic ideals in the country's revolutionary past already characterized the textbooks of 1985. The books studied here do, however, reveal a shift in their presentation of the history of Enlightenment ideas. The books of 1985 present Voltaire, Rousseau, and company as links in the chain of international intellectual history. These textbooks indicate that the British concept of habeas corpus and philosophers such as Locke influenced the French *philosophes*, and that the American Revolution helped inspire revolutionaries in France:

> From England the idea of liberty won over the rest of the world. In America, the inhabitants of the English colonies also wanted to be free and regulate their own taxation. In 1776, they declared their independence. They were the first to proclaim that men are born equal, free, and that they have the right to happiness. The United States was born.
> (Nembrini et al. 1985: 85)

In the recent books, however, predecessors to French (and Swiss) thinkers vanish, and the American Revolution seems to have been inspired by French events, not the other way around. This change goes against broader trends of expanded international focus in these textbooks, so this more Francocentric approach appears all the more surprising. It is, though, in keeping with the textbooks' emphasis on France as the home of human rights.

As we saw in the previous chapter, the textbooks advocate commitment to a level of socioeconomic equality and solidarity within the nation-state, as well as internationally. They also express pride at this commitment. The history sections of these books emphasize the growth of the welfare state as a major form of progress. For instance, in its most recent edition, Hatier presents the Third Republic in the following terms:

> Under the Second Republic, democracy had progressed with manhood suffrage and the abolition of slavery in 1848. Under the Third Republic, it progressed further with the passage, by the representatives, of important laws. [. . .] Different laws reestablished the great liberties in France: freedom of assembly, freedom of opinion, freedom of expression, freedom to unionize, and freedom of association. At the end of the nineteenth century, republicans defined the civic and moral values, those of the rights of man and of justice, on which the republic should be founded [. . .].
> (Le Callennec 2011: 48)

Fraternity—defined in civic education sections as solidarity, including redistributive justice and the welfare state—is also shown as being at the heart of national identity and as a source of national pride. For instance, in its recent civic education textbook, Hatier states that fraternity is the third word of the national motto (after having presented the first two), adding "it is, then, one of the fundamental values of our country." The authors add that fraternity is the opposite of individualism, in which one only thinks of oneself (Le Callenec 2008: 98). Solidarity, then—including a vast welfare state—is quintessentially French, in opposition to individualism and, one can conclude, unfettered capitalism. This textbook emphasizes fraternity and solidarity by focusing on them in 17 (out of a total of 89) lessons. All French history and geography textbooks, as we saw in the previous chapter, emphasize poverty and the growing wealth gap in France and worldwide and highlight the work of NGOs, as well as the responsibility of governments and individuals to help the less fortunate. These books discuss this assistance to the less fortunate (in France and worldwide) as a duty, and label discussions on the topic as "civic education," thus emphasizing the quasi-official nature of this responsibility and its relationship to national identity.

Where the civic education lessons of the 1980s cited *liberté, égalité, fraternité* as the core national values, more recent books have made the significant addition of *laïcité*. The vehement secularism that has come to dominate much French discourse since the 1980s appears clearly in the recent civic education textbook, which defines these four ideals as the central values of France, explicitly showing *laïcité* as necessary for the protection of the other three values (Le Callennec 2008: 112–113). This textbook focuses in particular on the 2004 law banning ostentatious religious signs in public schools, explaining how it promotes the values of the Republic in schools: "In 2004, a law decided that, to guarantee the liberty of everyone's beliefs, equality between students, and the fraternity of all, neither teachers nor students have the right to wear visible religious signs at school" (113). The explanation is accompanied by the reproduction of a poster in cartoon style of the republican allegory Marianne pasting the text of the 2004 law on the side of school in a community of mixed ethnic groups.

This presentation of the topic demonstrates a major shift. In civic education textbooks of the 1980s, one of the two studied here does not mention *laïcité* at all (Bordas; Hanniet et al. 1987). The other, Nathan, mentions it only briefly and offers a different definition than post-2004 books: in an annotated version of Article 2 of the French constitution, the textbook authors define "secular" (*laïque*) as meaning "There is no official religion," and the commentary emphasizes that all religions are permitted in France (Billard et al. 1986: 19). There is no mention, as in later years, of the restriction of acceptable expressions of religion. Where the 1980s books either don't mention *laïcité* at all or only in two sentences, the 2008 civic education book dedicates a complete lesson to it. In addition, Nathan's 1987 edition only discusses secularism moving in one direction: lack of state intervention in religion. Hatier's 2008 book emphasizes the reciprocity of this arrangement. While history textbooks follow the curriculum and define *laïcité* regarding the 1905 law, they do not dwell on the subject. Their definitions are more similar to that of Nathan's 1987 edition (e.g., Le Callennec 2011: 49).

The vision of *laïcité* that predominates in the recent civic education textbook reflects politicized conceptions present in various government reports (Debray 2002; Haut Conseil à l'Intégration 2009, 2010; Loi d'orientation 2005), and it is largely ahistorical and instrumentalized. Though this is the only civic education textbook published for the 2008 primary school curriculum, it merits attention, as it may well foreshadow coming trends. *Laïcité* has already been emphasized for middle school pupils since 2009 and is set to become an object of focus from the primary grades through high school in light of the 2015 directive on teaching the values of the republic and the implementation of the related new moral and civic education curricula in fall of that year ("Programme" 2015). By omitting the various conflicts surrounding the evolution of secularism in 2004 as in 1905, textbooks give a teleological view of *laïcité*, thereby transforming it from national value to national myth.

Language, Culture, and Power in French Textbooks

Parallel to messages about national values, textbooks have increasingly emphasized other aspects of national culture. In line with curricula, textbooks now focus more on French language as a cultural good that both reflects national prestige and requires protection. Where history, geography, and civic education textbooks prior to 1995 did not mention the French language, recent books express pride over the reach of French in the world and urge students to defend the language.

Since 1995, textbooks have increasingly stressed defense of the language against the power of English. Some books show this situation as a "competition" between the two languages (e.g., Le Callennec 1998: 163). Some support opposition to the culture that the English language—and especially American dominance—promotes (Beyria et al. 2003 CM2: 125). Some advocate preserving French in the name of cultural diversity for its own sake: "This does not mean fighting the development of English but defending cultural diversity in the world: a world in which everyone would speak English and would have the same customs would be a dull world" (Le Callennec 2008: 179). Others defend this same cultural diversity, but in much more militant terms:

> [The *Organisation Internationale de la Francophonie*] is also a way for them [other Francophones] and for us, the French, to defend the diversity of our cultures which are threatened by the increasingly crushing domination of the English language.
>
> (Boëche 2010 CM2: 125)

It is noteworthy that, in neither colonial history nor the history of metropolitan France do textbooks mention the repressive policies of enforcing French as a national language. At most, they state that after the Revolution, leaders decided it would help the country's development to speak a common language—a utilitarian argument that glosses over the means of achieving so-called linguistic unity. The relative silence on this question contributes to reinforcing the impression that French is the natural language of France, thereby further legitimizing the nation-state.

Further emphasizing the pride and importance attached to the French language in these textbooks, to varying degrees, these books indicate that other countries (i.e., former colonies) have chosen to speak French. This information generally illustrates the good relations maintained between France and its former colonies. While shades of colonialist justification thus persist in the celebration of other countries' "choice" to speak French, this recent emphasis on a unified French-speaking world, its linguistic varieties, and shared goals represents a move away from previous more Eurocentric (and Franco-centric) approaches to discussing cultural diffusion. Some books in the mid-to-late 1980s showed awareness of avoiding Eurocentric bias. For example, Nathan, while still Franco-centric, states that other countries' different expressions "enrich" the French language (Hinnewinkel, Sivirine, and Duchesne 1985: 168). Most books of the period, however, reveal persistent colonialist positions. For instance, Hachette's 1991 geography textbook includes this statement on "The influence (*rayonnement*) of France," which is both baldly jingoistic and paternalist:

> France is one of the great world powers. She owes her rank to her economy, but also to her history and the talent of her artists and writers: Victor Hugo, Emile Zola, Jean-Paul Sartre, and Colette are read in the whole world. For a long time, French remained the language of culture and Paris the world capital of arts and literature.
>
> In Quebec, they have spoken French since Jacques Cartier's conquest in the sixteenth century. Until the 1960s, France possessed vast territories in Africa and Asia: the colonies. Millions of Africans and Asians learned our language. That is why, in the U.N., the representatives of more than thirty nations speak French.
>
> Today, French teachers and engineers take their knowledge and their help to the countries that want it.
>
> With the United States, the Soviet Union, China, and the United Kingdom, France is one of the "Great Five" responsible for peace in the world since 1945.
>
> (Nembrini et al. 1991: 15)

Recent books are certainly more uniformly anticolonialist, as we saw in Chapter One. If they still regard the French language as a source of pride, they also adopt a less Eurocentric view of its multiple varieties. Instead of referring to other cultures learning "our" language or "enriching" it, newer books take an approach more in line with sociolinguistics, stating that all varieties constitute French. In the only book of this study to discuss the role of the French language within France (Hatier), this linguistically inclusive approach also encompasses French regional variations. This textbook now states, for instance, that there are different varieties of French within metropolitan France and in the overseas French territories, and that "the French language is made up of all these varieties" (Le Callennec 2011: 176). Similarly, Hatier informs students, "every region of the world has its way of speaking French" (177).

The anti-Americanism—whether implicit or explicit—of these passages on the defense of the French language is consistent with the final category of proud statements that I wish to discuss here: those regarding France's culture, power, and independence in the world. In a variety of ways, French textbooks show France and, to a lesser extent, the European Union as righteously standing up against U.S. hegemony. Textbooks across the period studied here present the formation of the European Union as a concerted attempt to retain independence against the U.S. and U.S.S.R. (e.g., Boëche 2011 CM2: 68; Le Callennec 2011: 80; Nembrini et al. 1985: 147; Vincent et al. 1985 CM2: 106). Similarly, the most recent edition of Hatier, for instance, stresses regular opposition of Fifth Republic France to U.S. power (Le Callennec 2011: 89). The previous edition of this textbook mentioned with pride French opposition to the war in Iraq (Le Callennec 2004: 182). Likewise, in its 1985 edition, Hachette critiqued U.S. policy in Vietnam (omitting its connection to the French Indochina War [Nembrini et al. 1985: 151]).

Similarly, these books emphasize France's economic strength. The books of 1985 particularly emphasize the country's technological prowess, including such images as the Minitel, TGV trains, the European-built but French-launched Ariane rocket launcher, and French astronauts who traveled to the international space station. The books from 1985 to 2011 generally mention the that country is the world's fifth-largest economy, discussing French exports (such as cars and Airbus planes), and stating with pride that France is the world's number one tourist destination, thus linking economic pride to cultural pride.

However, these textbooks strike a balance between expressing pride in France's economic standing and critiquing "consumer society" and globalization for contributing to inequality. As such, they place even greater emphasis on France's commitment to solidarity and defending human rights, as well as the richness of French culture. For instance, in a lesson entitled "France among the Great World Powers," Hatier, in its most recent edition, explains that while France is no longer as powerful as it was in the nineteenth century, it remains disproportionately influential and wealthy relative to its size. The text states that France has only the world's twenty-first largest population and forty-seventh largest landmass: "Yet it is a rich country that produces and exports many riches [sic] (agriculture, industries, and services); it is the fifth economic power in the world after Germany" (Le Callennec 2011: 174). The text goes on to emphasize France's cultural superiority in a paragraph entitled "The Great Cultural Powers":

> American culture influences the whole planet: everywhere, people wear jeans, listen to American music, watch films and television series from the United States, and eat hamburgers. English acts as an international language of communication. Other cultural influences are more specific: Japanese anime and sushi, Italian pizza, Chinese cuisine, Brazilian music . . . France is known for its heritage (*patrimoine*), its ideas (the "homeland of the rights of man"), its gastronomy, its fashion . . .
>
> (175)

This assessment of cultural influences ties together with the anti-Americanism present elsewhere in these books (e.g., Boëche CM2: 125; Le Callennec 2011: 179). Furthermore, this passage is dismissive of and reductionist toward other cultures, whose material objects and quaint foods seem inconsequential compared to France's high-brow intellectual and cultural achievements.[4]

With the notable exception of the recent emphasis on *laïcité*, the French expressions of pride change little over the time period studied. They are rooted in the country's modern history and demonstrate a stable, consensual commitment to the ideals of social justice. The shifts in these books' representations of French culture and identity stem from changed approaches in curricula and textbooks to fighting racism and reducing ethnic tensions within France. On the one hand, this goal takes the form of increased cultural sensitivity and attempts to foster a (multiethnic) French community. The textbooks demonstrate increased attention to avoiding Eurocentric bias when discussing former colonies, turning geographically diverse support for Francophone language and cultures into a source of pride and cultural distinctiveness in the face of Anglophone (and particularly, American) dominance. On the other hand, this goal takes the form of emphasizing more rigid secularism and assimilationism in a way that seems to target and stigmatize Muslims as being frequently outside the national community.

Freedom, Power, and Patriotism in U.S. Textbooks

Expressions of pride in the U.S. textbooks, by contrast, change more visibly in several significant ways between 1982 and 2003. All these books express pride in the country's guarantees of freedom. The most clearly defined aspect of this freedom in more recent books relates to economic liberties, and this emphasis on capitalism represents a notable change from older books. The editions of 1982 and 1997 were already required by the Texas curriculum guidelines to teach about the "benefits of free enterprise" (as seen in Chapter Three). They normally did so in a few sentences scattered throughout the books, most often regarding the economy in the British colonies in North America and when explaining the appeal of the United States for immigrants. For example, in its conclusion to a chapter on life in the British colonies, McGraw-Hill (1997) states:

> Today the economy of the United States remains a free enterprise system in which people run many types of businesses. This legacy of colonial times has drawn people to our country for well over two hundred years. [. . .] Through patience and determination, [the colonists] built a legacy of independence and hard work—a legacy that is still an important part of our country's free enterprise economy.
>
> (Banks et al. 1997: 233–234)

This type of narrative ties together multiple founding myths of the U.S. as a land of opportunity (thanks to market capitalism) and as a nation of hard-working immigrants drawn to this freedom and prosperity.

However, these books also show negative aspects to economic relations in U.S. history. As we have seen in the previous chapter, the books of 1982 and 1997 critique the inequalities and the exploitation of laborers during the age of mass industrialization. In some cases, these books acknowledge that capitalist society in the nineteenth century was built on a less-than-equal playing field. This egalitarian, anti-materialist interpretation undergirds the myth of self-reliance tied to pioneer culture and spirit that these books promote. Scholastic, for instance, explains:

> The frontier offered land, adventure, and a chance to begin again. This pioneering spirit is what made the U.S. grow. It is a spirit passed on to us. It is part of our heritage as Americans today. Pioneer life was not easy. It required strength and patience. Pioneers could not be afraid of hard work. [. . .]
>
> **The New American**
>
> The Declaration of Independence said, "All men are created equal." Still, money and family background gave some people an advantage in the new country. However, on the frontier, there was a new kind of spirit. The pioneers did not believe that anyone was better than anyone else. It didn't matter how much money a family had. There was no place to spend it. It didn't matter how important someone's parents were. Being important didn't cut down trees or put meat on the table. To the pioneers, all that mattered was how well you could shoot, chop, cook, spin, and weave.
>
> As more people headed west, this idea spread in the U.S. A person was judged on what she or he did. All people started with the same

> things: a gun, an ax, a bag of corn, a few pots, perhaps a spinning wheel, and a dream.
>
> (Klein et al. 1982: 198)

This presentation of the pioneer spirit perpetuates a Protestant work ethic (Weber 1905/1920/2012) but does so in a way that criticizes the market economy as we know it today.

All of these characteristics change in the books of 2003. As we have already seen (in Chapter Three), textbooks are no longer as uniformly critical of inequalities during the industrial age. They no longer contain statements like the one above indicating that wealth is often hereditary. Most strikingly, the recent books emphasize the "free enterprise economy" in a way that their predecessors—even those published just six years prior—certainly did not. The 2003 textbooks all include a separate section (of two to five pages) explicitly dedicated to presenting the "free enterprise economy" (Banks et al. 26–27; Berson et al. 632–637; Boyd et al. 18–22) They use this terminology (which is found in the Texas curriculum guidelines), rather than ever referring to the more negatively connoted "capitalism," or even simply "market economy." These sections emphasize the opportunities provided by such an economy: the possibilities for fortune and success, the variety of goods available to consumers, and the fostering of invention. They encourage children to become entrepreneurs, even urging them to start their own businesses now. These texts promote the myth of equal opportunity. For instance, McGraw-Hill added a statement in its 2003 edition that: "This system allows equal opportunity for people to own and operate their own businesses" (Banks et al. 26). Displaying both the myth of opportunity and the attempt to transmit an entrepreneurial spirit, Scott Foresman cites the first female African American millionaire, known as Madam C. J. Walker, and features a large photo of her accompanied by her words in large print: "Don't wait for opportunities to come. Get up and make them!" (Boyd et al. 22).

Above all, these textbooks emphasize that capitalism is a fundamental freedom. Scott Foresman, for instance, uses the words "free" and "freedom" 30 times in four pages of text presenting the "free enterprise economy." To illustrate these lessons, these textbooks show multiple images of abundance and personal wellbeing. For instance, Harcourt shows a quaint scene of a smiling, white-haired woman selling jams outside a red-painted wooden shop in Vermont and an entrepreneurial couple lucky enough to work from home (Berson et al. 2003: 636–637). McGraw-Hill and Scott Foresman show piles of money (Banks et al. 26–27; Boyd et al. 18).

While the definition of economic freedom has become more precise and celebrated over time, other aspects of "freedom" have become more vague. These changes are particularly evident when comparing editions that are otherwise very similar from 1997 and 2003. For instance, in an introductory section presenting the American people, both editions of McGraw-Hill's text and illustrations emphasize diversity, discussing different customs as well as common culture, including values. The 1997 text states that Americans share a belief in "freedom to worship and to earn a living as one chooses [. . .], fairness and equal treatment of people [. . .]." The text continues:

> Most important, you will probably find that people in the United States share similar values about the rights and freedoms they enjoy as Americans. Values are the beliefs or ideals that guide the way people live. Americans also respect the laws and the government that protect those rights.
>
> (Banks et al. 1997: 8–9)

This message of shared values is repeated several times, emphasizing that Americans are united by their shared belief in "liberty and justice for all" (11).

If this text already seems to define liberty rather vaguely, this trend is even more pronounced in the 2003 edition. Here, even the references to such specific liberties as religious freedom disappear, and the only "value" that is explicitly emphasized in the same section is patriotism. After stating that the United States is often described as a "nation of immigrants," and that these immigrants have brought "cultural diversity" to "our country," the text states:

> This diversity can be seen in the many religions, languages, values, and traditions that are found in our nation. Values are the beliefs that guide the way people live. One important value is patriotism, or love for and loyal support of one's country.
>
> (Banks et al. 18)

This emphasis on a vaguely defined patriotism and loyalty is characteristic of the 2003 textbooks and is consistent with subtle shifts in the presentation of pride in the United States' power and influence in the world. The textbooks of 1997 already emphasized the country's growing power throughout the twentieth century and showed the U.S. as a beacon to the world. For instance, McGraw-Hill introduced its final unit, on the U.S. after the Second World War, with a two-page spread including large-print text and several illustrations. This collage features in large, red print Martin Luther King's phrase "I have a dream." The largest illustration, occupying a full page, shows Neil Armstrong in a space suit apparently floating in front of the moon. Other illustrations show a recruiting poster featuring Uncle Sam, portraits of Franklin Roosevelt and Supreme Court Justice Sandra Day O'Connor, and King leading a march. The text reads:

> The dream that Martin Luther King, Jr., spoke of is a dream shared by many in the United States. Yet the American dream has many forms. It is the dream of freedom, equality, peace, and prosperity. It can be as grand as exploring the moon and as simple as buying a family home.

> In the second half of the twentieth century, the United States has become the leading power in the world. From far and wide, people in other countries look to it as a symbol of liberty, economic opportunity, and hope for world peace. The future of liberty, equality, and democracy lies in the hands of the people of the United States.
>
> (573)

The books of 1997 all showed American might in conjunction with universal hopes for peace. Images of American spacecraft, with the U.S. flag prominently displayed, accompanied text on the beauty of earth from outer space and the degree to which all humanity is connected (e.g., Bednarz et al. 530–531; Boehm et al. 634–635).

In the books of 2003, these lessons are similar, but the emphasis is more military in nature, focusing more on security than on Enlightenment values. For instance, after discussing the U.S. response to the attacks of September 11, 2001, Harcourt states:

> As the United States works to make our nation and world more secure, the Constitution will continue to protect our basic freedoms as Americans. Once again the American people are united, working together to make sure that our nation and nations around the world remain strong and free.
>
> (Berson et al. 2003: 601)

We might also note the emphasis on the Constitution's power and incarnation of national identity, reminiscent of the originalism that is characteristic of right-wing movements (Hartman 2015; Lepore 2010). This devotion to the Constitution echoes statements in the curricula and prefigures changes in the 2010 TEKS, with their renewed focus on the "founders." The increased emphasis on military power in this excerpt is not surprising, given the intervening events, but when combined with all the other changes discussed so far, the overall effect is a clear move toward more conservative definitions of national values.

In addition, the 2003 textbooks emphasize select core values explicitly through a series of featured biographies, which present Americans, both famous and unknown, and highlight in the biography titles a character trait or value that each person exemplified. A tally of these values and traits reveals a clear hierarchy and consensus across the three textbooks. "Courage" is by far the most celebrated virtue (appearing a total of eight times across the three books of 2003). "Responsibility" and "Loyalty" each appear at least once per book, and "Justice" or "Fairness," "Compassion" or "Caring," and "Leadership" appear in at least two of the books of the period. Harcourt dedicates one of these biographies to "patriotism" and two to "civic virtue." Beyond these biographies, all the books also emphasize patriotism multiple times in the narrative, showing it to be essential for the national good. Harcourt concludes its presentation of U.S. history with a sub-chapter entitled "Working Together," which returns to the founders to emphasize that American citizens must cooperate to preserve the country and its system of government. Speaking of the founders' intentions, the text concludes:

> The country would need good citizens—citizens who would work for the common good.
>
> Past republics, like that of ancient Rome, broke up partly because the people grew greedy and selfish. To keep the nation strong, Americans would have to keep the spirit that had given the nation its independence and its Constitution. They would need to show patriotism, or love of country. Patriotism is more than simply waving the American flag at special times. The writers of the Constitution knew that Americans would have to be good citizens all the time.
>
> (Berson et al. 643)

The definition of good citizenship provided by these books is a conservative one. They do not promote a critical, progressive patriotism (as many educators advocate). Where the textbooks of 1982 charged students with the responsibility to improve the United States and the world, already by 1997, the accent was less on duties of citizenship and progress that remains to be made than on the advantages and privileges of being a U.S. citizen. Rather than encouraging children to act now to protect the environment (see Chapter Six) or help the less fortunate (see Chapter Three), to the extent that they define responsibilities at all—beyond, simply, "patriotism"—these books and subsequent editions stress respect for laws, voting, and recognizing the qualities of a leader. In lessons on citizenship, the 2003 books also mention "volunteering" but without elaborating on what this might entail, as the older books did, and they mention military service and fighting terrorism (e.g., Boyd et al. 2003: 664). For example, in a discussion on the meaning of citizenship, McGraw-Hill notes, "some citizens, such as General Colin Powell, help defend our country" (Banks et al. 2003: 23). This is a vision of citizenship that not only legitimizes and encourages acceptance of the status quo; it celebrates it. Why should children be charged with a mission to improve upon what is already nearly perfect? This transformation is particularly clear when comparing the final lesson in Harcourt's editions. Its 1997 textbook emphasizes improving the world and human relations. The book ends with a photo of Earth taken from the space shuttle and quotes an astronaut saying that all people on Earth are neighbors. The text comments,

> People's views of our world today depend a lot on where they live. Many problems still cause conflict among neighbors on Earth. But in places around the world people are trying to work together to help solve those problems.
>
> (Boehm et al. 1997: 634)

This statement contrasts sharply with the 2003 edition, whose final lesson stresses capitalism and patriotism. Indeed, rather than being told to strive for cooperation or greater equality, children are now told to love their country and start their own business.

CONCLUSION

This chapter has demonstrated the growth of nationalistic expression in both France and the United States from the early 1980s to the 2000s. Curricula and textbooks from the 1980s onward plainly aim to shape students into citizens not just in the political sense, but also to instill affective attachment to a national culture and impart a sense of belonging to a clearly defined community. The definition of this community has changed, as French textbooks have moved away from Eurocentric positions, and U.S. books more systematically promote ethno-racial diversity. Concurrently, textbooks' claims to national superiority are, if anything, heightened. In U.S. textbooks, the extraordinary proliferation of U.S. flags and other symbols seems to have occurred (at least partly) in direct reaction to conservatives' complaints that the editions of the 1980s and even 1990s, with their supposed "emphasis" on racist oppression, were not "patriotic" (e.g., Jones 1997; Warren 1997). And yet, even in France, where there have not been calls for increased displays of patriotism *per se*, the number of images depicting national symbols has grown. As in Part One of this book, these similar changes point to broader processes of national regeneration that reach beyond the vagaries of country-specific political activity. This more visible nationalism is attributable to increased debates over national identity in the wake of social and demographic changes. In addition, in the case of France, certain expressions of nationalism reflect a defensive stance against the country's loss of power, particularly to U.S. hegemony, but perhaps also regarding the loss of France's empire. As such, French assertions of pride focus on cultural superiority, continued power and influence in the world, and moral superiority in the form of commitment to social justice as a brake on the unfettered capitalism associated with the American model.

The comparison of the two countries' curricula and textbooks highlights several significant differences regarding the basis of their national identities and the evolution of their nationalism. Both countries' textbooks have expressed pride in their national culture consistently over the period studied. French national pride—in the 1980s as in the 2010s—rests on a collective self-conception as bearers of a humanist tradition. The recent books (more than those of the 1980s) recognize that the country has not always lived up to this ideal in the past. However, as we also saw in Chapter Three, they only very rarely indicate that ideals of equality and solidarity may not always be met today. In this way, the more recent books often avoid the most controversial issues at the heart of contemporary debates over national identity while adhering to official colorblind discourse. Similarly, the recent emphasis on *laïcité* (which is subtle in history textbooks, but prominent in the lone recent civic education textbook) reflects this firm assimilationism. Yet these books have a strong aspirational focus on building a better future through commitment to these ideals, and the critical stance that they take on discrimination in French history might prepare students to be more critical of contemporary issues.

Where French books clearly posit that a degree of socioeconomic equality and the solidarity that makes redistribution possible are necessary to maintaining liberty, U.S. books define both liberty and equality much more narrowly as political rights to representation and equality before the law. In this view "freedom" is allied with more conservative rhetoric, where belief in "liberty" justifies rejection of government efforts to redistribute wealth.

Both countries' textbooks turn values into symbols of national identity. Yet the values that receive the most attention and that inspire the most praise in textbooks point to different conceptions of national identity and goals for the country's future. In French textbooks, though equality, liberty, and (increasingly) *laïcité* also hold symbolic weight, the dominant such value is solidarity. Solidarity becomes a symbol, source of collective pride, and the primary vector for maintaining current status and achieving future national greatness. It is the ideal that binds the nation through time and holds the promise of France's continued existence as a unique, exceptional community. In U.S. textbooks, "freedom" is that symbol. These conceptual symbols are perhaps more powerful than flags or other icons, which stand for unity but whose meaning is more clearly hollow. In both of these cases, the interpretation of these values is malleable. In France, a symbolically charged commitment to solidarity could obscure differences within the national polity. In the U.S., freedom is now defined as the special province of capitalism. It therefore seems that U.S. textbooks associate national iconography as well as ideology with patriotism of the right.

Despite these differing values, French and U.S. curricula and textbooks share a renewed emphasis on national symbols and discourse, which promote civic loyalty to the nation-state. However, as the next chapter shows, they diverge in how they present another major nationalist resource—heroes.

NOTES

1. Some French scholars contend that the term *laïcité* is untranslatable, arguing that it is uniquely French (Scott 2007: 15; see also A. Goldhammer's translation of Baubérot 2011). This logic seems to me to be caught up in particularist, nationalist thought. As such, I will employ the English term "secularism" interchangeably with the French *laïcité*.
2. The *Marseillaise* has been met with booing at several soccer matches, ostensibly from second- and third-generation French citizens of Algerian origin. The

first highly remarked incident occurred in October 2001 at a friendly match opposing France and Algeria in the *Stade de France* outside Paris.

3. See, for instance: California 2000/2005; Massachusetts 2003; Michigan 2007; NYSED (1999).
4. Regarding the "Americanization" of the world, see for example: Guéhenno (1999). Regarding anti-Americanism, see for instance: Meunier (2006). This assessment corroborates Vincent Martigny's conclusions concerning anti-Americanism and French cultural nationalism (2012: 447–540).

REFERENCES

For the complete list of textbooks analyzed, see Chapter One.

French Textbooks Cited

Beyria, Patrick, et al. 2003. *A Nous le monde! Cycle 3, 3e année, CM2: Histoire, géographie, sciences, éducation civique.* Paris: Sedrap.

Billard, Jacques, et al. 1986. *Education civique CM: "Vivre ensemble."* Paris: Nathan.

Boëche, Sandra, ed. 2011. *CM2: Les Reporteurs histoire, géographie, histoire des arts, développement durable.* Toulouse: Sedrap.

Chevalier, Jean-Pierre and Roselyne Le Bourgeois, eds. 2010. *Histoire, histoire des arts, instruction civique, CM2.* Paris: Nathan.

Dorel-Ferré, Gracia and M. Dhainaut. 1985. *Cours moyen: Histoire.* Paris: Armand Colin.

Hanniet, J.-P., et al. 1987. *Education civique, CM1, CM2.* Paris: Bordas.

Hinnewinkel, Jean-Claude, Jean-Michel Sivirine, and Anne Duchesne. 1985. *CM Géographie.* Paris: Nathan.

Le Callennec, Sophie, ed. 1998. *Histoire-géographie, Cycle 3, niveau 3, CM2.* Paris: Hatier.

Le Callennec, Sophie, ed. 2004. *Histoire, géographie, CM2, Cycle 3.* Collection Magellan. Paris: Hatier.

Le Callennec, Sophie, ed. 2008. *Education à la citoyenneté, Cycle 3.* Collection Magellan. Paris: Hatier.

Le Callennec, Sophie, ed. 2011. *Histoire, géographie, CM2.* Collection Magellan. Paris: Hatier.

Nembrini, Jean-Louis, Pierre Polivka, and Jean Bordes. 1985. *Histoire CM.* Pour connaître la France. Paris: Hachette écoles.

Nembrini, Jean-Louis, Pierre Polivka, and Jean Bordes. 1985/1991. *Géographie CM.* Collection Pour connaître la France. Paris: Hachette écoles.

Vincent, Marc, et al. 1985. *CM2: Histoire: La France au fil du temps, de 1789 à nos jours.* Collection Télémaque. Paris: Nathan.

United States Textbooks Cited

Banks, James A., et al. 1997. *United States: Adventures in Time and Place.* New York: Macmillan McGraw-Hill.

Banks, James A., et al. 2003. *Our Nation.* New York: Macmillan McGraw-Hill.

Bednarz, Sarah, et al. 1997. *Build Our Nation. We the People.* Boston, MA: Houghton Mifflin

Berson, Michael, et al. 2003. *Harcourt Horizons: United States History.* Orlando, FL: Harcourt.

Boehm, Richard G., et al. 1997. *America's Story: Stories in Time*. New York: Harcourt-Brace.
Boyd, Candy Dawson, et al. 2003. *The United States, Social Studies*. Glenview, IL: Scott Foresman.
Klein, Stanley, et al. 1982. *Our Country's History: Level E*. New York: Scholastic.

Curriculum Guidelines and Official Reports

California Department of Education. 2000/2005. History-Social Science Framework for California Public Schools. Retrieved 19 Jul. 2015 (http://www.cde.ca.gov/ci/cr/cf/documents/histsocsciframe.pdf).
"Chapter 113: Texas Essential Knowledge and Skills for Social Studies." 1998. *Texas Essential Knowledge and Skills*. Texas Education Agency. Retrieved 20 Dec. 2000 (http://www.tea.state.tx.us/rules/tac/ch113.html#s1137).
"Chapter 113: Texas Essential Knowledge and Skills for Social Studies." 2010. *Texas Essential Knowledge and Skills*. Texas Education Agency. Retrieved 5 Nov. 2013 (http://ritter.tea.state.tx.us/rules/tac/chapter113/index.html).
Debray, Régis. 2002. L'enseignement du fait religieux dans l'Ecole laïque, Rapport au Ministre de l'Education Nationale.
Framework for the Social Studies. 1980. Austin: Texas Education Agency.
Haut Conseil à l'Intégration. 2009. Faire connaître les valeurs de la République: Faire connaître, comprendre et respecter les valeurs et symboles de la République et organiser les modalités d'évaluation de leur connaissance. Avis à Monsieur le ministre de l'immigration, de l'intégration, de l'identité nationale et du développement solidaire. Paris: République Française.
Haut Conseil à l'Intégration. 2010. Rapport au Premier Ministre pour l'année 2010: Les Défis de l'intégration à l'école et Recommandations du Haut Conseil à l'intégration au Premier minister relatives à l'expression religieuse dans les espaces publics de la République. Paris: République Française.
"Horaires et programmes d'enseignement de l'école primaire." 2002. *Bulletin officiel de l'Education nationale*. Special issue 1 (14 Feb.).
"Horaires et programmes d'enseignement de l'école primaire." 2008. *Bulletin officiel de l'Education nationale*. Special issue 3 (19 June).
"Horaires, objectifs et programmes. Cycle Moyen." 1980. R.L.R. 514-3.
"Horaires, programmes et instructions pour l'école élémentaire, 1985." 1986. *Bulletin officiel de l'Education nationale*. Special issue 1 (16 Jan.).
"Loi d'orientation et de programme pour l'avenir de l'école." 2005. *Bulletin official* 18 (5 May). Retrieved 20 Aug. 2015 (http://www.education.gouv.fr/bo/2005/18/MENX0400282L.htm#loi).
Massachusetts Department of Education. 2003. Massachusetts History and Social Science Curriculum Framework. Retrieved 19 Jul. 2015 (doe.mass.edu).
Michigan Department of Education. 2007. Grades K-8 Social Studies Content Expectations. Retrieved 19 Jul. 2015 (https://www.michigan.gov/documents/mde/SSGLCE_218368_7.pdf).
Ministère de la Jeunesse, de l'Éducation nationale et de la Recherche: Direction de l'enseignement scolaire. 2002. "Histoire et géographie cycle des approfondissements (cycle 3)." Collection Ecole: Documents d'application des programmes. Paris: Centre national de documentation pédagogique.
NYSED (New York State Education Department). 1999. Social Studies Core Curriculum. Retrieved 19 Jul. 2015 (http://www.p12.nysed.gov/ciai/socst/ssrg.html).
Proclamation 1994 of the State Board of Education Advertising for Bids on Instructional Materials. 1994. Austin: Texas Education Agency.

"Programmes de l'école primaire." 1995. *Bulletin officiel de l'Education nationale* 48 (28 Dec.).

"Programme d'enseignement moral et civique." 2015. *Bulletin officiel* 6 (25 Jun.). Retrieved 7 Jul. 2015 (http://www.education.gouv.fr/pid25535/bulletin_officiel.html?cid_bo=90158).

République Française. 2015. Grande mobilisation de l'Ecole pour les valeurs de la République. Retrieved 26 Feb. 2015 (http://cache.media.education.gouv.fr/file/01-janvier/49/4/2015_DP_mobilisation_Ecole_complet_385494.pdf).

Texas Education Agency. 2002. "Transcript of July 17, 2002 Public Hearing Before the State Board of Education." Retrieved 23 Aug. 2003 (http://www.tea.state.tx.us/textbooks/proclamations/proc2000/july17hearing.pdf).

Works of Reference

Baubérot, Jean. 2011. "Laicity." In E. Berenson, V. Duclert, and C. Prochasson, eds. Trans. A. Goldhammer. *The French Republic: History, Values, Debates*. Ithaca, NY: Cornell University Press, pp. 127–135.

Billig, Michael. 1995. *Banal Nationalism*. London: Sage.

Breuilly, John. 1982/1993. *Nationalism and the State*. 2nd ed. Chicago: University of Chicago Press.

Elgenius, Gabriella. 2011. *Symbols of Nations and Nationalism: Celebrating Nationhood*. Houndmills, UK: Palgrave Macmillan.

Eriksen, Thomas Hylland. 2007. "Some Questions About Flags." In T.H. Eriksen and Richard Jenkins, eds., *Flag, Nation and Symbolism in Europe and America*. London: Routledge: 1–13.

Guéhenno, Jean-Marie. 1999. "Américanisation du monde ou mondialisation de l'Amérique?" *Politique Etrangère* 64.1: 7–20.

Hargreaves, Alec G. 2007. *Multi-ethnic France: Immigration, Politics, Culture, and Society*. 2nd ed. New York; London: Routledge.

Jones, Jeanie. 1997. "Reviews of 5th Grade U.S. History Texts." *1997 Elementary Social Studies Information*. Longview, TX: Educational Research Analysts.

Lepore, Jill. 2010. *The Whites of Their Eyes: The Tea Party's Revolution and the Battle over American History*. Princeton, NJ: Princeton University Press.

Martigny, Vincent. 2012. *Le Nationalisme culturel français: Récit national et usages politiques de la culture en France (1981–1995)*. PhD dissertation, Institut d'Etudes Politiques de Paris.

Meunier, Sophie. 2006. "The Distinctiveness of French Anti-Americanism." In Peter J. Katzenstein and Robert O. Keohane, eds., *Anti-Americanisms in World Politics*. Ithaca, NY: Cornell University Press, pp. 129–156.

Noiriel, Gérard. 2007. *A quoi sert « l'identité Nationale »*. Marseille: Agone.

Scott, Joan Wallach. 2007. *The Politics of the Veil*. Princeton, NJ: Princeton University Press.

Smith, Anthony D. 1999. *Myths and Memories of the Nation*. Oxford: Oxford University Press.

Warren, Carol. 1997. "Reviews of 5th Grade U.S. Social Studies Texts." *1997 Elementary Social Studies Information*. Longview, TX: Educational Research Analysts.

Weber, Max. 1905/1920/2001/2012. *The Protestant Ethic and the Spirit of Capitalism*. Trans. Stephen Kalberg. New York: Routledge.

5 National Heroes

Founding heroes are a key element of national identity, whose stories provide direction, meaning, and cohesion to the national community. Long after they have played roles in establishing the modern nation, they serve as symbols of national values and greatness, and they act as models for the citizenry to emulate.

This chapter demonstrates that, in the wake of 1960s social and epistemological changes, the place of national heroes in history education has evolved very differently in France and the United States. This divergence presents one of the clearest indicators that French textbooks have moved toward treating history as a discipline while U.S. books have increasingly embraced pedagogy of memory, in line with more conservative nationalism.

Heroes are more than simple historical figures, yet they are different from other types of national myths and symbols: they are incarnations of the nation, meeting a psychological need for identification with people one admires and helping to provide a sense of community in the process. They represent the beliefs that a community holds about itself, thus reflecting and reinforcing members' self-image and sense of belonging to a group (Campbell 2008; Porpora 1996: 209–210; Zelinsky 1988: 20, 21, 28). In addition, most often, they are perceived as having made personal sacrifices (frequently including martyrdom) for the sake of the nation, thus justifying the national idea: if such great and good people are willing to give so much to defend or promote the nation, then we must treasure it.

The symbolic and pedagogical power of heroes was recognized by early nationalists, who put edifying tales of "great men" at the center of national history education. In France, hagiography predates the modern state and was very deliberately developed during the Revolutionary era in order to foster a sense of national republican consciousness and identity (Amalvi 2011; Bell 2001/2003: 107–139). The place of national heroes in history education was reaffirmed and heightened with Jules Ferry's expansion of public education and late nineteenth-century policies aimed at turning "peasants into Frenchmen" (Weber 1976), aided by the long-lived commercial success of *Le Tour de France par deux enfants* by Augustine Fouillée (under the pseudonym G. Bruno) first published in 1877, which celebrated the heroes of the French Republic and was a staple of classrooms of the Third Republic until the First World War.

Similarly, in the U.S., even as the Revolution was still ongoing, its heroes fueled the national imaginary (Schwartz 1987; Zelinsky 1988: 30). Teaching about their lives and showing them as models of good citizenship and sources of patriotism quickly became the norm, as evidenced, for instance, by Mason ("Parson") Weems' extraordinarily popular (largely apocryphal) biography of Washington, first published in 1800, and Noah Webster's more accurate, though no less glowing, accounts of Washington's role in U.S. history in his schoolbooks. Thus, from the late eighteenth century, and increasingly through the nineteenth century, public education in both countries relied heavily on biographies and stories of national heroes to instill in children values, character, and a sense of belonging to the nation.

However, from the 1960s onward, historians came to reject the "great men" approach to history. These historiographical shifts led to controversy over the place of heroes in history teaching in France as well as the U.S. The ensuing debates, though, have taken different forms in each country and have led to different outcomes.

These controversies are not only over whether to focus on heroes, but also over which heroes and what they represent. Like other symbols and myths, heroes are subject to vastly different interpretations. Opposing groups of citizens may champion different heroes, or they may seek to appropriate the same figures for different causes. Where the national flag or other more content-neutral symbols can be appropriated by different groups for different purposes, the historical meaning of these symbols as such is not generally called into question: the flag stands for the nation-state, however defined. National heroes, however, are by nature more controversial. The very act of admiring heroes tends to idealize them. Their lives are simplified; the complexities that characterize human interaction—the study of which largely defines history as a discipline—are erased from popular conceptions and memory (on this simplification, see Zelinsky 1988: 21).

France turned away from teaching history as a succession of great events by great men after the 1960s (Amalvi 2011). This shift reflected historians' influence over history education, as well as broader pedagogical trends as embodied by the *éveil* methods of the 1970s. In addition, the memory of the Vichy government and Marshal Pétain's overt nationalist manipulations of school curricula most likely contributed to public wariness regarding hagiography in the post-war years. However, in the early 1980s as historians and politicians alike called for a return to transmitting national identity through history education, they included certain traditional heroes among the cultural references children should learn.[1]

U.S. textbooks certainly also moved away from older models centered on glowing accounts of traditional heroes of the nation. However, they did not incorporate as much social history as did their French counterparts, as previous chapters in this book have demonstrated. In addition to the differences in curricula and textbook production that give popular history a larger role in U.S. educational materials than in France, the place of heroes in U.S. history teaching has never been questioned to the extent that it has been in France. Throughout the American "culture wars," there have never been significant calls to stop teaching about national heroes, though there have been calls to teach about them in a different manner.[2] Particularly as regards elementary education, there is general agreement among educational actors that heroes play an important pedagogical role. There is some disagreement, however, over which heroes children should learn about and how they should be represented.

PRINCIPAL FINDINGS AND OUTLINE

French curricula and textbooks reflect the search for balance between wishing to transmit national culture and aiming to teach history in a way that is consistent with the academic discipline. On the whole, they have increasingly rejected heroic accounts and now present most key national figures as historical subjects, revealing their complexities and contradictions.[3] There are, however, significant exceptions to this generalization, as certain tropes of national memory remain. U.S. textbooks, on the other hand, have continued to transmit mythical visions of certain national heroes, clearly approaching this aspect of history education for the primary schools as a vector of national memory and culture. The focus on traditional founding heroes has grown in more recent curricula and textbooks, thus reflecting the rightward shift we have seen in previous chapters.[4]

This chapter begins by examining curricula instructions regarding historic individuals. It then provides an overview of the people regularly pictured in illustrations, considering the types of people thus featured and the nature of textbooks' presentations of them. Finally, I examine in more detail textbooks' evolving approaches to the most prominent people.

CURRICULA

In the period studied here, curricula in both France and the United States have become increasingly specific in mentioning individual people to be included in history lessons, reflecting growing commitment to transmitting traditional aspects of cultural memory. However, the forms that this process has taken and the impetus behind it are different in the two countries, as French curricula have been shaped more by historians, while the increased influence of citizen activists and politicians in Texas has led to curriculum guidelines that use increasingly celebratory language about individuals in the country's past.

In France, since the implementation of the 1985 curriculum reinstating history teaching as a separate subject in primary school, the Education

Ministry's guidelines have become increasingly specific and detailed, continually adding names with which students should be acquainted and emphasizing the importance of studying individuals. The very brief curriculum of 1985 only mentioned periods with which students should be familiar, just twice defining these periods in terms of political leaders ("the monarchy and formation of the state from Philippe Auguste to Louis XI"; "the era of Napoleon Bonaparte" ["Horaires . . ." 1985: 19). Otherwise, this curriculum does not mention any specific names, leaving the choice of focus largely up to individual teachers (and textbook writers) and more importantly, reflecting a vision of history teaching grounded not in individual actors but in the *longue durée*, with only a few key events standing out, marking the turning points from one period to the next.

The curriculum of 1995 marks a clear shift toward transmitting national culture, as it explicitly lists 20 names of people with whom students should be familiar by the end of primary school. The 2002 curriculum keeps this list and adds to it, giving 14 names that students are required to know and another 21 suggested figures, among whom educators can select those they wish to study (Ministère . . . 2002; "Programmes . . ." 1995). The more concise 2008 curriculum removes 15 names from the 2002 list (adding five new ones), for a net decline, down to 25 people ("Horaires . . ."). Overall, we must bear in mind that this pedagogical shift did not entail a full retreat to pre-1960s political and military history, and social history remains prominent in the curricula and textbooks.

In addition to the numerical increase of listed people, since 1995, the French curricula make increasingly explicit the nationalistic aims of teaching about well-known individuals. The curriculum guidelines of 2002 are particularly expansive on the subject and are worth quoting at length:

> **Major Figures and Anonymous Groups: Women's Place in History**
>
> Each era has been marked by several major figures, not only heads of state or great military leaders, but also writers, poets, painters, musicians, scientists, and inventors. Some, like Victor Hugo or Marie Curie, have been selected for multiple reasons. These figures are presented to students both as special witnesses of their time and as individuals with exceptional lives, whose personalities or exemplary behavior can be emphasized in terms of values. By the end of primary school, students should already be familiar with several of them, constituting a first cultural "pantheon" which will continue through middle school. These references can vary somewhat according to region, language studied, and even from one school to another. The names are presented here as indications, as a foundation that can be used in other subjects, or to foster reflection on civic education, such as Gandhi or Martin Luther King's non-violence. Whenever possible, the role of women in

> public life should be highlighted, all the while pondering their relative absence. Similarly, an effort should be made to show, in relation to different events or the day-to-day life of a given period, the role of more anonymous groups, whether social (knights), gender (women during the Revolution), or by age group. Thus, thinking about the lives of children in different eras can provide a change of scenery and be a means of comparison.
>
> We have been attentive not to limit the selection only to French figures, though they normally make up the great majority of people to be studied. Here again, the list is deliberately very long, without aiming to be exhaustive: figures that should be known to everyone are indicated in bold print. These men, women, and groups, (and this also applies to events) can be presented through narratives of the time and can also help teachers to "tell the story" of history.
>
> (Ministère . . . 2002: 8–9)

Though the exact meaning of "pantheon" is unclear, it seems to imply admiration, not just familiarity with national culture. The ministry strives, however, to leave the specific contents of that "pantheon" somewhat open, allowing teachers to skip certain suggested figures and substitute others. This individualistic approach is also tempered by a stated commitment to social history. As discussed in previous chapters, the 2008 curriculum (written with great secrecy under Education Minister Xavier Darcos and without the usual involvement of historians), removes these complex explanatory passages. It thus gives less weight to social history, women's history, and the small amount of pluralism that the 2002 guidelines allow. Instead, the 2008 curriculum states: "The events and people listed here in italics constitute indispensable points of reference, to which the teacher may add according to his or her pedagogical choices. Pillars of national history, they form the basis of a shared culture" ("Horaires . . .": 24).

By contrast, Texas curriculum guidelines of 1980, 1994, and 1998 require teaching about "significant individuals" but do not emphasize heroism, and neither do they discuss any wider purpose in teaching about these people. Like the French curricula, though, Texas guidelines have become more specific over the years, adding names of people to be taught. In the 1980 document, no one is mentioned by name. For the elementary program, only general goals and objectives are outlined ("Citizenship Education," "Crime Prevention and Drug Education," "Economic Education," "Career Education," and "Multicultural Education" [*Framework* . . . 1980: 13–14]), and teaching about individuals is only mentioned in conjunction with multicultural education:

> Content should be organized for: [. . .] examining the historic record of individuals from many groups whose achievements helped build a state and nation [. . .]. Support for the multicultural theme may include: [. . .]

> identifying specific contributions of individuals and groups representing various cultures in American society.
>
> (*Framework* . . . 1980: 15)

The broader implications of these statements regarding multiculturalism are discussed in Chapter One. For our present purposes, it is significant to note that while the curriculum requires teaching about individuals and their actions, it does not give any specific names. The same is true regarding the secondary school curriculum of 1980, which requires teaching about key figures of U.S. history but gives no examples. Perhaps this lack of detail indicates a sense that there was widespread agreement over who these key figures were, so that it was not necessary to list them.

By 1994, the curriculum guidelines are more extensive and specific, though they still list no names for fifth grade (however, lists and examples of important people for the previous grades surely indicate the authors' intentions and assumptions about who should be included in the fifth-grade U.S. history course). The fifth-grade history curriculum guidelines require students to: "identify significant Americans of various racial, ethnic, and cultural groups who contributed to change in the United States (e.g., explorers, statesmen, reformers, inventors, military leaders, entertainers, sports figures, literary figures)" (*Proclamation* . . . 1994: A-24).

The 1998 guidelines (the Texas Essential Knowledge and Skills, or TEKS), by contrast, are much more detailed, mentioning by name or by category people to be studied. As a reminder, the 1998 TEKS were more directly influenced by the elected State Board of Education and its appointed advisors than were previous curricula. The language in the guidelines, however, is vague enough that these specific figures do not have to be included in textbooks, and the list is not exhaustive. The general instructions require the following:

> An overview of major events and significant individuals of the late-19th century and the 20th century is provided. [. . .] Students describe customs and celebrations of various racial, ethnic, and religious groups in the nation and identify the contributions of famous inventors and scientists.

In descriptions of different eras, the TEKS list examples of key figures. For instance,

> [. . .] The student is expected to: [. . .] identify the contributions of significant individuals during the revolutionary period, including Thomas Jefferson and George Washington; [. . .] identify the accomplishments of notable individuals such as Carrie Chapman Catt, Dwight Eisenhower, Martin Luther King, Jr., Rosa Parks, Colin Powell, and Franklin D. Roosevelt

> who have made contributions to society in the areas of civil rights, women's rights, military actions, and politics.
>
> (1998: "Chapter 113" 1998: §113.7.b.2a)

Most of these names are technically given as suggestions, not as requirements. In addition, Texas legislation only requires textbooks to meet half of curriculum guidelines in order to be considered acceptable.

Though the Texas curriculum guidelines of 1998 for Grade Five do not include sweeping statements regarding the importance of teaching about heroes, this does not necessarily mean that heroes are absent from their conception of history teaching. In the section concerning third grade, the TEKS state:

> In Grade 3, students learn how individuals have changed their communities and world. Students study the effects inspiring heroes have had on communities, past and present. Students learn about the lives of heroic men and women who made important choices, overcame obstacles, sacrificed for the betterment of others, and embarked on journeys that resulted in new ideas, new inventions, and new communities. Students expand their knowledge through the identification and study of people who made a difference, influenced public policy and decision making, and participated in resolving issues that are important to all people. Throughout Grade 3, students develop an understanding of the economic, cultural, and scientific contributions made by individuals.
>
> ("Chapter 113" 1998: §113.5.a.1)

The 2010 TEKS more explicitly emphasize heroes throughout primary social studies education. These standards require fifth graders to:

> identify the Founding Fathers and Patriot heroes, including John Adams, Samuel Adams, Benjamin Franklin, Nathan Hale, Thomas Jefferson, the Sons of Liberty, and George Washington, and their motivations and contributions during the revolutionary period.
>
> ("Chapter 113" 2010, §113.16.b.4a)

The phrase "Founding Fathers and Patriot heroes" (which is repeated throughout the 2010 curriculum) here replaces the more neutral language from the 1998 curriculum, "significant individuals." In addition, the 2010 curriculum expands on the list of names, including more of the revolutionaries and creators of the Constitution, in accordance with the wishes of the Christian Right (see Erekson 2012). As we will see, officially emphasizing traditional founding heroes by including them in the curriculum was hardly necessary, given the prevalence of these figures already in existing textbooks.

OVERVIEW OF ILLUSTRATIONS IN TEXTBOOKS

As we have seen previously, illustrations indicate which people textbook editors choose to emphasize, and they have pedagogical as well as ideological significance, particularly in the U.S., where they can play a major role in textbook selection (Amalvi 1984; Bliss 1990; Duchastel 1983; Farr and Tulley 1985: 470; Finn and Ravitch 2004; Marshall 1991: 127). The following analyses of representations of heroes in textbooks thus begin by briefly considering their prevalence in illustrations.

In French textbooks, the figures featured adhere to the lists given in the curricula. Textbooks generally attribute a two-page spread to the most prominent of these individuals, including a maximum of five illustrations depicting them. Though all books follow the curriculum guidelines, emphasizing the same historical figures, there is variation over time and between books of the same period in how much attention they devote to each figure and how they represent certain individuals.

Although several of these historical people are presented in a positive manner, the French textbooks do not use heroes for the purpose of character education. The more prominent figures in these books represent a combination of the cultural "pantheon" recommended by the curriculum and a compendium of figures known not as celebrated national heroes but for the important roles they have played in history. French textbooks generally present in a positive light the scientists, philosophers, and authors included in the curricula. Marie Curie (as discussed in greater detail in Chapter Two), Victor Hugo, Louis Pasteur, Jean-Jacques Rousseau, and Voltaire are all represented positively, along with their accomplishments. (Hugo is somewhat emphasized in recent books, not just for his literary achievements but also for his political convictions, particularly his defense of and service to the Republic. [e.g., Boëche CM2: 34; Le Callennec 2011: 30–31, 47]). Similarly, Jean Moulin is presented in a positive light for his role in the Resistance and the sacrifice of his life to this cause (Boëche CM2: 54; Chevalier and Le Bourgeois 85). However, textbooks do not greatly emphasize these figures, as they dedicate between one paragraph and two pages to presenting them, and on average, these people appear in one to two illustrations per book. As Christian Amalvi argues, these are among the rare consensual figures in French history, those who are widely seen as the "benefactors of humanity whose genius contributed to the universal influence of France: inventors, scientists, artists, writers, to whom are added after 1945 the constructors of European unity" (2011: 157). Including these individuals certainly contributes to giving a positive image of France's history and is consistent with the general sense of pride expressed in textbooks in France's technical, scientific, and humanitarian achievements (see Chapter Four). Nevertheless, the brief, unadorned presentations of these figures hardly constitute hero worship.

Similarly, these books do not generally use the term "hero." Only one book grants importance to the concept of heroism and commemoration of heroes. In its 2010 edition, Hatier (the same book that consistently presents national myths and explains their history; see Chapter Four) includes a section on the Pantheon. The Pantheon is first mentioned in conjunction with Marie Curie:

> Louis Pasteur and Marie Curie are famous because they made major discoveries that allowed many lives to be saved. Marie Curie, in addition, proved that women can, as much as men, study and work as scientists. This is why her ashes were transferred to the Pantheon in Paris, the resting place of people whom the French Republic wishes to honor.
> (Le Callennec 2011: 37)

Students are then instructed to find out who else is in the Pantheon and what they "did for France" (37). The book mentions the Pantheon again in the section about the Resistance to Nazi rule and policies. Here, Hatier lists several "French figures present in the Pantheon": Voltaire, Jean-Jacques Rousseau (inaccurately depicted as French), Victor Hugo, Emile Zola, Jean Jaurès, Alexandre Dumas, Jean Moulin, and Marie Curie (73). The authors then ask students to reflect on or research commemorations of Resisters in their town. This book is alone in drawing even moderate attention to people whom the country has commemorated.

Among people pictured in the textbooks are many foreign figures, thus further indicating that French textbooks do not, on the whole, select illustrations in order to demonstrate admiration for national heroes. Though the focus in CM1 and CM2 (equivalent to U.S. Grades Four and Five) is on national history, the books do not present French history in isolation but, at least to a certain extent, within the international context and, as European law requires, the European context. In addition, the presence of people known for destructive actions further shows that illustrations are not just about celebrating national history but about familiarizing students with key actors in history.

By contrast, U.S. textbooks place much greater emphasis on individuals than do their French counterparts and employ the term "hero," designating a large group of American people as such, and clearly aiming to combine history and character education. Unlike the French books, U.S. books frequently repeat images of the same people, thus emphasizing them. Both of these practices have become increasingly common in more recent textbooks. In addition to referring to historical figures as heroes (e.g., "Theodore Roosevelt became a national hero" [Boyd et al. 2003: 582]), these books include a series of biographies, set apart from the main narrative text, focusing on an individual, whom they hold up as a moral example. As mentioned in the previous chapter, the textbooks explicitly associate a character trait with each person thus featured (for instance, courage, loyalty, and civic virtue), and Scott Foresman (Boyd et al.) labels these biographies with the title "Citizen Hero." Through the combination of these approaches emphasizing individuals, the U.S. books thus establish a large group of national heroes.

As we have seen in Part One of this book, textbooks' choices of which historical figures to emphasize reflect to some extent a wish to depict diversity. However, overall, these choices seem to reflect the wishes of conservative right activists, as they focus more on Anglo-American history and particularly the founding period. In reaction to multiculturalist changes, including the addition of more women and minority heroes to textbooks and the increased visibility of inequality in U.S. history, Christian Right education activists have repeatedly called for renewed emphasis on traditional heroes. These groups focus on traditional heroes as something of a litmus test to determine textbooks' patriotism and, therefore, acceptability. For instance, among prominent Texas activists, the Gablers' Educational Research Analysts described their preferred 1997 fifth-grade history textbook as "very patriotic" because it "glorif[ies] our nation's greatest heroes and what our country is all about. [. . .] [I]t teaches patriotism! Especially great on American revolution [sic] and George Washington" (Warren 1997; see also Educational Research Analysts 1982: 6).

These books only emphasize American people who contributed in a positive way to national history. The 14 people who appear in at least three illustrations on average per textbook in the 2003 editions are the leaders of the American Revolution (George Washington, Benjamin Franklin, Thomas Jefferson, John Adams, Alexander Hamilton) and writers of the Constitution (James Madison), explorers of the national territory (Columbus, Lewis, Clark, and Sacagawea), Civil War leaders (of both sides; Abraham Lincoln, Ulysses S. Grant, and Robert E. Lee), a proponent of expansionism (Theodore Roosevelt), and (as the lone civil rights activist of this core group), Martin Luther King Jr. The choice of these figures focuses attention on the country's founding and growth, including a narrative of progress, which allows for a positive (and often teleological) way to incorporate women and minorities into the national story. However, the vast majority of those emphasized are the traditional heroes and founders of the nation-state.

Through their focus on individual figures and explicit association of these people with patriotism and civic virtues, the U.S. textbooks are more traditional, reminiscent of the "great men" approach, unlike their French counterparts. This difference is even more striking when we consider the most prominent people featured in the textbooks of each country.

PROMINENT HISTORICAL FIGURES IN TEXTBOOKS

Leading French Figures

The following people appear in illustrations three times or more on average per book in the most recent French CM1 and CM2 textbooks (in decreasing order of prevalence): Charles de Gaulle (5), Joan of Arc (4.7), Louis XIV (4.3), Napoleon Bonaparte (4.3), Henri IV (3), and Louis IX (3) (also known as Saint Louis).[5] Interestingly, of these six, all but Henri IV fall into the category that Christian Amalvi defines as the "most strongly contested heroes":

> The memory of the five figures [. . .] presents the following paradox: no one dares contest their historical importance, but, at the same time, the evaluation of them is often, still today, violently contested. Therefore, because of the deep marks (or perhaps, despite them) that Saint Louis, Joan of Arç, Louis XIV, Napoleon, and Charles de Gaulle have left on the collective memory, any consensus about them seems improbable.
> (2011: 227)

Amalvi's statement here corroborates the evidence on the contested nature of national symbols—the key national figures are precisely those who inspire the most heated debate. The stakes of this symbolic importance make them worth fighting over.

The way in which the textbooks present these people shows a shift from the 1980s to the present. The older French books contain the last vestiges of a more simplified narrative in which several key figures were presented as heroes representing a particular vision of the nation. The more recent books take a more complex approach in which all of these people appear as important figures in the country's past. Yet, while textbooks still transmit certain tropes of national memory, they do not engage in hagiography.

Broadly speaking, among these most prominent figures, we can identify three groups. Charles de Gaulle and Henri IV are presented positively, but without being mythologized, in books from 1985 to the present. Louis IX and Joan of Arc remain the most symbolically potent people in the French textbooks. Louis XIV and Napoleon are represented in a critical manner. However, while representations of Louis XIV remain essentially unchanged between 1985 and the present, Napoleon's image has evolved during that time. In this section, I will discuss textbooks' representations of these people in this order.

Charles de Gaulle (1890–1970)

Leader of the Free French forces during the Second World War, president, and founder of the Fifth Republic, Charles de Gaulle is perhaps the closest that the French textbooks come to representing a modern political and/or military leader as a major national hero. They simplify certain elements of his history (notably, controversy over the Algerian War as well as the protests of 1968 and de Gaulle's subsequent resignation), thus making him appear as a more consensual figure, which could be seen as a step toward mythologizing him. However they do not turn him into a national symbol, nor do they idealize him or heavily emphasize his historical importance.

Though today Charles de Gaulle is still associated with the center-right, his image has become increasingly depoliticized in recent years, making him a less controversial figure than the other prominent French heroes discussed here. Since 1990, previous partisan controversy surrounding de Gaulle has abated, and the general has become part of the national heritage, viewed favorably by four out of five French people (Amalvi 2011: 274.). The Fifth Republic, initially rejected by the left as giving too much power to the president, was implicitly legitimated in the eyes of critics by François Mitterrand's election in 1981 as the first socialist president. Resentment felt by some on the right toward de Gaulle over Algerian independence faded with time. These changes left a vision of de Gaulle as the figure of a powerful leader who stood up against oppression, resisting Nazi rule, going on to give the country its current republican constitution, women's suffrage, and key aspects of the social welfare system. We might, then, expect more recent textbooks to discuss more readily de Gaulle's accomplishments and actions in addition to leading the Resistance. We might also expect a more consensual vision of de Gaulle to appear across the more recent textbooks. In practice, presentations of de Gaulle have become more homogenous over time, but his role in the Resistance is emphasized less than it might have been, as are his actions as president.

De Gaulle's role as head of the Resistance puts him in the position of national savior, a category that has resonated in French hagiography for centuries, like Vercingétorix against Rome, Robespierre (more controversially) against civil war and foreign invasion, and Napoleon (according to his admirers). De Gaulle's famous 1940 call to resistance is a model of patriotic discourse and defense, and de Gaulle himself, in his memoires published in the 1950s, developed this connection between the Resistance and patriotism, contributing to the "resistancialist myth," by equating the Resistance with the true, eternal France (Amalvi 2011: 270; Rousso 1987/1994; see also Chapter One).

The textbooks, for the most part, accept and perpetuate this vision. Though (as we saw in Chapter One) they do not omit the collaboration of the Vichy government with the Nazis, most emphasize the Resistance, indicating that it represents the true French spirit. Instead of allowing de Gaulle's narrative and image to act as a proxy for France, textbooks focus more on the Resistance overall than on de Gaulle's role, in keeping with their emphasis on social history. For the most part, older and newer books use similar language, which positions de Gaulle as a leader but also as representative of a broader trend of resistance, rather than a unique or exceptional individual. However, not surprisingly, given the chronological proximity, there is more variation among the books of 1985, with Armand Colin somewhat dramatizing de Gaulle's stance, making him stand out more as a strong leader. After painting a dire picture of occupied France, the authors state:

> However, one man refused defeat: General de Gaulle. From London, where he had taken refuge, he launched on June 18, 1940 a call to the

> Resistance. He asked the French to continue fighting beside the English [sic]. "France," he said "lost a battle, but she hasn't lost the war."
>
> (Dorel-Ferré and Dhainaut 1985: 147)

The other books of 1985, as well as more recent editions, use less emphatic tones. For instance, the 2011 edition of Sedrap, like all the recent books, includes de Gaulle's 1940 call from London but does not dramatize his role:

> Refusing the armistice signed by Marshal Pétain and wanting to continue the war against the Germans, General de Gaulle reached London on June 17, 1940. On London radio, on June 18, 1940, he issued a call to all French people. He asked them to refuse defeat and to resist the Germans who occupied the country. Some French people who received Radio London heard General de Gaulle's call, and the first groups of the Resistance were formed.
>
> (Boëche 2011 CM2: 49)

From there the narrative focuses more on the actions of Jean Moulin and anonymous Resisters (51).

Continuing to present de Gaulle in a favorable light, but without great emphasis or adulation, the recent books are generally even more concise in their discussions regarding his actions as president. Once again, older books exhibit more variation in their approaches. For instance, one book emphasizes in positive terms de Gaulle's progressive reforms, including women's suffrage (Nembrini et al. 1985: 141), while the others do not mention these significant changes at all (Dorel-Ferré and Dhainaut 1985: 157; Vincent et al. 1985 CM2: 121). For the most part, books of all periods state that de Gaulle created the Fifth Republic but do not expand upon this, and while they generally give positive accounts of the changes in policy effected under the Fifth Republic, they do not attribute these changes to de Gaulle. For instance, in its 2011 edition Hatier explains that French people elected de Gaulle to replace the disorganized, quarrelling government leaders in 1958 because they credited him with France's liberation. The text then states that de Gaulle proposed the Constitution of the Fifth Republic, which was approved via referendum. It then ceases to refer to de Gaulle and summarizes major events and trends in French society under the Fifth Republic, all of which date from after de Gaulle's tenure (Le Callennec 2011: 86, 88).

While textbooks do not emphasize de Gaulle's role in reforming the state, neither are they critical of him. The textbooks all omit discussion of his role regarding the protests of May 1968. Only two books in 1985 and one in 2010 even mention that he resigned the following year. Armand Colin states:

> In May 1968, a political and social crisis shook the country: student uprisings in Paris, amplified by a vast strike movement throughout France, rocked the political equilibrium of the Fifth Republic. General

> de Gaulle managed to overcome the conflict, but left the government the following year. The institutions that he put in place have been respected by his successors.
>
> (Dorel-Ferré and Dhainaut 1985: 157)

Among more recent books, only Sedrap (Boëche 2011 CM2) even mentions that de Gaulle resigned but gives no indication as to why. By leaving out the 1969 referendum and social divisions as causes of de Gaulle's resignation, the books improve his image and reputation, giving a simplified narrative and impression of consensus.

Despite this bit of simplification, de Gaulle is not presented in glowing, hagiographic terms. His actions are shown to have been positive for the country, but he, himself, is not idealized or celebrated, whether in the books of 1985 or in the most recent ones.

Henri IV (1553–1610)

French textbooks similarly avoid processes of heroification in their presentations of Henri IV. The more recent textbooks, however, dedicate more space to him than do most of the older editions. Henri IV, the king responsible for the Edict of Nantes, which established official tolerance of the Protestant religion, has traditionally "incarnated national unity" (Amalvi 2011: 193). He is also one of France's best-loved kings, as he is seen as concerned for his subjects' well-being (famously aiming to have a chicken in every French family's pot for Sunday dinner), and he was tragically assassinated by Ravaillac, who opposed Henri's policy of religious tolerance. In recent years, the Education Ministry has assigned civic education the task of teaching religious tolerance. It thus seems that, if the textbooks wished to use heroes to teach values, Henri IV would be an excellent model. (Indeed, Vincent's 1985 edition does exactly this, but it is the outlier; Vincent et al. 1985 CM1: 104–105.)

The textbooks (old and new) show him as reestablishing order and peace in the wake of the religious wars that opposed Protestants and Catholics during the sixteenth century. Most of the books emphasize progress made thanks to Henri's policies in civil rights (e.g., among the recent books, Hatier stresses religious tolerance [Le Callennec 2010: 82–83], and Nathan emphasizes minority rights; [Le Bourgeois 2010: 78–79]). The books show either Henri's affection for the people or theirs for him, although Hatier explains that the traditional image of the beloved king was not accurate, as he was disliked during his lifetime (however, this textbook still emphasizes the positive image, particularly by citing at some length Voltaire's *La Henriade*). The textbooks do not dwell on his assassination; only two of three recent books mention it, though they both state that a "Catholic fanatic" was the assassin. Nevertheless, only one of the most recent books emphasizes Henri's commitment to religious tolerance: Hatier implicitly ascribes Henri IV martyr status, by saying that he was a victim of religious intolerance, the very intolerance which he successfully fought against. Clearly, this representation also aims to promote values of religious tolerance in the present, opposing fanaticism (see also Chapters One and Four). Overall, the fact that only one of the three recent books emphasizes the issue of religious tolerance (and even that one book debunks myths about Henri IV) demonstrates the general lack of attention to heroes in French history teaching and reluctance to use them as models of civic virtue.

Louis IX ("Saint Louis") (1214–1270)

Louis IX, however, is something of an exception to this generalization. The idealized image of Louis IX, also known as Saint Louis, as propagated by nineteenth-century historian Jules Michelet, depicted the canonized king as a model of chivalry and fairness. The image of the king dispensing justice humbly seated beneath an oak tree in the woods of his Vincennes castle, accessible to all who sought him, is one of the most enduring tropes in the national consciousness (Amalvi 2011: 228, 231; Le Goff 1999). In keeping with this element of collective memory, nearly all of the textbooks from 1985 through 2011 present Louis IX in very positive terms, using more qualitative adjectives to describe him than to describe any other person. For instance, Le Callennec's 2010 edition explains: "Louis IX is better known by the name Saint Louis. Indeed, the Church considers him to be a saint. He led a simple life, in accordance with the message of the Gospel. He gave charity to the poor and helped the sick. He was also considered to be a fair king" (Le Callennec 2010: 17). The textbook—like most others of more recent years—cites Jean de Joinville's 1309 text praising the king for his simplicity and charity, and then resumes its commentary: "This image of a good and fair king, who takes care of his people as a father does of his children, served as a model to the kings who succeeded him. From 1610 to 1824, all the Capetian kings were named Louis in order to resemble him" (17).

There is, furthermore, a small move toward more myth-making concerning Louis in the more recent books. Like the older books, those of 2010 generally depict Louis IX as a model of Christian behavior and a caring, paternal king who genuinely wished to improve the well-being of his subjects, creating institutions to this end (a judicial system, hospitals, university . . .). Unlike most of the older books, though, the newer editions propagate the myth of the oak tree in the Bois de Vincennes. This shift is in line with more recent curricula's new focus on perpetuating national culture (and possibly reflects the influence of Jacques Le Goff, who held a prominent role in writing curricula and whose 1996 thousand-page biography of Louis IX drew renewed attention to the king).

Perhaps surprisingly, the most recent textbooks also continue to reflect the older, idealized image of Louis IX regarding his involvement in the Crusades, which they show in a positive light, without any modern judgment. Representations of Louis's role in the Crusades are discussed in greater detail in Chapter One. In general, the books justify Louis's participation in the Crusades in the name of his faith. One might argue that this approach to the Crusades respects history as a discipline (i.e., not imposing anachronistic judgment on the past). It certainly does not, however, reflect a commitment to multiculturalism (as, in this part of almost all the books, only the French viewpoint regarding the Crusades is shown).

These representations of the king ultimately legitimate aspects of the French monarchy as it existed in the Middle Ages. They constitute a romanticized ideal of a premodern, Christian France. In a way, Louis IX serves as a bridge between traditionally antagonistic Catholic and secular views of the French nation. Here, narratives about him ground the modern state (with the attributes and institutions that Louis IX created) in this honorable, Christian, premodern past. Still, if Louis IX appears as something of a hero, he is not a major national symbol, whether in society or in the textbooks. Beyond the textbooks and their reasons for eschewing hero worship, Louis' renown is not sufficiently broad to constitute major symbolic status, as he appeals primarily to practicing Catholics (Joutard and Lecuir 2000). Not all figures with religious importance, however, have such limited appeal.

Joan of Arc (c. 1412–1431)

The only person to appear in the most recent textbooks as a full-fledged national symbol—complete with multiple meanings, systematically iconic images, and a dramatic story—is Joan of Arc. Joan is already presented as a hero in the books of 1985. However, unlike other such figures, she retains her symbolic status in current books. Among the most frequently pictured figures in the textbooks, she is the only one who did not play an active public role for an extended period of time and who was not a head of state. Not only is her image emphasized disproportionately to her historical involvement, but textbooks also praise her personal qualities in a way that they do not for other prominent figures.

The reason for this emphasis is, most likely, represented in the curriculum guidelines of 2002: "The Hundred Years War, with its heroine Joan of Arc, gave birth to a first form of national consciousness, also facilitated by the emergence of the French language" (Ministère . . . 2002: 12). In a pedagogical approach designed to transmit national culture and consciousness, Joan's story is a key part of national mythology and offers one of the rare instances in which a figure from the distant past can be shown as a "national" martyr, free from the politicization of, say, Jacobin revolutionaries. Though Joan's legacy has been subject to competing claims and many conflicting interpretations over time, this malleability is precisely what allows her to be a durable national symbol. Joan has alternatively represented patriotism, sacrifice, martyrdom (for religious and/or nationalist causes and/or class conflict), strong womanhood, feminism, hysteria (in the antifeminist sense), madness, inspiration, leadership, delusion, Catholic faith, mysticism, France's Christian roots, anti-English sentiment, and betrayal; the list goes on (Amalvi 2011: 235–241; Jennings 1994).

Textbooks might well be skittish about how they can represent Joan of Arc. Though the left has often claimed her as a symbol, she is currently more frequently associated in the national psyche with the far right *Front National*, and she has a long history of being appropriated by right-wing movements, including the Vichy government. The conflicting interpretations of Joan and the extensive network of myths surrounding her raise a number of questions regarding textbooks' representations of her and her status as a historical figure versus national myth. How do the books—with their secular aims—present Joan's faith and the religious aspects of her story? Do they present her as a martyr? If so, to which cause(s)? That is, is she a Christian martyr, who died for her faith, and/or a nationalist martyr, sacrificing herself in the fight to save the "nation" (and possibly reaffirming the ties between Christianity and France, as French Catholics have long contended)? Or does she represent the betrayal of the peasant class by elites, as those on the left have, at times, argued (abandoned by Charles VII after she helped restore him to power)? Is she shown as the savior of France? How, in this age of Europe-building, do the books handle the role of the English in Joan's capture and execution? From the perspective of gender issues, how do they discuss the fact that she was a woman in a nontraditional role (condemned to die partly because she wore men's clothes)? Do the books take some distance from legend and explain that she is a national symbol? Is she shown as a tragic figure? A victim? A hero? And ultimately, why do the books dedicate so much attention her?

Understandably, these secular textbooks omit elements of the Joan mythology that bolster Christian myths about her. Clearly, they do not say that she was called by God but mention that she "believed" that she was called. They do not emphasize the elements of her story that have traditionally been explained as miracles. For instance, they do not relate the legend according to which she recognized the disguised king Charles VII, thus making the case for her divine guidance. One recent textbook (Le Callennec 2010, which often relates the traditional myths or reputations surrounding heroes and then explains how they were constructed) uses these points seemingly to question the authenticity of Joan's story:

> Historical sources about Joan of Arc are incomplete and, at times, contradictory. Historians do not all agree about her history. In addition, over time, elements of legend have been added to the truth. For example, it was long said that Joan of Arc was a little shepherdess who heard voices that told her to "kick the English out of France." But then, in that case, we don't know how to explain why she knew how to fight on horseback or why the king so easily agreed to entrust her with an army.
> (Le Callennec 2010: 53)

Nevertheless, there does seem to be a shift toward accepting discussing religion, as most of the newer books state that Joan was a devout Christian, an explanation most of the older books do not provide. This trend seems to be in keeping with the addition of religious history to the curriculum and textbooks since 2002 (see Chapter One). These changes perhaps show a new consensus: a decline in previous incompatibility of secular education and any mention of religious roots.

The books, however, do not present Joan as a martyr. They do not present her story in an emotional way or attempt to have pupils identify with her (the one major exception to this is Sedrap's 2003 edition[6]). Nor do they emphasize the unfairness of her death, though they all mention that she was burned alive, which might be sufficient to capture children's attention and sympathy but does not explicitly indicate that she suffered for the nation or any other cause. Regarding her capture and death, the older books do not mention the Bourguignons' role at all, whereas the newer books all do. Older books were split as to whether they blamed the English for her death, which all of the new books do. By mentioning both the Bourguignons and the English, the books are not only more accurate, but they also mitigate the potentially awkward effects for Europe-building of blaming solely the English for the death of a national hero.

Regardless of how they present her death, most textbooks do not present Joan as a tragic figure but as a warrior, both through their illustrations and explicitly in the text. All of the recent books include romanticized nineteenth-century images of Joan, with long hair and a feminine figure reflecting Romantic-era beauty standards, as well as Joan in armor (sometimes these features are combined in the same illustration). The combination of hyper-feminized images and Joan as a warrior subconsciously, if not more directly, evoke Marianne, the allegorical female incarnation of the nation and/or the republic since the Revolution, perhaps most famously depicted in Delacroix's painting, *Liberty Leading the People* (1830) (cf. Amalvi 2011: 236–237; see Figure 2.1).

This image of Joan as a national savior appears to varying degrees in most textbooks' accounts of her, though more so in 1985 than more recently. The books do not generally state explicitly that she alone "saved" France, though many—but not all—credit her with either leading to France being saved or contributing to saving the country. The older books credit her with getting the king crowned, where the newer books downgrade this to accompanying or encouraging him to be crowned in Reims. The older books are also more likely to dramatize the situation and Joan's role by stating that France seemed lost before she intervened, which the new books omit altogether. The books from all periods studied here credit her with saving Orléans, and most of the books credit her with creating a reinforced national sentiment. For instance, in its 1985 edition, Hachette gives this account, which is preceded by a dramatic setting of the scene before Joan's arrival:

> The English occupied a large portion of France: she then seemed lost.

Joan of Arc and the Rebirth of France

> A young girl from Lorraine, Joan of Arc, did not accept defeat or the English occupation. A shepherdess who was barely 16 years old, pushed by her Christian faith, she succeeded in convincing king Charles VII to take up fighting again. In 1429 she took Orléans back from the English and established the king's authority throughout the kingdom. Taken prisoner in Compiègne, she was judged, then burned alive, as a witch, by the English in Rouen in 1431.
>
> But her example gave courage to the French. The king reorganized his kingdom and created a new army that was well equipped and used the first canons. Charles VII began fighting again and drove the English from the territory. In 1453, the English only retained control over Calais.
>
> A new France, rallied around its king, was triumphant.
>
> From 1328 to 1453, France and England fought each other. Our country was ravaged by the war. Joan of Arc revived the courage of the king and the nation. France was liberated.
>
> (Nembrini et al. 1985: 49)

This textbook thus includes strongly nationalistic prose. It presents an anachronistic and teleological account of the nation, referring to the medieval kingdom as "our country." Hachette blames the English for Joan's death (which not all books do; e.g., Armand Colin does not), thus also reasserting national sentiment in defining France in opposition to England. Similarly to most other books, Hachette credits Joan with restoring French courage and motivation, as well as with saving Orléans, as if she accomplished this feat alone.

The most recent books also contain statements about Joan's importance and effect on the war effort and ultimately, France. With exceptionally nationalistic prose, Sedrap summarizes the section on Joan: "Within a few months, Joan of Arc restored the confidence of the king, the soldiers and the French population, all ready to fight for their nation: France" (Boëche 2011 CM1: 35). Hatier similarly concludes:

> Joan of Arc played an important role in the liberation of France and in the birth of national feeling during the Hundred Years War. [. . .]
>
> History remembers Joan of Arc for her courage, her heroism, and her determination to liberate France from the English. This is what makes her a figure of French history, on the same level as Vercingétorix, who attempted to prevent the Romans from invading Gaul. But we must not forget that her actions would have been impossible without the courage and heroism of the soldiers that she led.
>
> (Le Callennec 2010: 52–53)

As these passages demonstrate, the quantity of text and especially of illustrations dedicated to Joan of Arc place her in the select group of the most important figures in French history—in the oldest books of this study, she is surpassed only by Charles de Gaulle, Louis XIV, and Napoleon Bonaparte, and in the most recent books, only de Gaulle is pictured more than she is. The books' text does not offer a ready explanation for this focus on Joan. Perhaps the growing attention to the lack of women in French history textbooks is a factor, though the books do not address this question explicitly when discussing Joan, and neither do they make much of her gender (i.e., they do not proclaim it to have been terribly unusual for a young woman, rather than a young man, to have done what she did). This hypothesis is also somewhat undermined by the lack of other female figures in the books (as discussed in Chapter Two). It is possible that Joan's image has been progressively freed from association with Vichy France, thus removing reticence about depicting her. Overall, though, the emphasis on Joan in these books is, more likely, attributable to nationalism and to the commitment to transmitting national memory and myths to schoolchildren, as the various concluding statements from different textbooks show. In addition, it is possible that textbook publishers wish (consciously or not) to reclaim Joan and her story from the *Front National.* This hypothesis is supported by the dominance of more left-wing imagery surrounding her in the more recent books, which shows her as a woman of the people and a beacon of national sentiment and unity, a sort of Liberty leading the medieval (French) people.

Louis XIV (1638–1715) and Napoleon Bonaparte (1769–1821)

Though these last people to figure prominently in French history books have, at times, been depicted as heroes by certain segments of the population, they have never been as consensual as de Gaulle now is nor held as wide appeal as does Joan of Arc. Textbooks certainly show the historical importance of Louis XIV; however, none of the textbooks published between 1985 and the 2011 depict him as a hero. Nor do they use discussions of Louis XIV to focus on the greatness of France, as textbooks might once have done (see Amalvi 2011: 246). Louis is shown in a negative light in the textbooks of the 1980s as in the more recent editions, which indicate that his lavish lifestyle was financed at the expense of the nobles, whom he kept under strict control in his court, and still more unfairly, at the expense of the peasantry, who suffered hunger and great hardship due to Louis XIV's excessive taxation. Depicting Louis XIV and his anti-egalitarianism in a negative light undergirds the principles of the Revolution and the republic. In this manner, he serves as a sort of national antihero, which is also valuable as a national symbol.

While Louis XIV had already fallen into disfavor before the publication of the textbooks studied here, these books offer a telling look at the evolution of perceptions of Napoleon Bonaparte. There are some significant changes in the way Napoleon is represented in the textbooks between 1985 and 2011. There was not a consensual vision of Napoleon in 1985; textbooks published then exhibit varying degrees of criticism in their presentations of him.

Vestiges remain in these books of an idealized image of the emperor, which disappear completely from more recent books, where he clearly shifts from national hero to criticized historical figure. The older books depict Napoleon as continuing the missions of the Revolution, both within France (by protecting civil liberties) and throughout Europe, attempting to spread the Revolution's ideals (even if, these books state, his governors did not always respect these principles in the territories that they administered). These textbooks do not depict Napoleon as aggressive, seeking conquest, but as forced to fight by the hostile English. They also do not relate his limitations of civil rights within France—neither for the population at large (e.g., curtailing liberty of press), nor the inferior status that his civil code reserved for women and his reinstatement of slavery, which had been banned by the Revolutionary government. Armand Colin's account is particularly glowing:

> Bonaparte wanted to complete his work for domestic pacification with peace abroad. He signed the treaty of Amiens with the European countries (1802). His popularity was then enormous. Two years later, he succeeded in being proclaimed as emperor of the French. The pope himself came to crown him in Notre Dame of Paris (December 2, 1804) under the name Napoleon I.
>
> However, Napoleon was very quickly dragged into an interminable succession of wars. England had not renounced fighting. [. . .]
>
> These long years of war hide the lasting work of the First Empire. Napoleon was an effective and visionary head of state [. . .].
>
> (Dorel-Ferré and Dhainaut 1985:103)

Beyond the factual error (the pope did not crown Napoleon; he crowned himself, though the pope was present), this text gives an idealized view of Napoleon, excusing his aggression (even painting him as something of a victim of foreign aggression), omitting his abuses of power, and emphasizing only the good that he did for the country.

Current textbooks offer a sharply different view of Napoleon, presenting a far more complex vision that includes emphasizing the contradictions between his aims and reality, as well as his evolution from early popular leader to resented authoritarian. They also show him as aggressive in his foreign wars. These profound changes represent a shift away from jingoistic memory and a move from a more uniformly positive national self-image to a more nuanced approach to history. Changes in depictions of Napoleon are, in this way, reminiscent of and parallel to those regarding colonization (see Chapter One). The process of revising Napoleon's image seems to be ongoing, reflecting continuing debates among historians and the complexity of establishing a narrative about such a contradictory figure (see Amalvi 2011: 264–265). However, while recent books vary in their presentation of some details (such as how much popular support Napoleon seemed to have for his coup d'état), on the main ideas, they appear to reflect a certain consensus.

This fact is not surprising, given the official 2002 curriculum guidelines regarding Napoleon:

> The First Empire is another example of a rift between principles and realities. Initially a fervent republican, Bonaparte reestablished in his favor an authoritarian power in the form of a hereditary empire (Napoleon I). Nevertheless, he respected and consolidated the main victories of the Revolution in creating the Civil Code. Abroad, inspired by the memory of Charlemagne, he militarily conquered an immense empire that included more than half of Europe. This empire was ephemeral.
>
> (Ministère . . . 2002: 14)

This complex vision is faithfully reflected in recent textbooks. Hatier, for instance, explains:

> In 1799, a young general, who was popular for his victories in battle, Napoleon Bonaparte, took power through a coup d'état. He imposed himself in an authoritarian manner, but he reestablished order and thus obtained the support of the French people.
>
> (Le Callennec 2011: 23)

Then, after relating his soldiers' praise and affection for him, the text continues:

> In reality, the feelings of the French evolved over the course of Napoleon's reign: he was much loved at the beginning, but then the French tired of his authority and the wars that he constantly undertook and which caused many deaths. Abroad, Napoleon has always had a bad image: that of a conqueror who wanted to dominate Europe.
>
> The crowning of Napoleon in 1804 is characteristic of the ambiguity of the French: they wanted the liberty and equality that were gained during the Revolution, as well as the return to order, or even to the authority of a sovereign. In the nineteenth century, they would continue to hesitate between republic, monarchy, and empire.
>
> (25)

This type of narrative is a powerful instance of French history teaching in newer curricula and textbooks taking a more critical view of the national past and employing a pedagogical approach that presents complexity, multiple viewpoints, and the contradictions that constitute the study of history. Napoleon, then, appears to have still been a hero to certain textbook authors and publishers in 1985, but his symbolic legacy has eroded, as history teaching has come to reflect a more critical academic approach.

In their stated aim of transmitting national memory and culture while teaching history in line with certain academic trends and discipline, recent French textbooks for the elementary schools have adopted multiple approaches. They have moved away from representing certain historical figures as national heroes or symbols (such as Napoleon). They represent other prominent figures in a positive manner but do not praise, idealize, or emphasize them enough to constitute a process of heroification or an attempt to turn them into national symbols (as with de Gaulle or Henri IV). The books have, though, emphasized certain traditional figures of the premodern "nation," whom they present in a more subjective way, such as Saint Louis and Joan of Arc. In these instances, the recent textbooks continue to transmit memory, rather than teaching history strictly as an academic discipline. Nevertheless, this approach is rare in the French books. France has several prominent historical figures but no dominant, consensual founding hero of the modern nation. (If Vercingétorix could be viewed as embodying the Gallic spirit of resistance [Amalvi 2011], he is not glorified in these textbooks.)[7] Charles de Gaulle, Joan of Arc, and to a lesser extent, Louis IX certainly fulfill a nationalist function, but none is a key "founder" of the modern nation-state or serves in these books as a sort of spiritual ancestor of the nation. Thus, while French textbooks emphasize a few key figures, they can hardly be said to engage in hero worship.

Primary United States Heroes

The situation in the United States is distinctly different. George Washington provides the U.S. with an exceptional example of a national hero, a founder who, in many ways, embodies the very archetype of the spiritual "father" of the nation. Americans' near-deification of Washington began during his lifetime, and many are still devoted to him today. The Washington myth, which remains largely unchallenged, presents him as the father of the nation, a brave, selfless military and political leader, disinterested in power, who acted for the good of the country (Schwartz 1987; Zelinsky 1988: 30–35). The U.S. also has an additional key national hero, Abraham Lincoln, who presided over the national "rebirth"—the Civil War. Through the North's victory, the war confirmed the unity of the states and strengthened the national government, establishing its supremacy above the individual states, and ended slavery—thus bringing the country more in line with its egalitarian ideals (Grant 2003; Schwartz 2009; Zelinsky 1988).

Washington and Lincoln have long been, by all measures, the most prominent U.S. heroes (Zelinsky 1988: 34, 48). Washington remained the foremost American hero until the early twentieth century, when Lincoln surpassed him in popular memory and imagination (Schwartz 1987, 2009). Lincoln remains more prevalent in popular memory as well as among historians, with both groups ranking him as the greatest U.S. president in various surveys (Schwartz 2009). Lincoln also inspires more work by historians than does Washington, as well as a greater number of popular biographies and forms of entertainment (films, etc.). Both Washington and Lincoln played key roles in the two major periods of U.S. nation-building. Yet from the early 1980s to the 2000s, Washington's symbolic role, the prevalence, and status accorded to him in history textbooks grew, far surpassing those of Lincoln, whose importance and prestige appear diminished. This decisive shift demonstrates the influence of Texas Christian Right activists on textbooks and has significant repercussions for the vision of national identity presented in these books.

Washington is a powerful hero for promoting a conservative view of democracy. He was first elevated to mythic status during the Revolution, itself, embedding his symbolic importance deeply in the country's history. Barry Schwartz has convincingly argued that Washington was a uniquely American type of hero: celebrated not for great military skill nor for political genius but rather for strength of character. Washington's reputation was grounded in his self-discipline, perseverance, and above all, his image as a reluctant leader, who assumed power only when it was demanded of him, in service of his country (Schwartz 1987). In this way, Washington is an effective model in a democratic society: his great qualities are not innate but result from choice and effort. Anyone can aspire to emulate this vision of Washington. Though he was a revolutionary in his time, he was not a radical seeking to overturn the existing social order. Washington represents the United States itself in a "thin" or most basic conception of U.S. ideals and government. He is the human equivalent of the values that now dominate textbooks, as seen in the previous chapter. His role was military and political. As such, he is a prime incarnation of state-centered nationalism.

For Christian Right education activists, Washington's prominence and representation in curricula and textbooks have long been a test of patriotism and "accuracy," more so than for other heroes (see Gabler et al. 1985: 54). For instance, in protest against the proposed National History Standards in 1994, many commentators argued (inaccurately) that the standards omitted Washington. This argument clearly resonated with many Americans, as it was widely repeated and publicized (Nash, Crabtree, and Dunn 1997/2000).

Lincoln has a more complex legacy. As Barry Schwartz has shown (drawing on work by Merrill Peterson [1994]), in the early years of the twentieth century, Lincoln was celebrated by historians and in popular memory for five major reasons: as the savior of the Union, the great emancipator, man of the people, first (frontier) American, and self-made man (Schwartz 2009: 3). In what David Blight has called "reconciliationist memory" of the Civil War (and Lincoln's role in it), the conflict was seen as the "war that made the nation" (Blight 2008; Grant 2003: 189). In this vision, many Americans and other observers (including historians) saw the war as marking the birth of the modern United States. Reconciliation between white people in the North and the South was founded on a shared vision of the Civil War as a "war among brothers" over euphemistic states' rights or ways of life, thereby obscuring the importance of slavery in the war and in American history more broadly. Lincoln was thus celebrated primarily as the savior of the

Union. This was the dominant vision of the early twentieth century. However, with the growth of Progressivism and then the Civil Rights Movement, Lincoln increasingly became revered much more as the great emancipator (Schwartz 2009). As historiographical trends changed, the reconciliationist vision of the Civil War was increasingly rejected. Partly through the work of such scholars as Eric Foner, this vision of history has come to be seen by most mainstream historians as racist (Foner 1997: 85, 90–91). Many white Southern conservatives still adhere to the "Lost Cause" vision of the war as a war for states' rights and a romanticized vision of antebellum life (Blight 2008: 276). Lincoln as great emancipator, then, is not a symbol that resonates for all Americans, and he has ceased to be as consensual as a symbol as he once was.

In addition, Lincoln's prestige among progressive multiculturalists has ebbed, as more recent champions of civil rights have promoted equality in a way that is more attuned to current concerns. Nevertheless, while Lincoln may no longer be the powerful unifying symbol that he was for much of the twentieth century, he remains widely admired, as evidenced for instance by competing efforts of Democrats and Republicans to claim his legacy (Blight 2008: 269–282).

The remainder of this chapter will demonstrate how the Washington myth has grown in textbooks while Lincoln's importance has diminished from the early 1980s to the early 2000s. As I have argued in greater detail elsewhere (Hutchins 2011), it is almost certainly a sign of conservative influence that Lincoln, who had long been the second-most-pictured figure in U.S. history textbooks, drops to fourth place in the most recent books, now preceded not only by Washington, but also by Benjamin Franklin and Thomas Jefferson. This change reflects an increased emphasis on the founding era, as well as a more critical stance regarding Lincoln. Both of these changes are in line with conservative activists' wishes. Washington appears on average in 4.8 illustrations per textbook in 1982, 12.8 in 1997, and 17.7 in 2003. Lincoln appears 1.6 times in 1982, 7.8 in 1997, then 6 times in 2003. It is not only the number of illustrations that makes Washington by far the most prominent hero in these books but also the nature of the illustrations. The first president is presented in legendary style, as textbooks (despite their space constraints) often include multiple copies of the same images, which depict defining national moments, such as the famously difficult winter through which Washington led his Revolutionary soldiers at Valley Forge, as well as other battles, the Constitutional Convention over which Washington presided, and his inauguration as president. In all of these images, Washington stands out, physically above the others, in noble, impressive stances (Figure 5.1 [e.g. Banks et al. 2003: 320]).

The books exhibit no similar process for Lincoln, and in fact, they actually remove the elements of Lincoln's life that were most likely to contribute to transmitting a mythical vision of him that appeared in the older books (e.g., depicting his childhood on the frontier or legends and anecdotes that

Figure 5.1 Howard Chandler Christy, *Signing of the Constitution*, 1940.
Photograph credit: Architect of the Capitol.
Source: Flickr. Retrieved 29 Sept. 2015 (https://www.flickr.com/photos/uscapitol/6263666566).

illustrate his famed honesty), all the while increasing their focus on Washington's early years. Similarly, the older books dedicated long biographies to Lincoln (usually between five and seven pages in 1982), whereas by 2003, only Scott Foresman gives him a one-page biography (Boyd et al. 483). (Even then, this publisher appears to balance out the attention to Lincoln by including a sympathetic biography of Robert E. Lee; 497.) The more recent books also curb statements that emphasize his contemporaries' love for Lincoln, while including more such statements regarding Washington. For example, the books of 1982 declare Lincoln to have been a "great leader" and a friend to the South (as he hoped for quick reconciliation after the war), and they depict a country in mourning upon his death, saying, for instance: "many had learned to love the wise, kindly man in the White House" (Gross et al. 1980: 274). Such assertions disappear from later editions.

This is not, of course, to criticize the textbooks for decreasing their attention to Lincoln's boyhood or myths. This shift away from nationalist legend could have been considered as a step toward a more historical approach, were it not for the counterexample of the books' presentations of Washington. For instance, in discussions of Washington, summaries such as this one from Silver Burdett Ginn's 1997 edition are typical of textbooks published since then:

> George Washington was a brave, determined man. He faced many dangers in his life, yet he seldom panicked and never gave up. Instead, he

> worked his way through each problem as calmly and bravely as possible. [. . .] [H]e had earned a reputation as a man who could deal with anything. [. . .] In the end George Washington became a hero. He was more than just a good general. He had the ability to take command and inspire his soldiers to do the impossible. [. . .] When Americans were looking for their first President, it is no wonder they turned to George Washington.
>
> (Garcia et al. 1997: 172–73)

The textbooks praise Washington for his bravery and perseverance in battle, both as a young leader in the Seven Years War and during the difficult times of the Revolutionary War. Notably, the top-selling textbook of 2003 has added a highly visible reference to a myth with powerful religious associations that has been promoted by Texas Christian Right advocates. In large, bold print, Scott Foresman cites Washington's account of a battle during the Seven Years War: "I had four bullets through my coat and two horses were shot under me, and yet escaped unhurt" (Boyd et al. 2003: 249). The inclusion of and emphasis on this account is noteworthy in that David Barton focused upon the incident in a book he wrote entitled *Bulletproof George Washington* (2003). As a reminder, Barton is the founder of the education lobby the WallBuilders [sic], which publishers have consulted in order to obtain approval for their textbooks in Texas (Blakeslee 1999). Barton is also former vice chair of the Texas Republican Party, who was appointed by the State Board of Education in 2009 to participate in the rewriting of state history standards. In his 2003 book, Barton perpetuates myths according to which God protected Washington and destined him to lead the United States, thereby indicating that both the leader and the country are divinely blessed (Barton 2003). It thus seems plausible that Scott Foresman's decision to include this account reflects conservative wishes. Though the textbook does not go so far as to say that Washington was divinely chosen or protected, the story might well offer evidence for such a view.

More strikingly, textbooks make a clear concession to conservative wishes—in opposition to a multiculturalist stance—in the way that they handle Washington's slave ownership. Multiculturalists and many historians would like Washington to be understood as a man of his time, subject to contradictions and conflict between belief in Enlightenment values and being a slave-owner (Jordan and Bennett 1997: 155). Many conservatives, however, rail at presenting traditional heroes—and especially this ultimate founding hero—in any negative ways (see Gabler et al. 1985: 60). For instance, in their overall critique of 1997 U.S. history textbooks, the Gablers' Educational Research Analysts made the following statement, which reflects their general approach to traditional heroes:

> These textbooks have several goals—to divide the students racially, to tear down heroes of our past (at a time when students are in desperate

> need of heroes), to present our nation in a negative light, and to re-write American history. These textbooks must be rejected because they are unpatriotic and create a racist atmosphere of division instead of working to bring unity.
>
> (Warren 1997 [n.p.])

Concerning this most controversial aspect of Washington's history, the textbooks of 1982 do not mention that Washington (or any of the other founders) owned slaves. By 1997, two of the four books do discuss this fact, with one of these publishers (Harcourt) omitting it again in their 2003 edition (Banks et al. 1997: 323; Berson et al. 2003; Boehm et al. 282). The only 2003 textbook that does mention that Washington owned slaves does so in a rather distorted manner: McGraw-Hill's textbooks of 1997 and 2003 state that Washington freed his slaves after the Revolution (Banks et al. 2003: 292). This assertion is misleading, as he did not free them until after his death, in his will. The book also states that Washington's slaves were a gift from his wife's family (in what appears to be an attempt to dissociate him from the practice), though this is inaccurate (Higginbotham [2001: 116] shows that Washington himself had purchased most of his slaves). These inaccuracies may simply be unwitting errors, but the effect is significant.

The question of how to represent a president's stance on slavery is even more central regarding Lincoln. This issue reveals a significant rightward shift in certain textbooks and further illustrates the decline in Lincoln's prestige. Most textbooks of 1982, 1997, and 2003 reflect mainstream historiography by explaining that Lincoln was morally opposed to slavery but was above all committed to preserving the Union (e.g., Banks et al. 2003: 428–443; Boyd et al. 2003: 500; see Rothman 2011). There is, however, variation between the books over the degree of commitment to abolition that they attribute to Lincoln. Harcourt's editions are worth additional attention on this key point. In their 1997 edition, they show Lincoln as deeply committed on a moral level to abolition:

> Lincoln had been against slavery all his life [. . .]. By the stroke of his pen, Lincoln had launched a second American Revolution. He not only had helped end the shame of human bondage in America but had guaranteed the survival of American democracy. As he put it, "By giving freedom to the slave, we assure freedom to the free."
>
> (Boehm et al. 1997: 422–24)

In 2003, the publisher greatly decreases coverage of the Emancipation Proclamation (down from five pages in 1997 to just over one page in 2003) and implies that Lincoln was somewhat indifferent to the moral implications of slavery, presenting emancipation more as a response to public pressure and military strategy:

> To President Lincoln, the purpose of the war had been to keep the country together—to save the Union. It had not been to abolish slavery. [. . .] However, the move to end slavery grew stronger. Finally, after the Battle of Antietam Creek, Lincoln decided the time had come for an emancipation order. [. . .] The Emancipation Proclamation hurt the South's hopes of getting help from Britain and France. [. . .] Confederate President Jefferson Davis called Lincoln's proclamation "the most execrable measure recorded in the history of a guilty man." [. . .] By allowing freed slaves to serve in the military, the Emancipation Proclamation helped ease the Union army's shortage of soldiers.
>
> (Berson et al. 2003: 461–62)

There is, of course, support for both of these interpretations among the work of academic historians (Rothman 2011). The subject is complex. Yet, rather than present that complexity and embrace the opportunity to teach children nuanced critical thinking skills and historical reasoning, Harcourt moves from one extreme to another. By being thus more critical of Lincoln, Harcourt is less critical of the white South. Harcourt's 1997 textbook (Boehm et al.) received poor ratings from the prominent Christian Right activists, the Gablers' Educational Research Analysts. Harcourt's 2003 edition, on the other hand, received the Gablers' top endorsement. It therefore seems reasonable to wonder whether this stark change in the books' coverage of Lincoln and emancipation reflects influence (perhaps behind the scenes, or perhaps indirect) of Texas Christian Right activists.[8]

The only aspect of Lincoln's life that all of the textbooks now present in positive terms is the Gettysburg Address. This shift in focus has meaningful repercussions for textbooks' representations of Lincoln and the Civil War. Only one book of 1982 mentions the address. Since 1997, all the textbooks reproduce it in its entirety and emphasize it as a key part of the Civil War, thus elevating it to symbolic status as a revered founding text, akin to the Declaration of Independence and the Constitution. Two of the most recent textbooks explain that the speech emphasized national unity and indicated that the war was also being fought to end slavery. The third, Harcourt, avoids mentioning slavery explicitly (in keeping with the passage cited above), ambiguously speaking only of preserving the government based on liberty and equality (467–468). The books thus present Lincoln primarily as a great speaker, instead of for other personal qualities. He is no longer at the center of Civil War chapters in these books, which present less political history but more military history (focusing on strategy, key battles, as well as African American soldiers) and include short sections of social history (notably discussing women's wartime roles). By focusing on the Gettysburg Address, textbooks emphasize national unity and regeneration in the "new birth of freedom" (Bellah 1991: 176). This speech constitutes a powerful text in the cult of the nation, enshrining the sacralization of the homeland through heroic sacrifice (Smith 2008: 150). Consistent with this message, these books also continue to present the war as pitting brother against brother (literally referring to families fighting on opposite sides; e.g., Boyd et al. 492), and they show the true tragedy of Lincoln's death to have been the lost promise of reconciliation.

Through their idealization of and emphasis on Washington, in contrast to decreased and more critical coverage of Lincoln, textbooks have clearly turned Washington into the vastly predominant heroic figure of American history. This emphasis on Washington treats him not so much as a historical figure but as a national symbol, in contrast to the decreased symbolic status of Lincoln.

The decreasing emphasis on Lincoln's role coincides with a revision of the meaning of the Civil War and Reconstruction (see also Chapter One). In the last third of the twentieth century, in popular perceptions, the "reconciliationist memory" of the war was largely superseded by "emancipationist memory" (Blight 2008; Schwartz 2009: 131). While showing slavery to have been a cause of the war, textbooks in the early twenty-first century have come to promote a new compromise vision. In keeping with the conservative nationalist multiculturalism that has come to dominate these books, their presentations of Lincoln and the Civil War likewise combine elements of reconciliationist and emancipationist memories, so that all groups may celebrate "their" heroes, and the war is recognized as a milestone in the narrative of progress. If they so choose, conservative white Southerners can thus still cling to aspects of the older consensual myth that were consistent with "Lost Cause" ideology. Notably, they can focus on the bravery exhibited by soldiers of both sides (see Grant 2003: 200–201). As was mentioned in this chapter, textbooks emphasize this shared valor with their equal representations of generals Grant and Lee, and they adapt this conciliatory logic to certain demands of multiculturalism by including sections praising the bravery of black soldiers (as discussed further in Chapter One).

In this unifying myth all Americans fought, ultimately, for the union. Nevertheless, textbook publishers face complexity from the left and reticence from the right not so much over the history of Lincoln and the Civil War as over their place in American memory. Thus, beyond this seemingly consensual type of appeal to collective memory, recent textbooks have attempted to find consensus by reducing their attention to the subject. This choice contrasts with multiculturalists' and historians' invocations to teach about such controversies, including showing how and why historiography evolves. This decline in attention to Lincoln and the Civil War when considered in conjunction with textbooks' increased attention to Washington and the American Revolution reveals greater significance.

Textbooks' renewed fervor for the Revolution and its heroes reflects originalism (i.e., the idealized devotion to the founders that is characteristic of much conservative thought [Hartman 2015; Lepore 2010]). Instead of confronting the divisive myths in the United States' past, the shifts described in this chapter substitute a new consensual myth for the old one.

CONCLUSION

French curricula and textbooks aim to familiarize students with a variety of national figures, many of whom they present as positive forces in history. Curricula encourage transmission of national memory in requiring students to construct their own "pantheon" of heroes. Textbooks turn Joan of Arc into something of a national symbol, as they emphasize her role in helping to forge a national consciousness and defending the country. Similarly, they transmit certain classic images of national memory with their depictions of Louis IX. Outstanding French figures are those who defended French independence (such as de Gaulle and Joan of Arc), those who supported and advanced the structures and ideals of the republic (Hugo and de Gaulle), and those known for scientific achievement. All of these types of people advocate a sense of national identity and pride based on Enlightenment institutions and beliefs, including nationalism, as well as liberty and reason. Some of the French heroes establish ties with the premodern past (Joan of Arc, Louis IX, and Henri IV), but even among these, Louis IX and Henri IV are mostly discussed in relation to their contributions to modern institutions and beliefs in justice and tolerance. The emphasis is thus primarily on nationalism as grounded in modernism and is consistent with the vision of France as a bastion of universalist rationalism, as seen in the previous chapters. Nevertheless, overall, the French textbooks are more likely to adopt an approach more in line with academic historiography than are their U.S. counterparts, which engage much more in a pedagogy of memory and teaching through celebration of heroes.

U.S. textbooks idealize and celebrate George Washington above all. This is a key difference not only in each country's history education but also in each country's history. France simply has no George Washington, no consensual key hero of the nation. Its heroes are either controversial—admired by one segment of the population but disliked or ignored by another (e.g., Saint Louis) or subject to such diverging interpretations as to represent very different things to different people (e.g., Joan of Arc). In addition, the main actors of France's founding moments as a modern nation-state often tarnished their own legacy, as in the case of Robespierre or Napoleon. Washington, on the other hand, is an exceptional national hero, as, despite his many years in the public eye, he constitutes a sort of ideological blank slate. He stands for American independence and democracy (or, at least, for opposition to monarchy), but beyond that, he is not a partisan figure.

Even Lincoln, despite his much more complex legacy and the still-controversial questions surrounding representations of the Civil War and its aftermath, is more consensual than French heroes. He represents values that most mainstream Americans support (the end of slavery, national unity, self-sacrifice for the nation, and in the popular imagination, honesty and hard work), which accounts for his heroic status in the textbooks of the 1980s. However, Lincoln's place in these textbooks has declined, most likely for multiple reasons. In public memory, he once stood for many things but now stands mostly for abolition of slavery. In the political arena, this is a legacy that both parties want to claim (especially as Republicans struggle to attract minority voters). However, this association means that conservative Southern Christian textbook activists, who are the champions for many traditional American heroes, have little interest in Lincoln. This more narrow association—and the attendant decline in Lincoln's malleability as a symbol—may prevent Lincoln from continuing to be the powerful icon he once was. This symbolic limitation in conjunction with more nuanced historiography (i.e., a decline in hagiography among historians) and a shift among multiculturalist activists to advocating inclusion of other heroes of civic rights may signal a durable decline in Lincoln's symbolic role.

U.S. textbooks' intense focus on Washington may also reflect a difference between multiculturalist and conservative memory. Memory on the left appears more diffuse, embracing multiple heroes. This does not necessarily make it any less national or nationalist. Memory on the right focuses on a fairly homogenous group of founding heroes, with Washington at their core. The heroes of the left are individually pictured less frequently than Washington and the other traditional founding heroes, but (consensual) multiculturalist heroes are nevertheless given significant coverage as a group.

In addition French and U.S. textbooks' different pedagogical approaches to heroes, they also tend to highlight different types of people. French textbooks emphasize builders of the modern state, and while they accord some importance to military defenders of the nation-state, they do not turn them into idols. They explicitly show pupils models of other routes to serving humanity (not just the nation) through their more positive presentations of artists, philosophers, and scientists. However, few women and no minorities appear in all the textbooks, which instead focus on traditional figures. In U.S. textbooks, the most prominent heroes tend to emphasize a belief in freedom (vaguely and minimally defined; essentially a Lockean freedom from tyranny), military courage and achievement, and devotion and sacrifice in service of the nation (as we also saw in the previous chapter.) Thus, more martial expressions of commitment to the country are celebrated and promoted, depicting defense and promotion of the nation-state as the highest of callings.

Despite these differences, French and U.S. textbooks' depictions of heroes reveal a noteworthy similarity. Many scholars have studied the religious roots of nationalist hero worship (Bell 2001/2003; Durkheim 1925/1961; Schwartz 2009). Examining French and U.S. textbooks demonstrates the surprising endurance not just of the form of religious-style adulation but of the content. Notably, the primary French heroes in these textbooks are Catholic saints. These textbooks retain vestiges of the sacred associations with Joan of Arc and Louis IX despite the professed secularism—and even anticlericalism—of many French scholars and policymakers. The enduring symbolic power of these figures demonstrates the strength of the association of religion and nationalism: that which the collectivity once held as sacred appears to retain a hold on collective memory, even when the belief in the sacred has purportedly vanished. Similarly, both Washington and Lincoln have explicitly been seen as divine figures—not figuratively but very literally. Perhaps Lincoln's declining prevalence in textbooks may be partly attributed to the fact that the progressive Christian groups who historically saw him as a divine emissary no longer attempt to get public education to include religious interpretations of history. Only the Christian Right now seeks to incorporate their religious beliefs into public education, and they attribute sacred status not to Lincoln but to Washington and the other founders (as well as to various religious communities and leaders, as we will see in Chapter Six). As this book has shown repeatedly, Washington is a key figure in conservative Christian religious nationalism, which views the U.S. as a covenantal nation, with Washington as an anointed leader. This vision forms a powerful conception of the nation, which resonates for many Americans to the point that they invest significant effort in seeing that schools perpetuate it.

Nations need a broad array of heroes from different time periods and contexts to illustrate their greatness, progress, and continuity. Variety among this "pantheon" is essential, both to offer a complete vision of the nation and its excellence in different domains (political, social, economic, scientific, artistic, humanitarian . . .) and to allow members of the national community to identify with and admire different heroes, according to their own sensibilities. While a certain amount of continuity in the pantheon helps ground the nation in the past, regeneration of the store of heroes also seems valuable for perpetuating attachment to the nation in the present.

In France, with its long history that is commonly viewed as national, multiple heroes emerged from multiple eras of nation-building. This multiplicity may not be conducive to hero-worship focused on one or two consensual figures. Yet there is potentially a national hero for everyone, as the diversity of the pantheon could allow for identification with individual national patron saints, leading to common commitment to the multifaceted nation. Nevertheless, French textbooks have largely shifted away from a pedagogy of memory, particularly regarding heroes. In this domain, they rely instead on critical pedagogy and shared knowledge of the past to transmit national identity. The U.S. textbooks, by contrast, display two complementary paths for promoting national attachment. On the one hand, they promote a variety of heroes, thus offering multiple sources of identification. On the other hand, in their abundant and idealized representations of Washington, they promote a supreme, unified cult of the state. These books' presentations of heroes thus parallel other instances of nationalist multiculturalism, in which pluralism exists within a hierarchy of unity.

NOTES

1. Historian Christian Amalvi has argued that in France, historians' rejection of the "great men" approach has been countered in recent years by popular interest in national heroes (Amalvi 2011: 9–10). Indeed, there have been recent calls from the right in France to return to traditional history narratives with

their focus on national heroes and chronological lists of events (for examples, see: Brocard 2012; Rochat 2012; Sevillia 2012). However, even before these recent publications, history curricula had already begun to add lists of people with whom students must be familiar as part of the renewed emphasis on transmitting national culture.

2. The authors of the National History Standards, for instance, advocated a more active, critical approach to teaching history. Though they wanted to do away with rote learning and hagiography and to increase the teaching of social history, they have repeatedly argued that they did not seek to remove traditional heroes from curricula (Jones 1995; Nash et al. 1997/2000). Furthermore, if multiculturalists have wanted more social history, many of them also wanted not to do away with the national pantheon, but to add to it (cf. CIBC 1981: 44, 58; Zimmerman 2002; and see Chapter One in this book).
3. Géraldine Bozec has similarly concluded that textbooks no longer treat traditional heroes as myths (2010: 198), as did Soysal et al. regarding French and German high school textbooks (2005).
4. In his study of textbooks published between the 1970s and 1990, James Loewen (1995/2007) examined the prevalence of heroes and how the process of "heroification" simplified and bowdlerized the lives of those thus enshrined. The centrality of heroes in U.S. textbooks is clearly an enduring feature.
5. Christopher Columbus is a close seventh, appearing 2.7 times on average per book in the most recent publications. The attention paid to Columbus is interesting; French textbooks emphasize the importance of his "discovery" of America (as they still call it, in Eurocentric fashion), in an approach that is consistent with official calls to connect French history to European and world history. However, the multiple images of Columbus are somewhat surprising, given that no portraits were made of the navigator during his lifetime, thus undermining the authenticity of the textbooks' illustrations.
6. This edition (Beyria et al. 2003 CM1) dedicates an exceptional amount of space to Joan—six pages—and tells the story of the Hundred Years War exclusively as it relates to her. Throughout this book, the authors use a narrative device of a fictional account of time-traveling children from the present day. This technique creates an emotional bond with Joan and her death, emphasizing a sense of unfairness. This approach is a complete outlier among all the books, and Sedrap did away with it in its most recent edition (Boëche 2011 CM1).
7. Vercingétorix, leader of the unsuccessful last major effort of the Gauls to fight Roman conquest, is not among the most frequently pictured people in textbooks, but he merits brief discussion here. Though he is mentioned in the textbooks' narratives throughout the period studied here, he is not treated as a national symbol. On the contrary, in its most recent edition, Hatier explains how Vercingétorix became a legend in the nineteenth century and reveals the inaccuracies common in depictions of that era (Le Callennec 2009: 54–55).
8. That Harcourt consulted the Gablers' group about this textbook seems highly likely, especially since the group's director, Neal Frey, indicates that this was the case, at least in subsequent years, in a June 2009 newsletter (Frey 2009).

REFERENCES

For the complete list of textbooks analyzed, see Chapter One.

French Textbooks

Beyria, Patrick, et al. 2003. *A Nous le monde! Cycle 3, 2e année, CM1: Histoire, géographie, sciences, éducation civique*. Paris: Sedrap.
Boëche, Sandra, ed. 2011. *CM1: Les Reporteurs histoire, géographie, histoire des arts, développement durable*. Paris: Sedrap.
Boëche, Sandra, ed. 2011. *CM2: Les Reporteurs histoire, géographie, histoire des arts, développement durable*. Paris: Sedrap.
Chevalier, Jean-Pierre and Roselyne Le Bourgeois, eds. 2010. *Histoire, histoire des arts, instruction civique, CM2*. Paris: Nathan.
Dorel-Ferré, Gracia and M. Dhainaut. 1985. *Cours moyen: Histoire*. Paris: Armand Colin.
Le Bourgeois, Roselyne. 2010. *Histoire, histoire des arts, CM1*. Paris: Nathan.
Le Callennec, Sophie, ed. 2009. *Histoire, géographie, CE2*. Collection Magellan. Paris: Hatier.
Le Callennec, Sophie, ed. 2010. *Histoire, géographie, CM1*. Collection Magellan. Paris: Hatier.
Le Callennec, Sophie, ed. 2011. *Histoire, géographie, CM2*. Collection Magellan. Paris: Hatier.
Nembrini, Jean-Louis, Pierre Polivka, and Jean Bordes. 1985. *Histoire CM*. Pour connaître la France. Paris: Hachette écoles.
Vincent, Marc, et al. 1985. *CM1: Histoire: La France au fil du temps, de la Préhistoire à 1789*. Collection Télémaque. Paris: Nathan.
Vincent, Marc, et al. 1985. *CM2: Histoire: La France au fil du temps, de 1789 à nos jours*. Collection Télémaque. Paris: Nathan.

United States Textbooks

Arnsdorf, Val E., et al. 1982. *The United States and Its Neighbors*. Morristown, NJ: Silver Burdett.
Banks, James A., et al. 1997. *United States: Adventures in Time and Place*. New York: Macmillan McGraw-Hill.
Banks, James A., et al. 2003. *Our Nation*. New York: Macmillan McGraw-Hill.
Bednarz, Sarah, et al. 1997. *Build Our Nation. We the People*. Boston: Houghton Mifflin.
Berson, Michael, et al. 2003. *Harcourt Horizons: United States History*. Orlando, FL: Harcourt.
Boehm, Richard G., et al. 1997. *America's Story: Stories in Time*. New York: Harcourt-Brace.
Boyd, Candy Dawson, et al. 2003. *The United States, Social Studies*. Glenview, IL: Scott Foresman.
Garcia, Juan R., et al. 1997. *Our United States: Social Studies*. Parsippany, NJ: Silver Burdett Ginn.
Gross, Herbert, et al. 1980. *Exploring Our World: Americas*. 2nd ed. Chicago: Follett.
King, Allen Y., et al. 1982. *The United States and the Other Americas*. New York: Macmillan.
King, Frederick M., et al. 1981. *Understanding Our Country*. River Forest, IL: Laidlaw.
Klein, Stanley, et al. 1982. *Our Country's History: Level E*. New York: Scholastic.

Curriculum Guidelines

"Chapter 113: Texas Essential Knowledge and Skills for Social Studies." 1998. *Texas Essential Knowledge and Skills*. Texas Education Agency. Retrieved 20 Dec. 2000 (http://www.tea.state.tx.us/rules/tac/ch113.html#s1137).

"Chapter 113: Texas Essential Knowledge and Skills for Social Studies." 2010. *Texas Essential Knowledge and Skills*. Texas Education Agency. Retrieved 5 Nov. 2013 (http://ritter.tea.state.tx.us/rules/tac/chapter113/index.html).

Framework for the Social Studies. 1980. Austin: Texas Education Agency.

"Horaires et programmes d'enseignement de l'école primaire." 2002. *Bulletin officiel de l'Education nationale*. Special issue 1 (14 Feb.).

"Horaires et programmes d'enseignement de l'école primaire." 2008. *Bulletin officiel de l'Education nationale*. Special issue 3 (19 Jun.).

"Horaires, programmes et instructions pour l'école élémentaire, 1985." 1986. *Bulletin officiel de l'Education nationale*. Special issue 1 (16 Jan.).

Ministère de la Jeunesse, de l'Éducation nationale et de la Recherche: Direction de l'enseignement scolaire. 2002. "Histoire et géographie cycle des approfondissements (cycle 3)." Collection Ecole: Documents d'application des programmes. Paris: Centre national de documentation pédagogique.

Proclamation 1994 of the State Board of Education Advertising for Bids on Instructional Materials. 1994. Austin: Texas Education Agency.

"Programmes de l'école primaire." 1995. *Bulletin officiel de l'Education nationale* 48 (28 Dec.).

Works of Reference

Amalvi, Christian. 1984. "L'Iconographie des manuels d'histoire et la mémoire collective: de la mémoire scolaire à la mémoire buissonière." In Henri Moniot, ed., *Enseigner l'histoire: Des manuels à la mémoire*. New York: Peter Lang, pp. 205–215.

Amalvi, Christian. 2011. *Les héros des Français: Controverses autour de la mémoire nationale*. Paris: Larousse.

APHG (Association des Professeurs d'Histoire et de Géographie). 2010. "Motion à propos du projet de Maison de l'Histoire de France." APHG Aix-Marseille. 29 Nov. Retrieved 28 Oct. 2013 (http://www.aphgaixmarseille.com/spip.php?article1418).

Apple, Michael W. 1991. "The Culture and Commerce of the Textbook." In Michael W. Apple and Linda K. Christian-Smith, eds., *The Politics of the Textbook*. New York: Routledge.

Barton, David. 2003. *The Bulletproof George Washington*. Aledo, TX: WallBuilder Press.

Bell, David. 2001/2003. *The Cult of the Nation in France: Inventing Nationalism, 1680–1800*. Cambridge, MA: Harvard University Press.

Bellah, Robert N. 1991. *Beyond Belief: Essays on Religion in a Post-traditionalist World*. Berkeley: University of California Press.

Bingham, Marjorie Wall. 1997. "Washington: By Ability, Politeness, and Attention." *Social Studies* 88.4: 158–9.

Blakeslee, Nate. 1999. "McGraw-Hill Sees the Light." *The Texas Observer* 30 avril. <http://www.texasobserver. org/showArticle.asp?ArticleID=1051> (21 mars 2005).

Blight, David. 2008. "The Theft of Lincoln in Scholarship, Politics, and Public Memory." In E. Foner, ed., *Our Lincoln: New Perspectives on Lincoln and His World*. New York: Norton, pp. 269–282.

Bliss, Traci. 1990. "Visuals in Perspective: An Analysis of U.S. History Textbooks." *The Social Studies* 81.1(Jan./Feb.): 10–14.

Borne, Dominique. 2002. "Apprendre l'histoire et la géographie: inventaire critique." In Michel Hagnerelle, ed., *Apprendre l'histoire et la géographie à l'école.* Versailles: Centre régional de documentation pédagogique de l'académie de Versailles, pp. 17–24.

Brocard, Marie-Amélie. 2012. "Les Déclassés de l'histoire de France." *Le Figaro Histoire*, 4 (Oct.): 58–69.

Campbell, Joseph. 1949/2008. *The Hero with a Thousand Faces.* 3rd ed. Novato, CA: New World Library.

CIBC (Council on Interracial Books for Children). 1981. *Guidelines for Selecting Bias-Free Textbooks and Storybooks.* New York: Council on Interracial Books for Children.

Collins, Gail. 2012. "How Texas Inflicts Bad Textbooks on Us." *The New York Review of Books* 12 Jun. Retrieved 5 Nov. 2013 (http://www.nybooks.com/articles/archives/2012/jun/21/how-texas-inflicts-bad-textbooks-on-us/).

De Cock, Laurence and Emmanuelle Picard. 2009. *La Fabrique scolaire de l'histoire.* Marseille: Agone.

Delfattore, Joan. 1992. *What Johnny Shouldn't Read: Textbook Censorship in America.* New Haven, CT: Yale University Press.

Duchastel, Philippe C. 1983. "Text Illustrations." *Performance & Instruction Journal* 22.4(May): 3–5.

Durkheim, Emile. 1925/1961. *Moral Education: A Study in the Theory and Application of the Sociology of Education.* Trans. E.K. Wilson and H. Schnurer. New York: Free Press of Glencoe.

Educational Research Analysts. 1982. *1982 Textbook Ratings.* Longview, TX: Educational Research Analysts.

Educational Research Analysts. 1997. *1997 Elementary Social Studies Information.* Longview, TX: Educational Research Analysts.

Educational Research Analysts. 2003. *US History Textbook Standard Review Criteria.* Longview, TX: Educational Research Analysts.

Erekson, Keith A. 2012. *Politics and the History Curriculum: The Struggle over Standards in Texas and the Nation.* New York: Palgrave Macmillan.

Farr, Roger and Michael A. Tulley. 1985. "Do Adoption Committees Perpetuate Mediocre Textbooks?" *Phi Delta Kappan* 66.7(Mar.): 467–471.

Finn, Chester and Diane Ravitch. 2004. *The Mad, Mad World of Textbook Adoption.* Washington, DC: Thomas B. Fordham Institute. 29 Sept. Retrieved 25 Feb. 2015 (http://edex.s3-us-west-2.amazonaws.com/publication/pdfs/Mad%20World_Test2_8.pdf).

Foner, Eric. 1988/2002. *Reconstruction: America's Unfinished Revolution, 1863–1877.* New York: Perennial Classics.

Foner, Eric, ed. 1997. *The New American History.* Rev. ed. Philadelphia, PA: Temple University Press.

Frey, Neal. 2009. *Educational Research Analysts Newsletter.* Jun. 2009.

Gabler, Mel, et al. 1985. *What are they Teaching Our Children?* Wheaton, IL: Victor Books.

Garcia, Patrick. 2013. "Les Péripéties de la discipline." *Le Débat* 175: 8–17.

Grant, Susan-Mary. 2003. "'The Charter of Its Birthright': The Civil War and American Nationalism." In S.-M. Grant and P.J. Parish, eds., *Legacy of Disunion: The Enduring Significance of the American Civil War.* Baton Rouge: Louisiana State University Press, pp. 188–206.

Hartman, Andrew. 2015. A *War for the Soul of America: A History of the Culture Wars.* Chicago: University of Chicago Press.

Higginbotham, Don, ed. 2001. *George Washington Reconsidered*. Charlottesville, VA: University of Virginia Press.
Hutchins, Rachel. 2011. "Traditional Heroes and the Renegotiation of National Identity in United States History Textbooks: Representations of George Washington and Abraham Lincoln, 1982–2003." *Nations and Nationalism* 17.3: 649–668.
Hutchinson, John. 2005. *Nations as Zones of Conflict*. London: Sage Publications.
ISSP Research Group. 2003. International Social Survey Programme (ISSP): National Identity II. Distributor: GESIS Cologne Germany ZA4850, Data Version 2.0.0 (2009–10–29).
Jennings, Eric. 1994. "'Reinventing Jeanne': The Iconography of Joan of Arc in Vichy Schoolbooks, 1940–44." *Journal of Contemporary History* 29.4: 711–734.
Jones, Arnita A. 1995. "Our Stake in the History Standards." *OAH Magazine of History* 9.3: 5–6. Retrieved 27 Jan. 2005 (http://www.oah.org/pubs/magazine/standards/jones.html#Anchor-Ou-23757).
Jordan, Ervin L. Jr. and Clifford T. Bennett. 1997. "George Washington: A Hero for American Students?" *Social Studies* 88.4: 154–6.
Joutard, Philippe and Jean Lecuir. 2000. "Les Palmarès de la mémoire nationale." *L'Histoire* 242(Apr.): 33–35. Retrieved 20 Aug. 2013 (http://www.histoire.presse.fr/dossiers/les-heros-des-francais/le-palmares-de-la-memoire-nationale-01–04–2000–8418).
Le Goff, Jacques. 1996/1999. *Saint Louis*. Paris: Folio.
Legris, Patricia. 2010. "Les Programmes d'histoire en France: la construction progressive d'une 'citoyenneté plurielle' (1980–2010)." *Histoire de l'éducation* 126: 121–154.
Lepore, Jill. 2010. *The Whites of Their Eyes: The Tea Party's Revolution and the Battle over American History*. Princeton, NJ: Princeton University Press.
Loewen, James W. 1995/2007. *Lies My Teacher Told Me: Everything Your American History Textbook Got Wrong*. Revised Edition. New York: Touchstone.
Marshall, J. Dan. 1991. "State-Level Textbook Selection Reform: Toward the Recognition of Fundamental Control." In Philip G. Altbach, Gail P. Kelly, Hugh G. Petrie and Lois Weis, eds., *Textbooks in American Society: Politics, Policy, and Pedgagogy*. Albany: State University of New York Press, pp. 117–144.
Nash, Gary B. 1997. "The National History Standards and George Washington." *The Social Studies* 88.4(Jul./Aug.): 159–162.
Nash, Gary B., Charlotte Crabtree, and Ross E. Dunn. 1997/2000. *History on Trial: Culture Wars and the Teaching of the Past*. New York: Vintage Books.
Peterson, Merrill. 1994. *Abraham Lincoln in American Memory*. New York: Oxford University Press.
Porpora, David V. 1996. "Personal Heroes, Religion, and Transcendental Metanarratives." *Sociological Forum* 11.2: 209–229.
Ravitch, Diane. 2003. *The Language Police: How Pressure Groups Restrict What Students Learn*. New York: Knopf.
Rochat, Sébastien. 2012. "Trois livres engagent la bataille de l'histoire: Du Figaro à Pernaut, la défense des Grands Hommes s'organise." *Arrêt sur Image* 6 Oct. Retrieved 29 Oct. 2013 (http://www.arretsurimages.net/contenu.php?id=5260).
Rothman, Adam. 2011. "Slavery, the Civil War, and Reconstruction." In E. Foner and L. McGirr, eds., *American History Now*. Philadelphia: Temple University Press, pp. 75–95.
Rousso, Henry. 1990/1994. *The Vichy Syndrome: History and Memory in France Since 1944*. Trans. Arthur Goldhammer. Cambridge, MA: Harvard University Press.
Schwartz, Barry. 1987. *George Washington: The Making of an American Symbol*. London: Collier Macmillan.

Schwartz, Barry. 2009. *Abraham Lincoln in the Post-Heroic Era: History and Memory in Late Twentieth-Century America*. Chicago: University of Chicago Press.

Sevillia, Jean. 2012. "Qui veut casser l'histoire de France?" *Le Figaro* 24 Aug. Retrieved 29 Oct. 2013 (http://www.lefigaro.fr/actualite-france/2012/08/24/01016-20120824ARTFIG00298-qui-veut-casser-l-histoire-de-france.php).

Smith, Anthony D. 1999. *Myths and Memories of the Nation*. Oxford: Oxford University Press.

Smith, Anthony D. 2008. *The Cultural Foundations of Nations: Hierarchy, Covenant, and Republic*. Malden, MA: Blackwell.

Soysal, Yasemin Nohuğlu, Teresa Bertilotti, and Sabine Mannitz. 2005. "Projections of Identity in French and German History and Civics Textbooks." In H. Schissler and Y. Soysal, eds., *The Nation, Europe, and the World: Textbooks and Curricula in Transition*. New York; Oxford: Berghahn Books, pp. 13–34.

Warren, Carol. 1997. "Reviews of 5th Grade U.S. Social Studies Texts." *1997 Elementary Social Studies Information*. Longview, TX: Educational Research Analysts. [n.p].

Weber, Eugen. 1976. *Peasants into Frenchmen: The Modernization of Rural France, 1870–1914*. Stanford, CA: Stanford University Press.

Zelinsky, W. 1988. *Nation into State: The Shifting Symbolic Foundations of American Nationalism*. Chapel Hill: University of North Carolina Press.

6 National Territory

Representations of the national territory play a major role in definitions of national identity. Establishing the existence of authentic connections between the national community and the territory helps legitimize the political sovereignty of the nation-state. This chapter shows how French and U.S. textbooks anchor national identity in the territory. Both countries' history books draw on founding myths that legitimize the nation-state's existence through teleological accounts of ties to the land. Their approaches to teaching geography differ, however, with French books once again approaching the subject more as an academic discipline while U.S. books treat the landscape as another national symbol.

Nationalist relationships to the territory can take different forms in different historical and geographical contexts. In countries such as France, where the land was mostly settled before the modern age and the creation of the nation-state, the people's mark on the land can be interpreted by historicists to show the nation's connection to its territory.[1] In other words, the territory is defined as national because French people have historical ties to it and interact with it in productive, spatially specific ways. This historicist grounding of the nation in a territory is certainly also present in countries such as the United States, which had extensive inaccessible regions (for European-American settlers) during much of their history. However, in such settler-colonist countries this relationship to the territory exists alongside another process: the "naturalization" of the nation (Kaufmann and Zimmer 1998). Here, aspects of the landscape are attributed with forging the national character and thus creating a unique people. This mode of symbolic appropriation of the national landscape(s) developed under the influence of Romantic notions of the sublime in nature and particularly in wilderness. It is perhaps also particularly well suited to colonist states, where the founders of the modern country cannot claim ancient ties to the land.

National territory can also gain legitimacy through association with religious themes. If modern French identity strives to present itself as secular, vestiges of religious belief can nevertheless color interpretations of national borders. The reputedly hexagonal shape of metropolitan France can be seen as an indication that these borders were meant to be (Sahlins 1990: 1451). Similarly, the abundance of natural resources and variety of landscapes could be viewed as a sign of divine favor (Marienstras 1988: 328). More historically, Christianity can be interpreted as a major force that shaped the medieval kingdom, leading to present-day borders; the devout may see this process as another sign of providence. However, overtly religious interpretations are not dominant in the largely unreligious modern country and do not appear in discussions of educational content. Though certainly some French Catholics do still see the country as divinely ordained, as we have already seen, Catholic groups have not sought to influence French public education the same way that Christian groups have in the U.S. The rift between republicanism and Catholicism that lasted for more than a century after the Revolution may have left certain premodern religious heroes in the public consciousness (see Chapter Five) but did not, apparently, leave room for religious mythology surrounding the national territory. While premodern France embraced a sort of myth of divine election legitimizing the monarchy (as the *fille aînée de l'Eglise*, i.e., the oldest daughter of the church), this vision was transformed from the time of the Revolution into the *mission civilisatrice*. It was this resolutely secular mission that justified territorial conquest on and near the European continent, as well as colonization abroad (Conklin 1997).

The American case is quite different on many levels. Many European colonists moved to what would become the United States for economic reasons, and the modern state was founded in a colonial revolution based on Enlightenment values. Yet, many Americans have traditionally seen the Puritans of New England as the spiritual ancestors of the nation and see continuity between their belief in divine election and a national, divinely ordained mission of the United States. According to this belief, religious and national identities are fused and are intricately tied to the national territory: the promised land in the covenantal myth to which the Pilgrims subscribed. A belief in national chosenness and purpose drove the doctrine of "manifest destiny" and justified western expansion, and this conviction still colors many Americans' understanding of U.S. history and the country's current role and place in the world (including, notably, foreign policy; Bacevich 2002; Smith 2008: 172–173, 181; Stephanson 1995). This unified Christian vision of American history and identity is at the core of conservative Christian education activists' goals and strategies (e.g., Educational Research Analysts 2013; see Note 11 in Chapter One for examples).

In both France and the United States, history and geography have long been taught together, sharing the charge of shaping the national citizenry. This pairing highlights the fact that national history has, typically, been the story of conquering and expanding the national territory to its present borders.

PRINCIPAL FINDINGS AND OUTLINE

In curricula and textbooks of France and the United States, the relationship of the people to their territory is seen as unique and historically justified. French curricula and textbooks largely perpetuate traditional myths, depicting the national community as having deep historical roots in the contemporary French borders. In U.S. textbooks, on the other hand, origin myths have evolved in the wake of multiculturalist reform, though these newer myths also give the modern nation historical roots.

Differences in symbolic approach and types of territorial origin myths contribute to differences between French and U.S. textbooks' representations of geography. Where French curricula and textbooks ground a vision of national identity and pride in the variety of ways in which contemporary people interact with the land, U.S. textbooks' expressions of attachment focus much more on the beauty of the national territory.

This chapter begins by examining depictions of French and U.S. geography, including statements regarding natural and human-made beauty, the variety of natural resources, and more potentially controversial questions regarding ecology and conservation. It then explores contemporary versions of traditional myths about territorial expansion, demonstrating the ways in which textbooks present a teleological vision of national territorial rootedness. For France, these topics include the tradition of anchoring modern France in ancient Gaul, the Frankish kingdom, and Capetian dynasty. For the U.S., these subjects include the relationship between European colonization and Native Americans, as well as nineteenth-century westward expansion, and the doctrine of "manifest destiny."

TERRITORY AND GEOGRAPHY IN CURRICULA AND TEXTBOOKS

Utility, Beauty, and Unity in French Educational Materials

In the past thirty years, French curricula have adopted an increasingly explicit approach to the relationship between the national territory and the community, consistent with their overall emphasis on national identity. The history and geography curriculum of 1985 vaguely charges these subjects with transmitting the country's "political and cultural heritage" ("Horaires . . ." 17). The 1995 curriculum makes clearer and more frequent reference to familiarization with and conservation of the national heritage, which it more explicitly associates with geographical sites ("Programmes . . ." 28). This trend is further amplified in the 2002 curriculum. The accompanying documents (which are no longer officially in effect for the 2008 curriculum but which continue to influence textbook authors) discuss at some length the meaning of landscapes (*paysages*), concluding (in language whose denseness I have tried to replicate):

> The landscape accounts for multiple factors and allows for an approach to studying contact between man and his milieu; it can be imbued with a patrimonial value that refers to founding sites of a local or national

> identity (sites of the Pointe du Raz, the Mont-Saint-Michel, Sainte-Victoire mountain . . .), that are protected (natural parks, Coastal Protection Agency . . .), or to history (urban and industrial sites . . .). It can have a memorial function or artistic value. It can have economic value, like the speculative landscapes of downtowns or seasides. . . . Or it can be recreational, like places of leisure or tourism, often associated with an aesthetic value: the "beauty" (*le "beau"*) of touristic landscapes . . . the "picturesque" of guidebooks.
>
> (Ministère . . . 24; ellipses in the original)

Thus, while familiarizing students with sites of national memory and identity, the curriculum also shows that a nationalist attachment to the territory is an object worthy of study, representing one of the many ways in which people interact with their environment. Similarly, territorial beauty is seen as something of a commodity—an explanatory factor in how people interact with the environment—but it is not celebrated in a Romantic sense. On the contrary, this is a rather pragmatic approach to beauty, and the use of quotation marks indicates the subjectivity of its existence.

In addition to this more academically grounded approach, the 2002 curriculum also focuses on attachment to the territory and its variety as a source of unity and pride: "Like Europe, France is also characterized by a diversity of landscapes, which is accompanied on the part of the French by a profound feeling of the unity of their country, which is the fruit of a long history" (81). Thus, French specificity is rooted in its diversity, allied with affective unity (in which the curriculum explicitly includes the overseas territories).

The 2008 curriculum is considerably less expansive in its goals for geography teaching. In its much more concise instructions for the final three years of elementary school, it states that the primary goal is to familiarize students with how people interact with their environment, particularly in France (situated in its European context) ("Horaires . . ." 25). It also requires familiarizing students with various national "landscapes" (including urban and industrial), but this curriculum reserves its comments on *patrimoine* for art and literature, rather than geography.

In keeping with these curricula, the French textbooks from 1985 through 2010 teach geography as a discipline, focusing on the ways in which humans interact with the environment. They do not generally describe the landscapes in aesthetic or subjective ways. They present a variety of types of interaction between people and the environment, including various forms of industry, farming, and tourism. Even regarding tourism, most books do not cite beauty as a draw for tourists but more often refer to favorable climate (as for beaches) or activities (whether for Paris or for the mountains). The books that drew on the 1985 curriculum mentioned somewhat more often the beauty of the national territory, yet they did so in conjunction with a concern for environmental protection. For example, Armand Colin's 1993 geography textbook explains that natural beauty is a draw for tourists but mainly emphasizes how tourism damages the environment (Chagny and Forez 1993: 99). The photos that illustrate these books likewise focus on industry and economic activity. The national territory, then, is not idealized or assigned mythical status for its inherent qualities. Instead, its representations promote economic nationalism, giving the national community form and cohesion through pragmatic attachment to the land.

A key question regarding presentations of French territory concerns the degree to which the overseas territories are shown as part of the nation. The ways in which the textbooks present national geography tend to reinforce the centrality of metropolitan France. As we have seen in other chapters, though the French textbooks have increasingly included the overseas territories in national history and geography, many books continue to marginalize these regions of France in significant ways. In CM1 (equivalent of Grade Four), geography lessons are meant to focus on "France within Europe." Different textbooks take very different approaches to presenting the overseas territories in this context. Sedrap only includes one illustration of an overseas territory (Boëche 2011 CM1: 127) and generally focuses on metropolitan France. However, the other books make more of an effort to include the overseas territories. Nathan dedicates a ten-page chapter to the territories, though this is separate from the coverage of metropolitan France (Chevalier and Picrel 40–49). Hatier includes images of scenery from the territories to illustrate various lessons, thereby including the territories as part of "France." In the introductory lesson, Hatier explains that the overseas territories are part of the E.U. (Le Callennec 2010: 102–103). This textbook thus gives a political, rather than strictly geographical definition of "Europe." All books include the territories in two or three maps of France, but most maps (between 10 and 15 per book) show only metropolitan France.

The marginalization of the overseas territories has deep historical and cultural roots, well beyond the editorial practices of textbooks. The very terms that are commonly used—and that the books reproduce with no critical distance—to distinguish "metropolitan France" from the "overseas territories" are Eurocentric. In addition, these books continue to teach children that metropolitan France is often called "the Hexagon" (e.g., Boëche 2011 CM2: 121; Le Callennec 2011: 144). This label further pushes other territories to the periphery. It also has symbolic weight, carrying forward ideas of natural—or at least supremely rational—borders, making the shape of the country an object of pride (see Sahlins 1990 on the symbolic ramifications of seeing metropolitan France as a hexagon).

In familiarizing children with the national landscapes and economic activities, French geography education seeks to strengthen the bonds of community and territorial rootedness. Despite paying greater attention to the overseas territories than older editions did, the books still largely present them separately from continental France.

Utility, Beauty, and Unity in U.S. Educational Materials

U.S. geography curricula are similar to their most recent French counterpart, emphasizing technical, rather than ideological, aspects of geography. For instance, the 2010 TEKS focus primarily on teaching students to understand maps (in Grades K–5), and in Grades Four and Five, on familiarizing students with major landforms and cities and patterns of settlement and land use. The geography curriculum guidelines are considerably less detailed than the (already brief) history guidelines, and geography certainly does not receive the same type of public scrutiny as does history teaching in the U.S. As such, it seems that the curricula have not been subject to the same overt nationalizing that has characterized evolutions of the history curricula. Texas geography curricula require familiarity with the national territory, but they do not include any subjective assessments of the national territory and certainly do not mention its beauty.

The textbooks, however, take a vastly different approach. In keeping with the conclusions of previous chapters, over time, U.S. books have come to teach less about the interaction between Americans and their environment and more about celebrating the beauty of the scenery, which becomes a nationalist symbol akin to the flag or the Statue of Liberty. In 1982, only two books out of five had chapters celebrating the national territory. Both of these caption an illustration of a national park with text from the song "America, the Beautiful" (Helmus et al. 3, 261; Klein et al. 229). These books both explicitly ground national identity in the diverse territory. For instance, one states, "Few other nations have as many different and interesting kinds of people and places as ours" (Helmus et al. 2). The other is slightly more expansive: "Now you know something about the important landforms of the United States. You know that our large country looks different from one region to another. You have made an important step in learning about the land that all Americans share" (Klein et al. 25).

This nationalistic approach to territory reaches a zenith in the 1997 books. They offer a great deal more praise in their presentations of the territory than did the 1982 books, as three of the four 1997 textbooks (all but Harcourt Brace [Boehm et al.]) dedicate a full, lengthy chapter to celebrating the territory. We should note here that the difference between formats of U.S. and French books is significant, as the much longer and more lavishly produced U.S. textbooks are able to show a great deal more (both quantitatively and qualitatively) stunning photos of scenery.

The U.S. books of 1997 also develop the theme of unity through diversity, which becomes a dominant, recurring idea, as they draw parallels between the varied territory and the diverse population. This message is in keeping with the celebration of ethnic diversity, as discussed in Chapter One, as the 1997 textbooks emphasize seeing the U.S. land and people as varied, yet unified, stating that all Americans can be proud to share their magnificent land. All three of these books with chapters on the national territory start with a quote from a patriotic song about the land (two citing "America, the Beautiful," the other quoting from "This Land is Your Land"), all aiming to transmit emotional attachment to the nation as a whole, in its territorial beauty and variety. McGraw-Hill in particular (which received the highest ratings of 1997 from the Gablers' group, who appreciated its "patriotism") emphasizes this approach, as it dedicates a full page to illustrated sheet music of "America, the Beautiful," pictured against lush, bountiful farms. The narrative text ties together celebration of the country's beauty with appreciation for its abundant resources: "[. . .] the United States has many natural resources in addition to its forests. Such natural resources add to our country's beauty. Katharine Lee Bates wrote about this beauty [. . .]" (Banks et al. 46). This textbook also encourages students to celebrate the beauty of the U.S. or their region by writing a poem or song (48). The choice to print Bates' complete first verse, which ends with a prayer invoking God, seems surprising in a textbook for the secular public schools.

In addition, these books all focus on national parks and repeatedly use the words "wonderful" and "beautiful" when describing U.S. scenery. They also show the usefulness and enjoyment offered by U.S. territory and encourage tourism within the country. These textbooks praise the national parks system and through it, enshrine the territory as a national feature to be cherished and preserved. For example:

> Though the beauty of this country has shone for thousands of years, our national park system is less than a hundred years old. President Theodore Roosevelt loved the natural landscape of the United States so much that he asked Congress to set aside land simply to be enjoyed. He said: "Leave it as it is. You cannot improve on it; not a bit. The ages have been at work on it, and man can only mar it."
>
> The National Park Service was started in 1916 to protect the nation's natural treasures. Yosemite [pictured] is one of more than 350 national parks and historic sites all over the United States.
>
> (Bednarz et al. 1997: 14)

Twice this short excerpt emphasizes the almost timeless quality of the beauty of the national territory. The awe and intimations of eternity inherent in this approach are reminiscent of religious views of the U.S. as divinely ordained, and such statements ground the national territory and its beauty in the distant past, referring to the country long before it existed as such, thus using the territory for somewhat teleological purposes.

The textbooks of 2003 do not evolve exactly as one might expect, given the conservative shift in these books overall. Each of the three books studied here is different. McGraw-Hill adopts a more historical approach to celebrating the national territory than it did in 1997. It focuses on conservationist John Muir instead of Katharine Bates, though it quotes Muir's descriptions of "our magnificent land" and of the U.S. as a "great nation" (Banks et al.

2003: 3). In addition, this textbook includes a stunning two-page photo of Yosemite National Park, referring to its "great natural beauty." Thus, while the 2003 edition gives more factual descriptions of the country's regions than did the 1997 edition, which more frequently describes regions as "beautiful," it is still not a neutral, wholly academic presentation of the national territory. Similarly, Scott Foresman is less expansive than the 1997 editions, as it primarily discusses the beauty of the territory in relation to conservation, though it does contain some rather poetic prose describing the country's variety of landforms (Boyd et al. 24–30). Harcourt, then, is once again the outlier,[2] adopting the most overtly jingoistic tone: where its 1997 edition had no chapter on the national territory, its 2003 edition includes a lengthy chapter that celebrates the country's beauty, and begins by quoting "America, the Beautiful" beside a 1.3-page photo vista of Grand Teton mountain range (Berson et al. 16–17). This edition also gives a fairly long history of Bates' inspiration (18), thus according the song historical importance and enshrining it and its message among national symbols.

Even if two of the three 2003 textbooks take a somewhat more measured approach, they nonetheless all teach children about national territory through learning to appreciate its richness and beauty, rather than in a more social-scientific manner, as French books do. Compared to other aspects of national identity, territory is fairly neutral politically. It seems, perhaps, to provide a consensual means for textbook publishers to demonstrate their "patriotism" consistently with the wishes of conservative activist groups, and these celebratory approaches do not seem to have incurred criticism from geographers or other pedagogues. Indeed, the remarkable emphasis on the beauty of the national territory beginning with the 1997 textbooks seems to result from the same processes that led to the increased number of patriotic symbols in these books, as publishers sought to please the Gablers and company and met no opposition to this approach.

Resources and Ecology

Along with the beauty of the national landscapes, the wealth of natural resources has also been a traditional source of pride and attachment (Curti 1946/1968; Marienstras 1988). The variety of natural resources was long seen (and is still seen by some) as evidence of divine intervention and favor. Though it is not presented as such in textbooks for the public schools, this association might constitute a latent undercurrent in representations of resources. In addition, discussions of natural resources are necessarily connected to more controversial issues of environmental preservation.

Here, again, French and U.S. curricula and textbooks take divergent approaches. French curricula consistently emphasize ecology in conjunction with social studies. This issue is emphasized more in the science curriculum but also in geography, as the theme of "sustainable development" is integrated throughout the curriculum. Already in 1985 and 1995, French curricula discuss land use in conjunction with its impact on the environment and require teaching about ecological problems ("Horaires. . ." 1985: 19; "Programmes . . ." 1995: 43). Since 2002, the topic has been emphasized further, mentioned multiple times throughout the curricula. Likewise, environmental concerns are covered consistently by older as well as newer French textbooks and are a major focus in geography sections. Older books connected discussions of depletion of resources and concerns over pollution to more positive statements about the abundance of natural resources in France. The newer books have simplified the narrative and done away with more celebratory statements of the country's natural wealth, focusing more on ecology. This focus is integrated throughout the geography sections of these books, in relation to different types of regions and industries. For example, the books show how agriculture can be a source of pollution and highlight French farmers—both in metropolitan France and in the overseas territories—who are adopting more environmentally conscious policies (e.g., Boëche 2011 CM2: 98–99; Chevalier and Le Bourgeois 140, 145; Le Callennec 2011: 107). Likewise, these textbooks explain how tourist sites must—and do—strive to protect the environment from the dangers of excessive tourism. Sedrap, in particular, seems to have chosen to focus on areas with sound environmental policy (e.g., the port of Le Havre and its respect of wildlife and restrictions on pollution, and the newly built city of Val d'Europe [in Marne la Vallée] and its treatment of rain water, abundance of pedestrian spaces, and ecological city planning [Boëche CM2: 89, 93]). Though all three recent books (like their predecessors) focus on many forms of environmental protection, only Sedrap discusses climate change explicitly. This book dedicates two pages to the issue, first to the science, government actions, and what can be done individually (133), and then to human migrations due to climate change, showing that it is already a problem and will be a major danger in the future if nothing is done (137). Climate change is more likely to be discussed in science books, yet Sedrap shows it can logically also be included in geography studies.

There is no similar discussion of this issue in Texas social studies curricula or any of these American textbooks. Climate change is simply not mentioned at all. Even other, less controversial environmental concerns have become increasingly invisible in U.S. curricula and textbooks since the early 1980s.

The curricula have changed slightly on this issue over time. In the 1980 curriculum guidelines, education about environmental concerns was cited as a major goal of social studies teaching, though the topic did not receive the kind of more detailed presentation that, for instance, multicultural education did. Emphasis on ecology declined in the 1994 curriculum guidelines, which simply mention teaching about the positive and negative effects of human modification of the environment. This document also contains some vague language that could allow for discussion of serious environmental problems, but not necessarily: "identify environmental issues and discuss their effects on the United States" (*Proclamation* . . . A-24). The 1998 TEKS are more vague and avoid referring to "negative effects" on the environment, saying instead: "analyze the consequences of human modification of the environment in the United States, past and present" ("Chapter 113" §113.7.b.9.c). This document also contains a rather ambiguous instruction that students should: "analyze environmental changes brought about by scientific discoveries and technological innovations such as air conditioning and fertilizers" (§113.7.b.24.d). In one rare instance of the 2010 curriculum guidelines reversing slightly the conservative trend, they reinstate the language from the 1994 curriculum: "analyze the positive and negative consequences of human modification of the environment in the United States, past and present" (§113.116.b.9.b). Still, this is the full extent of their coverage of the issue.

Where the curricula seem to accord slightly less importance to environmental concerns over time, the contrast is much sharper in the textbooks. All five textbooks of 1982 emphasize the danger facing the environment and the importance of taking immediate action. All of these books emphasize the wealth of natural resources in the U.S. but do so in a way that is not so much celebratory or jingoistic as it is sensitive to the fact that not all countries benefit from a similar situation. In addition, all five of these books connect their discussion of resources to warnings about conservation and protection of the environment. They all make this point clearly, and four of them emphasize this theme heavily either in their general introduction or conclusion (i.e., all except for Scholastic [Klein et al.]). Silver Burdett's edition contains a particularly striking epilogue that presents two possible, extreme scenarios for the future: one is a dystopian vision, in which pollution and the depletion of resources have rendered the planet nearly unliveable; the other is utopian, in which environmental protection and international cooperation have led to high quality of life around the world (Helmus et al.: 463–465).

Statements in these textbooks about environmental problems drew consistent, heavy criticism from the Gablers' group in the 1980s. For instance, in reply to this statement in Macmillan's textbook: "Americans use more energy per person than any other people on the earth," (King et al. 1982) the Gablers' group argued, "This information is misleading. Students are not also told that America uses this energy to produce enough goods to support the many nations that cannot support themselves" (Educational Research Analysts 1982 [n.p.]).

As concerns over environmental change have intensified in society at large, with greater understanding of climate change, textbooks have increasingly adopted the conservative line, minimizing the importance of these issues. The books of 1997 appear considerably more optimistic regarding the outlook for the environment than their predecessors. Three of the four 1997 textbooks studied here explain that some U.S. natural resources are limited but stress that scientists are searching for solutions. This contrasts sharply with the older books, which transmitted a sense of urgency and charged students with the responsibility for doing their part to protect the environment, beginning immediately and as they grow up. The only responsibility more recent textbooks seem to give students for environmental protection is recycling. The 1997 textbooks emphasize instead the richness of resources in the United States, rather than preservation, thus embracing a considerably more conservative approach.

The 2003 books continue this rightward shift. Notably, Harcourt and McGraw-Hill state that nonrenewable resources cannot be replaced, but they do not elaborate on this issue, focusing instead on renewable resources (notably forests and soil, which they show people have been conserving for years already). Further, they state that scientists and the government are already searching for solutions, thus indicating that there is no cause for alarm. For instance, Harcourt explains:

> Once nonrenewable resources, such as minerals and fuels, are used up, there will be none left for future use. [. . .] However, as people use these resources, they often find ways to use them more efficiently. They may also discover new resources to take their place.
>
> (Berson et al. 41)

McGraw-Hill's similar presentation of the issue is particularly striking, as it represents a departure from the earlier edition of the same book, which dedicated four pages to the need for conservation (Banks et al. 1997: 42–46). Scott Foresman's edition is somewhat more attentive to the subject, though it is still far from the urgent tone of the 1982 books and from the emphasis in French textbooks. Like its contemporaries, Scott Foresman states that "scientists" are working to prevent pollution, but it also says it is important to conserve nonrenewable resources and to recycle. This book also features two conservationists in its biographies—Marjory Stoneman Douglas (Boyd et al. 39) and a contemporary young man who started a clean-up project in Oklahoma (40–41), thus emphasizing the topic a bit more, even though climate change is absent altogether, and concerns over fossil fuels are far from central.

Similar to the previous conclusions of this study, French curricula and textbooks adopt a more academically centered approach to teaching about geography than do U.S. books, which once again focus heavily on an uncritical pedagogy of memory. However, this observation does not mean that the French textbooks are not nationalistic: they draw more on historical myths of territorial rootedness than do U.S. textbooks.

HISTORY OF NATIONAL TERRITORY

Teaching history in a national framework lends itself to teleology and reifies the nation. A narrative that focuses on the current national territory before it became part of the modern state (as opposed to a broader geographical scope) tends to indicate that the territory was somehow destined be part of the modern nation-state and that all its previous inhabitants were (among the) ancestors of those living there now.

French Curricula and Textbooks

That being said, there are varying degrees of nationalism that can accompany narratives of how the state's present borders came to be. This is one rare instance of a way in which French curricula and textbooks adopt a more overtly nationalistic approach than their U.S. counterparts. As they have increasingly focused on transmitting national identity, French curricula have become more teleological regarding national history. The 2002 curriculum guidelines (which continued unofficially to affect textbooks published after the 2008 curriculum) refer to "our territory" in conjunction with prehistoric and ancient times, and they even use the term "our country" in an anachronistic manner (e.g., the curriculum qualifies Greek settlements on the Mediterranean coast as "the first cities of our country"). In addition, the curriculum projects national unity into the distant past, as it indicates that the French language began developing throughout Gaul, stating, "People spoke Latin, from which little by little the French language emerged" (Ministère . . . 11).

The projection of modern France into the premodern past is even more marked regarding the early Middle Ages. Of the Frankish conquests in the fifth century, the 2002 curriculum states:

> This period is decisive in our national past, with the very name of our country, the emergence of its capital, and at the same time the major regional identities. Decisive also for Europe, with, on the one hand, the linguistic differentiations, but also, on the other, an initial form of religious unity (Christianity), cultural, and artistic unity.
>
> ("Horaires . . ." 79)

While the focus is not exclusively national, French identity remains key. Similarly, the curriculum lists major facts for students to learn regarding this period: "birth of France: a royal state, a capital, a language" (79). Arguably, it is somewhat difficult to avoid teleology unless one explicitly refutes it, as the very name of the modern country asserts continuity, grounding "France" in the old kingdom. Nevertheless, curricula make no effort to differentiate the modern country from the kingdom. The curriculum overlooks complexities of transitions of power and changing borders when it states in a timeline: "987: Beginning of the Capetian dynasty, which governed our country without interruption until 1789" (12). Though these statements grounding France in the distant past were not repeated in the much more concise 2008 curriculum, the more recent instructions (worth repeating here) still make explicit the connection between prenational history and contemporary national identity:

> The events and people listed here in italics constitute indispensable points of reference, to which the teacher may add according to his or her pedagogical choices. These pillars of national history form the basis of a common culture [. . .].
>
> The Tautavel man approx. 500,000 years ago; Lascaux 17,000 years ago; Julius Caesar and Vercingétorix; 52 B.C.: Alésia; [. . .] 496: baptism of Clovis; 800: crowning of Charlemagne; 987: Hugues Capet, king of France; Saint Louis; Joan of Arc.
>
> ("Horaires . . ." 24–25)

While the curricula have become more teleological in recent years, projecting the modern nation-state more explicitly into the past, textbooks have moved somewhat away from more sweeping statements of this type, though they still contain anachronisms that result in exaggerating the longevity of the nation.

Attributing Gallic roots to modern France became common practice in the nineteenth century, notably in Fouillée's (a.k.a., Bruno) seminal *Le Tour de France par deux enfants*, and its famous reference to "our ancestors the Gauls." If this ethnic approach to national identity has since been largely discredited, textbooks nonetheless continue to assert a certain continuity between Gaul and France. They do this mainly by exaggerating the cultural unity of the Gauls and by equating the territory of Gaul with that of France.

As Gauls and Celts did not leave written records, recent scholarship reveals the complexity of studying these peoples, who are known through written accounts of outsiders (namely, Greeks and Romans) and through the work of archeologists. It seems that the terms grouping them into a unit were largely imposed by conquerors and that they, themselves, did not have a broad sense of community beyond individual tribes (Dietler 1994). Yet textbooks continue to exaggerate the unity of Gaul, referring to it in a way that is both tautological and anachronistic as an entity predating the Roman conquest, thus indicating that its existence was "natural," anchored in time immemorial, rather than a Roman administrative creation. More strikingly, some books explicitly refer to Gaul as "a country," the Gauls as "a people" and, at times erase the distance between France and Gaul with such statements as: "Long ago, our country was called Gaul. . ." (Le Callennec 2009: 48). This same textbook explains:

> Starting in the 7th century B.C., people from the center of Europe and around the Mediterranean arrived in our country and mixed with the descendants of the prehistoric peoples who lived there. Together they formed a people: the Gauls. The Gauls all had the same lifestyle and the same customs. They spoke the same language.
>
> (48)

While it attempts to go beyond nineteenth-century ethnic descriptions of national identity, Hatier nevertheless reinforces them in slightly updated form. This edition reprints the "our ancestors the Gauls" excerpt from Bruno's book without explicitly contradicting its deeply ethnic representation of these "ancestors." The cited passage of Bruno's text states: "Our ancestors, the Gauls, were large and robust, with skin white as milk, blue eyes and long blond or red hair. . ." (51). While stating vaguely that this text contains "the errors of its time," Hatier's only corrective to this racialized description is to add other (also Western European) ancestors to the family tree:

> In the nineteenth century, historians emphasized the fact that the Gauls are the ancestors of the French. But they are not the only ones: the French have quite a few other ancestors, including the Franks, who came later and gave their name to France.
>
> (Le Callennec 51)

Belin's edition is considerably more cautious in its descriptions. It avoids anachronistically referring to Gaul as "our country," but it does refer to the territory as "Gaul" even before the arrival of the Celts, thus giving it a sort of timeless quality (Chapier-Legal 45–53). Sedrap gives more historical detail on the origins of the Gauls but refers to the land as "our territory" (Boëche 2011 CE2: 28, 33). Despite variations between textbooks, clearly the myth of "our ancestors the Gauls" retains a powerful foothold in French history education. This overly simplified vision of proto-nationalist Gauls acts as a basis for contemporary projections of national identity. In addition, as Dietler convincingly argues, presenting the Celts, including the Gauls, as a people promotes a myth of pan-European roots, which in turn can serve to justify a certain French cultural hegemony as major bearers of Celtic tradition and culture (Dietler 1994: 596).

Regarding the early Middle Ages, textbooks reflect the 2002 curriculum instructions to show the period as providing the roots of much that is familiar about France today, including its name. However, one cannot perhaps fault textbooks for perpetuating this projected temporal link, as deconstructing the use of the country's name might be beyond the scope of history books for nine-year-olds. Nevertheless, the textbooks do make editorial decisions that contribute to reifying "France" via the distant past. The textbooks of 2010 focus on times of national unity, skipping over centuries of divisions. They generally skip from Clovis, to Charlemagne, to the kings who then "reunified France," only discussing the history of territory once it is French and showing unity as its proper state.

Similarly, the textbooks give an exaggerated sense of the continuity of French borders. Notably, all the books, in their coverage of centuries of various conflicts and contests over borders (e.g., from Hugues Capet, through subsequent kings, through the Hundred Years War) include maps showing the same borders for the "Kingdom of France" in which different regions are simply labeled as "occupied" by other powers at different times. This approach gives a sense that it was really "France" all along (e.g., Le Bourgeois 2010: 51). In addition, most books do not mention territories added or lost later than 1314 or at the latest, after the Hundred Years War, so it could seem like "France's" borders have been the same since the Middle Ages. Furthermore, the textbooks generally skip over details of how violent the process of expanding the French territory could be. Notably, they do not mention the Albigensian Crusade or the conquest of the Languedoc region.

Nevertheless, the newer books generally do not adopt the nationalistic language of the curricula, which was commonly reflected in the books of the 1980s. These older textbooks emphasized the early emergence of national consciousness in France (see also Bozec 2010: 196). These textbooks, unlike their more recent counterparts, took such steps as titling the unit on the Middle Ages: "A thousand years to make France" (Nembrini et al. 1985: 32), and showing the battle of Bouvines as marking the birth of national sentiment. For instance, "On the way back [from the battle of Bouvines], between Bouvines and Paris, the people welcomed the king, demonstrating a real national feeling that was reinforced and spread progressively" (Dorel-Ferré and Dhainaut 1985: 47). The French books thus project territorial (and cultural) roots of modern France into the distant past via an overly simplistic vision of Gaul and of the medieval kingdom of France.

The modern French nation-state thereby claims ties to the ancient inhabitants of the territory. Though the Gauls and Franks are not shown to be the only ancestors of modern French people, they are nonetheless depicted as the core ethnic component of national identity, which posits a degree of continuity for much of the current population.

Jumping ahead, from prenational history to current supra-national institutions, this chapter would be incomplete without discussing how curricula and textbooks present the European Union. Under the 1988 "Resolution of the Council and of the Ministers of Education meeting within the Council on the European Dimension in Education," in the 1990s, member states increasingly aimed to reinforce a sense of European identity among young people (see also Bozec 2010: 4). In France, where the curriculum of 1985 already required situating France in the European context, this increased attention to Europe led to greater emphasis on shared European culture and European citizenship. Notably by 2002, though the focus was still on the national community and its history, the curriculum stated:

> History and geography help students to construct an initial understanding of historic time and the diversity of spaces transformed by human activity. They give students the necessary cultural references so that the world of humans starts to make sense to them. While continuing to focus mostly on the history of France and of the French territory, these subjects open up a European and even global dimension that is indispensable today.
>
> ("Horaires . . ." 65)

The textbooks take different approaches to European identity. While all books certainly show the E.U. in a positive light, only rarely do they reflect efforts to create cultural or emotional attachments to Europe. For instance, Hatier and Nathan emphasize peace and cooperation (for example, through institutions and shared economic and social projects) but do not appear to foster emotional attachment (Chevalier and Le Bourgeois 96–97; Le Callennec 2011: 80–81). Only Sedrap tries to present Europe as a community and discusses cultural manifestations of it. In addition to talking about institutions and lasting peace, Sedrap emphasizes European cooperation and achievement through Airbus, Erasmus, and the Ariane-series rocket launchers, explicitly presenting the Ariane launchers as "another great symbol of the European Union" (Boëche 2011 CM2: 72). Sedrap argues that European unity is now a reality, thanks to mobility, communications, civic institutions, and cooperation. It also suggests reading Roald Dahl books, whom it cites as one of the greatest European authors for young people (73), thereby also providing a cultural component to European construction. Still, this textbook's approach is the exception, and most books reserve statements about culture and community for the national scale.

U.S. Textbooks

Historical differences between the U.S. and France lead to significant differences in their popular memory as well as the academic histories of their territorial roots and of the connection between the territory and national community. Traditionally, U.S. textbooks have focused on the history of the territory as conquered and ruled by European colonists and their descendants. However, in the wake of multiculturalist reforms, textbooks have sought to modify the narrative to be more inclusive. As we have seen in other chapters, these textbooks primarily tell the story of the state, yet the origin story for the prenational territory has changed significantly in the period studied here.

In 1982, textbooks generally dedicated one short chapter to pre-Columbian civilization in North America (approximately 16 pages, on average). While they did show European cruelty toward Native Americans (to varying degrees), their focus was Euro-centric. The recent books include more than three times as much information on pre-Columbian Native American cultures than did their older counterparts (approximately 50 pages on average in 1997 and 2003). The history of European arrival in the Americas, in particular, changes in important ways. The older books tended to focus on and glorify Columbus, telling the story as a dramatic, heroic tale, only from a European perspective. Since the mid-1990s, the textbooks have come to reflect some of the upheaval regarding the Columbus myth that accompanied the 1992 quincentennial commemorations.[3] If textbooks still present Columbus as an important figure, often reprinting excerpts of his questionably accurate journal, they no longer dedicate space to laudatory biographies of him. More significantly, perhaps, where in older books, Columbus's arrival in the Americas is heralded as a European triumph and the beginning of proto-U.S. history, the newer books have instated a replacement myth, in keeping with the recommendations of the National Council for the Social Studies and the Organization of American Historians (e.g., Bingham 1991; NCSS 1991). All three 2003 books incorporate the narrative of the meeting of worlds, entitling the unit "Time of Encounters" (Berson et al.), "Worlds Meet" (Banks et al.), and "Connections across Continents" (Boyd et al.). American history is now shown as emerging from the confluence of Native American, European, and African cultures. The newer books thus all show the perspective of the Taino people (the Caribbean people who greeted Columbus) as well as that of the navigator. Their approaches vary, however. For example McGraw-Hill explains that we know little about the Taino but shows how knowledge of them has been assembled from artifacts (Banks et al. 118–119). Harcourt, by contrast, includes a paternalistic fictional account of the Tainos' first impressions of Columbus's arrival, which makes them sound like simpleminded children, in a stark example of a Rousseauan myth of the "good savage." For example:

> [T]hey see three moving islands that gradually make their way across the water [. . .] In the first light, the floating islands give birth to small rafts that float away from their mothers and drift toward the beach, carrying the most unbelievable creatures. They look like people made of bright colors. [. . .] The people smile happily when the strangers admire their spears made of reeds and the lovely little ornaments of gold they wear on their ears and nostrils. The people cannot understand why the yellow metal is so fascinating to them.
>
> (Berson et al. 2003: 102–103)

After its antiquated presentation of the Taino, Harcourt gives no further information on their fate. The other two books, however, explain the effects of the Columbian Exchange, including the death of millions of Native Americans (Banks et al. 124; Boyd et al. 136).

Moving chronologically forward to the next period traditionally viewed as part of the roots of American identity (by Christian Right education activists and in textbooks published prior to the multiculturalist movement), the 1982, 1997, and 2003 books do not systematically mythologize the British colonies in America. The books of 1997 and 2003 increase the coverage of French and Spanish colonies, in addition to the British ones. They show economic reasons as driving most settlement and plainly discuss British colonists' treaty-breaking and violence toward Native Americans. The textbooks also present disputes over freedom of religion in New England, particularly as these led to the founding of new colonies. Thus, overall these books treat Pilgrims' and Puritans' religion in its historical context. However, the books' presentation of Thanksgiving is something of an exception.

Thanksgiving is a national holiday of unique proportions (after all, Americans do not travel for the Fourth of July the way they do for Thanksgiving). While the holiday is religious in tone, it is also celebrated across religions and by atheists. It is a prime example of what Gabriella Elgenius terms a "successful" national day (Elgenius 2011). Thanksgiving celebrates successful English settlement, allowing for a myth of—or at least emphasis on—good relations with Native Americans; it celebrates the bounty of the country, and in the eyes of many Americans, God's favor. It is a territorialized holiday that has perpetuated aspects of the Pilgrims' covenantal view of their settlement in New England. While the meaning of the holiday may be more or less literal for different Americans, the story of the so-called first Thanksgiving legitimizes European colonization in America and by extension, the existence of the United States. Americans generally see it as an authentic holiday, one that has not been commercialized in the way that many other holidays have been (as is reflected in historian James Baker's assessment of the holiday, 2010: 214). In addition, Thanksgiving links national history to family togetherness in embodied practice.

Thanksgiving holds an important place in elementary school textbooks. Though individual books emphasize it to different degrees, on the whole, the books of 1997 highlight the first Thanksgiving more than those of 1982 or 2003. For instance, McGraw-Hill's 1997 edition includes a separate two-page presentation of Thanksgiving, which features the famous Norman Rockwell painting of a family celebrating with a feast (Banks et al. 1997: 192–193). The 2003 edition removes this section and the Rockwell painting, though it still contains the longest explanation and description of the topic in books of that year (filling two pages). Among the 2003 books, Scott Foresman includes the most striking images depicting the event, as it chooses the J.L.G. Ferris painting to illustrate the title pages for the entire unit on European exploration and early settlement of the Americas, which means it repeats the image, covering three full pages with it (Figure 6.1 [Boyd et al. 125–127]). Scott Foresman and Harcourt present another departure from older editions, in that they specify that what we think of as the "first Thanksgiving" was, in fact, one among many such celebrations, and that thanksgiving feasts in the Spanish colonies almost certainly predated those in New England (Berson et al. 2003: 168; Boyd et al. 2003: 171). In addition, how the books present Thanksgiving is one of the Gabler group's criteria for evaluating textbooks. They were satisfied with coverage in two of the three books (Harcourt and Scott Foresman), as these made it clear that the Pilgrims were specifically thanking God (Educational Research Analysts 2003). Overall, multiculturalism has somewhat altered most of the books' presentations of this iconic holiday, but it remains prominent in their depictions of early colonial history and most often, presentations of it combine territorial and religious roots.[4] These presentations of the Pilgrims' Thanksgiving contribute to nationalizing the territory, anchoring U.S. existence and

Figure 6.1 J.L.G. Ferris, *The First Thanksgiving 1621*, c. 1912–1915.
Source: Library of Congress. Retrieved 29 Sept. 2015 (http://www.loc.gov/item/2001699850/).

identity in this group's adaptation to the land. However, textbooks do not otherwise idealize European settlement of New England.

Beyond Columbus' arrival and the Pilgrims' first Thanksgiving, the textbooks of all periods studied here vary in how critical they are of European interactions with Native Americans. The books of 1982 emphasize that Europeans' treatment toward the Indians they displaced was dishonest, unfair, and often cruel. However, they vary in how they present the roles of certain specific European-American actors. Notably, presentations of President Andrew Jackson's policies that led to the mass forced displacement known as the Trail of Tears range widely. Silver Burdett presents Jackson in highly favorable light, indicating that he relocated Native Americans for their own safety (Helmus et al. 142). Gross, which consistently highlights European-Americans' injustice toward Native Americans, omits Jackson and the Trail of Tears altogether. Scholastic also omits mentioning Jackson, but unlike the other books of its time, it emphasizes in both text and illustrations the hardship, suffering, and death of the Trail of Tears (Klein et al. 206–207). Among the most recent books, Scott Foresman most consistently denounces European actions, showing that the U.S. repeatedly broke treaties, and the U.S. government encouraged white settlers to kill buffalo in order to conquer Plains Indians (e.g., Boyd et al. 554–555). Similarly, McGraw-Hill clearly shows violent treatment by white settlers of Indians (including stating that the Puritans' "massacred" the Pequot [Banks et al. 184]) and denounces the actions of the United States government in breaking treaties and leading to many Indians' deaths (498). Harcourt, at the other end of the spectrum, mostly avoids the subject. It minimizes the brutality of European treatment of Indians, giving the impression that the Plains Wars (to which it dedicates about a quarter of the space that its competitors do) were less imbalanced in terms of each side's strength and resulted merely in getting Indians to live on reservations, downplaying the violence and trauma they endured (Berson et al. 491). However, all of the most recent books systematically criticize Jackson's actions that led to the Trail of Tears (Harcourt explicitly calls Jackson's policies "harsh and unfair"), unlike the varied approaches that characterized the books of 1982. Two of the three recent books studied here, then, have incorporated some significant multiculturalist shifts, by being more attentive to Native Americans' perspective and clearly and rather consistently showing how the U.S. was built on violence against them. Harcourt, however, tends to minimize Native American history when doing so would conflict with its positive Anglo-centric narrative.

Nevertheless, nationalism ultimately prevails in all the textbooks, and the death and displacement of Native Americans seems to have been an unfortunate side effect of desirable national growth. All the books studied here show that white Americans killed Indians and made them leave their land. However, overall, they present territorial expansion as beneficial for the country, as it led to prosperity and the enjoyment of beautiful natural scenery, thanks to the hard work of intrepid pioneers. For instance, Harcourt states that Americans gained new confidence in their country through territorial expansion, concluding: "The country seemed to have met its 'manifest destiny,' as it now stretched from sea to sea. Nothing seemed too difficult as Americans overcame one problem after another" (Berson et al. 2003: 412). This statement seems to include the original inhabitants of the conquered lands as a "problem" to be overcome. While nominally attributing belief in manifest destiny to the Americans of the time, Harcourt nevertheless does not discredit the notion, instead justifying and glorifying the country's maritime borders with the unquestioned use of the modified song lyrics "from sea to sea." Similarly, McGraw-Hill shows territorial expansion in a positive light, when discussing earlier pioneers: "Thanks to them, our nation continued expanding. It stretched from the Atlantic Coast to the Mississippi River" (349). This text also ties the contemporary U.S. to these pioneers (as opposed to the populations they displaced and killed) through the use of the marker "our."[5]

Representations of hardy, industrious, self-reliant pioneers and the exalted territory they encountered and inhabited have been essential elements in nationalizing American territories since well before Frederic Jackson Turner articulated his "Frontier Thesis." The Puritan settlers of New England, who saw the wilderness of their new home as forging the community's character, were forerunners to the larger-scale process of naturalizing the nation during westward expansion in the nineteenth century. Americans saw a virtuous cycle between the unique qualities of pioneers and the influence of the frontier on the European-Americans who settled there, which they credited with shaping a superior and unique national character (Kaufmann 1998; Kohn 1957: 33, 65; Turner 1893/1921; Zelinsky 1988: 161–162). Images and stories of both of these ages of nationalizing the territory and the territory shaping the nation have long been prevalent in U.S. cultural production, particularly when Americans have sought to affirm their unique identity through cultural realms.[6]

In the past few decades, as part of the postmodern turn and related growth of memory studies, historians have become more likely to study how representations of these periods have shaped national memory (Erll, Nünning, and Young 2008; Hoskins et al. 2008). Yet despite greater awareness among scholars of the role of myth and memory in traditional representations of the territory and its history, textbooks still reflect the legacy of processes of naturalization of the nation via western landscapes, thus legitimizing territorial expansion. These textbooks engage in myth-making surrounding pioneers and westward expansion, though it is perhaps not as iconographically charged as one might expect. These books all present pioneers as a group as courageous, emphasizing the hardships they faced and their determination to arrive at their destinations. Often the books dramatize these journeys in striking ways, such as through their focus on Narcissa Prentiss Whitman (Harcourt, for instance, highlights her as an example of "courage" in a featured biography [Berson et al. 2003: 405; see also Banks et al. 386; Boyd et al. 439]). Similarly, McGraw-Hill shares a pioneer's account in which physical hardship is tempered by appreciating the beauty of the land (Banks et al. 2003: 387). The books all present Mormons and their settlement in Utah in highly positive terms, relating that they had been persecuted (though omitting the reasons for this persecution) and thus fled where they had been living and established a new, thriving community through hard work and perseverance (Banks et al. 386; Berson et al. 406–407; Boyd et al. 441). Mormons thus appear to fit the archetype of religious pioneers, reenacting in secularized narrative a covenantal mission in establishing a new city on a hill (or in this case, on a lake). Among pioneer imagery, the textbooks all include Bingham's painting of Daniel Boone leading families through the Cumberland Gap into Kentucky, a painting that art historians point out was based on the imagery of Moses leading the Exodus from Egypt (Hughes 1991; Figure 6.2). Similarly, many of the books show "Davy" Crockett in a defiant, heroic pose facing certain death at the Battle of the Alamo (e.g., Berson et al. 2003: 403; Boyd et al. 2003: 428).

These books include photographs and paintings familiarizing students with iconic visions of various regions of the U.S. In addition to the vistas already discussed that adorn the geography sections of these books, many show wagon trains heading through the Great Plains or the Rocky Mountains (e.g., Banks et al. 2003: 342–343; Boyd et al. 2003: 393, 394–395, 399). Harcourt (the conservative Gabler group's favorite textbook of 2003)

Figure 6.2 George Caleb Bingham, *Daniel Boone Escorting Settlers Through the Cumberland Gap*, 1851–1852.

Source: Wiki Commons. Retrieved 29 Sept. 2015 (https://commons.wikimedia.org/wiki/File:Daniel_Boone_Escorting_Settlers_Through_the_Cumberland_Gap_by_George_Caleb_Bingham_1851–52.jpg).

strikingly introduces its chapter on "The New England Colonies" with a 1.3-page picturesque photograph of a colonial-style wooden church and tree covered in snow together with the Cotton Mather quote: "The New Englanders are a people of God. . ." in large print (Berson et al. 186–187). Yet, these books do not contain paintings of the Hudson River School showing the West in ways meant to the evoke the sublime and divine favor. The one exception included in 2003 books is a painting by Frederic Edwin Church, depicting Thomas Hooker leading his followers into Connecticut. The grandeur, composition, and lighting of this painting certainly conjure divine imagery, a sense of a promised land and covenantal mission (Berson et al. 2003: 196; Boyd et al. 2003: 178), but it is the exception, not the rule (Figure 6.3).

Beyond the details of the narratives and the illustrations, the very structure of most books lends itself to a teleological and celebratory approach to territorial expansion. Even if there were no language of praise for territory or new borders, the simple fact that these books cover westward expansion in its own chapter creates it as a category, something of a unified event, thereby making it seem more cohesive. Scott Foresman (Boyd et al.) is the exception. Unlike McGraw-Hill (Banks et al.) and Harcourt (Berson et al.), this textbook

Figure 6.3 Frederic Edwin Church, *Hooker and Company Journeying through the Wilderness from Plymouth to Hartford, in 1636*, 1846.

Source: Wiki Commons. Retrieved 29 Sept. 2015 (https://commons.wikimedia.org/wiki/File:Hooker_and_Company_Frederic_Edwin_Church.jpeg).

presents westward expansion chronologically, spread out over several chapters with others interspersed. It thereby seems less inevitable, more a series of historic events than a symbolic object unto itself.

As we have seen (in Chapter Four), U.S. overseas territorial expansion is shown uniquely as a source of pride in most books. Only Harcourt mentions opposition to it, and it is the only book to present financial gain as a motivating factor in the country's search for new land and new markets (Berson et al. 2003: 524). The other textbooks show the results of the Spanish-American War and other expansion in purely positive terms, as advancing the country's power. They focus on Theodore Roosevelt as a hero (explicitly so in Scott Foresman [Boyd et al. 2003: 582]) for his distinction in battle and contributions to U.S. territorial gains. Because the focus of these textbooks is on the development of the state rather than on international relations, they pay little attention to U.S. foreign policy, including expansionism. They mention in generally one sentence that the U.S. gained control of Puerto Rico, Guam, and the Philippines from Spain in the Spanish-American War and that Guam and Puerto Rico are today part of the United States. Two of the three recent books simply state that the Philippines became independent in 1946 (Berson et al. 527; Boyd et al. 581). Only McGraw-Hill explains that some Filipinos had been fighting for their independence from Spain and continued fighting under U.S. control (Banks et al. 521). The very small quantity of text dedicated to these issues indicates the general lack of importance accorded to the subject, except as a sign of growing U.S. power.

However, textbooks do treat the addition of new states in greater detail, and the case of Hawaii brings together questions of imperialism and national expansion in the fairly recent past. The fact that the territory is composed of islands at a great distance from the continental U.S. brings its annexation into sharper focus, perhaps, than for contiguous states whose borders were less bounded and where the spread of U.S. settlers could more easily be seen as "natural." It seems that textbooks struggle with establishing a narrative to explain Hawaii's statehood, as there is no consensus among them. Hawaii's last queen, Liliuokalani, who was overthrown by American planters, has recently become a fixture in these books, reflecting more consistent attention to indigenous peoples and victims of U.S. expansionism. Where no textbooks of 1982 included her portrait, all the books of 1997 and 2003 picture her at least once. Accordingly, the annexation of Hawaii has gained some prominence in the more recent textbooks. The books of 1982 reveal a complete lack of consensus on how to approach the subject. For instance, Scholastic dedicates only one sentence to the topic, much less than for any other state. In its chapter on World Power, which focuses mainly on the Spanish-American War, the full explanation reads: "In the same year, the Hawaiian Islands also came under the control of the United States" (Klein et al. 336). It is unclear whether the authors sought to avoid controversy by discussing a potentially upsetting topic in the relatively recent past or if it simply did not fit with their broader narrative. Follett, normally the most progressive among this group of books, has an even more surprising approach: it dedicates a full paragraph to Hawaii but emphasizes good relations between U.S. settlers and Hawaiians and indicates that the queen's overthrow was her own fault. Follett explains that, after years of American planters and Hawaiians getting along well, the queen made a power grab, so the Americans revolted (Gross et al. 331). Silver Burdett, on the other hand, is highly critical of the planters' actions, attributing them to greed, and criticizing their influence on the U.S. government in securing Hawaii's annexation (Helmus et al. 224). By 1997, all books discuss Liliuokalani's resistance to U.S. power, though they do so in varying amounts of detail and with different emphasis. Among the 2003 books, McGraw-Hill and Scott Foresman give little attention to the topic and only a brief factual account, which avoids judgment. This account relates that the planters had become powerful, the "queen wanted to restore power to native-born Hawaiians" (Banks et al. 519), so the planters revolted and overthrew her (Boyd et al. 579). By contrast, Harcourt is, in a rare occurrence, more critical of U.S. actions than its competitors. The 2003 edition's presentation of U.S.-Hawaii relations (as regarding U.S. overseas expansion more generally) is very similar to the 1997 edition, which was more systematically progressive. The text shows that American planters came to control most of the Hawaiian land and took away the authority of the king (who preceded Liliuokalani) when he tried to prevent the Americans from taking over (using language that implies the king was in the right). The text then states that as a result of U.S. expansion in Hawaii and elsewhere, "some people now accused the country's leaders of imperialism" (Berson et al. 2003: 526). Harcourt is the only recent book to list "imperialism" in the index. However, references to imperialism are perhaps mitigated by the chapter introduction, which promotes the image of the United States as an unwilling world power, as it shows a 1.3-page photo of an American battleship from the First World War accompanied by a large-print quotation of Alfred T. Mahan stating, "Whether they will or no, Americans must now begin to look outward" (523). Despite Harcourt's somewhat more critical approach, all of the books ultimately present Hawaii's annexation in positive terms, grouping it together with the acquisition of Alaska and expansion of power globally, stating that all of these events "contributed to our country's power" (e.g., Banks et al. 1997: 554).

CONCLUSION

Presentations and representations of the national territory and its history in French and U.S. textbooks draw on myths old and new, anchoring the nation in the land, and legitimizing contemporary borders. According to French textbooks, the ancestors of the modern inhabitants of France—a long-unified people—have cultivated the land since time immemorial. These books present simplified accounts of Gallic and medieval history, which project unity and proto-French (or frankly French) identity upon these prenational societies. French history is the history of the territory, going back to prehistoric times. All the groups that have lived in the territory that is now France are subsumed under French identity. The nation is thus shown as ancient, with a history and character that predate the modern state. Despite their general commitment to teaching history in line with academic techniques, French textbooks favor memory in this case, as they adopt ahistorical, teleological approaches to aspects of premodern history that have long been seen as key "national" myths. Notably, they continue to present the Gauls as ancestors whose culture and character already reflected modern French self-conceptions.

Presentation of the contemporary territory is more in line with geography as an academic discipline, as it focuses on interactions between people and the environment. This approach highlights economic connections to the territory and is also consistent with an emphasis on ecology and preservation (as is the general progressivism of these textbooks). French textbooks thus support the theory advanced by Kaufmann and Zimmer (1998), as they represent French territorial nationalism that is rooted in distant history and contemporary land use.

U.S. textbooks' approach is somewhat more complex to categorize. These books display many aspects of "naturalization" of the territory (Kaufmann and Zimmer 1998). That is, they rely heavily on affective presentation of the land as beautiful, and they present it as a national symbol in its own right, promoting pride and unity. Where the sublime and covenantal visions of the land overlap in many Americans' visions of national history and identity, textbooks include a modified, mostly secularized version of the sublime.

This emphasis on beauty is consistent with the increased influence of conservatism on these textbooks. The changing presentation of the territory provides another example of the increase in pedagogy of memory over teaching history and geography as disciplines. The conservative shift is also reflected in these textbooks' sharp move away from environmental activism. This change parallels their shift from emphasizing social justice to celebrating opportunity and capitalism: in both cases, textbooks have come to idealize the status quo. U.S. textbooks emphasize conservation only as it relates to national parks (including some historic sites). Conservation of key sites of historic events and natural beauty is an aspect of national commemoration, anchoring memory in space and giving the nation form and continuity through time (Elgenius 2011; Lowenthal 1985; Smith 2008).

Regarding historical presentations of the territory, multiculturalism and secularism have altered the founding myths somewhat, especially regarding the arrival of Columbus and "manifest destiny," which are no longer presented in the purely triumphalist tones of the early and mid-twentieth century. Textbooks now promote a narrative of the U.S. as emerging at the confluence of "three worlds," thus incorporating Native Americans and the pre-Columbian territory, as well as African Americans, into the national narrative in a way that the story of Columbus and nation-building beginning with the British colonies did not. Ironically, perhaps, these efforts to better incorporate previously excluded groups into the national story result in taking a less classically civic approach to national identity; instead of focusing only on the history of the state, U.S. textbooks now focus more on the prenational history of the territory. As such, a certain amount of teleology in the American context is a means of inclusion. However, this new myth can be used to obscure the destruction wrought upon indigenous people. While textbooks do show European-American cruelty toward Native Americans, they do not always make clear the scope of the consequences.

Similarly, other origins myths remain prevalent in presentations of U.S. national territory. In these textbooks, hardworking pioneers have spread the founders' vision of the democratic state across the land and brought freedom to many parts of the world. U.S. textbooks appear to seek balance by presenting Native Americans as the original inhabitants of the territory who were wrongfully killed and driven from their land. However, the history of the nationalization of U.S. territory remains, ultimately, a triumphant account of the expansion of the nation-state and the growth of power at home and abroad.

In both France and the United States, the territory is a source of unity. In both countries—with their histories of migration—national culture is shown as tied to the territory, rather than to kinship. Territorial grounding of the nation is thus an essential component of the cultural nationalism that characterizes French and U.S. history, geography, and social studies education.

NOTES

1. Anthony Smith has elaborated on this process of nationalization of the territory: "The passage of generations has wedded [populations] to the land, both in fact and in their (and others') perceptions. Their modes of production, patterns of settlement and folk cultures spring from their diurnal round of work and leisure, itself formed out of their ceaseless encounter with a particular environment" (Smith 1986: 183).
2. As a reminder, Harcourt went from producing the textbook that earned the lowest ranking from the Gablers' group in 1997 to the highest ranking with its 2003 edition.
3. See for example articles in the *Magazine* of the Organization of American Historians and position papers of the National Council for the Social Studies, which reflected the push within the history profession to change how the topic was taught (e.g., Bingham 1991; NCSS 1991; Sale 1991). These changes may also have been furthered by James Loewen's bestselling *Lies my Teacher Told Me* (1995), which emphasized the massive discrepancies between scholarship such as Howard Zinn's and the state of history textbooks.
4. We should also note that McGraw-Hill includes a rather surprisingly inaccurate etching of the Pilgrims' and Wampanoags' Thanksgiving celebration, in which we see the bare torsos of Wampanoag people, which would have been unlikely in November in New England (Banks et al. 2003: 168). This type of stereotypical image has been criticized by Native Americans and various multiculturalist activists for decades (e.g., CIBC 1981; Guidelines 1975). In addition, on the opposite page, the textbook pictures a statue of Massasoit, also bare-chested, with the Eurocentric caption, "This statue in Plymouth, Massachusetts, honors Massasoit, a great friend to the Pilgrims" (169).
5. The recent books define "manifest destiny," generally employing neutral language that neither supports nor refutes the idea (which is a sound approach in terms of historical pedagogy, though is certainly not progressive social studies). Older books, on the other hand, generally did not mention the doctrine. The reasons for this are unclear. Perhaps the older books simply were not sure how to approach the issue for young children or wanted to avoid the controversy of dealing with underlying religious themes (an explanation that would be consistent with the fact that the newer books are more likely to discuss religious history, as seen in Chapter One).
6. The strength of these two eras of territorial conquest as defining myth shows in popular culture (e.g., film and television westerns), as well as the visual arts (e.g., paintings of the Hudson River School), the performing arts (e.g., American efforts to establish a characteristic opera repertoire; see Hutchins 2004), and in early national historiography, including Turner's work (see Kaufmann 1998; Zelinksy 1988).

REFERENCES

For the complete list of textbooks analyzed, see Chapter One.

French Textbooks Cited

Boëche, Sándra, ed. 2011. *CE2: Les Reporteurs histoire, géographie, histoire des arts, développement durable*. Toulouse: Sedrap.

Boëche, Sandra, ed. 2011. *CM1: Les Reporteurs histoire, géographie, histoire des arts, développement durable*. Toulouse: Sedrap.

Boëche, Sandra, ed. 2011. *CM2: Les Reporteurs histoire, géographie, histoire des arts, développement durable*. Toulouse: Sedrap.

Chagny, Victor and Jean Forez. 1993. *Géographie. Cycle des approfondissements: CE2, CM1, CM2*. Paris: Armand Colin.

Chapier-Legal, Geneviève. 2010. *Histoire, géographie, histoire des arts, CE2*. Paris: Belin.

Chevalier, Jean-Pierre and Martine Picrel. 2010. *Géographie: CM1*. Paris: Nathan.

Chevalier, Jean-Pierre and Roselyne Le Bourgeois, eds. 2010. *Histoire, histoire des arts, instruction civique: CM2*. Paris: Nathan.

Dorel-Ferré, Gracia and M. Dhainaut. 1985. *Cours moyen: Histoire*. Paris: Armand Colin.

Le Bourgeois, Roselyne, ed. 2010. *Histoire, histoire des arts, CM1*. Paris: Nathan.

Le Callennec, Sophie, ed. 2009. *Histoire, géographie: CE2*. Collection Magellan. Paris: Hatier.

Le Callennec, Sophie, ed. 2010. *Histoire, géographie: CM1*. Collection Magellan. Paris: Hatier.

Le Callennec, Sophie, ed. 2011. *Histoire, géographie, CM2*. Collection Magellan. Paris: Hatier.

Nembrini, Jean-Louis, Pierre Polivka, and Jean Bordes. 1985. *Histoire CM*. Pour connaître la France. Paris: Hachette écoles.

United States Textbooks Cited

Banks, James A., et al. 1997. *United States: Adventures in Time and Place*. New York: Macmillan McGraw-Hill.

Banks, James A., et al. 2003. *Our Nation*. New York: Macmillan McGraw-Hill.

Berson, Michael, et al. 2003. *Harcourt Horizons: United States History*. Orlando, FL: Harcourt.

Boehm, Richard G., et al. 1997. *America's Story: Stories in Time*. New York: Harcourt-Brace.

Boyd, Candy Dawson, et al. 2003. *The United States, Social Studies*. Glenview, IL: Scott Foresman.

Gross, Herbert, et al. 1980. *Exploring Our World: Americas*. 2nd ed. Chicago: Follett.

Helmus Timothy M., et al. 1982. *The United States and Its Neighbors*. Morristown, NJ: Silver Burdett.

King, Allen Y., et al. 1982. *The United States and the Other Americas*. New York: Macmillan.

Klein, Stanley, et al. 1982. *Our Country's History: Level E*. New York: Scholastic.

Curriculum Guidelines and Official Reports

"Chapter 113: Texas Essential Knowledge and Skills for Social Studies." 1998. *Texas Essential Knowledge and Skills*. Texas Education Agency. Retrieved 20 Dec. 2000 (http://www.tea.state.tx.us/rules/tac/ch113.html#s1137).

"Chapter 113: Texas Essential Knowledge and Skills for Social Studies." 2010. *Texas Essential Knowledge and Skills*. Texas Education Agency. Retrieved 5 Nov. 2013 (http://ritter.tea.state.tx.us/rules/tac/chapter113/index.html).

Framework for the Social Studies. 1980. Austin: Texas Education Agency.

"Horaires et programmes d'enseignement de l'école primaire." 2002. *Bulletin officiel de l'Education nationale*. Special issue 1 (14 Feb.).

"Horaires et programmes d'enseignement de l'école primaire." 2008. *Bulletin officiel de l'Education nationale*. Special issue 3 (19 Jun.).

"Horaires, programmes et instructions pour l'école élémentaire, 1985." 1986. *Bulletin officiel de l'Education nationale*. Special issue 1 (16 Jan.).

"Horaires, objectifs et programmes. Cycle Moyen." 1980. *R.L.R. 514–3*.

Ministère de la Jeunesse, de l'Éducation nationale et de la Recherche: Direction de l'enseignement scolaire. 2002. "Histoire et géographie cycle des approfondissements (cycle 3)." Collection Ecole: Documents d'application des programmes. Paris: Centre national de documentation pédagogique.

Proclamation 1994 of the State Board of Education Advertising for Bids on Instructional Materials. 1994. Austin: Texas Education Agency.

"Programmes de l'école primaire." 1995. *Bulletin officiel de l'Education nationale* 48 (28 Dec.).

Works of Reference

Bacevich, Andrew J. 2002. *American Empire: The Realities and Consequences of U.S. Diplomacy*. Cambridge, MA: Harvard University Press.

Baker, James W. 2009. *Thanksgiving: The Biography of an American Holiday*. Durham: University of New Hampshire Press.

Bingham, Marjorie W. 1991. "Teaching the Columbian Quincentenary." *OAH Magazine of History* 5.4: 7–9.

Bozec, Géraldine. 2010. *Les héritiers de la République: Eduquer à la citoyenneté à l'école dans la France d'aujourd'hui*. Unpublished doctoral dissertation, Institut d'Etudes Politiques de Paris, Paris.

Conklin, Alice L. 1997. *A Mission to Civilize: The Republican Idea of Empire in France and West Africa, 1895–1930*. Stanford, CA: Stanford University Press.

CIBC (Council on Interracial Books for Children). 1981. *Guidelines for Selecting Bias-Free Textbooks and Storybooks*. New York: Council on Interracial Books for Children.

Curti, Merle. 1946/1968. *The Roots of American Loyalty*. New York: Atheneum.

Educational Research Analysts. 1982. *1982 Textbook Ratings*. Longview, TX: Educational Research Analysts.

Dietler, Michael. 1994. "'Our Ancestors the Gauls': Archaelogy, Ethnic Nationalism, and the Manipulation of Celtic Identity in Modern Europe." *American Anthropologist* 96.3: 584–605.

Educational Research Analysts. 2003. *2003 5th Grade Social Studies Textbook Rating*. Longview, TX: Educational Research Analysts.

Educational Research Analysts. 2013. *Newsletter* Oct. Longview, TX: Educational Research Analysts.

Elgenius, Gabriella. 2011. *Symbols of Nations and Nationalism: Celebrating Nationhood*. Basingstoke: Palgrave Macmillan.

Erll, Astrid, Ansgar Nünning, and Sarah B. Young. 2008. *Cultural Memory Studies: An Interdisciplinary and International Handbook*. Berlin: Walter de Gruyter.

Guidelines for Creating Positive Sexual and Racial Images in Educational Materials. 1975. New York: Macmillan.

Hoskins, Andrew, Amanda Barnier, Wulf Kansteiner, and John Sutton. 2008. "Editorial." *Memory Studies* 1.1: 5–7.

Hughes, Robert. 1991. "How the West was Spun." *Time Magazine* 13 May. Retrieved 3 Jun. 2015 (http://content.time.com/time/magazine/article/0,9171,972933,00.html).

Hutchins, Rachel D. 2004. "The American Opera Boom of the 1950s and 1960s: History and Stylistic Analysis." *La Revue LISA/LISA e-journal* 2.3: 145–163. Retrieved 3 Jun. 2015 (https://lisa.revues.org/2966).

Kaufmann, Eric. 1998. "'Naturalizing the Nation': The Rise of Naturalistic Nationalism in the United States and Canada." *Comparative Studies in Society and History* 40.4: 666–695.

Kaufmann, Eric and Oliver Zimmer. 1998. "In Search of the Authentic Nation: Landscape and National Identity in Canada and Switzerland." *Nations and Nationalism* 4.4: 483–510.

Kohn, Hans. *American Nationalism: An Interpretative Essay*. New York: Macmillan, 1957.

Lowenthal, David. 1985. *The Past is a Foreign Country*. Cambridge, UK: Cambridge University Press.

Marienstras, Elise. 1988. *Nous, le peuple: Les Origines du nationalisme américain*. Mayenne, France: Gallimard.

NCSS. 1991. "The Columbian Quincentenary: An Educational Opportunity." National Council for the Social Studies. Retrieved 9 Sept. 2004 (http://www.ncss.org/positions/columbus/).

Sahlins, Peter. 1990. "Natural Frontiers Revisited: France's Boundaries Since the Seventeenth Century." *The American Historical Review* 95.5: 1423–1451.

Sale, Kirkpatrick. 1991. "The Columbian Quincentenary: A Necessary Reassessment." *OAH Magazine of History* 5.4: 20–23.

Smith, Anthony D. 1986. *The Ethnic Origins of Nations*. Oxford: Blackwell.

Smith, Anthony D. 2008. *The Cultural Foundations of Nations: Hierarchy, Covenant, and Republic*. Malden, MA: Blackwell.

Stephanson, Anders. 1995. *Manifest Destiny: American Expansionism and the Empire of Right*. New York: Hill and Wang.

Turner, Frederick Jackson. 1893/1921. "The Significance of the Frontier in American History." In F.J. Turner, ed., *The Frontier in American History*. New York: Henry Holt and Company, pp. 1–38.

Zelinsky, Wilbur. *Nation into State: The Shifting Symbolic Foundations of American Nationalism*. Chapel Hill; London: University of North Carolina Press, 1988.

Conclusion

SUMMARY OF PRINCIPAL FINDINGS

By the first decade of the twenty-first century in France and the United States, demographic, social, and epistemological changes had led to heightened expressions of nationalism in policy directives, curricula, and textbooks. This reaffirmed commitment to nationalism accompanied active renegotiation of national identity in these educational materials.

Curricula and textbooks for the primary schools in France and the U.S. both promote forms of cultural nationalism, but there are significant variations in the nature of that nationalism and the vision of national identity it projects. These different models of nationalism are correlated with different pedagogical approaches to history education, which result at least partly from differing processes of knowledge production. The French system for writing curricula and textbooks is more top-down and gives historians predominant power over the books. The process in the U.S. is much more democratic and thus gives a much larger role to more popular history. This system, combined with the broader political, social, and epistemological context, has led to French textbooks that aim to teach history as an academic discipline while also seeking to transmit aspects of national memory, resulting in a form of progressive cultural nationalism. U.S. textbooks do not, for the most part, aim to teach history as an academic discipline—using critical approaches—but instead engage in pedagogy of memory, resulting in a more conservative cultural nationalism.

French curricula and textbooks demonstrate significant recent changes in incorporating a critical pedagogy of French colonial history, involvement in the trans-Atlantic slave trade, France's role in the Holocaust, and more aspects of women's history. However, on the whole, these books still present a largely white, male nation, where the overseas territories remain "other" and women's history is usually limited in quantity and separate from the broader narrative arc.

These books transmit a sense of the importance of socioeconomic differences as a driving force of history. This pervasive class awareness lays the foundations for a focus on social justice in contemporary society.

Accordingly, these books promote the values of the French creed, presenting equality as a condition of liberty and solidarity as a cornerstone of national identity. They express pride in these values, but they are not as overtly nationalistic in their presentations of other possible symbols. Notably, they have moved away from hagiographic representations of traditional national heroes, and their discussions of the national territory focus on how people interact with the land and the importance of ecology, rather than on aesthetic qualities. Such presentations are consistent with France's self-conception as a bearer of rational Enlightenment values, as opposed to more Romantic notions of history and geography.

However, despite their apparent commitment to solidarity and critical self-examination, the curricula and most textbooks omit difficult questions regarding contemporary inequality and exclusion. Furthermore, books published since 2008 show increased emphasis on secularism, which is likely to continue to grow following the 2016 curriculum. They have shifted toward staunchly assimilationist positions that reflect implicit stigmatization of Muslims. They depict France as the bearer of universalist, rationalist, secular republicanism, yet they also show its Christian roots, including Catholic saints as heroes. They thus assert a progressive yet immutable vision of national identity, which reflects the dominance of the Catholic ethnic majority.

U.S. textbooks present a more resolutely multiethnic vision of the nation than do their French counterparts, and this focus on diversity throughout U.S. history has increased over time. Similarly, U.S. textbooks include more women than do the French textbooks (though men still far outnumber women). They incorporate certain multiculturalist approaches in discussing the cruelties of slavery and the use of violence and illegal means to deprive African Americans of their rights during and after Reconstruction. They mention women's rights' movements, including the Seneca Falls convention of 1848, suffragists of the early twentieth century, and feminists of the 1960s and 1970s. However, recent textbooks relegate discussions of racism and sexism to distant times and have increasingly come to indicate—whether through omission or through positive statements—that poverty, discrimination, and systemic injustice are things of the past. They further idealize the country as they celebrate the national territory in aesthetic terms; they celebrate national heroes in moral terms; they celebrate capitalism as a fundamental freedom.

Recent textbooks' increasing emphasis on individuals as well as military and political history reaffirms their commitment to more traditional history narratives, as opposed to the social history approaches common among historians and that foster more progressive education. In addition, their selection of heroes of both genders and all ethnicities is deeply nationalistic, as these figures focus attention on the country's founding and growth, including a narrative of progress that allows for incorporating women and minorities without fundamentally altering the national story. Moreover, among named individuals, traditional, white male heroes still far outnumber women and minorities, thus also reflecting the persistence of traditional narratives. Furthermore, these books move away from multiculturalist positions where these become irreconcilable with conservatives' wishes to avoid emphasizing conflict and inequality among groups of Americans and to protect the image of government leaders—especially those of the early republic.

The marginalization of race as a dividing line for national solidarity in the U.S. has led to subtler forms of exclusion. Through their pedagogy of memory and renewed adherence to the narrative of progress, textbooks have eradicated the progressive nationalism of the early 1980s. In rendering invisible institutionalized racism and the continuing inequalities caused by racist and sexist discrimination, in "including" minorities and women in the national narrative almost exclusively as paragons of nationalist virtue, social studies textbooks have embraced a conservative patriotism according to which unity and equality are not just the ideal but represent reality. In this way, U.S. textbooks demonstrate the strength and enduring power of nationalism, which has absorbed aspects of multiculturalism and feminism by transforming them. The result is a more inclusive vision of national identity. However, these shifts legitimize only nationalist variants of diversity, thereby delegitimizing more radical approaches through omission.[1]

EXPLANATIONS AND HYPOTHESES

As approaches to multicultural history became more sophisticated and mainstream, U.S. textbooks' underlying values became more conservative. This process defies simple explanation. It is partly a result of Texas politics and institutions. It is partly a result of long-term neoconservative plans to gain power and popularity on local, state, and national levels. It is partly a result of negotiations and compromise between textbook publishers and various decision-makers in Texas. It may also reflect a pessimistic turn. Textbooks of the early 1980s—with their chronological proximity to a wave of social movements—could inscribe calls to promote social justice and environmental protection within the continuity of a hopeful narrative of progress. However, from the 1980s onward, as these progressive movements ebbed, the continued existence of racism and sexism, growing fears over climate change, and the widening of the wealth gap perhaps made it more difficult to maintain the narrative of progress, which is an enduring feature of U.S. social studies textbooks.

Perhaps above all, it is not a coincidence that textbooks seem to have embraced diversity more while becoming increasingly conservative. It is the growth of multiculturalism, broadly speaking—including expanding rights for African Americans in the 1950s and 1960s, broader ethnic movements of the 1970s, and third-wave feminism—that has fueled the rise of the right. Neoconservative gains in the wake of these progressive movements have drawn on nationalist discourse, which has largely focused on education as a primary contested site of power in which to define the nation. Conservative politicians and education activists have fought—and continue to fight—for education not just for its own sake but as a powerful symbolic victory to rally broader support for the cause. Many of these activists promote with apparent sincerity the mythical, ahistorical vision of an idealized United States—a classless society where discrimination is a thing of the past and hard work puts success within reach of all. Yet, paradoxically, the same people who see their country as the greatest and most powerful nation in the world also see it as fragile, facing constant threat of decline or destruction from those who question its greatness. The enemies of the nation in this vision are the progressive multiculturalists and feminists.

A similar process may be occurring in France. Identity politics also fueled the rise of the far-right *Front National* and has led more centrist parties to emphasize and support culturally protectionist assimilationism (Brubaker 2001; Thomas 2012). In history education, this interaction between growing calls for diversity and concern with traditional national identity seems to be reflected in the fact that textbooks are including more women in history, but without fundamentally altering the nationalist narrative. Similarly, they include more ethnic minorities and colonial history and pay greater attention to the overseas territories in geography textbooks. However, these topics, too, are added onto the "national novel" (as Suzanne Citron famously called it; 1987/2008), which remains the main focus. Nevertheless, there is a significant difference with U.S. books, in that the French textbooks' commitment to progressive (though assimilationist) nationalism means that they are also able to show the persistence of gender and economic inequalities in the present in a way that still promotes nationalism.

In their critical approaches to injustice in history, French textbooks most often impugn actions carried out by the government, rather than by individuals. In this way, for instance, colonization appears to have been the responsibility of the abstract state in the nineteenth century. Similarly, the image of the French people regarding the Holocaust is somewhat protected by attributing collaboration to the Vichy government and focusing not on those individuals who collaborated with the Nazi occupation but on the Resistance. Sometimes critiques also implicate economic elites (for instance, regarding the French role in the international slave trade) but never the wider population or societal norms themselves. Solutions to unjust situations appear to have come from activism among the French intelligentsia (e.g., Victor Hugo and Victor Schoelcher regarding slavery) or local resistance as regarding decolonization, which then led to laudable legal action by new republican governments.

In U.S. textbooks, on the contrary, the U.S. government is usually shown as the solution to problems rather than being guilty for them. These books minimize the role of racism and the extent of systemic and institutionalized oppression and inequality. They also minimize the role of civil society in fighting ethnic and sexist discrimination as well as exploitative labor practices that affected workers of all ethnicities in the early twentieth century by focusing only on a few leaders and the government officials who ended slavery, segregation, other civil rights abuses, and unsafe working conditions.

This difference raises a deeper point: though both French and U.S. textbooks promote forms of cultural nationalism that include attachment to values and institutions of the state, in French textbooks, the French people are seen as distinct from their government but not from the state. French nationalism idealizes the abstract concept of the republic and the people, particularly the working classes, thus reflecting founding myths going back to Sièyes and the Revolution (Sieyès 1789/1970). American nationalism idealizes the state and its leaders. Perhaps this is a defining trait of left- versus right-leaning nationalism. Perhaps there is less French identification with past actions of the government, and national identity is, instead, more grounded in traditions of seeking social justice. This difference may also stem from the fact that since the Revolution, France has had five republics, two periods of empire, and several monarchies, while the U.S. (minus the Confederacy) has had the same Constitution since 1791. Thus, French republican government is shown as incarnating progress over monarchy, and each successive republic (with the exception of the short-lived Fourth Republic) is shown as morally superior to the last. While grounded in the past, this vision of nationalism is focused on the future.

This difference is also consistent with other variations in the two countries' histories. France sees itself as being much older than the modern state. The nation is still resolutely discursively grounded in the Gallic, Gallo-Roman, and Frankish past. While modern philosophy and the form of the state define the contemporary nation, curricula and textbooks show that it is still widely seen as having a character that predates these. In the dominant view, this character is based on reason, culture, and language. French high culture and Enlightenment ideals are thus posited as mythic, almost timeless: the core of national identity before the Enlightenment and the Revolution and still valid today.

U.S. textbooks reflect a conception of the nation as having been consolidated after the creation of the state.[2] As such, they ground national identity in the country's modern position as a world power and a continental presence, tying national identity more to the state than do French textbooks. They convey devotion to the state, which can facilitate diversity by allowing assimilationists and pluralists alike to share a common focus. However, this approach appears to have conservative ramifications, as textbooks' reverence for the state parallels their reluctance to criticize it. Considering implications beyond textbooks, this situation may create a positive feedback loop, in which focus on the state as the heart of national identity leads to conservatism, which leads to deference for the state. Indeed, this conception of the state is consistent with Tea Party and other conservative positions, which reflect a form of worship for the Constitution and the founders (see Lepore 2010 and Hartman 2015 on originalism).

Different self-conceptions and founding myths may also help account for the fact that French textbooks do not glorify heroes as much as the U.S. books do. French identity as depicted in these books embraces many collectivist goals. This is consistent with textbooks' greater emphasis on social history and weaker attachment to heroes. By contrast, individual achievement is a key part of American mythology and loyalty to the state; being able to recognize and admire high achievers is essential for furthering that mythology. These different stances are also consistent with the different civic values promoted in each country's current textbooks, as the French books promote solidarity and the U.S. books promote capitalism.

Finally, differences between French and U.S. history and social studies education may be partly attributable to different conceptions of the role of intellectuals. The French system of curricula and especially textbook production largely defers to academic experts. This deference partly reflects the commitment to—and pride in—Enlightenment ideals of education as a means to securing the greater good as well as individual improvement. The U.S. system—notably in Texas—has increasingly limited the role of historians and other academics in favor of citizen groups and elected officials. That so many Americans believe history education should reflect popular conceptions rather than those of professional historians shows the strength of populist anti-intellectualism and its ties to nationalism. Critical thinking and especially critical approaches to history are antithetical to the nationalist religious fundamentalism advocated by influential Christian right activists.

This book has shown that broader political trends and activism greatly influence textbook content. Thus, French textbooks have become more diverse, but do not discuss thornier issues of socioeconomic inequality along ethnic lines, despite their general commitment to promoting social justice and solidarity. Perhaps continued pressure from associations could lead to such a change. However, this shift would require a reversal of the country's colorblind policies via a challenge to established views of national identity. In the U.S., there is academic support for education focused on social justice, but there has not been sustained, broad-based activism equivalent to that of conservative Christians that has resulted in similar political pressure and action. This situation may be in the process of changing in the U.S., as more moderate and liberal Americans come to realize how much power conservative groups wield over public education (see, e.g., Blue 2014; Erekson 2012; Texas Freedom Network n.d.). For the time being, this key arena of knowledge production and construction of national identity is disproportionately influenced by the Christian conservative right.

Despite the differences in pedagogical approach and the political slant of each country's nationalism, this book has also shown how resilient certain traditional myths are: textbooks in both France and the U.S. still glorify their founding civic values, turning them into symbols and boundary markers as much as beliefs. Both countries' books also demonstrate the endurance of the visions that have long legitimized the states' borders as national borders, showing that the modern nation-state and the territory are coextensive. These visions may evolve to reflect current sensibilities, as in the removal of ethnic connotations regarding "our ancestors the Gauls" or more strikingly, the "meeting of three worlds" modifying the Columbus "discovery" myth. However, the function of the myths persists: certain teleological practices continue in both countries' textbooks, turning all inhabitants of the current national territory across time into ancestors of the nation.

The endurance of traditional myths and their slow evolution point to the need to consider the *longue durée* regarding educational materials. The move away from teaching history in a nationalistic way in France in the 1970s and the progressivism of U.S. books of the early 1980s were both overturned by more conservative nationalist backlash. This process has been seen before. For example, the Muzzey Reader, first published in 1911, was the most popular textbook of its time. It followed a period of conservative-dominated history education, and it taught that citizens must be ever watchful of "the corruption of government by money power." However, this textbook and its imitators were soon rejected in favor of a more conservative, celebratory approach to U.S. history and government (FitzGerald 1979). Yet perhaps we should not think of this process as cyclical, exactly: alternation between conservative and progressive influence still allows for long-scale evolution of the dominant narratives. Renegotiation of national identity can appear to happen quickly, when a key event or series of events changes the perception of many people in a short amount of time, as was the case regarding the rapid rise of progressive multiculturalism in the late 1960s and 1970s. Such changes, textbook analysis suggests, are often met with backlash. Most often, enduring changes in how members of a nation see themselves occur over the long term.

It is not surprising that nationalism should be so closely connected to history, for history and social studies teaching, like representations of the nation, link the past to the present and project a vision of the future, giving the national community a legitimacy and grounding in the national territory and an identity that transcend time. Historicity—with its backward- and forward-looking dimensions—makes the nation seem eternal. Education, with its focus on shaping the next generation of citizens, ties together the practical and symbolic needs of the nation-state. History and social studies education share with national identity the essential trait of being continually renewed. Conflict over them reflects and feeds a sense of their importance. Without the impression that national identity (and history and social studies education) is under threat (whether from opposing viewpoints or from international competition), it might lose its salience.

POLICY IMPLICATIONS

Arguing about curricula and textbooks is important. It brings to light different viewpoints about how different members of the nation perceive their sociopolitical collectivity. It can lead to healthy, fruitful debate that can change ideas and lead to better mutual understanding.

Studying these textbooks is also important. The comparative approach used in this book shows how and why they change over time, and examining the ways in which they differ from one country to another helps to highlight possible alternatives while showing the effects of broader trends.

However, while politicians, activists, academics, educators, and the media have continued seeking to shape social studies curricula and textbooks, somewhat ironically (after so many years of such ardent debate), as of this writing in mid-2015, social studies may be losing ground in schools. In France, history teachers bemoan the reduction in hours allocated to the subject (e.g., Benoit 2015). However, French schools seem very unlikely to reduce history education below a certain threshold. Political commitment to civics education (tied to history) has, if anything, been renewed in the wake of the events of early 2015. In addition, there are also simple structural factors. For instance, the sheer number of history teachers tenured in the civil service means the government has an interest in keeping them employed.

In the U.S., on the other hand, textbooks have been made more conservative by activists who represent groups that increasingly do not frequent public schools (Hartman 2015: 212–215). A growing number of Christian conservatives homeschool their children and advocate for vouchers that would allow them to send their children to private religious schools using state funds. Because the most conservative families increasingly opt for homeschooling, the consensual textbooks—no matter how conservative one may find them—are still rejected as being too liberal by homeschooling families.

Even more significantly, studies have found that as testing and accountability have increased, teachers are paying less attention to social studies (Britt and Howe 2014; Heafner and Fitchett 2012). In the U.S., there has already been a significant decrease in the time allotted to social studies in the primary grades (down from approximately 3.5 hours of instruction on average per week in the 1993–1994 school year to 2.5 in 2007–2008, after the implementation of No Child Left Behind). This trend seems likely to continue and perhaps worsen as school and teacher assessment and funding are increasingly tied to student performance on standardized tests, which do not test social studies in 38 of the 50 states (Britt and Howe 2014).

Where the "educational crisis" of the early 1980s led to renewed focus on social studies—and particularly history—education, politicized reform efforts in the 2000s and 2010s often hold teachers responsible for the perceived failure of U.S. schools (Kumashiro 2012; Leonardatos and Zahedi 2014). The resulting focus on evaluating students' performance in English language skills and math embodies the neoconservative goal of the "return to basics" (Hartman 2015). In so doing it has shifted ideological debates away from the content of history education, making teachers, instead of curricula, the scapegoats for systemic and socioeconomic problems that lead to "failing schools."

The move away from focusing on history education as essential may also reflect a pragmatic neoconservative solution to the battles of the "history wars." Multiculturalism may not have led to a radical overhaul of education, but it nevertheless led to significant changes in including the history of oppressed minorities in the U.S. Teaching a 1950s-style triumphalist narrative is no longer possible. Perhaps reducing government involvement in this ideologically charged subject serves a conservative agenda. Though textbooks did shift to the right between 1997 and 2003, education moves further rightward still by leaving only enough instructional time to cover basic chronology and to "Celebrate Freedom."[3]

The resulting shift has two major potential repercussions. In teaching students less about history and social studies, they may become less competent, less informed citizens (Pace 2007). They may also develop less of a sense of common identity—and therefore, of solidarity—with those beyond their local community. History education will not cease completely, and neither will efforts to shape it. However, these seem poised to become less widespread and of less interest to the general public (Hartman 2015: 288).

Ceasing to debate history and social studies education on a wide scale may have repercussions for broader society. Progress toward greater inclusion and justice has never been linear. However, viewed over the long term, upheavals and more subtle changes in social studies education have led to a renegotiated form of national identity that is still short of democratic ideals of equality and solidarity but has made tremendous strides toward marginalizing racism. To increase social justice within the United States, as well as beyond national borders, we must continue to make social studies a priority in schools and to fight for it.

IMPLICATIONS BEYOND FRANCE AND THE U.S., AND DIRECTIONS FOR FUTURE STUDY

The endurance of nationalist history education has repercussions beyond the cases of France and the United States that invite further research within the field of education studies and in other aspects of cultural history and sociology. This book has shown the renegotiation of national identity and the perpetuation of nationalism in history and social studies education through the power of nationalism to ally itself with and transform other—potentially competing—ideologies. This study shows how a range of debates over pedagogy as well as politics is grounded in existing conceptions of the nation. Awareness of the nationalist dimension of education should inform both study and practice of reform efforts.

The observations in this book point to the need for further research, as these two case studies may have implications for similar countries. Both countries' textbooks have evolved in reaction to growing, officially accepted ethno-cultural diversity. French curricula and textbooks have reaffirmed traditional progressive values while showing increased commitment to assimilationist cultural nationalism. U.S. curricula and textbooks celebrate ethno-cultural diversity yet display heightened commitment to traditional conservative nationalism and civic values. These findings may indicate that societies with a more conservative consensus (or lack of consensus) can better tolerate cultural pluralism, while states with a stronger commitment to redistribution of wealth tend toward greater homogeneity. However, further research is required to isolate the most salient independent variable, as it may well be that the relevant difference is not mass opinion at all but instead whether knowledge production is controlled by elite experts or from the bottom up. Historians and educators in France and the U.S. tend to promote similar epistemological and pedagogical tools, which lend themselves to more progressive history teaching. In France, these experts largely shape history and social studies curricula and textbooks, whereas in the U.S., their role is constrained by a more democratic process, which gives greater power to electoral politics and citizen intervention. It thus seems likely that the means of creating curricula and textbooks may be the determining factor in shaping official representations of national identity. In order to confirm or refute this hypothesis and better understand the relations between knowledge production, consensus, national identity, and education, further studies could examine, on the one hand, whether countries with similar historic approaches to ethno-cultural pluralism, but different means of establishing social studies curricula, emphasize similar visions of national identity. On the other hand, studies could examine outcomes in countries with different historical approaches to pluralism but similar means of creating educational content. Similarly, further research is required to determine the conditions that foster the growth of cosmopolitan education.

This book's demonstration of the enduring power of nationalism also has policy implications regarding more cosmopolitan aims. That nationalists of all political leanings have strong affective attachment to their vision of their nation renders history education particularly contentious. Thus, cosmopolitan education that seeks to transcend national allegiances faces significant obstacles. Those seeking to promote more cosmopolitan attachments could have more success by accommodating national attachments. After all, just as nationalism has not undone allegiances to smaller units (family, town, province or state, and region), there is no reason to believe that attachment to supra-national or universal communities is a zero-sum game.

A significant first step to increasing solidarity beyond national borders might be to teach about the political, intellectual, and cultural history of nationalism and the rise of nation-states so that future citizens understand that national identity is not eternal but is somewhat arbitrary. This self-aware nationalism need not prevent a sense of affective attachment to one's nation—just as close bonds of friendship or love thrive even though we recognize the somewhat arbitrary circumstances of such encounters. Nationalism is arguably the dominant ideology of the modern world. By learning about it in a similar way to how we learn about other ideologies, we demystify it and take the first step to freeing ourselves from unknowingly being influenced by it.

NOTES

1. See also Stuart Foster (2006) and VanSledright (2008) regarding continuity in U.S. social studies education over time and coopting diversity into the narrative of progress.
2. This does not exclude earlier roots, as many Americans (and especially conservatives) trace the nation's roots back to the core of the Anglo-American colonies. In light of multiculturalist changes, Native American, African American, and Hispanic history also ground the modern nation and its diverse inhabitants in its prenational territory.
3. Beginning with legislation introduced in March 2001, the Texas Education Code requires dedicating the designated "Celebrate Freedom Week" to "educate students about the sacrifices made for freedom in the founding of this country and the values on which this country was founded" through study from Grades Three through Twelve of the Declaration of Independence and Constitution (Texas Legislature 2013).

REFERENCES

Benoit, Bruno. 2015. "Editorial: L'enseignement de l'histoire-géographie." *Historiens & Géographes* 431. Retrieved 20 Sept. 2015 (http://www.aphg.fr/EDITORIAL-L-enseignement-de-l-Histoire-Geographie).

Blue, Miranda. 2014. "Texas Approves Textbooks with Moses as Honorary Founding Father." *Right Wing Watch* 22 Nov. Retrieved 20 Sept. 2015 (http://www.rightwingwatch.org/content/texas-approves-textbooks-moses-honorary-founding-father?_ga=1.37661920.1942459606.1443229956).

Britt, Judy and Mandi Howe. 2014. "Developing a Vision for the Common Core Classroom: What Does Elementary Social Studies Look Like?" *The Social Studies* 105.3: 158–163.

Brubaker, Rogers. 2001. "The Return of Assimilation? Changing Perspectives on Immigration and its Sequels in France, Germany, and the United States." *Ethnic and Racial Studies* 24.4: 531–548.

Citron, Suzanne. 1987/2008. *Le Mythe national: L'histoire de France revisitée*. Rev. ed. Paris: Les éditions de l'Atelier.

FitzGerald, Frances. 1979. *America Revised: History Schoolbooks in the Twentieth Century.* New York: Vintage.

Foster, Stuart. 2006. "Whose History? Portrayal of Immigrant Groups in U.S. History Textbooks, 1800-Present." In S.J. Foster and K.A. Crawford, eds., *What Shall We Tell the Children? International Perspectives on School History Textbooks*. Greenwich, CT: Information Age, pp. 155–178.

Hartman, Andrew. 2015. *A War for the Soul of America: A History of the Culture Wars*. Chicago: University of Chicago Press.

Heafner, Tina L. and Paul G. Fitchett. 2012. "Tipping the Scales: National Trends of Declining Social Studies Instructional Time in Elementary Schools." *Journal of Social Studies Research* 36.2: 190–215.

Kumashiro, Kevin K. 2012. *Bad Teacher! How Blaming Teachers Distorts the Bigger Picture*. New York: Teachers College Press.

Leonardatos, Harry and Katie Zahedi. 2014. "Accountability and 'Racing to the Top' in New York State: A Report from the Front Lines." *Teachers College Record* 116.9: 1–23.

Lepore, Jill. 2010. *The Whites of Their Eyes: The Tea Party's Revolution and the Battle over American History*. Princeton, NJ: Princeton University Press.

Nussbaum, Martha C. 2012. "Teaching Patriotism: Love and Critical Freedom." *University of Chicago Law Review* 79: 215–251.

Pace, Judith L. 2007. "Why We Need to Save and Strengthen Social Studies." *Education Week* 27.16: 26–27.

Sieyès, Emmanuel Joseph. 1789/1970. *Qu'est-ce que le Tiers-Etat?* Geneva: Droz.

Texas Freedom Network. [n.d.] Fighting Textbook Censorship. Retrieved 20 Sept. 2015 (http://www.tfn.org/site/PageServer?pagename=issues_public_schools_textbook_censorship).

Texas Legislature. 2013. Education Code. Section 29.907. Retrieved 20 Sept. 2015 (http://www.statutes.legis.state.tx.us/Docs/ED/htm/ED.29.htm).

Thomas, Elaine R. 2012. *Immigration, Islam, and the Politics of Belonging in France: A Comparative Framework*. Philadelphia: University of Pennsylvania Press.

VanSledright, Bruce. 2008. "Narratives of Nation-State, Historical Knowledge, and School History Education." *Review of Research in Education* 32.1: 109–146.

Index